RISE OF THE INDO-PACIFIC

Perspectives, Dimensions and Challenges

RISE OF THE INDO-PACIFIC

Perspectives, Dimensions and Challenges

Edited by

Chintamani Mahapatra

INDIAN COUNCIL OF SOCIAL SCIENCE RESEARCH
NEW DELHI

PENTAGON PRESS LLP
NEW DELHI

The book is an outcome of a seminar, sponsored and financially supported by the Indian Council of Social Science Research, New Delhi.

Rise of the Indo-Pacific: Perspectives, Dimensions and Challenges
Edited by Chintamani Mahapatra

First Published in 2019

ISBN 978-93-86618-87-0

Published by
Indian Council of Social Science Research
(Ministry of Human Resource Development)
Aruna Asaf Ali Marg, New Delhi-110067

in association with
PENTAGON PRESS LLP
206, Peacock Lane, Shahpur Jat,
New Delhi-110049
Phones: 011-64706243, 26491568
Telefax: 011-26490600
email: rajan@pentagonpress.in
website: www.pentagonpress.in

Printed at Aegean Offset Printers, Greater Noida, U.P.

Contents

Preface

Defining a region in international politics is a difficult proposition. At various stages of history of International Relations, various powerful entities have defined different regions reflecting both their geopolitical understanding as well as goals of the leadership. Many such geographical definitions developed for political and security reasons often overlap. For example, there are many countries which are part of the Middle East as well as West Asia.

Since the early years of 1990s, 'Asia-Pacific' as a region came to prominence. Even this particular region had no clear-cut geographical boundary that could be acceptable to all the members of the International community. For example, India was never considered a member of the Asia-Pacific region in sharp contrast to inclusion of Pakistan in the South East Asia Treaty Organisation in 1954. Significantly, all Asian countries and all Pacific countries were never considered part of the Asia-Pacific either by the scholars or by the governments.

In recent years, a new concept of 'Indo-Pacific' has entered into the geopolitical discourse and the lexicon of International Relations. Like in earlier instances, there is no unanimity of views on this emerging concept of Indo-Pacific. Yet, Indo-Pacific region as a new geopolitical concept appears to have come to stay. The present book is actually a by-product of two days of intense deliberations among large group of scholars on various issues and challenges faced by the countries of the Indo-Pacific region. The book has been divided into three major sections. Section one consists of chapters related to the perspectives of major powers in the Indo-Pacific. Five scholars have contributed on American, Japanese, Indian and Chinese perspectives and policies in the Indo-Pacific region. The second section consists of six chapters related to critical regional security issues, such as sovereignty issues in South China Sea, the rise of QUAD, role of soft power, challenges to ASEAN centrality and regionalism. The third section of the book consists of five chapters devoted to non-traditional security threats, such as terrorism, nuclear proliferation, environmental degradation, drugs trafficking and health hazards. No effort has been made to add, subtract or modify the content of the contributors while editing the manuscripts and thus individual authors are responsible for the content of their respective articles.

One of the significant highlights of this volume is contributions by large number of younger faculty, senior research scholars in addition to some senior faculty members of various universities. I would like to express my gratitude to Indian Council of Social Science Research (ICSSR) for providing financial contribution to hold the conference and for its willingness to take charge of the publication of this book. I owe a great debt of gratitude to Vice-Chancellor of JNU, M. Jagadesh Kumar, Vice-Chancellor of HNB University (Gharwal), Prof. Annpurna Nautiyal, Vice-Chancellor of Central University of Kerala Prof. Gopa Kumar, his Excellency Ton Sing Tanh, Ambassador of Vietnam and Ms. Fienth eMaritje Suebu, Deputy Chief of Mission, Embassy of Indonesia to India and Prof. Virendra Kumar Malhotra, Member Secretary of ICSSR for actively participating in the conference and making their valuable contributions.

I express my sincere thanks to Ambassador R. Rajagopalan, Ambassador Sheel Kant Sharma, Prof. R. Rajagopalan and Dr. Upendra Choudhury for making valuable observations while chairing various sessions

I must acknowledge that all student volunteers of Centre for Canadian, US and Latin American Studies (CCUS&LAS), SIS, JNU worked incessantly for the success of the conference. However, my special thanks go to Souravie, Upma and Sachin for undertaking all kinds of painstaking exercises during the preparation of this manuscript. If there is any mistake of omission or commission I take the entire responsibility.

Chintamani Mahapatra

Editor and List of Contributors

Prof. Chintamani Mahapatra is currently Rector (Pro-Vice Chancellor) of Jawaharlal Nehru University and Professor of American Studies at the School of International Studies of JNU. He is also the Editor of *Indian Foreign Affairs Journal*. He has held positions, such as Member, UGC Review Committee, Area Studies Programme; Member, Fellowship Expert Committee, ICSSR; Editor, Indian Foreign Affairs Journal; Member, Editorial Board, Strategic Analyses, IDSA; Member, Editorial Board, Diaspora Studies and Member, Committee on Studies, Academy of International Studies, Jamia Millia Islamia.

Recently, he was Tagore Chair Professor at Yunnan University of China. He has conducted research in several US Presidential Libraries and US National Achives; British Public Record Office in London. Prof. Mahapatra has authored four books, one edited volume, and has contributed chapters to more than 30 edited books. He has published more than 70 research articles in reputed journals.

He has been awarded a number of international fellowships, such as Fulbright Fellowship, Commonwealth Fellowship, and Visiting Fellowships to undertake research in the US, UK, Austria, Australia and many other countries. He has been a visiting faculty in several UGC-run Academic Staff Colleges, the Foreign Service Institute of the Ministry of External Affairs, National Defense College, Army War College, Naval War College and the College of Air Warfare. He is also a regular commentator in newspapers and on audio-visual media on international affairs.

Huo Wenle is a Junior Fellow at Centre for South Asian Studies at Shandong University, Jinan City, China. He is working on his PhD thesis titled "Sino-Indian Maritime Security Relations: A Case Study of the Indian Ocean, 2000-2016" at Centre for East Asian Studies, Jawaharlal Nehru University, New Delhi, India. His research interests include Sino-Indian maritime security and China-India relations.

Prof. K.P. Vijayalakshmi is Professor of US Studies and Chair at the Centre for Canadian, US and Latin American Studies, School of International Studies, JNU, New Delhi and Adjunct faculty at the International Strategic Studies Programme (ISSP,) National Institute of Advanced Studies (NIAS), Indian Institute of Science Campus, Bangalore. She is a resource person at the Army War College, Foreign Services Institute, and Indian Institute of Public Administration. Serving as a teaching faculty of the Centre since 1990, she has been awarded Olive J. Reddick Award 1982; Gilmour Award of the Indian Association of American Studies 1992; Ford Foundation Faculty Fellowship 1997; Senior Fulbright Post-Doctoral Fellowship (1999-2000), University of Maryland; Salzburg Seminar Fellowship (1995, 1998, 2001) and Fulbright-Nehru Visiting Professor, Texas A&M University 2013.

Liu Jinxiu, is Assistant Professor in Hezhou University, Guangxi China. She was selected as Visiting Scholar to Edmonton, Canada for TEFL (Teaching English as a Foreign Language) Programme. Currently she is pursuing PhD in English Literature in School of language, Literature and Culture Studies, Jawaharlal Nehru University, and is also a guest faculty in the Centre of Chinese and South-East Asian Studies, Jawaharlal Nehru University

Merieleen Engtipi is a PhD. Scholar at Jawaharlal Nehru University in the Centre for Canadian, U.S. and Latin American Studies. She has completed her Masters in Politics with specialization in International Relations and MPhil. in the United States Studies, JNU. Her research interests lie in the area of Human Security, interactions between states and non-state actors, and peace and world order.

Dr. Monish Tourangbam is an Assistant Professor (Senior Scale) at the Department of Geopolitics and International Relations, Manipal Academy of Higher Education (MAHE), Manipal. He is the Coordinator of the North East Studies Centre at MAHE. He is Features Editor (Foreign Policy) for the Science, Technology, and Security Forum (stsfor.org) run by the Manipal Advanced Research Group (MARG). Formerly, he was Associate Fellow at the Centre for International Relations, Observer Research Foundation, New Delhi and also a visiting faculty at Ansal University, Haryana.

He was an international observer of the Russian Presidential Election held on 18 March 2018. He was a Visiting Faculty at the Department of Political Science, University of Cincinnati, Ohio. He was also a Visiting Fellow at the

Henry L. Stimson Centre, Washington D.C. He was a part of the Indian delegation at a BRICS Exchange Programme held in the People's Republic of China in 2017 organised by the Chinese Peoples' Association for Peace and Disarmament, Beijing.

Dr. Netajee Abhinandan is currently working as Assistant Professor of Political Science at Ravenshaw University. He is also the Director of Kalinga Institute of Indo-Pacific Studies (KIIPS), a premiere think-tank based in Bhubaneswar. He had done his M.Phil and Ph.D on Chinese foreign policy from Centre of East Asian Studies, Jawaharlal Nehru University. He was the recipient of prestigious Jawaharlal Nehru Memorial Fellowship. Apart from authoring China's Adaptation to Global Regimes: Dilemmas and Debates (2011), he has published numerous articles/chapters in reputed (national/ international) journals and books on diverse aspects of Chinese/Indian foreign policy, ASEAN, security and diplomacy in Indo-Pacific region. He is the chairman of Odisha's first campus radio station, Ravenshaw Radio and Editor of renowned Literary Quarterly of Epistolary Literature titled 'Chithi'.

Dr. Obja Borah Hazarika is Assistant Professor in the Department of Political Science, Dibrugarh University, Assam since 2013. She completed PhD in 2017 from Dibrugarh University and did her M.A. and M.Phil. from School of International Studies, JNU, New Delhi.

Prerna Chahar is currently pursuing Ph.D (1st Year) from United States Studies (CCUS&LAS), Jawaharlal Nehru University, New Delhi. Her area of interests includes United States Foreign and National Security Policy, United States strategies and policies in South Asia, Comprehensive and Non-traditional security, Indian Foreign Policy and Bilateral relations. She has published articles on "The Rise of Quadrilateral Tide: An Emerging Asian Order", *World Focus*, January, 2018. "Indo-Russian Investments in Pharmaceuticals: A Way Forward", *Diplomacy and Beyond*, 2018. "India-Mozambique: Charting a New Future through Trade & Economy", *Diplomacy and Beyond*, 2018

Prof. R.S. Yadav is Former Dean, Faculty of Social Sciences & Former Chairman, Department of Political Science, Kurukshetra University, Kurukshetra. Earlier he was also Director, UGC-Academic Staff College; Director, MGAIS Coaching Institute; and Director, UGC Gandhian Study Centre at the same University. He is also Professor Emeritus at Jain Vishwa Bharati Institute, Ladnun (Rajasthan). He has to his credit 8 books and more than 80 research papers in reputed national and international journals. He is editor of – *Political Discourse* – a peer-reviewed journal of Political Science. He is on the editorial board of 10 research journals of the discipline. He is member of Board of Studies and Advisory Committees of different Universities, Commissions and Institutions at State and National levels.

Sachin Tiwari is M.Phil. student at the Centre for Canada, US and Latin American Studies (CCUS&LAS) SIS JNU. His current research interest is on US Search for Cybersecurity: Domestic and international dimension. He has completed his M.A. in Political Science from Jamia Millia Islamia University and has earned Certificate in Public International Law from KU Leuven University Belgium. He has published articles on topics related to Indian diaspora and US pivot to Indo-Pacific.

Dr. Shantesh Kumar Singh is presently working as a Postdoctoral Fellow at the International Institute for Global Health, United Nations University, Kuala Lumpur, Malaysia. He also holds a regular faculty position in the Department of Political Science at the Shaheed Bhagat Singh College, University of Delhi, India.

Souravie Ghimiray is a Ph.D. scholar of American Studies program in JNU. Her M.Phil. dissertation was on "U.S. Counterterrorism policy: A Case Study of ISIS". Currently she is working on International Religious Freedom in US Foreign Policy as her Ph.D. topic. She has published articles on topics related to terrorism, and security issues, her primary research interests pertain to US politics, global security issues, political violence and armed conflict.

Sweta Kumari is currently pursuing M.Phil. from the Center for Canadian, US, and Latin American Studies, School of International Studies (SIS), JNU. For the same, she has submitted her dissertation on "A Study of Yogic Thought and Practices in the United States, 19th Century to the Present". She has done M.A. in International Relations from SIS, JNU. One of her articles titled "The US Defense Posture in the Asia-Pacific Region from Obama to Trump Administration and Present Debates on Rhetoric, Reassurance, Reliability, and Reality", got published in the January 2018 edition of *World Focus Magazine*.

Upma Kashyap is a PhD Research Scholar in United States Studies Programme, School of International Studies at Jawaharlal Nehru University, New Delhi.

Her research topic is "U.S. Nonproliferation Policy and the Role of Congress: A Case Study of Iran, 2001-2016." Earlier in 2017, Upma also did a specialized summer course on the 'United Nations and Global Challenges' from The Graduate Institute of International and Development Studies, Geneva, Switzerland. This involved her participation in workshops and interactive sessions at some of the leading Geneva-based international organizations such as the World Health Organization (WHO) on *Global Health Governance*, the United Nations High Commissioner for Refugees (UNHCR) on *UNHCR's Evolution and Contemporary Challenges*, and the World Meteorological Organization on *Women's Empowerment within the UN*.

Urbi Das is currently serving as Assistant Professor in the Department of Political Science, Jadavpur University, Kolkata. She has Bachelor's Degree in Political Science and Master Degree in Political Science with International Relations from Jadavpur University. She has M.Phil from the United States Studies Programme, School of International Studies, Jawaharlal Nehru University. She is currently pursuing her Doctoral Research. She has also served as Assistant Professor of Political Science in West Bengal Educational Services (WBES).

Dr. Vivek Mishra is an Assistant Professor in International Relations at the Netaji Institute for Asian Studies (NIAS), Kolkata. Vivek has completed his PhD in International Relations at Jawaharlal Nehru University (JNU), New Delhi on the topic, "American Maritime Strategy in the Indian Ocean in the Post-Cold War era; 1990-2012". He was a Fulbright-Nehru Doctoral Research Scholar at the Saltzman Institute of War & Peace Studies, School of International Public Affairs, Columbia University, New York for the academic year 2015-2016. Mr. Mishra is also Assistant Editor with the Indian Foreign Affairs Journal, run by the Association of Indian Diplomats. He is in the editorial board of the International Relations Magazine – The Geopolitics. Vivek has a Bachelor's degree in English Literature from University of Delhi. He has a double Master's degree in Linguistics and International Relations, besides M.Phil. in International Relations from JNU, New Delhi.

Foreword

M. Jagadesh Kumar, Vice Chancellor, JNU

If there is one region in the world where nearly half of the world's population resides and facilitates significant seaborne trade on the sea lanes of communications with a coalesced Gross Domestic Product (GDP) more than that of either USA or the European Union, then it is the Indo-Pacific region.

The Indo-Pacific framework consists of the Pacific and Indian Oceans bounded by the South East Asian archipelago. Scientists involved in marine science and hydrological research surveys already know the Indo-Pacific region as a geographical entity. However, now this region holds great promise in demographic, economic, political and maritime security spheres too. It is, therefore, no wonder that the world has begun to pay a greater attention to the Indo-Pacific region as a centre of global power in this century.

The Indo-Pacific region has also emerged as an undisputable geopolitical, geo-economics and strategic reality furthering the linkages among Australia, India, Japan and the United States of America. How countries in Indo-Pacific region form coalitions and strategic partnerships among themselves may eventually help create a balancing force against China, a revisionist power as some analysts argue, with a growing naval presence in Western Pacific Ocean, South China Sea and even in the Indian Ocean.

India, being a rapidly growing economic power and with its emphasis on "Act East" Policy, has greater stakes in Indo-Pacific region from the point of India's security, military strategy and economic prosperity. India is also strategically located between two global oil supply "choke points" – the Malacca Strait and the Strait of Hormuz. As a result, enhancing maritime security cooperation with India becomes inevitable for many countries. India has a strategic importance and the opportunity to play a leadership role in ensuring that we continue to sustain the regional balance in the Indo-Pacific region.

The challenge for India is, therefore, to strategize what we should do so that what is good for the Indo-Pacific region is also good for India in terms of its security and economic growth. These and several other questions have been examined in a two-day workshop on "Emerging Security Order in Indo-Pacific: Issues and Challenges" organized by jointly by Centre for Canadian, US & Latin American Studies of Jawaharlal Nehru University (JNU), New Delhi and Bhubaneswar based Kalinga Institute of Indo-Pacific Studies at Indian Council for Social Science Research (ICSSR), New Delhi, from 14-15 July 2018. The articles in this volume are a result of the extensive deliberations by experts drawn from different think-tanks. I believe that the ideas put together in this volume may help us devise our efforts in ways that promote improved cooperation across the Indo-Pacific region for creating a better world.

M. Jagadesh Kumar
Vice Chancellor
Jawaharlal Nehru University

Address by Ambassador of Vietnam: Ton Sinh Thanh

Challenges in Indo-Pacific

First of all, I agree with many ideas that the Indo-Pacific has become a hot topic as we are facing a complex and rapidly changing context of the world and the region, especially the assertive rise of China, the change in balance of power, and the increasingly serious challenges to peace, stability and development, particularly to maritime security in the Indo-Pacific region.

I would like to emphasise that the ongoing situation in the East Sea (South China Sea) represents one of the biggest threats to peace, stability, and freedom of navigation, over flight and trade in the Indo-Pacific region.

At present in the South China Sea, we witness not only the land-reclamation and construction of artificial islands, but also the militarisation through installing of equipment and weapons that are capable of controlling the entire South China Sea.

In addition, the littoral states are prevented from exercising their sovereign rights to exploit natural resources within their EEZs. By doing this, China is trying to realise their baseless claim on the Nine-dash Line.

These activities are threatening not only the sovereignty of the Southeast Asian countries but also the freedom of navigation, over flight and trade of the countries outside the region.

If these common challenges are not tackled jointly by nations inside and outside the region, the Indo-Pacific will be divided and the dream of an open and free ocean region will never become true.

Importance of Indo-Pacific to Vietnam

For Vietnam, the Indo-Pacific in general and the South China Sea in particular is extremely important. In the South China Sea, Vietnam has not only sovereignty over the Paracels and Spratly islands but also 3,000 other large and small islands.

With a coastline of 3,260 kilometers running from north to south, Vietnam claims more than 1 million km^2 as an EEZ in accordance with the UN Convention on the Law of the Sea.

The South China Sea is critical to Vietnam's economy as it is a huge resource of oil and gas, seafood and tourism for Vietnam. Oil and gas alone contributes over 20 per cent to Vietnam's GDP.

Moreover, after more than 30 years of 'doimoi' (renewal), Vietnam's trade with the outside world has become 2 times bigger than our GDP. The Vietnamese economy is now very open and heavily dependent on exports and FDI.

In this context, the South China Sea has become the main gateway of Vietnam to the world. The South China Sea is the living space of Vietnam. If the South China Sea is controlled by a monopoly, not only will Vietnam's security be threatened but Vietnam's economy will be severely affected.

Similarly, a broader Indo-Pacific region is vital to Vietnam because almost all Vietnam's largest strategic partners and economic partners are located in this region. China is Vietnam's biggest neighbor, the US is the largest importer of Vietnam, Japan and India are all indispensable economic partners for our country. Therefore, the challenges for the peace, security and development of the Indo-Pacific region are also challenges for Vietnam.

Convergence of visions on Indo-Pacific

Vietnam's vision on the Indo-Pacific region has been expressed for the first time by President Tran Dai Quang in his speech at the Nehru Memorial Library & Museum during his visit to India in early March 2018.

President Tran Dai Quang said that in coping with common challenges in the region, all countries should share a common vision for an open and rules-based region, and a common interest in the maintenance of peace, stability, and inclusive prosperity, wherein no country, no nation, and no group shall be left behind.

All countries need to join together in the effort to protect the freedom of navigation and unimpeded trade and not let the Indo-Asia-Pacific be balkanized into spheres of influence manipulated by power politics, hindered by protectionism, or divided by narrow nationalism.

They should make the effort to establish effective mechanisms to maintain peace, stability, and the rule of law, so as to ensure the common security, prevent conflict and war, and effectively address security challenges both traditional and non-traditional.

President Tran Dai Quang also said that India and ASEAN are geographically positioned at the heart of the Indo-Asia-Pacific. ASEAN has strong faith and great expectations in the vigorous growth of India, a power that is deeply aware of her responsibilities, a new hub of economic development, an important engine for peace, prosperity, and integration in the Indo-Asia-Pacific and playing an expanding role in the region.

President Tran Dai Quang appreciated Prime Minister Narendra Modi's statement at the ASEAN–India Summit in November last year, saying that India's 'Act East' policy "is shaped around ASEAN, and its centrality in the regional security architecture of the Indo-Pacific region".

So, it can be said that Vietnam's view on the Indo-Asia-Pacific has converged in many ways with India's vision for the Indo-Pacific, which Prime Minister Modi proclaimed in his keynote address at the Shangri-La Dialogue on June 1, 2018 in Singapore. We both emphasise the inclusiveness of all nations in the oceans as well as on the lands. We prefer engagement to confrontation in dealing with the problems in the region.

Thus, the objectives and principles set out in the visions of the two countries are almost the same, although the region may be called as Indo-Asia-Pacific by Vietnam or the Indo-Pacific by India.

In conclusion, it can be seen that the above said visions of both Vietnam and India are also shared by many other major powers and nations on the Indo-Pacific. In my opinion, this is a very important premise for building an open, free, peaceful and prosperous Indo-Asia-Pacific or Indo-Pacific.

Introduction
Emerging Trends in Indo-Pacific: Shifting Paradigms & New Power Coalitions

Chintamani Mahapatra

International scholars had got used to the geopolitical space, called Asia-Pacific, in recent discourses on international affairs. When scholars, diplomats and political leaders spoke of emerging 'Asian Century', 21st Century belonging to Asia, shifting of global economic power house from West to the East etc., they all meant Asia-Pacific. Economic maturity of Japan and South Korea, exceptional growth of the Chinese economy, economic dynamism of Association of South East Asian Nations, and energetic multilateralism in East and Southeast Asia at a time when Western economies had slowed down were the rationale behind the focus on 'Asia-Pacific'. Political upheavals, rise of Islamists, expanding footprints of religious extremists and terrorist groups in West Asia and continuing lacklustre status of Africa in the global political economy made 'Asia-Pacific' region look attractive, dynamic, energetic, and as an area of future economic growth and political stability on the geopolitical map of the globe.

All these observable specifics have transformed in last several years. Three major developments have taken place leading to emergence of the concept of 'Indo-Pacific' that does not replace but subsumes the geopolitical entity, hitherto known as the 'Asia-Pacific'. The newest development, of course, is the rise of India as an economic powerhouse and influential political actor in world affairs, particularly in Asian affairs. A country with a billion plus people, including a vast number of young population, with credible nuclear and missile capability and with an unmatched historical record as a prominent leader of the developing countries, now came to be known for its enviable economic growth rate, expanding middle class and its achievements in poverty alleviation.

As India's arch opponent, Pakistan, got embroiled in economic and energy crisis and terrorism and domestic violence and it's main competitor for global influence, China, was no longer in a position to pose an existential threat to it in view of New Delhi's substantial military muscle built since the late 1990s, India since the days of its economic liberalisation has attracted the global spotlight as a large democracy with an expanding economy and a sort of a new model of growth for the developing nations around the world. India is the third largest economy in the world in terms of Purchasing Power Parity (PPP). Last year in 2017, according to World Bank Report, India's nominal Gross Domestic product (GDP) surpassed that of France and thus India's economy became the sixth largest economy in the world.[1] It is a different matter that India, like China, has no place in the Group of Seven industrialised countries in the world. But India's economy grew by more than 8 per cent in last one decade that has caught the global attention.

Second most important development is China's assertive foreign policy and use of military strength to assert its sovereignty on disputed islands in the South China Sea. When Communist China altered its economic growth model, opened its market to the outside world and propagated a policy of 'peaceful rise of China', almost the entire world took note of it, myriad countries took steps to take advantage of the economic benefits from a rapidly expanding Chinese economy through trade and investment relationships with Beijing and many countries in Africa and Latin America were able to raise their income by selling commodities and natural resources to ever hungry Chinese industries and corporations.

However, when China sought to construct new roads along its border areas, began to reclaim lands in South China Sea and built military facilities, refused to settle disputes over sovereignty claims over several island groups in South China Sea through multilateral dialogues with all disputants and rapidly began to build up its comprehensive military strength, the notion of 'peaceful rise of China' was no longer credible. China came to be perceived as a new bully in regional affairs by the international community. China-Japan brawl over Shenkaku Islands, China-Vietnam scuffle over Spratley Islands, China-India standoff at Doklam, China-US gridlock over the issue of freedom of navigation rights and many more such events led to the rise of a Sinophobia that a more powerful China would turn it into a new hegemon and disrupt the contemporary global order in general and Asia in particular. China's evolution has been a story of a journey of a nation that has moved from its relative isolation to embrace incremental engagement with other nations to emerge as a powerful entity on the slogan of peaceful rise to finally rising as an aggressive and pushy hegemon.

Alongside the unique rise of India and China, the third important development is erosion of self-confidence of a regional grouping in the Asia Pacific that had emerged as a leader in regional multilateralism. Association of Southeast Asian Nations (ASEAN) that emitted confidence as a triumphant political grouping in a region of extreme diversity in terms of political system, economic philosophy, religious beliefs and socio-cultural traditions, continued to remain united but began to lose its cohesion in collective decision making on regional and global issues. The inclusion in this organisation of three communist countries of Indo-China and Myanmar brought new challenges to this collective in the new context of the post-Cold War era. ASEAN persistently sought to play a central role in managing strategic stability in the Asia-Pacific region by establishing ASEAN Regional Forum, promoting East Asia Summit and diplomatically navigating the Asia Pacific Economic Forum (APEC), but the ascent of China as an assertive actor brought enormous new challenges to this grouping. Spread of uneven Chinese influence among the ASEAN members made it difficult for ASEAN to develop a cohesive or consensus position on various aspects of Chinese behaviour, including evolving a unified position on South China Sea disputes. In a near desperate effort ASEAN leaders looked up to India, Japan and the United States for more proactive role in the region. But in the meantime, difficulty faced by ASEAN to lead in multilateral diplomacy became increasingly discernible.

Japan, Australia, South Korea and Indonesia are regional heavyweights, but none of them alone were in a position to take the lead in sustaining the geopolitical notion of 'Asia-Pacific'. Growing dependent of China on the natural resources of Africa and energy resources of West Asia made the country reach beyond the confines of Asia-Pacific and search for naval and other footholds in the Indian Ocean region as well. China's presence in the Indian Ocean was effected through massive Chinese economic assistance to regional countries, cultivating the political leaders of various countries and making all necessary arrangements to acquire facilities that someday could be turned into naval facilities. Myanmar, Bangladesh, Sri Lanka, Maldives, Pakistan, Djibouti and many other countries in the Indian Ocean witnessed Chinese inroads into their domestic political economy. China subsequently coloured its strategic design by promoting 'One Belt, One Road' or 'Belt and Road' initiatives.

Partly in response to perceived China's empire building inventiveness, India came up with its idea of 'Sagarmala' as a first step. Naval modernisation and coastal security must accompany integrated port developments along India's coast.[2] In the midst of debate and discussion on perceived 'string of pearls' strategy of China to encircle India, India's naval modernisation drive was expedited as well. The United States took note of changes occurring in the Indian Ocean region and began to focus more on Indian Ocean than before. As it evolved, the United States saw more meaning and usefulness in combining its strategy and developing a unified Pacific and Indian Ocean strategy rather than keep the two oceans apart in its naval strategy.

Many articles have been written about how the 'Indo-Pacific" terminology began and how different countries used it in diverse perspectives. It is understood how Japan, Australia, India and the United States separately began to articulate 'Indo-Pacific' concept through statements, research papers and media commentaries and that there was no concerted grand plan by a group of countries in giving a name and meaning to the concept of 'Indo-Pacific'. Yet, China from the very early stages of the use of the term 'Indo-Pacific' expressed its reservations. Chinese scholars read a 'containment' strategy in use of this term. Chinese argument was based on the perception that the US wanted to rope in India into its strategy of containment of China by extending its Pacific strategy to Indian Ocean and making India part of it. Obama Administration's characterisation of India as 'linchpin' of its 'pivot to Asia' strategy and growing Indo-US defense and security ties actually fed suspicion in the Chinese mind.

However, one fails to understand why the US would begin to support the idea of 'Indo-Pacific' to make India part of a containment strategy, if any. Indo-US strategic partnership precedes 'Indo-Pacific' concept. Secondly, as Chinese themselves say Indian Ocean is not India's Ocean, although they claim South China Sea to be China's Sea. 'Indo-Pacific' thus is not India and Pacific. It is Indian Ocean and Pacific Ocean. China actually should have logically floated the idea of a concept of Ideally, China should have the first to propose and work towards an Indo-Pacific strategy. Importance of Africa and West Asia for sustainable Chinese economic growth is beyond dispute. What China has already been doing to safeguard its interest in those regions and the Indian Ocean that carries Chinese trade through its sea lanes could have been given a policy dimension by the Chinese Government. Strangely, China never thought about it and when others began to articulate geopolitics in Indo-Pacific, China not only backtracks but also grumbles.

ASEAN likewise does not welcome the new formulation of geopolitics in the shape of an 'Indo-Pacific' region. ASEAN was so intoxicated with Asia-Pacific as a reference point that its leaders and scholarly community failed to observe major changes in a region adjacent to theirs and change their policy or scholarly formulations accordingly. While simmering apprehensions about Chinese domination were there in almost all ASEAN member countries, understanding India was at least half baked in the region. One group of scholars kept on highlighting the negative sides of India to conclude that India would always have limitations in playing a significant role in the Asia Pacific. There was no effort on the part of ASEAN to make India a member of the APEC. The leadership in ASEAN actually was beholden to China that systematically sought to deny India a meaningful entry into the multilateral interactions and serious dialogues on questions of peace and stability. There were other group who looked at India as a potential alternative to a bullying China, but they remained ineffective.

If only ASEAN could have made a well-thought, well-planned and well-executed diplomatic initiative to encourage a larger Indian role in Asia Pacific affairs, its current hesitation to embrace Indo-Pacific formulation could have been avoided. Can India be faulted for its own lack of forceful diplomatic drive? Perhaps yes, the 'Look East' policy that was launched in early 1990s was innovative and relevant, but its implementation was lacklustre. It was only when the new NDA Government came to power in 2014 under the leadership of Narendra Modi that India was able to project its real worth in international affairs. Credit should go to the Modi Government for acknowledging a central role for ASEAN in the peace and stability of the Indo-Pacific region. ASEAN should capitalise on this Indian policy and end its hesitation to embrace the Indo-Pacific concept as a relevant frame of reference. ASEAN scholarly community need to do more serious work on India, India's strength and it's potential by going beyond studies on traditional social science subjects.

The only country that has debated, discussed, adopted and evolved a policy towards Indo-Pacific is Australia. Significantly, Australia has been self-aware for long of its geographical position as both a Pacific and Indian Ocean rim country. Yet, Australia for long gave priority to Asia-Pacific and neglected Indian Ocean region in its economic as well as foreign policy engagements. Reasons are many and Cold War logic always bounces back to explain behaviour of nations, yet Canberra has made timely shift to focus its attention on the

Indo-Pacific region and its defense white paper and foreign policy documents duly highlight the significance of Indo-Pacific region for its national interests.

Japan since 2007 has viewed Indian Ocean as an increasingly important region where it would like to play an active role to serve Japanese national interest. The address by the visiting Japanese Prime Minister to the Indian Parliament left a testimony of what foreign policy innovations Tokyo would undertake when the idea of a 'confluence' of two oceans to promote growth and development was underlined. For more than a decade now, Japan has actively sought to play a proactive role where India is one of the key partners. Japan, which was traditionally constrained by its constitution and foreign policy compulsions to look beyond Asia-Pacific, appears out of the shackles and is all poised to be an influential actor in the Indo-Pacific region by being prepared to invest heavily in infrastructure developments and industrial promotions in the Asia-Africa Corridor.

It is a fact that UPA Government, preceding the NDA Government, was not too willing to accept and use the term 'Indo-Pacific' in its formulation of foreign policy. One needs to carefully search in Prime Ministerial, Ministerial and Secretarial speeches to get a ready reference of usage of the term 'Indo-Pacific'. But the Modi Government has clearly articulated a policy towards the 'Indo-Pacific' region. Speaking at the Shangrilla Dialogue in 2017, Prime Minister Narendra Modi described the Indian view in the following words:

> The Indo-Pacific is a natural region. It is also home to a vast array of global opportunities and challenges. I am increasingly convinced with each passing day that the destinies of those of us who live in the region are linked. Today, we are being called to rise above divisions and competition to work together....
>
> India does not see the Indo-Pacific Region as a strategy or as a club of limited members. Nor as a grouping that seeks to dominate. And by no means do we consider it as directed against any country. A geographical definition, as such, cannot be. India's vision for the Indo-Pacific Region is, therefore, a positive one. And, it has many elements....
>
> It stands for a free, open, inclusive region, which embraces us all in a common pursuit of progress and prosperity. It includes all nations in this geography as also others beyond who have a stake in it....[3]

Last but most significant, the United States government has revised its strategy, adopted an 'Indo-Pacific' strategy and even redefined the geographical contours of its Pacific Command and renamed it as 'Indo-Pacific Command'. The US

National Security Strategy Report issued by the Donald Trump Administration says:

> A geopolitical competition between free and repressive visions of world order is taking place in the Indo-Pacific region—a region, which stretches from the west coast of India to the western shores of the United States, represents the most populous and economically dynamic part of the world. The U.S. interest in a free and open Indo-Pacific extends back to the earliest days of our republic....
>
> Our vision for the Indo-Pacific excludes no nation. We will redouble our commitment to established alliances and partnerships, while expanding and deepening relationships with new partners that share respect for sovereignty, fair and reciprocal trade, and the rule of law. We will reinforce our commitment to freedom of the seas and the peaceful resolution of territorial and maritime disputes in accordance with international law. We will work with allies and partners to achieve complete, verifiable, and irreversible denuclearisation on the Korean Peninsula and preserve the non-proliferation regime in Northeast Asia.[4]

To be fair, India, Australia, Japan and the United States are the four Indo-Pacific powers who have begun to frequently use the term 'Indo-Pacific' and have adopted policies towards this region. These four countries have also set up a dialogue forum, popularly known as Quad or Quadrilateral, to informally hold discussion on various issues of the Indo-Pacific region. Indonesia and Vietnam have begun to articulate their policies towards this larger region that actually subsumes the Asia-Pacific region. Some European countries, such as Britain and France, have also accepted the concept of China opposes the concept of Indo-Pacific, but negatively accepts it by criticising it. Russia is a Pacific country, it has closer ties with Indian Ocean rim countries and has little objection to Indo-Pacific concept.

In other words, Asia-Pacific as a region to understand and shape regional affairs has slowly been replaced by 'Indo-Pacific'. This new term has entered into the lexicon of international relations and global affairs and it would remain so into the foreseeable future. Keeping in mind, all these developments, the Centre for US, Canadian and Latin American Studies of JNU's School of International Studies and Bhubaneswar based Kalinga Institute of Indo-Pacific Studies organised a two-day international conference with the support of the Indian Council of Social Science Research of New Delhi. A wide range issues by a large team of senior scholars and young researchers were discussed and the outcome is the present volume.

It seems quite clear now that there is a paradigm shift in the ways nations conduct their diplomacy. The rise of the Trump Phenomenon in the United States, consolidation of power by President Xi Jinping in China and President Vladimir Putin in Russia, role of strong leadership in India with Narendra Modi at the helm of affairs, rise of a new nuclear power in the Korean Peninsula—North Korea—turmoil in the hydrocarbon rich West Asia and scramble for power and influence in Africa among major powers all have contributed to an international milieu where traditional theories and approaches to understand nations' behaviour are no longer adequate.

The European Union, which had turned out to be a model regional grouping, got a severe jolt in the wake of the British withdrawal from the organisation. The consequences of BREXIT for Britain and the EU, the immigration problem arising out of Middle Eastern political upheavals, economic impact of great recession since the 2008 and the rise of European rights symbolising new nationalism in the era of globalisation and, concomitant spread of anti-globalisation sentiments all have contributed to paradigm shift in ways nations conduct diplomacy. Russian assertion and Chinese aspiration for superpower status have already unleashed a mini-Cold War between Washington and Moscow and a Cold Confrontation between the United States and China. Consequently, neither liberalism nor realism nor traditional Marxist thoughts can guide leaders for conducting diplomacy. Newer coalition of nations has risen and disappeared in diverse permutations and combinations. Traditional alliances are no longer full proof and cohesive in all aspects of international affairs. Even adversaries have tried to join coalitions aimed at achieving limited goals. All these can be seen in power play and interactions among countries of the Indo-Pacific. No discernible pattern of state behaviour has emerged and is unlikely to be witnessed in the foreseeable future.

All these paradigmatic alterations in relations between nations and rise and fall shifting coalitions of countries make the Indo-Pacific region volatile, uncertain and unpredictable.

NOTES

1 Firstpost, 12 July 2018.

2 Ministry of Shipping, GOI, http://sagarmala.gov.in/about-sagarmala/vision-objectives

3 Ministry of External Affairs, GOI, https://www.mea.gov.in/Speeches-Statements.htm?dtl/29943/Prime+Ministers+Keynote+Address+at+Shangri+La+Dialogue+June+01+2018

4 National Security Strategy, 2017, https://www.whitehouse.gov/wp-content/uploads/2017/12/NSS-Final-12-18-2017-0905.pdf

MAJOR POWER PERSPECTIVES ON INDO-PACIFIC

1

American Perspective on the Indo-Pacific

Prof K.P. Vijayalakshmi

ABSTRACT

The Asia-Pacific has been an important part of the US Grand Strategy for years: however, the 'rise of China' has reignited its importance since the last decade. The region gained focused attention from the Obama administration under the 'Pivot to Asia' strategy. Asia Pacific essentially consisted of Southeast Asia, Northeast Asia and East Asia. Arising out of the growing emerging markets in the 1980s, it was an economic rather than a security conception. The Indo-Pacific region, on the other hand, ranges East Africa's coast, across the Indian Ocean, to the Western part of the Pacific and recognises the deep connections between them. It is both a strategic and an economic space that consists of important sea lines of communication (SLOC) that connect the two oceans. Most importantly, it recognised the transition of power from the west to the east and places India at the centre of the framework.

As China began to increase its presence in the region, the US began to place India at the middle of this larger maritime space. During the visit of Japanese PM Shinzo Abe (2007) to India, he described Indo-Pacific as a 'confluence of the two seas'; this shift in US thinking has important implications for India and the region.[1]

The debate over this new strategic framework to describe this pan-Asian region reached an interesting level since the election of US President Donald Trump. The Trump administration used the term not only in official government documents but also at various multilateral gatherings. In NSS 2017 and during his maiden Asia trip in 2017, Trump elevated 'Indo-Pacific' as a top-level priority region with vast geopolitical and strategic significance for the US. With the aim to counter China's "economic inducements and penalties; influenced operations and implied military threats to persuade other states to heed its political and security agenda", the US aimed at boosting its ties with regional allies.[2] The Quadrilateral Security Dialogue, conducted on the sidelines of East Asia Summit between Australia, India, Japan and US in 2017 led to the like-minded democracies taking their first step towards a possible future alliance. In the Trump administration's view, the term Indo-Pacific also emphasises India's status as a global power, with a focus on improving New Delhi's integration with the East especially in the light of its 'Look and Act East Policy'. Furthermore, by envisaging a region spreading across two oceans, the Trump administration has supported India's 'leadership role in the Indian Ocean's security'. Illustrating this thinking, the US Secretary of Defense, Jim Mattis (2018), only a day before the Shangri La Dialogue began, declared that the US Pacific Command will be renamed to US Indo-Pacific Command.[3] Thought to be symbolic at present, this move has emphasised how the Indo-Pacific has become a critical strategic, diplomatic and geopolitical construct for US foreign policy.

However, this term change has only added more issues to the US-Sino relations. The announcement came just a week before the strategically significant Malabar 2018 naval exercise, an annual military event that involves India, United States and Japan. This event is more crucial at a time of territorial disputes between China and some of its neighbors in resource abundant South China Sea region. China has been following an aggressive policy towards it by expanding its military bases on disputed islands which could ultimately strengthen its overall claim.

At another level, this foreign policy calculation by the US also coincides with its 'America First' policy, aimed at revitalising economic power of the country. The region gives umpteen opportunities to the US to advance its industrial and trade relations within the region, at a time when US trade deficits are at an all-time high. It also gives an opportunity to counter Beijing's economic clout that is fast overtaking the US both in terms of trade and free trade deals in the region.

This chapter assesses how and why the shifts in the US thinking and approach regarding the Indo-Pacific region occurred. What are the imperatives that guided the US to change the term to 'Indo-Pacific' and what gains does the US expect to achieve from this? It contends that analysis of the US perspective is both relevant and necessary in order to outline the key strategic shifts in the US policy vis-à-vis China. Taking into account the Indian response to these developments, it argues that the US has finally declared an India policy that is pervaded by persistent strategic convergence.

Introduction

In recent months, the US has made pointed references to the Indo-Pacific region that demonstrates the significance it has in their foreign policy calculus. Remarks made by President Trump and other officials of his administration on the American strategy on the Indo-Pacific on various occasions, present the vision, goals, strategy and the nature and extent of US engagement towards the Indo-Pacific. This has been accompanied by an increasing attempt to provide conceptual clarity and reassurance to allies and friends that the US is firmly committed to being an Asia Pacific power, which has no intention of withdrawing from this region. These assurances conveyed that Trump administration expects to continue the Asia focus started during the Obama administration with the 'Asia Pivot Policy' later changed to 'Rebalance Strategy towards the Asia Pacific'. Further, various changes were made to the nomenclature of the defense command in which the US 'Pacific Command' was renamed as 'Indo-Pacific Command'. Clearly, this announcement notified that America "...is particularly focused on the Indo-Pacific ... which includes New Zealand and the vast swath of the Western and South Pacific, will be the most consequential part of the globe this century".[4] The US emphasis on the centrality of India in this strategy signalled to the Chinese that there was convergence between the two on preventing Chinese domination. This strategy was in the making from the very first year of Trump Presidency and the subsequent years could see the implementation of it. It also seemed that the US supported both aspects: 'Free and Open' as an interlinked part of the strategy towards the Indo-Pacific.

The American perception of threat from China and the placing of India in its Indian Ocean strategy is a vital part of the former's understanding of the geoeconomic and geostrategic changes. As the strategy of the US on India pointed out, "The history of the 21st century will largely be the story of the Indo-Pacific region, and the trajectory of the US-India relationship will be one of the most important chapters".[5] Moreover, the India-centric strategy outlined by the Principal Deputy Assistant Secretary Alice Wells, alluded India and US as an 'all weather partner', and that 'India played a central role in US national security'.[6]

However, the current articulation of US interests and motivations in the region are part of a continued assessment of former administrations. Thus, to understand the US perspective of the region it is necessary to trace its genesis and evolution from previous years. In addition, a critical examination of the drivers that explains the shifts in US policy towards China (both domestic and international) in order to assess the implications of such changes is essential.

Beginnings of the China Threat Perception

Post the disintegration of Soviet Union, the US enjoyed a brief unipolar phase, during the shift of presidential power from George H.W. Bush to Bill Clinton. This was the time when the nation welcomed a new era with a youthful president, signifying a 'Globalised World' led by the 'Dot Com revolution'. With the successful containment of the Russia threat, there was fresh vigour to tackle a new world order, not only amongst the American public, but also amongst the policymakers. This was also the time when the US articulated plans to deal with America's 'next big challenge'. Documents on national security outlined the vision, strategy and goals of the US in this post-Cold War world that provided a sharp contrast to the Cold War era. The National Security Strategy presented by the Reagan administration was the first report after the Congressional Goldwater-Nichols Act that reflected the USA's then strategic thinking, emphasising how the tools of statecraft would be used. Subsequently, through other reports that followed, the shifts in the USA's view of the strategic affects of China's economic rise were becoming evident. In the initial reports, the US appeared eager to embrace China within the global economic system, with the hope that there would be democratic reform in China. "Change is inevitable in China, and our links with China must endure" stated the NSS of President George H.W. Bush in 1991.[7] Thus began a policy of engagement that focussed on integrating a democratically reformed China with the West, and yet how "…we must carefully watch the emergence of China onto the world stage and support, contain, or balance this emergence as necessary to protect US interests".[8] The key alliance in the Pacific was however with Japan.

At this time the United States had unparalleled strategic influence in the region and the concept of 'Asia Pacific' was not part of the US' calculus. The larger issue was the redefinition of US strategic intentions and the rationale for the US to maintain a substantive military deployment in Northeast Asia (with hopes of stabilising the Korean peninsula and making Japan a 'normal state'). As a report from the Council on Foreign Relations suggested at that time,

> "…that the United States maintain regional security by preserving a credible military presence and a viable regional training and support structure.... That will help prevent both intraregional conflict and domination by outside powers".[9]

Literature on the subject suggests that there was a broad consensus that Asia is important to the US and vice versa. However, in the post-Cold War era, scholars argued that the US role in Asia needed to refocus on emerging issues in regional security and re-examine its role as an offshore balancer/ security guarantor to smaller countries in the region. Significantly, focus on the US engagement with China and perception about the role China would play in America's post-Cold War Asia policy was reignited from the Clinton Presidency. As policymakers grappled with renewed threats in the region, China emerged with divergent security interests in Asia that led to the US contemplating China as a latent adversary. A re-examination of these policy shifts from the Clinton Presidency would contextualise how the US eventually and implicitly placed China at the core of its current 'Indo-Pacific Strategy'.

It was clear that from the start that Clinton was determined to stay engaged in the region. Both his trade and security policies demonstrated the high premium he placed on US-China ties. His first official trip overseas was to East Asia which highlighted his commitment to US engagement to the Asia Pacific region.

Clinton initially felt that the US China policy was soft on the grounds of human rights and a threat to its non-proliferation objectives. His NSS in 1994 stated, "China maintains a repressive regime even as it assumes a more important economic and political role in global affairs ... and (US must) press China to formalise its earlier MTCR [Missile Technology Control Regime] undertakings. 'The strategy was however to engage China economically and strategically': We are developing a broader engagement with the People's Republic of China that will encompass both our economic and strategic interests. That policy is best reflected in our decision to delink China's Most Favoured Nation (MFN) status from its record on human rights."[10] Clinton reiterated that US is committed to China's development towards an open market and economy which accepts the international trade norms. He further added that China's participation in the regional security architecture was crucial for peace and stability of the region.

Even though the White House and the State Department held an optimistic stance towards US engagement with China, the Department of Defence voiced its concern on China's military prowess. The Quadrennial Defense Review in 1997 stated that, "China has the potential to become a major military power in Asia".[11] Report by the National Defense Panel too reached a similar conclusion. Warnings on the 'China Threat' began to circulate in 1999 from the Office of Net Assessment (ONA), through a study titled 'Summer Study Report: Asia 2025' the conclusions of which were as follows:

- The main threats in the future for the US comes from Asia, largely from China;
- China in the future could grow consistently or become unstable, both scenarios are equally challenging for the US;
- As Middle Eastern oil flow was directed towards Asia, Asian sea lines of communications would spearhead global naval activities;
- Formal alliances formed during the World Wars/Cold War era could be side-lined for flexible arrangements which include non-traditional allies;
- South and Central Asia's internal dynamics could affect or be affected by the China-India rivalry;
- As China could become a strong competitor to the US, it would need important strategic partners, even if at the 'cost of selective nuclear proliferation';
- India in the future could be an ideal partner for the US and the US-India partnership can be the key to avoid China-India collaboration.[12]

Interestingly, in 2000, a Quadrennial Defense Review Working Group paper by the National Defense University attempted to assess the future security environment till 2025. A sharp focus on China was revealed in the threat assumptions. For instance:

- In the years beyond 2015 there could be regional great power or global competitor, with Russia or China having that potential;
- Russia and China will continue to increase their world trade for the next twenty five years;
- China could possibly work towards various alliances that could diffuse America's hegemony;
- China's economic power could be cited as a precursor to a politico-military confrontation with the US;
- China has the greatest likelihood among the current military powers to spark regional conflicts to achieve political aims and the three transition states, i.e. Russia, China and India possess the 'theoretical resources and sufficient independence of interest' to become larger competition for the US.[13]

The development of a plausible military competitor of the US in the near future, competition from actors of various regions, threat of space warfare, and the downfall of traditional alliance system were impacting the American perception towards China.[14] The US Congress passed the National Defense

Authorisation Act for Fiscal Year 2000, which took two important steps regarding China: there would be "limitation on military to military exchanges and contacts with the Chinese People's Liberation Army and; an annual report on military and security developments involving China would be submitted each year (at least till January 2021) by the Secretary of Defense to the specified congressional committees".[15] Some of the important aspects to be included in this report were specified in the Act:

> "...goals and factors shaping the Chinese military/security strategy; trends in Chinese security and military behaviour; size, location and capabilities of Chinese strategic land, sea and air force; capabilities of China's space and counter space programs; activities of PLA navy and so on".[16]

The Congress also put forward the idea of establishing the 'Center for the Study of Chinese Military Affairs' at the National Defense University, which was considered a crucial step to analyze the strategic relationship of US and China in the coming years.[17] With the intention of furthering research on China, legislative action was taken to create US-China Economic and Security Review Commission with the aim to "monitor, investigate, and submit an annual report to the Congress on the national security implications of the bilateral trade and economic relationship between US and China".[18]

The United States' China Policy under the Clinton administration was beset by the differing views held by people surrounding the President. The debate was essentially over whether China will be the great enemy or a worthy competitor in the near future. Some were convinced that the future course of action for the US was to take on China. The so called 'Blue Team' consisting of a "loose alliance of members of Congress, congressional staff, think tank fellows, Republican political operatives, conservative journalists, lobbyists from Taiwan, former intelligence officers and a handful of academics, (were) all united in the view that a rising China poses great risks to America's vital interests".[19] Clinton faced three possible choices for dealing with China: 1) the Blue Team voiced for a "Cold War era policy of containing and isolating China with the aim to weaken the Communist regime"; 2) others similarly opposed engaging with China but on different grounds, namely the power it would give China which would continue the oppress its peoples; and 3) yet others felt that US could have a significant impact on Beijing and its choices, therefore integrating it into the international security/economic systems could give US a leverage to hold China accountable.[20] Clinton eventually opted for the third method of dealing with the rise of China.

While many in the Department of Defense and in the Congress pushed for treading cautiously, Clinton-Gore administration stressed on comprehensively engaging with the Chinese. One of the most important milestones in the US-China relations came in the form of the US-China Relations Act of 2000[21] that led to China's acceptance in the World Trade Organisation and opened Chinese market for the US businesses. (US Congress 2000) The President stated:

> "...with this agreement China has chosen reform despite the risks. It has chosen to overcome a great wall of suspicion and insecurity, and to engage the rest of the world. The question for the United States therefore is do we want to support that choice or reject it, becoming bystanders as the rest of the world rushes in. That would be a mistake of truly historic proportions ... as we debate about China here ... it's easy to forget that the Chinese leaders and their people are also engaged in a debate about us there. And many of them believe that we honestly don't want their country to assume a respected place in the world. If China joins the W.T.O., but we turn our backs on them, it will confirm their fears."[22]

But Clinton's National Security Strategy (2000) cautioned:

> "Given its growing economic potential and already sizable military force, it is essential that China not become a security threat to the region.... The third pillar of our policy in building a new Pacific community is to support the wave of democratic reform sweeping the region".[23]

In the end the Clinton era was based on a constructive approach of engagement towards China on both economic and strategic issues while highlighting the prospects of trade. The 1999 NSS reported that the US and China were working together on regional security issues in South and East Asia, on non-proliferation and on high technology cooperation.

Bush Years: Strategic Competitor Versus Cooperative Partner

Under George W. Bush, the US policy towards China witnessed both continuity and change from the Clinton period. During his campaign, Bush described China as a strategic competitor that was poised to push back American interests. The expectation was that there would be harsher measures put in place to tackle China.

George Bush had been an ardent critic of Clinton's China policy of engagement, especially vis-à-vis US stance on Taiwan. A shift in the administration's views towards China occurred since 2000, largely due to the United States' changed priorities after 9/11 and Beijing's 'strong and unambiguous' support for US efforts to combat terrorism. Bush decided on a less confrontational policy. Given that the Republican Party extensively opposed Clinton's Policy on China, cooperation with China on Taiwan, seemed to denote continuity with Clinton's policy. As experts pointed out, the softer rhetoric and emphasis on cooperative ties with China in 2004 and integrating it to the West seemed remarkably different from 2000. China too reciprocated by softening its rhetoric.[24] The focus was clearly on the Middle East due to the preoccupation with the GWOT.

Even though the US military attention was focused towards the Middle East, the US Pacific Command (PACOM) was given instructions by Department of Defense to continue its operational commitments to the Pacific. The administration however clarified that China was part of such a policy with an important shift. It noted that China was "...pursuing advanced military capabilities that can threaten its neighbours in the Asia-Pacific region" even as it was helping in stabilising the Korean peninsula and the War on Terror.[25]

Amidst the reshuffling and reassessment of America's future strategic goals in the post-9/11 world, Bush struggled to develop a strong China policy with many in his administration differing with each other on the exact nature of the challenges from China. For instance, then Secretary of State Condoleezza Rice preferred closer US-Japan relations and made efforts to distance herself from the Chinese government.[26] Similarly many in the administration preferred closer US-India relations, a move to balance China's rise in the region and global influence.[27]

Eventually opinions of new members in the administration gained attention from the President. The person who supported increased engagement with China contrary to those with the opinion of it being a 'Strategic Competitor' during the Bush presidency was Clark T. Randt Jr, US' longest serving ambassador to PRC.[28] His personal relationship with Bush gave him exclusive access and he was successful in steering the policy towards engagement rather than a possible confrontation. Apart from him, Christopher Hill (the Assistant Secretary of State for the East Asian and Pacific Affairs) helped in moulding America's policy towards China in the post-9/11 era and played a crucial role in the Six Party Talks.[29]

The second term of the Bush presidency provided significant changes. The early discussions for Quadrilateral initiative occurred under the Bush presidency. In 2007, Japan and Australia penned the Japan-Australia Joint Declaration on Security Cooperation (JDSC)[30] and few months before the signing, Japan and India produced a joint statement on Strategic and Global Partnership.[31] In April, Japan hosted US and Australian officials, who agreed to include India in their Ballistic Missile Defense collaboration, and eventually "American & Indian navies moved their annual Malabar manoeuvres from the Arabian Sea to the South China Sea (for the first time) with Japanese warships joining up in another strategic triangle, adjoining China".[32] The naval cooperation which was strengthened in the aftermath of 2004 Tsunami impacting the Indian Ocean region, was furthered ahead between US, Japan, India and Australian officials in Manila (met on the sidelines of ASEAN Regional Forum), which inaugurated the 'Quadrilateral Security Dialogue'. Even though it was Japan's Shinzo Abbe that pushed the most for such a dialogue between the four in a bid to strengthen Asian Security,[33] America welcomed this development. The involved states reiterated that the Quad meeting was not targeted towards any specific country, but policy makers in Beijing felt apprehensive of the initiative. Eventually, Quad's structure started emerging with important back to back visits by Australian Defense Minister Brenden Nelson,[34] Admiral Russell Shalders Commander of the Australian Navy,[35] Japanese PM Shinzo Abe[36] and Japanese Defense Minister Yuriko Koike[37] to New Delhi.

By his second term, the US began to formulate a hedging strategy against Chinese military growth amidst continued hope for a more transparent and reformed China in trade. As the NSS 2006 stated, "China can make an important contribution to global prosperity and ensure its own prosperity for the longer term if it will rely more on domestic demand and less on global trade imbalances to drive its economic growth".[38]

At this time, American military supremacy in the Middle East and emerging economic challenges posed serious questions to the future of American leadership. The military expenditure of American missions in Afghanistan and Iraq created immense financial burden for the Bush administration. Finally, the financial meltdown of 2007-2008 exposed American vulnerabilities and prodded a rethink on the strategic direction of the US foreign policy. This assessment was reflected in the National Intelligence Council report that analysed global trends furthered by the economic recession:

- the emergence of a multi polar order with the rise of China, India and others;

- more countries might be attracted to china model than the western politico-economic model;
- growing middle class escalates the probability of political liberalisation and potentially greater nationalism in China;
- shift of economic power from West to East amongst others.

They concluded that America would continue being the most powerful country but 'less dominant' in future.[39]

Bush's second term presented another shift: the deepening of ties to India. As the lively debate on the motivations of both countries revealed, China factor was implicit part of the equation. While the Indo-US Nuclear Deal caught the headlines, the maritime cooperation was equally relevant especially as the US concluded a Maritime Agreement with India in 2006. The heightened focus on the maritime domain coincided with the US assessment that the future would rest on sea power. In addition, the conceptual convergence of the two oceans Indian and Pacific, with emphasis on maritime cooperation with India presented a new shift in US thinking.

The growing US perspective on the Indo-Pacific region under Bush could be derived from the 2007 Maritime strategy, called 'A Cooperative Strategy for 21st Century Sea power'. The strategy advocated the use of sea power to maintaining safe, global commerce operations across the seas. It acknowledged that the global system of connected economies depended on "the freedom of movement across the maritime commons especially, since 90 per cent of the world's commerce by weight and volume transited through these seas". Calling on the seapower of the US to be prepared to combat changes to the system caused by regional frictions, terrorist activities, natural calamities, and war, the strategy enunciated the shift towards the holistic role of the 'sea services' in the era of globalisation.

This doctrine marked a significant shift in the US policy perspective on the Indo-Pacific. Analysis of this strategy revealed that the US clearly articulated how and why the maintenance and security of SLOC, particularly those that linked the United States with its important partners in the Indian and Pacific Oceans, was at the very core of US interests. This strategy enabled "the US to sustain credible combat power in the Western Pacific and Arabian Gulf/Indian Ocean so as to preclude attempts at interrupting vital sea lines of communication (SLOCs) and commerce".[40] Furthermore, the United States' strategic interests and the possibility of either state or non-state actors disrupting the Indo-Pacific SLOC to global economic prosperity were safeguarded by this renewed commitment to maritime security. This document was the basis on which the recent revised Maritime strategy of 2015 was unveiled.

The release of this strategy had manifold objectives: first, the US was a *Pacific* maritime nation, closely linked with Asia and the Pacific and was determined to put to rest that Asia's rise was America's decline. Second, it was a tacit recognition of the Chinese naval doctrine and hoe maritime cooperation was foundational principle in countering threats to long term security objectives. Third, security and economic interests of the US were integrally tied to those of Asia. As then Secretary of Defence Gates highlighted, US "...commitment to free and open commerce; a just international order that emphasises the rights and responsibilities of nations and fidelity to the rule of law; open access by all to the global commons of sea, air, space, cyberspace; and the principle of resolving conflict without the use of force", a veiled reference to the North Korean behaviour with South Korea.[41] The point was the linking of these critical sea lanes from the Pacific, extending into the Indian Ocean. Therefore, Indo-Pacific sea lanes were not only critical to the states involved in carrying the cargo but also to those where they terminated. Further, this articulation not only provided strategic guidance but "*...since its inception, CS21 has provided the common principles guiding maritime strategic decisions and served as a vital reference for leaders at all levels in the US sea services*".[42]

Thus, while the US perceived cooperation with China to moderate North Korea's actions as necessary, it was equally concerned that China's doctrine in the maritime domain would have the potential to disrupt commerce beyond Chinese territory. For instance, the inclusion of 'anti-SLOCS operations' as one of the 'six offensive and defensive campaigns identified in official Chinese naval doctrine' was based on its key capabilities in anti-access/area denial (A2/AD) capabilities. This perception drove change in the policy apparatus of the Department of Defense. In 2007, the office of the Assistant Secretary of Defense for Asian and Pacific Security Affairs, or ASD (APSA) came into existence. The creation of such an office was clearly an outcome of the DOD's importance to the nations and international organisations in the Asia Pacific region. The ASD (APSA) would work closely with 'the United States Pacific Command, United States Central Command, and the Asia-Pacific Centre for Security Studies' and represent the USD(P) and the Secretary of Defense in interagency policy discussions and international negotiations associated with the Asia-Pacific region. Thus, by the end of Bush presidency, the 2007 Maritime Doctrine and the policy process for role of the US in the key theatre of Indian Ocean region set the stage.

US Pivot to Asia: Obama Administration

With his election in 2009, Barack Obama faced a global economic crisis, two ongoing wars and a weak US standing amongst its allies across the world. China's growing influence and the systemic turbulence generated as power shifted from the west to the east and the future of Sino-US power relations loomed large.[43] In the US centred on how 'China and the United States are inescapably engaged in a power transition process, which is, on top of all other issues, about the future of international relations'.[44]

The US-China relationship was one of the most important bilateral relationships of the Obama tenure. The inclusion of three members of Asian descent, of which two were Chinese Americans in his first-term cabinet, highlighted the significance of a discourse with China on strategic and economic issues.

Obama administration's initial appraisal pointed to China being one of the key centres of influence, (along with Russia and India) that the US was looking to build deeper and effective partnership.[45] The strategy of the US also focussed sharply on monitoring China's modernisation program with respect to its military, to ensure no harm to US interests and that of its allies both regionally and globally. In particular, the approach to Asia Pacific region continued to revolve around the convergence of the Pacific and Indian Ocean. The 'Pivot or Rebalance to Asia' strategy with 'Transpacific Partnership' were the outcomes of such appraisal.

Thus, it was clear that an Asia Pacific strategy was going to be given priority as numerous high level delegation visits counting that of Secretary of State Hillary Clinton to Beijing and other Asian capitals occurred in the first few months. Discussions on the ongoing financial crisis, security and climate change issues along with other humanitarian concerns were on the agenda.[46] In an effort to convince China that the US supported its rise, media reports highlighted that Deputy Secretary of State James Steingberg called for 'a core, if tacit, bargain' between US and China. He also reiterated that China should guarantee that its rise 'will not come at the expense of the security and well-being of others'.[47]

The upbeat mood continued as the Defense Policy Co-ordination Talks held in Beijing where David Sedney, then Deputy Assistant Secretary of Defence for Asian and Pacific Affairs assured Beijing that America supported China's growth, despite misgivings with regard to their military expansion. These talks were seen as a step forward in Sino-US relations, given that China had called off bilateral military exchanges in 2008, due to the US arms deal with Taiwan.[48] However, there were signs of a quick breakdown. Not only did China see this approach as weak, it also wanted an immediate halt of both US surveillance activities off the Chinese coasts and arms trade to Taiwan.

A month after the talks, a couple of Chinese ships pursued a US Navy ship in the South China Sea. According to the US Defence Department, the Chinese vessels 'shadowed and aggressively maneuvered in dangerous proximity with USNS Impeccable', an American surveillance container, that was conducting usual operations in the South China Sea in 2009. Chinese aggression towards American Navy ships continued in the area for longer.[49] China's capability to carry out anti-SLOC operations along with its gradually assertive maritime behaviour thus became a driver to US security establishment's view of China as dangerous and disruptive to freedom of navigation. However, global economic revival as well as the North Korean and Iranian nuclear plans continued to be discussed with China. The 2009 visit to China by Obama begun with great expectations did not deliver.

The dilemma for the Obama administration was whether to continue to support China's rise and influence in the region or challenge China's power with the help of allies and partners in the region and widen influence of the US over the region. This policy dilemma was eventually resolved by choosing the path of challenging China.

In deciding to challenge China, the US focussed on the Asia-Pacific for the following reasons: the increasing economic prominence of the Asia-Pacific to the United States' future; the growing military capabilities of China, its aggressive assertions to disputed maritime territory, the slow withdrawal of US troops in Afghanistan and Iraq; and the domestic endeavour to reduce the budget of the US federal government, especially the defence budget, that further created a fear in the public sphere that US commitment to the Asia Pacific region will lessen.[50]

It was in this context, the White House brought out a series of official announcements regarding the US Pivot towards the Asia policy. The intention was to intensify and expand the already existing US presence in the Asia Pacific and reassure allies that it was here to stay. Former Secretary of State Hillary Clinton explained the prominence of the region by stating that 'The future of politics will be decided in Asia, not Afghanistan or Iraq, and the United States will be right at the centre of the action'. While the US has invested enough and more in the allocation of resources in these countries, the need to be 'smart' and 'systematic' would require devoting more time in the Asia Pacific region, '...so that it can put itself in the best position to sustain its leadership, secure its interests, and advance its values'.[51]

The strategy was also referred to as 'forward-deployed' diplomacy. The aim was to deploy their diplomatic resources such as their various agencies, top officials and field experts to different parts of the region. This was to be carried out with six major steps: "deepen relationships with emerging powers, including with China; strengthen bilateral security alliances; expand trade and investment; engage with regional multilateral institutions; forge a broad-based military presence; and advancing democracy and human rights".[52]

Hillary Clinton reiterated that in order to carry out their strategy in the region, it was important to build new partnerships. India and Indonesia were two countries that found a specific mention in the strategy proposed by Clinton. The US strategy thus broadened in the Asia Pacific as partnership with these countries would be the key to countering China given "their strategic location, growing economy, large population and democratic governance system".[53]

During his visit to India, Leon Panetta, former US Secretary of Defence brought up India as the 'lynchpin' of the US Rebalancing Strategy in Asia. This further highlighted the vital role India played in the overall plan.[54] Another US government report conveyed that, "The United States is also investing in a long-term strategic partnership with India to support its ability to serve as a regional economic anchor and provider of security in the broader Indian Ocean region".[55] A.K. Antony, former Indian defence minister was quick to respond to Panetta's statement, clarifying the need to boost the multilateral security architecture in the Asia Pacific region "at a pace comfortable to all countries concerned".[56]

China's continued aggression in the South China Sea along with Obama's bumpy summit in China triggered the change in the Obama administration's attitude towards China.[57] With the onset of the political conflict in Syria at the time, and conjectures of a likely US military attack, the strategy faced stark scrutiny as political analysts were of the opinion that the US focus would have to shift towards West Asia and Pivot policy would now be of lesser priority. This worry was further addressed by a statement by Chuck Hagel, then US Secretary of Defence during an official tour of South East Asia, where he reaffirmed that "Asia Pacific would continue to be a significant part of redefining international affairs" despite issues elsewhere.[58]

This was followed by a US federal government shutdown which lasted for 16 days, further denting US image across the region as this resulted in President Obama having to cancel his South East Asian tour which consisted of high level summits such as APEC, East Asia and ASEAN and separate visits to Malaysia and Philippines. Apart from boosting security ties, an important agenda of the tour was to also promote the TPP initiative. The cancelation of his tour was seen as a negative for the US image.[59]

A number of political analysts were of the opinion that the absence of Obama at APEC was not taken well in Asia "where symbolism is everything".[60]

John Kerry, Obama's representative at the APEC meeting in Bali and then US Secretary of State, said, "I believe that those standing in the way (of a resolution) need to think long and hard about the message that we send to the world when we can't get our own act together".[61]

The US Rebalancing Strategy thus formed with the conviction that the core of US foreign policy should be realigned towards Asia, reaffirming its allies of US commitment to lead from the front seemed to be faltering under both domestic and Chinese actions.

In the final analysis, the Obama years moved away from the strategic reassurance to one of rejection of China's actions. As the NSS 2015 strongly stated, "We reject illegal and aggressive claims to airspace and in the maritime domain and condemn deliberate attacks on commercial passenger traffic. On territorial disputes, particularly in Asia, we denounce coercion and assertive behaviour that threaten escalation. We encourage open channels of dialogue to resolve disputes peacefully in accordance with international law. We also support the early conclusion of an effective code of conduct for the South China Sea between China and the Association of Southeast Asian States (ASEAN)".[62]

While US worked towards boosting its security prospects in Asia Pacific, trade continued to play a vital role. In November 2015, the Obama government brought out the largest free-trade agreement in US history, the Trans-Pacific Partnership, calling it an irreplaceable element of America's policy in Asia that linked 12 countries on the Pacific excluding China. Apart from trade, Congressional debates played a crucial role in shaping US perspective. In his testimony to the House Committee on Appropriations in March 2015, Admiral Locklear brought out the relevance of USPACOM's strategy in 'Indo Asia Pacific' region which he described in great detail. "The region also contains seven of the ten largest standing militaries, five nuclear nations, and five of the

US's seven mutual defense treaty alliances. The socioeconomic diversity and population density throughout the USPACOM area of responsibility (AOR) create strategic long-term challenges. These challenges include: political instability, social inequality, poverty, increased sensitivity to climate change and natural disasters, risk of pandemic disease, and epidemic drug use and distribution." He further reinstated that the US should continue to safeguard its access to air and sea lanes, deter North Korean aggression, monitor the activities of extremists in the Indo Asia Pacific, and push for peaceful resolution of maritime and territorial disputes in and around East and South China Sea.[63]

Congressional Committees in the Senate and House dealing with Foreign Affairs and Armed Services listened to successive PACOM Commanders on this theme and concluded that "the United States must continue to sustain a favourable military balance in the Asia-Pacific region... (due to) implications of China's rapid military modernisation".

Further, in the Congress' view, the US "...must continue to help our allies and partners in the Asia-Pacific region to build their maritime capacity, an initiative that this committee seeks to further in the fiscal year 2016 National Defense Authorisation Act [NDAA]".

The Congress shared Admiral Harris' view that "The United States is a maritime nation and the importance of the Asia-Pacific region to our Nation's security and prosperity cannot be overstated. Almost 30 percent of the world's maritime trade, as the chairman said, over $5 trillion, transits the South China Sea annually. This includes $1.2 trillion in ship-borne trade bound for the United States. The Asia-Pacific region is critical for our Nation's economic future".

India was seen as the obvious choice to counter China: "Rebalancing also means building a bridge between the confluence of two oceans, the Indian and Pacific, strengthening ties between India and East Asia".[64]

By the time the Trump administration came in, the Congress in a hearing held on April 26, 2017, decided to support what Admiral Harris noted as "Our five bilateral defense treaty alliances anchor our joint force efforts in the Indo-Asia-Pacific".[65]

India–Asia-Pacific to Indo-Pacific Strategy: Perspective under Trump

The 'India-Asia-Pacific' region had garnered major attention under the Obama administration and produced the 'Asia-Pivot/Rebalancing' strategy to tackle the issues identified. Separately, military and economic strategies were also announced to provide a comprehensive policy framework for the region. While Pentagon consistently pointed to the China threat, other executive departments came to similar conclusions due to a variety of factors. Ultimately, there was a consensus that American footprint, with help of old allies and new partners (India) should remain large in the region.

Trump administration devised a new strategic framework to describe region. From 'India Asia-Pacific' the term 'Indo-Pacific' came to acquire a fresh momentum. President Trump's campaign was highly critical of the Obama 'Asia rebalancing' strategy. As a result, Trump after coming to office not only abandoned the 'Rebalancing Asia' strategy and the Transnational Pacific Partnership, but acknowledged the region as 'Indo Pacific' elevating the region status as a top-level priority with vast geopolitical and strategic significance for the US. While analysts have argued that it was US Secretary of State Hillary Clinton who for the first time employed the phrase 'Indo-Pacific' in order to recognise India's role in new power dynamics[66], it was President Trump's trip to Asia in November 2017 that the term 'Indo-Pacific' was officially substituted for India-Asia-Pacific.

After Trump administration declared the 'rebalance' to Asia dead, the 'Free and Open Indo-Pacific' strategy acquired a central stage that aimed at pursing similar goals like containment of assertive China's presence in the region and aiming at strengthening relations with key regional countries like Australia, India & Japan and ASEAN.

In a special briefing to the press, Alex N. Wong, Deputy Assistant Secretary, Bureau of East Asian and Pacific Affairs, on April 2, 2018 gave a succinct outline of the American strategy in the Indo Pacific. He stated that the US, under President Trump, introduced a strategic concept called the "Free and Open Indo-Pacific Strategy" underscored by him during his 13-day visit to Asia in November 2017, wherein he spelt out this concept in numerous meetings and speeches in Seoul and Da Nang. Of particular interest was the mention of India as key to maintaining a "free and open Indo-Pacific." US emphasis on the centrality of India in this strategy signalled to the Chinese that there was convergence between the two on preventing Chinese domination. This strategy was in the making from the very first year of Trump Presidency and the subsequent years could see the implementation of it. It also seemed that the US supported both aspects: 'Free and Open' as interlinked part of the strategy towards the Indo Pacific.

To its allies the US emphasised, "Our vision for the Indo-Pacific is a region is for every nation big and small to have a rules-based order that allows all to interact as sovereign and equal nations" said Walter Douglas, Deputy Assistant Secretary, Bureau of East Asian and Pacific Affairs, during his visit to New Zealand in 2018.[67] In continuance with the strategy, in a ministerial consultation meeting held in June, the US, India, Australia and Japan agreed to examine how to achieve shared goals including "development and connectivity; good governance; regional security, including counterterrorism and non-proliferation; and maritime cooperation".[68]

US Secretary of State Mike Pompeo emphasised that even though the US is not motivated solely by economic interest, it is at the heart of the strategy which is why the "US seeks to promote free, fair, and reciprocal trade and investment in priority areas, such as digital trade, intellectual property rights enforcement, automobiles, electronic payments, and agricultural goods."[69]

In the above statements, there was a concerted effort to appear universal and inclusive while the main reason for the accelerated policy announcements vis-à-vis, China and its behaviour, was hidden in plain view. Arguably, the elevated importance of India in the US strategic calculations for the region could be a sign that US–India ties are set to deepen further.

The sour Sino-US trade relations and harsh accusations from the Trump administration regarding China's obstructive attitude, military operations in the region has provoked Chinese reaction. Chinese analysts have stated: "The US Indo-Pacific strategy seeks to use political (emphasising democratic values), economic (exclusive institutional economic and trade arrangements), diplomatic (strengthening bilateral alliances and sowing discord between China and other countries), military (joint military exercises and arms sales) and other means to co-opt China's neighbouring countries to undermine China, contain China's rise, and ultimately maintain US hegemony".[70]

The revival of Quadrilateral Security Initiative (QSI), on the sidelines of East Asia Summit, 2017 was the first significant step towards a possible future alliance in the region. The idea of 'Quad' for emerged under the George W. Bush the first time. Under the Trump administration, it appears specifically as a counterweight to Beijing. Though Quad is in nascent stage and its potential in the future to contain China is being questioned, yet coming together of like-minded democracies (Australia, India, Japan and US) has been considered timely and necessary to counterbalance assertive Chinese actions in the region.

The increasing importance of the region for the Trump administration can be witnessed by the usage of the term 'Indo-Pacific' multiple times in the US official documents as well as in number of other multilateral meetings. In NSS 2017 and during his maiden Asia trip in 2017, Trump elevated 'Indo-Pacific' as a top-level priority region with vast geopolitical and strategic significance for the US. In National Security Strategy (NSS), 2017 the current administration acknowledges the growing instability in the region with "geopolitical competition between free and repressive visions of world order taking place in the Indo-Pacific".[71] In this document there is an open recognition that the rise of belligerent China is threat to the US presence and therefore it would aim to counter China by boosting ties with its major regional allies in the region. The reports stated:

> "China has mounted a rapid military modernisation campaign designed to limit US access to the region and provide China a freer hand there. China presents its ambitions as mutually beneficial, but Chinese dominance risks diminishing the sovereignty of many states in the Indo-Pacific...to counter China's economic inducements and penalties; influenced operations and implied military threats to persuade other states to heed its political and security agenda...we will redouble our commitment to established alliances and partnerships, while expanding and deepening relationships with new partners that share respect for sovereign, fair and reciprocal trade, and the rule of law".[72]

James Curran argues that the Trump administration strategy of 'Free and Open Indo-Pacific' is essential not only for the US but also for its major partners in the region to contain Chinese increasing military presence and its abilities to dictate in 'Asia waters, Asia trade, and Asia diplomacy'. He further states that the strategy explicitly calls for "freedom of navigation in Pacific waters, to assertively and publicly call out Beijing for violating free navigation in areas of the Pacific, work with Asian states to promote high-quality bilateral free trade deals, and also emphasises states' sovereignty, essentially rejecting large multilateral coalitions".[73] The strategy is also in line with the Trump's 'America-First' policy, that aims at reinvigorating economic power of the country. Further, Trump administration's NSS and NDS report calls out China as a 'revisionist power' and a 'strategic competitor'[74] respectively. The usage of these terms by Trump administration, its 'Indo-Pacific' strategy and revival of Quad has made China more assertive and only added more issues to the US-Sino relations.

Trump 'Indo-Pacific' strategy also indicates that the US is ready to work with other likeminded countries in the region not just to counterweight China's actions and strategies but also to prioritize its ties with other major democracies. In the recent Shangri la Dialogue, Secretary of Defense James Mattis's speech outlined Trump administration's Indo-Pacific strategy. His remarks affirmed the US commitment to ASEAN centrality and partnering with ASEAN and ASEAN-led institutions.

This framework for the future regional model will seek to reward member nations that support freedom of navigation, norms and rules in international waters. James Mattis, United States Defence Secretary just before the beginning of the Shangri La Dialogue, declared that 'US Pacific Command' to be now referred as 'US Indo-Pacific Command' projecting Washington's new set of national interests.

With the onset of the 21st century the growing importance of India in the US strategic thinking is continuously increasing. Pentagon report (Jan. 2012) stated, "India as the only valuable strategic partner in the region and that the United States is also investing in a long-term strategic partnership with India to support its ability to serve as a regional economic anchor and provider of security in the broader Indian Ocean region"[75] The Trump administration too is continuously signalling to upgrade its US-India strategic partnership. The Trump administration focus towards the region is driven by the aim to improve New Delhi's integration with the East especially in the light of India's 'Act East Policy'. Furthermore, the usage of the term 'Indo-Pacific' emphasises on India's status as a global power and supports the leadership role of India to ensure security in the Indian Ocean. This move of Trump signifies the importance of Indo-Pacific region in US foreign policy strategic, diplomatic and geopolitical construct.

> Ashley Tellis in the testimony on "The challenges facing the United States in the Indo-Pacific region" to the Senate Armed Services Committee stated that for Trump administration "there is a need for clear public commitment to the preservation of US global primacy and its regional pre-eminence in the Indo-Pacific for preserving a balance of power that favours freedom in its own self-interest".[76]

Furthermore, in the testimony he highlights that the Trump administration should aim at materialising the efforts taken by key regional actors like Japan, Australia and India to increase security cooperation in the region. The key objective of US should be to actively engage in military exercises, encourage consultations, and build deeper cooperation and liaison relationship, with Quad members to balance China in Asia.

In light of these statements of policy, it is clear that the US perspective on the Indo-Pacific connects strategic, security, economic and commercial aspects as key pillars of the strategy. Further, the strategic reassurance on the continued US focus on the Indo Pacific to allies and others reveals that this strategy is set to play a major part in the US foreign policy in the coming years.

NOTES

1 C Rajamohan (2017), "The Confluence of Two Seas", *Carnegie India*, 26 October 2017, available at https://carnegieindia.org/2017/10/26/confluence-of-two-seas-pub-73560

2 The White House (2017), "National Security Strategy of the United States of America", p.46, available at https://www.whitehouse.gov/wp-content/uploads/2017/12/NSS-Final-12-18-2017-0905.pdf

3 Department of Defense (2018), "Remarks by Secretary Mattis at Plenary Session of the 2018 Shangri-La-Dialogue", 2 June 2018, available at https://dod.defense.gov/News/Transcripts/Transcript-View/Article/1538599/remarks-by-secretary-mattis-at-plenary-session-of-the-2018-shangri-la-dialogue/.

4 US Department of State (2018), Remarks by Walter Douglas on "New Zealand, the United States and the Indo Pacific", March 26, 2018, available at https://www.state.gov/p/eap/rls/rm/2018/03/279557.htm

5 US Department of State (2018), Integrated Country Strategy: India, 3 August 2018, available at https://www.state.gov/documents/organization/285254.pdf

6 The Hindu (2018), 2+2 Dialogue an Important Opportunity to Enhance Engagement with India: US, 21 August 2018, available at https://www.thehindu.com/news/international/22-dialogue-important-opportunity-to-enhance-engagement-with-india-us/article24742816.ece

7 University of South California US-China Institute (2017), China in US National Security Strategy Reports, 1987-2017, available at https://china.usc.edu/sites/default/files/article/attachments/china-in-us-national-security-strategy-reports-1987-2017.pdf

8 The White House (1993), National Security Strategy of United States, January 1993, available at http://nssarchive.us/NSSR/1993.pdf

9 Kerry, Robert. J and Manning, Robert A. (2001), The United States and Southeast Asia: A Policy Agenda for the New Administration, Council on Foreign Relations, Task Force Report, July 2001, (New York: CFR Press), available at https://www.cfr.org/report/united-states-and-southeast-asia

10 The White House (1994), National Security Strategy of Entanglement and Enlargement, 1 July 1994, available at http://nssarchive.us/national-security-strategy-1994/

11 US, Department of Defense, (1997) Quadrennial Defense Review, May 1997, available at https://history.defense.gov/Historical-Sources/Quadrennial-Defense-Review/

12 US State Department (1999), Under Secretary of Defense Policy, Summer Study Final Report: Asia 2025, July 25 to August 1999, US Archives, available at https://archive.org/

stream/UnderSecretaryofDefenseUSDPolicy1999SummerStudyFinalReportASIA2025/Under+Secretary+of+Defense+USDPolicy+1999+Summer+Study+Final+Report+ASIA+2025_djvu.txt

13 Tangredi, Sam J (2000), All Possible Wars? Toward a Consensus View of the Future Security Environment, 2001-2025, *National Defense University*, Mc Nair Paper 23, available at https://www.files.ethz.ch/isn/10896/doc_10927_290_en.pdf

14 Ibid.

15 Congressional Act, 106th Congress (1999), National Defense Authorization Act 2000, Public Law 106-65, 5 October, 1999, US Government Publishing Office, Washington DC, available at https://www.congress.gov/bill/106th-congress/senate-bill/1059

16 Ibid, available at https://legcounsel.house.gov/Comps/106-65.pdf

17 Ibid.

18 US China Economic and Security Review Commission, October 2000, available at https://www.uscc.gov/about

19 Kaiser, Robert G and Mufson, Steven (2000), Blue Team Draws a Hard Line on Beijing: Action on Hill Reflects Informal Group's Clout, *The Washington Post Archives*, 22 February 2000, available at https://www.washingtonpost.com/wp-srv/WPcap/2000-02/22/004r-022200-idx.html?noredirect=on

20 Osius, Ted (2001), Legacy of the Clinton-Gore Administration's China Policy, *Asian Affairs*, 28(3), Fall 2001, p 125.

21 US Congress (2000), 106th Congress, H.R. 4444 China Trade Bill, US Library of Congress, Washington DC, available at https://www.govtrack.us/congress/bills/106/hr4444/text

22 Bill Clinton (2000), "Speech on China Trade Bill" delivered at Paul H. Nitze School of Advanced International Studies at John Hopkins University, Maryland, 9 March, 2000, available at https://www.iatp.org/files/Full_Text_of_Clintons_Speech_on_ China_Trade_Bi.htm

23 US-China Institute, 2017, China in U.S. National Security Strategy Reports, 1987-2017, available in https://china.usc.edu/sites/default/files/article/attachments/china-in-us-national-security-strategy-reports-1987-2017.pdf, accessed on 28 July 2018.

24 Hathaway, Robert M and Wilson Lee (2005), George W Bush and East Asia: A First Term Assessment, Woodrow Wilson International Centre for Scholars Report, Asia program, available at https://www.wilsoncenter.org/sites/default/files/bushasia2rpt.pdf

25 The White House (2002), National Security Strategy of United States, September 2002, available at https://www.state.gov/documents/organization/63562.pdf

26 Wang, Chi (2009), George W. Bush and China: Policies, Problems and Partnership, (UK: Lexington Books), p. xiii.

27 Ibid.

28 Ibid.

29 US, Department of State, 2008, Media Note, Conclusion of the Sixth Round of the U.S.-China Senior Dialogue, available at https://2001-2009.state.gov/r/pa/prs/ps/2008/dec/113230.htm.

30 Government of Japan (2007), Japan Australia Joint Declaration on Security Cooperation, Ministry of Foreign Affairs of Japan,13 March 2007, available at https://www.mofa.go.jp/region/asia-paci/australia/joint0703.html

31 Government of India (2006), Joint Statement Towards India-Japan Strategic and Global

Partnership, Ministry of External Affairs,15 December, 2006, available at http://mea.gov.in/bilateraldocuments.htm?dtl/6368/Joint+Statement+Towards+IndiaJapan+Strategic+ and+Global+Partnership

32 Ali, S. Mahmud (2015), *US-China Strategic Competition: Towards a New Power Equilibrium*, (London: Springer), p.20.

33 Sekhon, Harinder (2018), India and Japan: New Strategic Dimension in Gauri Khandekar and Bart Gaens (eds), *Japan's Search for Strategic Security Partnership*, (Oxon: Routledge), p. 58.

34 Dikshit, Sandeep (2007), First Joint Naval Exercise with Australia in September, The Hindu, July 12, 2007, available at https://www.thehindu.com/todays-paper/tp-national/First-joint-naval-exercise-with-Australia-in-September/article14792645.ece

35 Singh, Rahul (2007), China Miffed at India Ties with 3 Nations, Hindustan Times, August 21, 2007, available at https://www.hindustantimes.com/india/china-miffed-at-india-ties-with-3-nations/story-YJsqY9g1kH8ONzQV9MTCzL.html

36 Government of Japan (2007), Joint Statement on the Roadmap for New Dimensions to the Strategic and Global Partnership Between Japan and India, Ministry of Foreign Affairs of Japan, August 22, 2007, available at https://www.mofa.go.jp/region/asia-paci/pmv0708/joint-2.html

37 Dikshit, Sandeep (2007), Japanese Defense Minister Meets Antony, The Hindu, August 25, 2007, available at https://www.thehindu.com/todays-paper/Japanese-Defence-Minister-meets-Antony/article14822457.ece

38 The White House (2006), National Security Strategy of United States, March 2006, available at https://www.state.gov/documents/organization/64884.pdf

39 National Intelligence Council (2008), *Global Trends 2025: A Transformed World*, November 2008, available at https://www.files.ethz.ch/isn/94769/2008_11_global_trends_ 2025.pdf

40 Bradford, John F (2011), "The Maritime Strategy of the United States: Implications for Indo-Pacific Sea Lanes." *Contemporary Southeast Asia*, 33(2): 183-208, available at http://www.jstor.org/stable/41288826.

41 Ibid.

42 Ibid.

43 Joseph Nye Jr., "Understanding 21st century Power Shifts", *The European Financial Review*, 24 June 2011, available at http://www.europeanfinancialreview.com/?p=2743

44 Lai D (2011), "The United States and China In Power Transition", US Army War College, Carlisle, p ix, http://ssi.armywarcollege.edu/pdffiles/pub1093.pdf

45 The White House (2010), National Security Strategy of United States, May 2010, available at http://nssarchive.us/national-security-strategy-2010/

46 US Department of State (2009), "Secretary Clinton: Travel to Asia", February 2009, https://2009-2017.state.gov/secretary/20092013clinton/trvl/2009/116166.htm

47 Pomfret, John (2016), "America vs. China: A competitive face-off Between Two Pacific Powers", *The Washington Post*, 18 November 2016, available at https://www.washingtonpost. com/graphics/national/obama-legacy/relations-with-china.html

48 Asian News International (2009), "US-China defense talks the "best" in more than a Decade", *The Free Library*, available at https://www.thefreelibrary.com/US-

China+defense+ talks+the+%22best%22+in+more+than+a+decade%2C+says...-a0212343984

49 Morgan, David (2009), "US Says Chinese vessels harassed Navy Ship", *The Reuters*, https://www.reuters.com/article/us-usa-china-navy/u-s-says-chinese-vessels-harassed-navy-ship-idUSTRE52845A20090309

50 Congressional Research Service (2012), "Pivot to the Pacific? The Obama Administration's "Rebalancing" Toward Asia", 28 March 2012, https://fas.org/sgp/crs/natsec/R42448.pdf

51 Clinton, Hillary "America's Pacific Century", *Foreign Policy*, November 2011, also see http://www.foreignpolicy.com/articles/2011/10/11/americas_pacific_century?wp_login_redirect=0

52 Ibid.

53 Clinton, Hillary, "Asia's Pacific Century", *Foreign Policy*, 11 October 2011, see http://www.foreignpolicy.com/articles/2011/10/11/americas_pacific_century

54 US Department of Defence (2012), "Remarks by Secretary Panetta at the Institute of Defence Studies and Analyses, 6 June 2012, available at http://archive.defense.gov/transcripts/transcript.aspx?transcriptid=5054

55 S. Amer Latif, India and the New US Defence Strategy, *Centre for Strategic and International Studies*, 22 February 2013, available at http://csis.org/publication/india-and-new-us-defense-strategy.

56 India and US Hold Defence Talks Asia Pacific Countries Should Settle Bilateral Disputes as per International Law, *Press Information Bureau*, 6 June 2012, available at http://pib.nic.in/newsite/erelease.aspx?relid=84715

57 Landler, Mark, "Obama's Journey to Tougher Tack on China", The New York Times, 20 September, 2012, available at https://www.nytimes.com/2012/09/21/us/politics/obamas-evolution-to-a-tougher-line-on-china.html.

58 Abraham M. Denmark, "Will Syria Kill the Asia Rebalance?", *The National Interest*, 5 September 2013, available at http://nationalinterest.org/commentary/will-syria-kill-the-asia-rebalance-8995?page=1

59 Joshua Kurlantzick (2013), "How Damaging is the Cancellation of Obama's Trip?" *Gateway House*, 5 October 2013, available at http://www.gatewayhouse.in/how-damaging-is-the-cancellation-of-obamas-trip/

60 James Hookway, Natasha Brereton-Fukui and Peter Nicholas, "Obama Absence Gives China Opening", *The Wall Street Journal*, 4 October 2013, available at https://www.wsj.com/articles/obama-cancels-asia-trip-leaving-more-space-for-china-1380870951

61 Matthew Lee (2013), "John Kerry Warns Congress: Think 'Long and Hard' About Government Shutdown's Global Message", *Huffington Post*, 5 October 2013, available at https://upload.democraticunderground.com/11093560

62 The White House (2015), National Security Strategy of United States, February 2015, available at http://nssarchive.us/wp-content/uploads/2015/02/2015.pdf

63 Adm. Samuel J. Locklear III (2015), Remarks Before the House Appropriations Committee, 18 March 2018, available at http://www.pacom.mil/Media/Speeches-Testimony/Article/581146/pacom-before-the-house-appropriations-committee-remarks/

64 Congressional Hearing, 113th Congress (2013), Session I, House of Representatives Committee on Armed Services, H.A.S.C. No. 113-49, Statement Of Dr. Patrick M.

Cronin, Senior Advisor And Senior Director Of The Asia Program, Center For A New American Security, Rebalancing To The Asia–Pacific Region And Implications For U.S. National Security, July 24, 2013, available at https://www.gpo.gov/fdsys/pkg/CHRG-113hhrg82464/pdf/CHRG-113hhrg82464.pdf

65 Congressional Hearings, (2017), US 115 th Congress, Session 1 st, House of Representatives, Committee on Armed Services, Hearings, Military Assessment of the Security Challenges in the Indo Pacific Region, 26 April 2017, (US Government Printing Office: Washington. DC), available at https://www.gpo.gov/fdsys/pkg/CHRG-115hhrg25822/html/CHRG-115hhrg25822.htm

66 Hillary Clinton, (2011), "America's Pacific Century" *Foreign Policy,* October 11, 2011 http:://www.foreignpolicy.com/articles/2011/10/11/americas_pacifc_century

67 US Department of State (2018), Remarks by Walter Douglas on "New Zealand, the United States and the Indo Pacific", March 26, 2018, available at https://www.state.gov/p/eap/rls/rm/2018/03/279557.htm

68 Australian Department of Foreign Affairs and Trade (2018), Media Release on "Australia-India-Japan-United States Consultations", June 7, 2018, available at https://dfat.gov.au/news/media/Pages/australia-india-japan-united-states-consultations.aspx

69 Department of Defense (2018), Remarks by Secretary of State Michal R. Pompeo at a Business Community Reception, 8 July 2018, available at https://www.state.gov/secretary/remarks/2018/07/283892.htm.

70 Peng, Wang (2018), "China's Counter Measures to US Indo Pacific Strategy, *CGTN*, 22 August 2018, available at https://news.cgtn.com/news/3d3d674d79636a4e79457a6333566d54/share_p.html

71 The White House (2017), "National Security Strategy of the United States of America",p.45, available at https://www.whitehouse.gov/wp-content/uploads/2017/12/NSS-Final-12-18-2017-0905.pdf

72 Ibid, p.46

73 Kurlantzick, Joshua (2018), "Trumps Indo-Pacific Vision: A Solid Idea Hard to Pull Off" *Aspenia,* 19 February, 2018, available at https://www.aspeninstitute.it/aspenia-online/article/trumps-indo-pacific-vision-solid-idea-hard-pull

74 Department of Defense (2018), "Summary of the 2018 National Defense Strategy of The United States of America: Sharpening the American Military's Competitive Edge", pp. 1, available at https://www.defense.gov/Portals/1/Documents/pubs/2018-National-Defense-Strategy-Summary.pdf

75 US Department of Defense (2012), *Sustaining US Global leadership: Priorities For 21st Century Defense,* p. 8, available at http://archive.defense.gov/news/defense_strategic_guidance. pdf

76 Ashley J. Tellis (2017) "Protecting American Primacy in the Indo-Pacific", *Carnegie Endowment for International Peace,* available at http://carnegieendowment.org/2017/04/25/protecting-american-primacy-in-indo-pacific-pub-68754

2

Indo-Pacific Region and Japan's Security Dilemma

R.S. Yadav

ABSTRACT

In the post-Cold War era, geo-political game in Indo-Pacific is more becoming a strategy of containment and encirclement rather than accommodation. Consequently, it may present a picture of instability and conflict heightening tensions in the times to come. Besides, rise of emerging power centres like China and India and shift in global economy from Atlantic to Pacific have added impetus to this phenomenon. As a result, there emerged not only the driving power of global economy, but also brought change about the balance of power in the region. Even non-traditional threats in the form of piracy, terrorism, narcotic drug trafficking, etc., are creating problem of governance in the area. Concerns are also being raised towards an attempt to challenge the status quo by force and destabilising the existing order in the region. Since geographically it is very proximate to Japan, hence latter is bound to face severe dilemma for its security from the contemporary developments in the Indo-Pacific.

Japan's security outlook towards Indo-pacific is determined by three-fold considerations: Its overall foreign policy moorings; its global alignments with power-centres; and, its geo-political settings. In its overall foreign policy orientations Japan has earlier been dependent on US security umbrella. Presently it is working as strategic partner of America's 'pivot of Asia' policy in this region. Simultaneously, it is involved as co-anchor in India's evolving Indo-Pacific security coalition that seems to take shape potentially as a counter-weight to China's menacing rise endangering Asia's security. Besides, through its 'Free and Open Indo-Pacific' policy it is engaged to enhance connectivity, boost infrastructure, increase investments and development in the region. As a result, high priority is given to the neighbours to create a peaceful and stable regional community underpinned by rule of international law and a free and open integrated regional economy.

Japan's 'free and open Indo-Pacific' strategy provide its geo-economic and geo-political vision towards this region. Geo-economically, this has been aimed at combining the dynamism of Asia and Africa, envisioning a greater regional integration along the coastlines of Indian and Pacific oceans, by promoting high standard infrastructure building and enhanced connectivity. Geo-politically, it has to counter balance vis-à-vis growing Chinese influence and presence in Eurasia and Africa under President Xi Jinping's 'one belt, one road' (OBOR) initiative. To operationalise this Japan has tried to build goodwill at bilateral levels towards its neighbours and countries of ASEAN and India. That is why, nearly two-third of total ODA was given by Japan to countries of East and Southeast Asia. At the multilateral level as well, Japan operationalise it by joining various frameworks like: Japan-ASEAN; Japan-Mekong Cooperation; ASEAN+3; East Asia Summit (EAS); ASEAN Regional Forum (ARF); and Asia Pacific Economic Cooperation (APEC). Besides, it is supported by Japan-US alliance as linchpin of its Indo-Pacific policy. Thus, through bilateral and multilateral naval exercises, particularly its joining of trilateral (Japan-India-USA) and quadrilateral (Japan-India-USA-Australia) groupings, it has further leads to strengthen its security scenario. It has further strengthened its position by creating synergies of its policy of 'free and open Indo-Pacific policy' and India's 'Act East policy'. In this context, Japan has perceived its membership of 'Quad' as 'Asia's democratic security diamond'.

But everything is not smooth for Japan's security arrangements in the Indo-Pacific region. Economically, if on the one hand, globalisation has enhanced interdependence and connectivity, then on the other hand emergence of protectionism and inward-looking trends are also manifest. Proliferation of Free Trade Agreements (FTAs) are there in Indo-Pacific, but China has emerged as leading trade partner of most regional economies. Changing maritime dynamics due to surging trade flows, regional powers have started for access, influence and relative advantage. Japan's vulnerability also lies in her near total dependence on fuel, feed, food (except rice) and virtually all the essential industrial raw material, as well as, corresponding dependence on fair access to foreign markets for her exports. Geo-politically, China's potential to endanger Japanese security, both by direct action (coercive politico-military brinkmanship) and through proxy use of North Korea, is serious problem for it. This is further aggravated by the prevailing politico-security milieu in the tri-polar structure involving USA, Russia and China. Thus, this region has developed a certain 'grey zone' situation due to insufficient institutionalisation of cooperative security framework. Besides, Donald Trump's uncertain policy initiatives like withdrawal from Trans Pacific Partnership (TPP), non-agreeing to climate change issues, changed attitudes towards North Korea and China, etc., have further created a disadvantageous position for Japan in this region. As a consequences of these developments, efforts towards forging of new alignments by India-China- Russia on the one hand, and initiation of USA-Russia dialogue on the other hand, have further created uncertainties in the region which are going to have significant bearing for the security of Japan.

In the given scenario, Japan is left with twin options to ensure its security in the Indo-Pacific area. On the one hand, it has to enhance its capabilities through developing strong ties with its neighbours along with fast tracking military capabilities in the areas of ballistic missiles interceptors, ballistic missiles shields and preparing for cyber and space wars. Simultaneously, Japan has to engage itself with the changed region and global scenario in such a way to evolve an integrated larger Asian economic community with a common security framework for Indo-Pacific.

Post-Cold War Scenario

In the post-Cold War era, geopolitical game in Indo-Pacific is more becoming a strategy of containment and encirclement rather than accommodation. Consequently, it may present a picture of instability and conflict heightening tensions in the times to come. Besides, rise of emerging power centres like China and India and shift in global economy from Atlantic to Pacific have added impetus to this phenomenon. As a result, there emerged not only the driving power of global economy, but also brought change about the balance of power in the region. Even non-traditional threats in the form of piracy, terrorism, narcotic drug trafficking etc. are creating problem of governance in the area. Concerns are also being raised towards an attempt to challenge the status quo by force and destabilising the existing order in the region. Since geographically it is very proximate to Japan, hence latter is bound to face severe dilemma for its security from the contemporary developments in the Indo-Pacific. It is because Japan has to face new kind of geostrategic and geoeconomic scenario, as both regional and global power dynamics are transforming in a significant manner. Hence, it became pertinent to analyse the reasons for the involvement of Japan in the Indo-Pacific region. What are its security concerns in this area? What types of strategies is Japan going to adopt for the realisation of such objectives? What are the likely irritants it is going to face towards the attainment of its security goal? What will be the future of Japan's security engagements from the Indo-Pacific? Therefore, here a modest effort has been made to find out the answer to such related questions.

Historical Perspective

Japan's interest in the Indo-Pacific region goes back to Shinzo Abe's speech entitled 'Confluence of Two Seas' delivered in the Indian Parliament on 22 August 2007; where he commented that the 'Confluence of the Indian and Pacific Oceans' as 'the dynamic coupling as seas of freedom and prosperity' in the 'broader Asia'.[1] For the safety and security of this region he suggested the cooperation among like-minded democratic states of the USA, India, Japan and Australia on certain fundamental values such as "freedom, democracy and the respect for basic human rights as well as strategic interests."[2] This idea was reiterated by him in December 2012 when he proposed a new security coalition among these states declaring it as 'Asia's Democratic Diamond'. Japanese leader might has perceived such idea due to their perceptions from "North Korea's nuclear threat, a rapidly rising China, and an unpredictable Trump..."[3] As a result, Japan's new Indo-Pacific strategy might have been aimed at to improve connectivity between the Pacific and the Indian Ocean. Thus, Indo-Pacific strategy is "threat-driven cooperation among like-minded maritime countries to promote a rule-based regional order. It is also a reaction to the rapid strategic and power structural changes characterised by China's assertive behaviour in the region, which poses increasing challenges to the US and its allies in the Pacific and Indian Ocean."[4] In this process Japan is most affected of them all due to its proximity and unique geographical setting.

Japan's Security Concerns

Japan's security outlook towards Indo-Pacific is determined by three-fold considerations: Its overall foreign policy moorings; its global alignments with power-centres; and, its geopolitical settings. Japan attained sovereignty status after the signing of San Francisco Treaty on 8 September 1951 (effective on 28 April 1952), which normalise its relations with all the allied powers, except Soviet Union. Simultaneously, on the same day it also signed 'Mutual Security Assistance Pact' with the USA, which allowed the latter to maintain the bases and troops on Japanese soil. Thus, since its inception, Japan accepted the security umbrella of the USA. Whereas with other countries it adopted the policy of 'omnidirectional diplomacy' which was essentially a policy of political neutrality and economic cooperation. Hence, Japan's post-World War II foreign policy orientation has been to regain economic viability and credible peace loving nation. But its national security was entrusted to protective shield and nuclear umbrella of the USA.

In the early 1970s, slight shift in Japan's policy towards the USA has been noticed due to emerging US-China rapprochement, America's withdrawal from

Indo-China region through Guam doctrine and the oil crisis in the Middle East. However, due to Islamic revolution in Iran and later Afghanistan crisis, America military presence in the region was restored. This again entrusted Japan's interest towards the USA. Later, currency realignment between them in 1980s increased the growth of Japanese trade, aid and investments, particularly in Asia. Consequently, Japan not only became the world's largest creditor nation in the decade, but also became major investor in the USA and contributor to international debt relief, financial institutions and other global assistance efforts. In the post-Cold War years, Japan has to adopt itself to the altered strategic and economic global milieu. As a result, Japan's influence increased in World Bank, IMF and other international financial institutions. However, its reliance for security guarantee on the USA continued as before despite changed world order. In its overall foreign policy orientations Japan has earlier been dependent on US security umbrella and it continues to work as strategic partner of America's 'pivot of Asia' policy in this region.

Simultaneously, it is involved as co-anchor in India's evolving Indo-Pacific security coalition that seems to take shape potentially as a counter-weight to China's menacing rise endangering Asia's security. Besides, through its 'Free and Open Indo-Pacific' (FOIP) policy it is engaged to enhance connectivity, boost infrastructure, increase investments and development in the region. As a result, high priority is given to the neighbours to create peaceful and stable regional community underpinned by rule of international law and free and open and integrated regional economy.

Strategies toward Indo-Pacific

After Shinzo Abe's renewed focus towards, the Indo-Pacific, Japan adopted the strategy of 'Free and Open Indo-Pacific'. This was later on revised and clarified in its plan of the 2013 ASEAN-Japan Vision Statement and further given boost through its August 2017 release of the—*Revised Implementation Plan of the Vision Statement on ASEAN-Japan Friendship and Coöperation: Shared Vision, Shared Identity, Shared Future.*[5] On the basis of these documents one can discern that Japan's strategies towards this region can be summed up in three-fold issues: (a) Trade; (b) Security; and (c) Development.[6]

(a) *Trade:* Geo-economically, in the post-Cold War era Japan's aim has been to combine the economic dynamism of Asia and Africa. This has been envisioned by creating a greater regional integration along the coastlines of Indian and Pacific oceans, by promoting high standard infrastructure-building and enhanced connectivity.But withdrawal of the USA from the Trans-Pacific Partnership (TPP), under the regime of Donald Trump, has created serious setback towards trade activities in the region. It is because economically USA constitutes for nearly 60 percent of total GDP of the TPP member states. Therefore, it has substantially reduced the influence of the states on global trade. Even this deficit in no way facilitate the growth of trade by the other neighbouring states of Southeast Asia. The only alternative to such withdrawal can be the formation of Regional Comprehensive Economic Partnership (RCEP) in the region comprising the East Asia Summit (EAS) group of 10+3+3 with ASEAN states on the driving seat. But experts are of the view that such kind of arrangement is likely to facilitate the growth of Free Trade Areas (FTAs) by reducing tariffs which may not be a substitute for quality trade. Therefore, it is time for Japan to lead this group of eleven states. It is because Japan now accounts for nearly fifty percent of the total GDP of this group. Its recent policies seem to have been moving in this direction. Its current negotiations with the states of TPP have resulted in the formation of Comprehensive and Progressive Agreement for Trans-Pacific Partnership (CPTPP) in March 2018. This trade initiative has not only provided leadership to Japan, but also may make it a greater partner in the economic activities with the countries of this region.

(b) *Security*: Geopolitically, Japan has to deal with both traditional and non-traditional threats emanating from this region. If on the one hand, it has to counter balance vis-à-vis growing Chinese influence and presence in Eurasia and Africa under President Xi Jinping's 'one belt, one road' (OBOR) initiative, then on the other hand, it has to confront the threats of terrorism, piracy, freedom of sea lanes, environmental issues, humanitarian assistance/disaster relief etc. To operationalise this Japan has tried to build goodwill at both bilateral levels towards its neighbours, particularly countries of ASEAN and India; and to be part of multilateral forums for concerted efforts. Thus to cultivate goodwill among its neighbourhood Japan is extending nearly two-third of total ODA to countries of East and Southeast Asia.[7] At multilateral level as well, Japan is operationalising its policies by joining various frameworks like: Japan-ASEAN, Japan-Mekong Cooperation, ASEAN+3, East Asia Summit (EAS), ASEAN

Regional Forum (ARF); ASEAN Defence Ministers Meeting-Plus (ADMM-Plus), and, Asia Pacific Economic Cooperation (APEC). It is also involved in Japan-ASEAN Ship Rider Cooperation Programme, Japan-ASEAN Joint Exercise for Rescue Operation Programme and Japan-ASEAN Disaster Relief Study Tour. Besides, it is supported by Japan-US alliance as linchpin of its Indo-Pacific policy. Thus, through bilateral and multilateral naval exercises, particularly its joining of trilateral (Japan-India-USA) and quadrilateral (Japan-India-USA-Australia) groupings, it has further strengthened its security scenario. In addition it has strengthened its position by creating synergies of its policy of 'free and open Indo-Pacific policy' and India's 'Act East policy' and joining the USA, India and Australia in the 'Quad' and perceived its membership of the latter as 'Asia's democratic security diamond'.

(c) *Development:* Development of infrastructure and connectivity are two issue of vital importance for Japan's interest in the Indo-Pacific. It aims to build both 'hard' (road, railway and telecommunication) and 'soft' (human development, environmental protection, transparency) infrastructure that facilitates connectivity and integration of the region.[8] This is done through its cooperation both at bilateral and sub-regional levels. This cooperation of Japan is manifest through its 'Partnership for Quality Infrastructure' (2015) and 'Expanded Partnership for Quality Infrastructure' (2017) policies towards this region. It is also estimated that Japan is going to contribute approximately US$ 110 billion until 2020 for such projects.[9] At sub-regional level, at present Japan is engaged in the development of Brunei-Indonesia-Malaysia-Philippines East ASEAN Growth Area (BIMP-EAGA) and Indonesia-Malaysia-Thailand Growth Triangle (IMT-GT). At bilateral level, it is engaged in the projects like—Patimban Port and Jakarta Mass Rapid Transit (MRT) in Indonesia; Trans-Sumatran Highway and the high-speed railway with Singapore and Malaysia; Phnom Penh City Transmission and Distribution System Expansion Project in Cambodia, etc. Similarly, Japan is also involved in the growth and development of numerous infrastructure and connectivity in different states in this region. Thus, through these activities Japan is developing infrastructure in this region at sustainable level to contain the impact of 'belt and road initiative' of China. That might have been the reason that in June 2018, the state-backed Japan Bank for International Cooperation made an investment of US$50 billion to help finance state-of-art infrastructure projects in the Indo-Pacific region. Simultaneously, it is sharing the burden of global multilateral financial institutions like World Bank and Asian Development Bank.

Problem Areas

But everything is not smooth for Japan's security arrangements in the Indo-Pacific region. Japan is facing serious irritants of both geoeconomic and geopolitical nature in this region.

(i) Geoeconomically, if on the one hand, globalisation has enhanced interdependence and connectivity, then on the other hand, emergence of protectionism and inward-looking trends are also manifest. Proliferation of Free Trade Agreements (FTAs) are there in Indo-Pacific, but China has emerged as leading trade partner of most regional economies. Japan is making serious efforts to contain Chinese activities by transforming Trans-Pacific Partnership (TPP) into Comprehensive and Progressive Trans-Pacific Partnership (CPTPP), but USA's withdrawal has created impediment in the success of such initiative. On the contrary, China is aggressively pushing her agenda through its belt and road initiative. Hence, cooperation under 'Quad' cannot tackle this problem without an alternative sound economic framework. Besides, these countries still lack a coordinating effort to integrate the existing grouping of APEC, CPTPP and Regional Comprehensive Economic Partnership (RCEP). Changing maritime dynamics due to surging trade flows, regional powers have started for access, influence and relative advantage. Japan's vulnerability also lies in her near total dependence on fuel, feed, food (except rice) and virtually all the essential industrial raw material, as well as, corresponding dependence on fair access to foreign markets for her exports.

(ii) Geopolitically, China's potential to endanger Japanese security, both by direct action (coercive politico-military brinkmanship) and through proxy use of North Korea, is serious problem for it. This is further aggravated by the prevailing politico-security milieu in the tri-polar structure involving USA, Russia and China. Thus, this region has developed certain 'grey zone' situation due to insufficient institutionalisation of cooperative security framework. Besides, all of Japan's strategies in the region are based on the support from the US leadership. But with the coming of Donald Trump to power there are always uncertainties about the US support for its allies. This is evident from recent foreign policy moves of the present government. For instance, Donald Trump's 2017 NSS is the only document in the past seventeen years that did not mention protection of its allies by the USA. It manifests about the strategic retreat by the America from its commitment from the 'Quad' arrangement. Trump's uncertain policy initiatives like withdrawal from Trans Pacific Partnership (TPP) on 23 January 2017, non-agreeing to Paris Climate Agreement on 1 June 2017, changed attitudes toward North Korea and China, etc., have further created disadvantageous position for Japan in this region. As a consequences of these developments, efforts towards forging of new alignments by India-China-Russia on the one hand, and initiation of USA-Russia dialogue on the other hand, have further created uncertainties in the region which are going to have significant bearing for the security of Japan.

Prospects

In the given scenario, Japan is left with twin options to ensure its security in the Indo-Pacific area. It has to enhance its capabilities through developing strong ties with its neighbours along with fast tracking military capabilities in the areas of ballistic missiles interceptors, ballistic missiles shields and preparing for cyber and space wars. Simultaneously, Japan has to engage itself with the changed region and global scenario in such a way to evolve an integrated larger Asian economic community with a common security framework for Indo-Pacific. For this it has to build an entente cordiale of cooperative dialogues and arrangements with like-minded countries with shared values and convergent interests in the larger strategic frame of Indo-Pacific region. To operationalise this Japan has to adopt following multi-pronged strategies:

(a) First of all it must realise that Japan-USA security alliance is likely to remain the cornerstone of its security policy towards the Indo-Pacific region in the times to come. For time being some uncertainties may be there due to unstable policies of the Trump administration, but in the long run US interests are going to converge with that of the Japan. Both are likely to support Japan's 'Free and Open Indo-Pacific' (FOIP) approach and their common concerns regarding the aggressive policies of China in this region.

(b) Second, to implement its FOIP policy, Japan has to make serious efforts to develop a sync between states of ASEAN and 'Quad'. Though, it is a fact that consensus in the states of ASEAN about threat perception towards China is missing, yet it is certain that without involvement of ASEAN goal of security in this region cannot be ensured. Besides, ASEAN states are cognizant of their geostrategic and geoeconomic situations and all the states are not succumbed to Chinese pressure. Even in the long run, it is likely that interests of powers of 'Quad' and ASEAN are going to converge. Since cooperation between the two is inevitable, hence policy makers in Japan have to seriously initiate in this direction.

(c) Third, in the present world order, relations among the states are involving complexity of both competition and cooperation. Therefore, manifest hostile strategy towards China may not work fruitful, rather Japan has to adopt a nuanced approach in this matter. Besides, both ASEAN and 'Quad' have multi-layered and complex relations with China based on their respective interests and compulsions. Japan has to be patient in the realisation of free and open Indo-Pacific.

Thus, in the given scenario of post-Cold War global order Japan's dilemma for security has not improved much. It is only nature and types of threats have undergone change, rather establishment of peace and tranquillity. Earlier it has to create a balance between the two superpower within a comparatively stable world order. Now it has to deal with an unstable non-polar world order involving multi-layered complexities. In the present scenario both traditional and non-traditional threats are emanating from a proximate region of Japan where assertion for hegemony and dominance became very rampant. This is manifest not only in geostrategical matters, but also apparent in geoeconomic area in the form of trade war between the USA and China. Therefore, Japan is facing very delicate scenario where uncertainties are looming large at its door steps. This situation is likely to prevail for some more time until unless a stable and peaceful global order evolves. Hence, Indo-Pacific region is going to remain crucial for the security of Japan.

NOTES

1 Govt. of Japan, Ministry of Foreign Affairs, Speech by H.E. Shinzo Abe, Prime Minister of Japan, at Parliament of Indian Republic, 22 August 2007 at http:// www.mofa.go.jp> speech-2

2 Ibid.

3 Yujen Kuo, "Japan's Roles in the Indo-Pacific Strategy", *Prospect Journal*, no.19, in http:/ / www.pf.org.tw>files, p. 31.

4 Ibid., p. 36.

5 For details see, Kei Koga, "Redirecting Strategic Focus in the Age of the Indo-Pacific," *Comparative Communications*, vol.20, no.1, May 2018, pp.129-138.

6 Ibid., p. 130.

7 For details see, Table-1 (Annexure at the end).

8 For details see, K.Yhome and Rajeev Ranjan Chaturvedy, eds., *Emerging Trans-Regional Corridors: South and Southeast Asia*, New Delhi, 2017.

9 Koga, n.5, p. 132.

ANNEXURE
TABLE 1*

Region-wise ODA Disbursement by Japan, 2011-2016
(Unit: 100 million Yen)

		2011	*2012*	*2013*	*2014*	*2015*	*2016*
1	East & South East Asia	9,741.16 (69.8)	11,779.80 (76.0)	19,667.79 (66.4)	6,410.49 (55.7)	15,550.49 (65.2)	12,712.81 (61.2)
2	Oceania	131.66 (0.9)	250.38 (1.6)	138.10 (0.9)	137.50 (1.2)	497.93 (2.1)	159.94 (0.8)
3	Central Asia & Caucasia	265.80 (1.9)	70.80 (0.5)	433.36 (3.0)	1,095.48 (9.5)	240.65 (1.0)	122.51 (0.6)
4	Middle East & North Africa	1401.73 (10.1)	1,366.28 (8.8)	1,551.84 (10.7)	1,153.42 (10.0)	2,467.55 (10.3)	1,864.29 (9.0)
5	Sub-Sahara Africa	1,240.01 (8.9)	1,538.58 (9.9)	1,597.64 (17.0)	1,870.92 (16.3)	2,795.15 (11.7)	2,155.90 (10.4)
6	Latin America & Caribbean	860.07 (6.2)	462.72 (3.0)	1,086.23 (7.5)	685.88 (6.0)	317.70 (1.3)	3,744.37 (18.0)
7	Europe	306.48 (2.2)	39.78 (0.3)	95.08 (0.7)	152.5 1(1.3)	1,981.89 (8.3)	25.32 (0.1)
8	Global Total	13,946.91 (100)	15,508.34 (100)	14,570 (100)	11,506.21 (100)	23,851.36 (100)	20,785.14 (100)

**Source:* International Bureau, MOFA, *Priority Policy for Development Cooperation, FY 2017*, at http://www.mofa.go.jp>policy>oda

3

Peace and Stability in the Indian Ocean: An Indian View

Vivek Mishra

ABSTRACT

As global powers try and re-anchor themselves in maritime Asia, the larger Indo-Pacific area and more specifically the Indian Ocean have assumed enhanced relevance in the context of an already emerging or even a coming 'grand-strategic and multi-contestant' great game. This paper will look at the current security map of the Indian Ocean with the small, middle and major powers involved. More specifically, it will try to assess the balanced approach of Indian's endeavour vis-à-vis the Indian Ocean Region (IOR) which looks to prioritize strategic necessity to maintain a regional upper hand simultaneously with engagement, especially through its approach of engaging with all partners and antagonizing none. Further, it will analyze India's responses to the changing strategic picture of the IOR and whether India's careful balancing in the Indian Ocean is a sustainable strategy given the rapidly shifting nature of the regional great game. So, is there a middle ground for India in its IOR diplomacy?

Introduction

The question of peace and stability in the Indian Ocean is an issue that dates back to the 1970s, yet holds contemporary significance. In a consequential move initiated by Sri Lanka, the Indian Ocean was declared a Zone of Peace at the 26th United Nations General Assembly (UNGA) in 1971. This was consequential for the adoption of a resolution which recognised the Indian Ocean as a Zone of Peace, with aerial space and ocean-bed stipulations to be estimated.[1] This meant that "the Indian Ocean within limits to be determined, together with the air space above and the ocean floor subjacent thereto, is hereby designated for all time as a zone of peace."[2] There were two primary interpretive spin offs that came out of this UN declaration: first, the declaration resulted in an alteration regarding the manner in which the Indian Ocean has been defined as a peace zone—not in the stereotyped binary of peace and war but with specificity regarding the need for great powers to halt and banish all bases, military installations and logistical facilities. This rather new conception of Indian Ocean seen as a zone of peace harped on the conception of collective security without building military alliances. In the following years as the Ad Hoc Committee on the Indian Ocean was constituted, the peace agenda in the region further divided world's major powers. China was the only permanent member of the UN that supported the original draft of the committee with the US, UK and France deciding to sit outside.[3] As such, regional stability and peace concerning the Indian Ocean region only managed to ensure a fractured mandate with powers divided over the issue.

Today, the geopolitical and geostrategic circumstances in the Indian Ocean have not just coaxed powers to recalibrate their approach but have realigned small, middle and major powers themselves in the IOR, often in contrast to these powers' Cold War alignments. However, in contrast to the past, the Indian Ocean's zone of peace paradigm that began in the early 1970s experiences an epistemological break today; with China likely to be on an ironical opposite end of a presumed IOR consensus. In other words, in the 1970s the conceptualisation of a zone of peace vis-à-vis the Indian Ocean split up world's major powers with China as the only permanent UNSC member supporting the original draft of the Indian Ocean Ad Hoc Committee, while major powers like the US, UK and France chose to sit out. Today, China would presumably be standing at the opposed end of the spectrum of a possible Indian Ocean consensus on security, particularly with the emergence of a loose alliance of sorts against it being led by the US.

Since the Cold War years, the Indian Ocean has remained an area of great power competition and only the players seem to have transformed in the period following the end of the Cold War era. As such, the agenda of stability and peace in this region has remained as a long lasting desire, even as regional complications have been compounded due to persistent strategic rivalries. Such rivalries have intensified due to various strategic binaries or groups of binaries that have come up in maritime Asia owing to rising nature of powers versus established powers. To be sure, the issue of peace and stability in the Indian Ocean has once again reared its head, with regional leaders like India emphasising the need for Indian Ocean to remain a zone of peace. On December 01 2014, India revisited the idea of Indian Ocean as a Zone of Peace (IOZOP) at the Galle Dialogue led by India's National Security Adviser.[4] In his address, he laid down India's position that in order to remain a peaceful and stable domain, the Indian Ocean should remain a zone of peace as was the call in the past. It was precisely to deter any hegemonic apprehensions in the IOR that the erstwhile UNGA Resolution 2832 (XVII) defined a 'zone of peace' in the context of the need for great powers to halt and eliminate all military bases, military installations and logistical facilities from the IOR. With the increasing involvement of regional and external players in the IOR, these are exactly the apprehensions that India faces in the IOR and the Indo-Pacific today. Even today, one of the strongest persuasions for revisiting the idea of IOZOP is to prevent any one country from holding sway over the Indian Ocean—most conspicuously China!

The question of peace and stability in the Indian Ocean cannot be dealt with substantially unless one has a measure of the threats involved. As such, in the following sections this paper will raise three important questions probing into the security structure of the IOR and try to find answers to them. The first question will deal with the comprehensive security picture from an Indian point of view, the second question would concern probing the most suitable regional template that India should adopt for a 'stable and peaceful' IOR, and the answer to the third question will evaluate whether India's strategy of careful balancing between increasing stakeholders in the IOR and the Indo-Pacific, especially under rapidly shifting interests of players, is a sustainable strategy?

The Broad Security Picture of the IOR

In its current context, the Indian Ocean is not very different from the Cold War history, except for a different set of players and somewhat altered interests. The IOR has become a complex maritime area involving world's major powers like the US, China, India, Japan, Australia, France, etc., all competing for their varied interests which align at times and don't at other. The strategic milieu of the Indian Ocean is rapidly changing, whereby the region is moving towards a new strategic order where a number of middle and major powers are jostling for increasing their influence in the region.[5] Among the major powers, the US continues to dominate the Indian Ocean through its presence and reach, particularly through the best Blue Water Navy in the world. The importance of the IOR for the US has remained very high as the region continues to dominate with world's major trade routes, making the littoral of the IOR extremely critical to the country's 21st century geopolitical interests. Geostrategically, the Indian Ocean is situated between its US Fifth Fleet stationed at Bahrain in the Gulf and US Seventh Fleet in Japan, with its Military Support facility Diego Garcia as a mid-oceanic node. However, changing players, interests and power alignments have necessitated a change of strategy by the US in the Indian Ocean. The presence of the US in the Indian Ocean has historically been concentrated on the western part of Indian peninsula (mostly in the Arabian Sea area).[6] However, more recently the US has now moved to course correct this imbalance through its Indo-Pacific strategy. There have been persistent efforts, both rhetorically and action-oriented, to incorporate the Indian Ocean in its Asia-Pacific strategy by the US. Starting with the Obama Administration's strategy of 'pivot-to Asia' which culminated in a more intentionally sober 'Rebalance', the US has constantly aimed to merge the Pacific and the Indian Oceans in its bid to create a seamless maritime connectivity deterrence to China from the Pacific Ocean to the Indian Ocean and retain its dominance in Asian waters.

Although the US remains the predominant player and influencer in the Indian Ocean it faces a complex set of circumstances in the Indian Ocean today. Despite announcing its Free and Open Indo-Pacific Strategy,[7] very little sense seems to have concretized in what this strategy means for the Indian Ocean. Amidst such uncertainty about the US presence in the Indian Ocean, an important Assumption that has led the discourse is that as the shale gas exports of the US picks up further along with simultaneous depletion in Gulf's energy resources, the security commitments of the US to the IOR are likely to reduce, forcing other major powers like China and India to assert in the region besides allowing other powers like Australia, Japan, France along with some Gulf and East African countries to play a significant role. The focus of the US is going to shift in future to individual countries in the IOR that would be export destinations for US energy supplies.

However, owing to a sobering account of success with US strategy of separate and distinct focus on the Indian and the Pacific oceans, the Trump Administration has focused specifically on its Indo-Pacific strategy. Alyssa Ayres has noted in this regard that, "The Donald J. Trump administration has adopted the term Indo-Pacific to describe its larger strategic area of interest across the pan-Asian region." She cautions, however, that the US' Indo-Pacific strategy needs more of the Indian Ocean than is currently being accommodated under this strategy.[8] For boosting the connectivity bid through its Indo-Pacific strategy, the US has sought to strengthen connectivity networks across the region and boost trade through a robust and secure Indo-Pacific Maritime Corridor (IPMC). This has advanced the role of India as an Indo-Pacific country. With regards to security, the primary concern for the US' Indo-Pacific security is increasing Chinese footprints in the Indian Ocean, primarily being advanced through its One Belt One Road (OBOR) initiative. Specifically with intention of tackling this issue, the incumbent administration under Donald Trump has reinvigorated the New Silk Road (NSR) along with the Indo-Pacific Economic Corridor (IPEC) promising to establish vital connections between South Asia and Southeast Asia. The revival of two infrastructure projects linking South and Southeast Asia by the US is at least conceptually stacked against Beijing's own infrastructural push to its west through the OBOR.[9] These connectivity networks are bound to involve strategic choices in accordance with the interest of their patron countries or groups.

In his CSIS speech, the then US Secretary of State Rex summed up the need for cooperation between the US and India in the Indo-Pacific:

> In particular, India and the United States must foster greater prosperity and security with the aim of a free and open Indo-Pacific. The Indo-Pacific, including the entire Indian Ocean, the Western Pacific and the nations that surround them, will be the most consequential part of the globe in the 21st century. Home to more than 3 billion people, this region is the focal point of the world's energy and trade routes. Forty percent of the world's oil supply crisscrosses the Indian Ocean every day, through critical points of transit like the Straits of Malacca and Hormuz.[10]

From the aforementioned, it is more than clear that for the US, the Indian Ocean and the larger Indo-Pacific region represents an area of growing interests which converge with regional powers such as Australia, India and Japan. For the US, the Indian Ocean retains its importance as a crucial trade route and passage for energy supplies. Chinese presence threatens to upset the regional balance of power which is currently in the favour of the US, at least militarily. As such, maintaining economic and military pre-eminence within the existing rules-based order in the IOR has become strategic priority for US.[11] Both India and the US have pitched for a free and open Indo-Pacific region with shared history and value of lasting democracies. Strategically, both countries have projected and safeguarded their common interests in the IOR and beyond through the Malabar naval exercises which now includes Japan, extending the area of common operation.

The Indian Ocean is critical to emerging US-India relations, especially with increasing defense ties between the two sides with definite implications for the IOR. For instance, the US has sold quite a few Poseidon-8I aircraft to India which are being used for reconnaissance in various parts of the IOR. Both the sides have signed the Logistics Exchange Memorandum of Agreement (LEMOA) to allow mutual use of each other's ports for refueling, resupplies and joint training. The US is also keen on eliciting more clarity from India on a regional grand strategy in the Indo-Pacific. It is a different matter that the Trump administration itself is not very clear about the future course of its Indo-Pacific strategy. However, the US of late has been voicing support for India's centrality in its Indo-Pacific strategy. Recently, a Trump administration official clarified in this regard that, "We have strong and growing ties with India. We talk about 'Indo-Pacific' in part because that phrase captures the importance of India's rise."[12]

The single biggest transformation in the security architecture of the IOR, however, has been in the form of China's 21st Century Maritime Silk Road passing through parts of the IOR. China's maritime and continental connectivity project, the Belt and Road Initiative (BRI), relies on Indian Ocean ports and sea lanes with three possible routes opening in the Indian Ocean.[13] Interestingly, there are three components to China's Maritime Silk Road all of which open in the Indian Ocean:

(a) First, through the CPEC which enters the Indian Ocean through Gwadar port in Pakistan
(b) Second, connects the Bay of Bengal through the Kyakpyu port in Myanmar to China, and
(c) Third, connecting China through the Strait of Malacca, across the Indian Peninsula on to the Atlantic

Chinese entry into the Indian Ocean has accompanied a sense of apprehension about the country's domination in the IOR. Recent patterns in Chinese partnerships across IOR littoral countries such as Sri Lanka, Maldives, Bangladesh, Myanmar, etc., have shown deepening concerns within India about increasing Chinese sway with these countries. Boosting its command over the IOR littoral countries, China has already built two naval bases in Djibouti and Gwadar along with another naval base and airfield planned in Jiwani, 60 kms west of Gwadar. Besides, Chinese plans to build bases in the IOR also include the eastern Indian Ocean, especially in waters closer to Australia. China is positioned comfortably apropos regional strategy in the IOR, especially in its probable long-term need to protect the east-west stretch of the IOR. These estimations have been heightened by the growing number of Chinese vessels, both ships and sub-surface, that frequent various parts of the IOR. In the coming years, the number of Chinese vessels in the IOR could grow as much as 20 at a given time.[14]

It is also a common assessment that China is unlikely to stop with the advances it has made in the IOR, even as it continues to gain further grounds in the southern and western parts of the Indian Ocean. Some analysts also anticipate a possibility of another Chinese naval facility in Tanzania, which along with the naval base in Djibouti is likely to comprehensively account for security of passage and sea-denial strategies in future for the country. China has opened a comprehensive training centre near Bagamoyo, Tanzania. China is also in negotiations with Tanzania to build a major port in Bagamoyo.[15] Among other Chinese strategies, speculations are rife about China sending its 'magic island-making' ship to the Indian Ocean. China has embarked on a new expansive journey led by its new dredging ship which helps in the creation of isolated islands reminiscent of some of those that China has already dredged up in the South China Sea.[16] "The vessel has a highly symbolic name: Tian Kun Hao—a legendary enormous fish which can turn into a mythical bird."[17] The gap between this legend and reality are being bridged by China's activities in Asia's maritime domain each passing day! This is likely to make the Indian Ocean more multipolar and a more strategically complex arena.

In so far as devising a regional grand strategy is concerned, the current set of circumstances has necessitated a counter-intuitive response from India that has often veered to take a multilateral form. The latest US National Security Strategy (NSS) prioritizes working with allies, friends and partners in the Indo-Pacific region, "including boosting quadrilateral cooperation with Japan, Australia, and India," also referred to as the Quadrilateral Initiative or simply the Quad.[18] As a host of countries including the US, France, Japan and Australia are keen to reorient their role in the Indian Ocean and the Indo-Pacific, India's challenge would lie in balancing its efforts between excessively militaristic and benign positions apropos other powers in the IOR. India has responded in various measures, most recently by gaining port access to Duqm in Oman,[19] economic and military access besides right to develop coastal infrastructure in Sabang in the Aceh province in Indonesia,[20] ongoing negotiations with Seychelles to bring a post at Assumption Island,[21] besides a recent decision to operate the 'world's emptiest airport' on a joint venture with Sri Lanka.[22] India's emphasis on getting port access to a host of IOR littoral countries has found equal justification in the need to develop a sound regional maritime strategy as a responsible power as well as in the need to counter Chinese strategies in the region.

The Duqm port located strategically on the southeastern tip of Oman, opening in the northeastern Indian Ocean, not only makes up for the strategic deficit that India has had apropos port access in the western Indian Ocean but also adds another nodal port in its own attempt to complete a strategic loop of port access across the Indian peninsula. The port of Duqm also has a special economic zone with the potential to create opportunities for Indian investment in future. India's economic and military access to the Indonesian port of Sabang gains heightened importance due to its proximity to the crucial Strait of Malacca, through which about 40 percent of Indian trade passes. The strategic importance of Sabang is heightened as the port is 40 meters deep and is ideal for submarine docking, an important counterstrategy that India could employ. Moreover, India together with Indonesia has agreed to boost connectivity links between its strategically critical Andaman and Nicobar Islands and parts of Indonesia's Sumatra Island. Both the countries have established a dedicated task force for facilitating and advancing this linkage to promote trade, tourism and people-to-people contacts.[23] With reference to maritime partnership with Seychelles, Prime Minister has observed, "India and Seychelles are major strategic partners. We respect the core values of a democracy and share the geostrategic vision to maintain the peace, security and stability in the Indian Ocean."[24] India is currently in talks with Seychelles to build a naval base on the latter's Assumption Island marking a potentially key node in India's bid to provide a more comprehensive role as net security provider in the IOR. Finally, India's decision to take over Sri Lanka's Mattala Rajapaksa International Airport in Hambantota which has been running into losses, also called 'world's emptiest airport', is a bid to cut the strategic advantage of China through its operation of the Hambantota sea port. Besides, India has also reached out to other countries within ASEAN such as Brunei and Vietnam for developing maritime linkage and fostering connectivity and cooperation. In a similar vein, India has recently established a Data Reception and Tracking and Telemetry Station located in Ho Chi Minh City, Vietnam. This reception centre is expected to be fully functional soon and is anticipated to work in tandem with a similar facility present in Indonesia. India has also set up a similar facility in Brunei.[25] These nodes to India's east, besides enhancing presence in Southeast Asia, will be crucial in data collection and monitoring activities in the South China Sea, an area of growing importance for India.

As such, India has taken quite a few steps in the recent past to navigate carefully between its reliance on and expectations from major powers in the region, mainly by developing its own regional capacities gradually. India has created a new strategic reach in the Indian Ocean by including ports in Oman (Duqm), France (Reunion), US (Diego Garcia, Central Command in Bahrain and the Indo-Pacific Command in Hawaii), Assumption islands in Seychelles and Indonesia (Sabang) through various agreements. India's mutual base sharing agreements with the US, France, Oman and Indonesia has reshuffled the security deck in the IOR, at least theoretically. This new outreach map of the Indian Navy has complimented its Security and growth for All Regionally (SAGAR) vision and Project Mausam which intend to harness the soft power potential of cultural ties and combined legacy with other regional countries. Besides, India is also working in areas of the Indian Ocean that it was hitherto understood to have traditional deficit, like the western and southern parts of the Indian Ocean.

India's Template for a 'Peaceful and Stable' IOR

The broad template that India has adopted in the past and should continue with is one which bases itself on the idea of collective security without building military alliances. As such, India's efforts to build stable and peaceful security architecture in the IOR and the larger Indo-Pacific region would necessarily have to be multilateral. Although this emerging multilateralism is currently being shaped and reshaped due to changing behaviour and uncertainty of actors. Some believe that the nature of the Indo-Pacific would depend entirely on China's behaviour and regional responses to it by other stakeholders.[26] Such future regional formulations stare at the possibility of two opposed groups of multilateral parties. If one were to place that analogy in today's fraught geopolitical circumstances in Asian waters, one would have China on one side with a loose United States-led regional consensus on the other. The BRI, IPMC AAGC, INSTC, etc., would be various manifestations of such intentionally conflicting yet regionally connecting designs. In the current scenario, the Indo-Pacific maritime and continental expanse has the criss-crossing of various multilateral networks. While China has floated the BRI, India has partnered with Japan for the Asia Africa Growth Corridor (AAGC) which intends to bridge the Indo-Pacific region with the African continent, besides coming together with the US, Japan and Australia for the QUAD. These have not just made the IOR a game-changing region apropos connectivity but the larger Indo-Pacific region an economically vibrant corridor and an arena for a great game. These developments are already reshaping the alignment and security templates for India in the Indo-Pacific region.

However, too many multilateral associations are likely to conflict with India's regional aspirations and goals as a major power in the region. For India to gain a unique place in the IOR and the larger Indo-Pacific, it will have to lead form the front regionally and expand its maritime vision beyond immediate waters. Its aspiration of developing blue water navy will have to be reconciled with its regional challenges and long term goals. For instance, rising global expectations from India to play the net security provider in the Indo-Pacific needs to be measured and worked upon from a capability perspective. The Indian Navy is still running on huge manufacturing and capability deficit emerging out of procedural and acquisitive delays, slow manufacturing, poor maintenance and red tape. Over the years, lackluster performance in the aforementioned sectors have resulted in surface and sub-surface capacity deficit for the Indian Navy, severely marring hard power projection capabilities in the IOR. India's current underwater capabilities and future above surface strength do project an enhanced maritime capability future but they still remain distant dreams.

Owing much to the capacity, capability and political will deficits, multilateralism becomes an understandable template for India to project in regional waters. To be sure, there are two strands of multilateralism emerging from India's regional maritime behaviour, which often merge in themselves. The first approach tethers itself upon the concept of holistic regional growth, propelled by India's traditional policy which relates to the growth-for-one-is-growth-for-all school of thought. And the second approach harps on multilateral structures for attaining advantageous position vis-a-vis other regional and extra-regional players and the regional balance of power. India's recent decision to initiate conceptual and pragmatic consolidation of the region by working with all countries through its Security and Growth for All Regionally (SAGAR) is an example of the first approach. The vision outlined through SAGAR by Prime Minister Modi in March 2015 was essentially an effort to concretize India's strategic design for the Indian Ocean. The SAGAR initiative focuses on,

> "enhancing capacities to safeguard land and maritime territories & interests; deepening economic and security cooperation in the littoral; promoting collective action to deal with natural disasters and maritime threats like piracy, terrorism and emergent non-state actors; working towards sustainable

regional development through enhanced collaboration; and, engaging with countries beyond our shores with the aim of building greater trust and promoting respect for maritime rules, norms and peaceful resolution of disputes."[27]

A related concept that has emerged out of the SAGAR initiative is the concept of 'Blue Economy' which aims to integrate regional economies of the IOR through initiatives in the areas of "areas of marine bio-technology, exploration and sustainable exploitation of ocean mineral resources, sustainable fishing practices, and harnessing of ocean energy".[28] Besides, India's idea of a seamless regional connectivity should integrate its SAGAR and Sagarmala Initiatives (which propels the idea of a port led growth) creating an inland-coastal-territorial waters-high seas continuum that will effectively bind the agenda of harnessing blue economy and align it with domestic as well as regional growth and development.

India's other multilateral efforts towards consolidating regional strategy include the biennial MILAN exercises and the Indian Ocean Naval Symposium (IONS). The biennial MILAN exercises bring navies of the IOR spanning from the Gulf and east African coast to New Zealand under one multilateral framework while the IONS brings the IOR navies under one multilateral structure.

In its effort to balance its growth perspective in the IOR and the Indo-Pacific India has focused on partnering with some middle and major powers to boost its own position vis-a-vis China, while still enhancing its own interests in the region. India has partnered with the US, France and Japan primarily, besides other countries such as Oman, Indonesia, Vietnam, etc., to gain a position of advantage vis-a-vis other players in the IOR and beyond. India has also signed White Shipping agreements with a host of countries including with the US and France to cooperate in the area of information sharing related to maritime traffic and maritime domain awareness in the IOR.

Whither India's Careful Balancing in IOR?

Despite the aforementioned efforts by India to enhance its footing in regional waters and beyond, one could ask, how willing is India or even the other players including the US when it comes to forming a collective security consensus in the IOR? India still sits out of big regional multilateral security apparatus such as the Combined Maritime Force (CMF) and its various components, willfully cringes when it comes to Quad, keeps Australia out of

Malabar exercises, etc. These half-hearted attempts have corroborated that India is still relying on its tactics of careful balancing between partners, opponents and enemies. Then one could ask, is India's careful balancing between stakeholders in the Indian Ocean and the Indo-Pacific sustainable, especially under rapidly shifting nature of the regional great game?

The strategy for India, going forward, shouldn't be mere benign strategies, as they are likely to burn out and will not be sustainable unless some semblance of assertiveness in India's IOR strategy are evinced from time to time to draw assurances from partners and depict readiness and will. Strong resistance strategies in the IOR will have to be coupled with political will to expand India's maritime security ambit. The recently 'mission based deployments'[29] do serve the intended purpose somewhat peripherally but stops short of creating substantial extra-regional ambitions, which form an important part of a growing power's strategies.

Finally, if India were indeed to sustain its careful balancing approach with strong presence in the IOR, certain steps have to be taken. As such, India should:

(1) increase naval deployment, readiness and enhance domain awareness in the Arabian Sea—traditionally a strategically deficit area,
(2) infuse some clarity on the military components of its IOR strategy, and
(3) increase coastal surveillance through its radars for coastal surveillance that have been installed—6 in Sri Lanka, 8 in Mauritius and 1 each in Seychelles and Maldives, beside increasing maritime reconnaissance in the western and southern parts of the Indian ocean.

More importantly, India's careful balancing strategy has officially distanced itself from the narrative that singles out China in the emerging security mix of the IOR. But it equally makes dealing with China strongly, a difficult option for India. While careful navigation in the IOR does send the message of peace and stability fairly strongly from India, on its flip side, it could lead to loss of traditional influence, as was evident in the recent case of Maldives. For India, the recent Maldivian crisis[30] signified loss of influence in a traditional area of influence in the IOR, at the cost of China's gain. There are costs and gains involved on either side of India's careful balancing strategy in the IOR and demands astute assessments based on its long-term national interest.

NOTES

1 "1971 The Indian Ocean - Zone of Peace", *United Ntaions.un.org*, available at http://lk.one.un.org/7060/en/the-indian-ocean-zone-of-peace, accessed pm 1 July 2018.

2 U.N. Document, A/Resolution/2832 (xxvi), 16 December 1971

3 Akshay, K. (2014), "Indian Ocean Zone of Peace: An Old Issue with Old Solutions", Dec 17, 2017, available at https://gurumavin.com/indian-ocean-zone-of-peace-an-old-issue-with-old-solutions/, accessed on 2 July 2018.

4 M. Srinivasan (2014), "Indian Ocean has to remain a zone of peace: Ajit Doval". *The Hindu*, 1 December 2014.

5 D. Brewster. "Welcome to the New Indian Ocean". *The Diplomat*. Feb 21, 2018, available at https://thediplomat.com/2018/02/welcome-to-the-new-indian-ocean/, accessed on 29 June 2018.

6 A. Pillalamarri, "A Brief History of the US Navy in the Indian Ocean". *The Diplomat*. Oct 14, 2014, available at https://thediplomat.com/2015/10/a-brief-history-of-the-us-navy-in-the-indian-ocean/, accessed on 30 July 2018.

7 Remarks by President Trump at APEC CEO Summit. *Ariyana Da Nang Exhibition Center*. Da Nang, Vietnam. November 10, 2017, available at https://www.whitehouse.gov/briefings-statements/remarks-president-trump-apec-ceo-summit-da-nang-vietnam/, accessed on 24 July 2018.

8 A. Ayres, "The U.S. Indo-Pacific Strategy Needs More Indian Ocean". Council on Foreign Relations. May 25, 2018, available at https://www.cfr.org/expert-brief/us-indo-pacific-strategy-needs-more-indian-ocean, accessed on 2 July 2018.

9 "To Counter China's OBOR, US Revives Two Infrastructure Projects in Asia". *The Wire*, 24 May 2017, available at https://thewire.in/business/obor-china-us-india, accessed on 4 July 2018.

10 R. Tillerson (2017), "Defining Our Relationship with India for the Next Century: An Address by U.S. Secretary of State Rex Tillerson". October 18, 2017. *Center for Strategic and International Studies*, available at https://www.csis.org/analysis/defining-our-relationship-india-next-century-address-us-secretary-state-rex-tillerson, accessed on 5 July 2018.

11 "Strategic Objectives of the United States in the Indian Ocean Region", Workshop Report. *Future Directions International*. Sep 29, 2011.

12 "We have strong and growing ties with India. We talk about 'Indo-Pacific' in part because that phrase captures the importance of India's rise." *Times of India*. Nov 5, 2017.

13 V. Mishra (2018), "China Is Moving into the Indian Ocean". *The National Interest*. April 14, 2018, available at https://nationalinterest.org/feature/china-moving-the-indian-ocean-25380, accessed on 5 July 2018.

14 D. Brewster (2018), "China's play for military bases in the eastern Indian Ocean", *The Interpreter, Lowy Institute*. 15 May 2018, available at https://www.lowyinstitute.org/the-interpreter/china-s-play-military-bases-eastern-indian-ocean, accessed on 5 July 2018.

15 C.R. Mohan, "Trailing China". *The Indian Express*. July 24, 2018.

16 D. Brewster (2018), "China's new network of Indian Ocean bases" *the interpreter, Lowy Institute*. Jan 30, 2018, available at https://www.lowyinstitute.org/the-interpreter/chinas-new-network-indian-ocean-bases, accessed on 5 July 2018.

17 "What is China's 'magic island-making' ship?". *BBC.* Nov 06, 2018, available at https://www.bbc.com/news/world-asia-china-41882081, accessed on 6 July 2018.

18 See n. 8.

19 S. Roy. "India gets access to strategic Oman port Duqm for military use, Chabahar-Gwadar in sight". *The Indian Express.* February 13, 2018.

20 "Indonesia Gives India Strategic, Military Access to Sabang Seaport". *The Quint.* May 18, 2018, available at https://www.thequint.com/news/world/india-indonesia-military-island-cooperation, accessed on 6 July 2018.

21 "India, Seychelles agree to work on Assumption Island naval base, respect concerns". *The Times of India,* 25 June 2018.

22 "India to operate "world's emptiest airport" in Sri Lanka". *The Hindu,* 6 July 2018.

23 "India, Indonesia to set up task force to enhance connectivity between Andaman and Sabang", *The Times of India,* 30 May 2018.

24 See n. 19.

25 D Chaudhury, "New base: Satellite monitoring station in Vietnam to give India room in South China Sea region". *The Economic Times,* 12 July 2018.

26 M. Sethi, "China And The Shape Of The Indo-Pacific". *IPCS.* Jul 18, 2018, available at http://www.ipcs.org/comm_select.php?articleNo=5496, accessed on 22 July 2018.

27 S. Swaraj (2018), "SAGAR – India's Vision for the Indian Ocean Region". Address delivered by Smt. Sushma Swaraj,Minister of External Affairs, Government of India, on 31st August, 2017 at the 2nd Indian Ocean Conference at Colombo, Sri Lanka organised by India Foundation, available at https://www.indiafoundation.in/sagar-indias-vision-for-the-indian-ocean-region/, accessed on 8 July 2018.

28 S.K. Mohanty (et. al.), "Prospects of Blue Economy in the Indian Ocean". *Research and Information System for Developing Countries,* available at http://www.ris.org.in/sites/default/files/Final_Blue_Economy_Report_2015-Website.pdf, accessed on 10 October 2018.

29 "New Mission-Based Deployment concept to result in greater presence and visibility in IOR – Admiral Sunil Lanba ". *Press Information Bureau.* Oct 27, 2018, available at http://pib.nic.in/newsite/PrintRelease.aspx?relid=171983, accessed on 24 July 2018.

30 Ashok Sajjanha (2018), "The Maldivian Crisis: What Can India do?" *Institute for Defense Studies and Analyses.* Feb 08, 2018, available at https://idsa.in/idsacomments/the-maldivian-crisis-what-can-india-do_asajjanhar_080218, accessed on 24 July 2018.

4

Maritime Tension in Indo-Pacific: Study of the US Approach to Access and Stability in the South China Sea

Obja Borah Hazarika

ABSTRACT

Tensions revolving around the South China Sea (SCS) have involved both resident and non-resident powers. The contentious claims of the littoral states include both jurisdiction of the maritime waters and sovereignty of territories in the SCS. The United States of America (US) is not a claimant of the territories in the SCS but has been involved in the region in several ways making it one of the major non-resident powers involved in the occurrences of the SCS. It has spelt out its position on the SCS, issues related to land reclamation, competing claims of sovereignty, and militarisation on many platforms. It has also taken other positions on the issue such as conducting Freedom of Navigation Operations (FONOPS) in the region. The stand of the US on the SCS has been one of the irritants of the overall US-China ties and has also impacted the ties of the US with the littoral countries of the SCS. The challenges posed by China, specially its activities relating to the SCS issue have also been addressed in many of the security and strategy-related documents released by the US. The US approach is pegged on maintaining the international order that it has propped up since the Second World War. The US approach towards the SCS will be the focus of this piece with an emphasis on the stands of the US on the SCS especially with regard to its views and positions on the freedom of navigation in the SCS.

Introduction

There have been certain discernible features, which have been identified related to the policy of the US towards the developments in the SCS. For instance it has been pointed out by Taylor Fravel (2016), that the US's involvement in the SCS is directly proportional to the rise in tensions among the littoral actors of the region. During periods of stability, there is an absence of involvement or change in policy of the US towards the SCS. The US involvement in the SCS is also based on ensuring neutrality towards the littoral countries with contending claims. The US has attempted to be non-partisan towards the countries involved in the SCS so as to prevent the SCS from becoming a defining feature of the already fraught US-China ties. The US has stressed the need to manage conflicts and tensions between the contending actors through the establishment of mutually acceptable codes of conduct. The US has attempted to structure China's conduct by underscoring the heavy costs, including deterioration of ties of China with its littoral neighbours while that of the US improves, of pursuing claims that are not supported by international law.

There is therefore a visible hedging, bordering on prevarication, in the approach of the US towards the SCS. While on the one hand the US proclaims neutrality, on the other, it seeks to shape the behaviour of China, and not any of the other claimants in the disputes of the SCS. The US harps on neutrality but is wary of being overtly reproachful of the activities of any of the claimants apart from China. In addition, the US seeks to emphasise the need for China to adhere to international law, while the US itself remains an outlier to the foremost international law governing conduct of countries over the High Seas—the United Nations Convention on the Law of the Seas (UNCLOS), having signed but not yet ratified it. Furthermore, the US seeks to shape China's approach to the developments in the SCS but at the same time is wary of being involved in an issue which China perceives as dealing with its sovereignty.

Such hedging tactics of the US towards the developments of the SCS has been discernible in the measures undertaken by the US on the issue. Such tactics are symptomatic of the conduct of a status-quoist power facing a revisionist power. Such tactics are also indicative of a status-quoist power, which has not signed the UNCLOS thereby preventing it from launching a less contradictory response to what it considers as China's assertions. The US involvement in the SCS will likely continue till tensions continue among the claimants. The balancing approach of the US towards the SCS, which intermeshes management of disputes, neutrality, and attempts to curate China's behaviour, is intended to prevent the SCS issue from foiling the tenuous nature of overall US-China ties while at the same time to ensure that the world order generated by the US in the aftermath of the Second World War is not drastically changed and replaced by rules imposed by China.

South China Sea: US Interests

The United States is interested in maintaining access as well as in allaying and preventing the escalation of crisis, which could upturn stability in the South China Sea.

With regard to Access: the US is keen to ensure access to the waters of the SCS remain unobstructed. The US is a firm believer in the principle of freedoms of the high seas for all countries beyond the 12 nm territorial seas allocated by the UNCLOS to coastal states over which they enjoy sovereignty. The US did not ratify the UNCLOS as when it was being negotiated thirty years ago, then "US President Ronald Reagan objected to it because, he argued, it would jeopardise US national and business interests, most notably with respect to seabed mining (Wright: 2012)." Nonetheless, the US maintains that it adheres to the principles slated in the UNCLOS as they are also a part of customary international law. Accordingly, the US contends that vessels, both commercial as well as military, enjoy unfettered access as outlined in UNCLOS (articles 56 and 87). In defense of such freedoms, since 2007, the US has been conducting multiple operational assertions in the waters of China, Vietnam and Malaysia. Access in the South China Sea waters is of interest for the US as trillions of dollars worth of trade passes through the SCS annually, out of which more than one trillion dollars associated with the US. Access in the SCS is also important for the US as it would permit it to project its power in the region as well as allow its navy to pass through the region and reach the Persian Gulf and Indian Ocean. Maintenance of the freedom of navigation in the SCS is linked to the US intention of ensuring that the principle of freedom of navigation is upheld everywhere else in the world.

The US faces threats to access in the SCS. China has interpreted its rights in the Exclusive Economic Zone and its recourse to legal arguments have been aimed to prevent activities of the US related to reconnaissance and surveillance in the SCS. Such concerns are also due to China's claims founded on its historic rights of the SCS which have been demarcated by the nine-dashed line. The modernisation of the PLA Navy (PLAN) could also be used to inhibit US access to the SCS. However, the SCS is approximately three million sq. kms. in area which makes is improbable that China would be able to control it completely. According to Fravel (2016), China's "South Sea Fleet has roughly

8 destroyers (5 of which are modern) and 19 frigates (4 or 8 of which are modern)."

With regard to stability: The US is keen to ensure that the SCS and adjoining regions remain stable as that translates to continued economic expansion for the US as a crisis could threaten freedom of navigation, thereby adversely impacting trade and investment of the US. Instability may lead to competition between the regional powers that would be debilitating to the aims of the US to maintain freedom of navigation. The developments in the SCS have been threatening regional stability in various ways. Competing claims of the littoral actors raise the possibility of armed conflict over maritime rights and territorial features of the SCS. Such confrontations have taken place between Vietnam and China in 1974 over the Paracel Islands' Crescent group and in 1988 over the Johnson Reef. Such confrontation over the land features in the SCS is susceptible to uncontrollable security competition between the other littorals and their allies. Stability in the region is also threatened by the use of coercive methods by the claimants to back their agenda. China has articulated its aversion towards Indian and American companies involved in the South China Sea. Such articulations can breed instability in the region. Stability in the region is also threatened by naval modernisation by the claimants in the region as such activities would impact the balance against certain of the claimants while lending undue advantage to the others. China is not the only littoral which is modernising its fleet in the SCS. Vietnam has also been enhancing its capacities, both in the air and naval departments. It has bought kilo-class submarines from Russia for bolstering its own ability to ensure area denial to other actors. Such modernisation of naval capacities among the littorals can segue into a naval acquisition race and heightening insecurity which may lead to a major crisis. Instability can also emerge as a result of attempts by the US and China to respond to each other's stance with regard to the developments in the SCS. While China has been seen to bolster its capacities in the SCS by acquiring anti-ship ballistic missile which the Western powers have said is part of China's overall 'anti-access/area denial' capabilities, US has initiated a concept called Air Sea Battle to ensure that in case of war the US has access to the SCS. The arrangements of the US and China to maintain access in the event of war can catapult to heightened insecurity and instability.

The US is also keen to ensure that, apart from ensuring access and maintaining stability in the SCS, its allies are sufficiently supported while at the same time ensuring that US is not seen to be breaking its commitments to neutrality in dealing with particular disputes involving its allies. The US is also interested in ensuring that the SCS does not become a debilitating issue in the overall framework of US-China ties.

US Policy towards the South China Sea Disputes

The US has responded to the disputes in the SCS based on its principles of maintaining freedom of navigation in the high seas and neutrality. In 1994 there emerged a dispute among the littorals when China occupied Mischief Reef in the South China Sea. In a daily press briefing of the US State Department in 1995, the US outlined its stand on the dispute.[1] The statement mentioned that the US favoured peaceful resolution of all disputes competing claims should not be resolved by force and instead restraint was to be pursued. It also mentioned that the US was keen to enhance stability as well as peace in the SCS. It stressed the interest of the US to maintain freedom of navigation whereby ships and aircrafts in the SCS were to be ensured unobstructed passage. The US's neutrality on the sovereignty-related claims to the land features of the SCS by the littorals was also iterated. It also mentioned that the US was concerned about any violation of international law, especially the 1982 United Nations Convention on the Law of the Sea."

The Press Briefing stated that following on the matter related to the developments of the South China Sea which in essence has continued to be the stance taken by the US till the present times:

> "The United States is concerned that a pattern of unilateral actions and reactions in the South China Sea has increased tensions in that region. The United States strongly opposes the use or threat of force to resolve competing claims and urges all claimants to exercise restraint and to avoid destabilising actions. The United States has an abiding interest in the maintenance of peace and stability in the South China Sea. The United States calls upon claimants to intensify diplomatic efforts which address issues related to the competing claims, taking into account the interests of all parties, and which contribute to peace and prosperity in the region.... Maintaining freedom of navigation is a fundamental interest of the United States. Unhindered navigation by all ships and aircraft in the South China Sea is essential for the peace and prosperity of the entire Asia-Pacific region, including the United States. The United States takes no position on the legal merits of the competing claims to sovereignty over the various island, reefs, atolls, and cays in the South China Sea. The United States would, however, view with serious concern any maritime claim or restriction on maritime activity

in the South China Sea that was not consistent with international law, including the 1982 United Nations Convention on the Law of the Sea."[2]

The ASEAN and China commenced negotiations of a code of conduct incase of SCS related disputes and by 2002 they formulated a *Declaration on the Conduct of Parties in the South China Sea* (DOC) which also consisted of a commitment to formulate a code of conduct in the future which was binding in nature.[3] The DOC mentioned:

> "The Parties reaffirm their respect for and commitment to the freedom of navigation in and overflight above the South China Sea as provided for by the universally recognised principles of international law, including the 1982 UN Convention on the Law of the Sea; The Parties concerned undertake to resolve their territorial and jurisdictional disputes by peaceful means, without resorting to the threat or use of force, through friendly consultations and negotiations by sovereign states directly concerned, in accordance with universally recognised principles of international law, ... The Parties undertake to exercise self-restraint in the conduct of activities that would complicate or escalate disputes and affect peace and stability including, among others, refraining from action of inhabiting on the presently uninhabited islands, reefs, shoals, cays, and other features and to handle their differences in a constructive manner."

In Manila on 6 August 2017, the ASEAN and China endorsed the framework for the Code of Conduct for the South China Sea (COC) which reiterated the principles endorsed in the DOC of 2002. Unlike the DOC of 2002, the COC of 2017 makes "a new reference to the prevention and management of incidents, as well as a seemingly stronger commitment to maritime security and freedom of navigation. However, the phrase 'legally binding' is absent, as are the geographical scope of the agreement and enforcement and arbitration mechanisms" (Storey: 2017).

From 2007 onwards there were growing claims on the land features and water on the part of the littorals in the SCS. Some of these claimants such as China started taking action to defend their claims. Such actions increased possibility of denial of access and instability in the region, which were antithetical to overall US interests in the region. China had begun to assert its rights in the region by threatening the involvement of companies on non-resident actors such as the US and India in the SCS; it was also claiming continental shelf rights of an extended nature in the SCS; it began to impose moratoriums on fishing in parts of the SCS as well as detain Vietnam's fishermen in the Paracel Islands; China's marine patrolling and naval drills in the contested waters also increased; China was also involved in encumbering access to the USNC Impeccable near the Hainan Islands. China was not the only country that was becoming more assertive in the SCS to defend its claims. Leaders of Vietnam and Malaysia began to visit the contested Spratly Islands as symbolic gestures to back their claims and Philippines passed a law demarcating a baseline that outlined its claims to the Spratly Islands (Fravel 2016: 394).

US Approaches to the SCS: The Obama Years

US concerns were heightened due to the threats received by its oil companies from China for operating in the SCS as that inimical to the economic interests of the US, and due to China's obstruction of the passage of the USNS Impeccable, which was indicative of the threat to the principle of the freedom of navigation on the high seas. The Obama administration responded to these new developments in the SCS in 2010 when Secretary of State Hillary Clinton reiterated the principles that were articulated in response to the Mischief Reef dispute in 1995 and also added that the US policy was based on ensuring the coercion was not used in resolving disputes. Clinton also affirmed that the US was keen to support diplomatic processes amidst the competing claimants to the SCS, which was collaborative, and to facilitate measures that were consistent to the Code of Conduct that was decided by the ASEAN and China in 2002. She also asserted that the US was supportive of claims of maritime jurisdiction derived from claims that were legitimately based on land features in the SCS. In her remarks, Clinton mentioned:

> "The United States, like every nation, has a national interest in freedom of navigation, open access to Asia's maritime commons, and respect for international law in the South China Sea.... The United States supports a collaborative diplomatic process by all claimants for resolving the various territorial disputes without coercion. We oppose the use or threat of force by any claimant. While the United States does not take sides on the competing territorial disputes over land features in the South China Sea, we believe claimants should pursue their territorial claims and accompanying rights to maritime space in accordance with the UN convention on the law of the sea. Consistent with customary international law, legitimate claims to maritime space in the South China Sea should be derived solely from legitimate claims to land features. The US supports the 2002 ASEAN-China declaration on the conduct of parties in the South China Sea. We encourage the parties to reach agreement on a full code of conduct."[4]

These declarations did not mention China by name but were interpreted as being aimed at China's actions in the SCS. The instance of collaborative measures by the US can be understood as inferring multilateral approach in contradistinction to the approach taken by China, which was premised on bilateralism. In addition, the US instance on its support for only those maritime claims that were legitimately based on land features can be comprehended at aiming at challenging China's claims of maritime jurisdiction based on its nine-dashed line, which was not accepted by other countries. While not debunking its neutral position, the US, with such declarations was more intensively involved in the region but enunciating its stance on the manner in which disputes were to be managed and resolved (Fravel, 2016: 395). Such articulations by the US prompted notions that US may begin to become directly entangled in the SCS developments. Several states also expressed their concerns about security in the SCS. Yang Jiechi, who was the Foreign Minister of China, delivered a harsh rebuke of such statements by the US and other countries. Jiechi noted that the SCS was peaceful and not dangerous; that there was regional consensus on ways of resolving disputes in a friendly manner; that there was no freedom of navigation problem in the SCS; that there was no point of mentioning coercion as China had legitimate concerns which should not be interpreted as coercion and that internationalisation of disputes would hamper peaceful resolution of disputes.[5]

The 2010 declarations of the US made clear the intentions of the US to continue to maintain neutrality where rival claims were concerned but also made clear its intentions to be involved in the disputes according to the legitimacy of competing claims as determined by it. The US was keen to ensure that freedom of manoeuvrability and operations of its oil companies in the region were not hampered by the developments in the SCS or the claims of the littorals. Prevention of the use of force, preference of peaceful resolution of disputes, significance of dialogues and support for a mutually agreed upon code of conduct among the powers with rival claims remained the main tenets of US policy. During this period countries such as India, which also had economic concerns in the SCS, were also expressive about their concerns regarding the assertiveness of China and possible destabilisation of the region.

In 2012, China and the Philippines had an impasse over their claims on the Scarborough Shoal in the SCS. The ASEAN was divided on the issue and was unable to issue a joint statement for the first time in its history. The navy of the Philippines tried to arrest fishermen from China who were near the shoal. China and the Philippines agreed to a deal arranged by the US to withdraw forces but the deal came apart when China reneged on the terms. Cambodia succumbed to Chinese pressure to reject a request by the Philippines to mention the Scarborough in an ASEAN joint statement in 2012. In 2012 it was also announced by China that it would upgrade the status of the SCS islands by constructing Sansha City, which would be of a prefecturial level and would be based on the Woody Island in the Paracels where a new garrison was constructed by China (Tiezzi, 2016). In 2012, Vietnam conducted its first ever air patrols over the Spratlys with Su-27 fighter and issued a national maritime law that contained its sovereignty claims over the Spratly and Paracel Islands. In response to China's actions, the US State Department spokesperson issued a statement, which reaffirmed US interests to maintain stability and peace in the SCS, but it also addressed China's activities especially its creation of Sansha City and actions around the Scarborough. The statement which was delivered by Patrick Ventrell (2012) read as follows:

> "We are concerned by the increase in tensions in the South China Sea and are monitoring the situation closely. Recent developments include an uptick in confrontational rhetoric, disagreements over resource exploitation, coercive economic actions, and the incidents around the Scarborough Reef, including the use of barriers to deny access. In particular, China's upgrading of the administrative level of Sansha City and establishment of a new military garrison there covering disputed areas of the South China Sea run counter to collaborative diplomatic efforts to resolve differences and risk further escalating tensions in the region."

Ties with littoral states such as the Philippines and Vietnam have been bolstered by the US during the course of the disputes over the SCS. Port visits, naval exercises, and dialogues on security form a part of US ties with these states. US-Vietnam relations have witnessed a fillip following the disputes in the SCS. These countries have held assistant secretary of state level annual dialogues covering political, security and defense spheres. A comprehensive partnership was announced during the visit of Vietnam's President Truong Tan Sang to the US in 2013 which covered a gamut of areas of intended cooperation including "political and diplomatic relations, trade and economic ties, science and technology, education and training, environment and health, war legacy issues, defence and security, protection and promotion of human rights, and culture, sports, and tourism" (Fravel 2016: 399). With regard to military relations, the US and Vietnam commenced annual dialogues on defence policy in 2010. They also began naval engagement activities that comprised of exchanges and exercises. The US navy has also used Vietnam's Cam Rahn Bay for servicing and repairing its ships. The US and Vietnam have also signed an agreement codifying existing exchanges under the Memorandum of Understanding in 2011 on Advancing Bilateral Defense Cooperation.

The US and the Philippines have close military ties which have been somewhat precarious after the coming into power of Rodrigo Duterte as President in the Philippines. They have held joint exercises called Balikatan since 1991. They cooperate on counter-insurgency as well. Both maritime and diplomatic cooperation have been on an upswing in the ties between the Philippines and the US in the recent years. A bilateral strategic dialogue took place between the two countries in 2011 with an intention to bolster patrolling abilities of the Philippines in its maritime waters. The Philippines acquired a Hamilton-class Coast Guard cutter from the US in 2011 for its navy. The Manila Declaration of 2011 reiterated the commitment of the US and Philippines to cooperation in security related to maritime issues, freedom of navigation, and collaboration in diplomatic and multilateral processes. In 2012, ministerial level talks were held with diplomats and defense officials during the second Bilateral Strategic Dialogue which stressed cooperation to enable the development of a minimum credible defense posture for the Philippines. Regarding maritime domain awareness of the Philippines the US pledged a 3-year US$40 million programme in 2013 (Fravel 2016: 400).

The US, during President Obama's regime, announced a rebalance policy to the Asia-Pacific and held a string of hearings in 2014 on this policy. A congressional testimony of Daniel Russel, the Assistant Secretary of State for East Asia and the Pacific in 2014 as part of these hearings was instrumental for the US policy on the SCS. Several new tensions had occurred related to the SCS including: China exerting pressure by positioning its vessels around the Second Thomas Shoal held by the Philippines; concerns about the establishment in the SCS of an Air Defense Identification Zone (ADIZ) given the formation in 2013 of the ADIZ in the East China Sea; concerns emanating the oath-taking ceremony at James Shoal which is located close to Malaysia aboard naval ships of China at James Shoal in 2014. It was asserted in the testimony that China's actions amounted to an incremental effort to establish control over the SCS. The testimony mentioned China by name as the country, which was responsible for increasing tensions in the SCS. No other country was identified in the testimony as being responsible for the tensions. The testimony also stressed the US stand that land features had to be the basis on which claims related to maritime jurisdiction were derived. The stand of the Philippines to seek intervention of the International Tribunal of the Law of the Sea was supported by the US as a method of peaceful resolution of disputes.

With regard to the US concerns in the region emanating from Chinese actions, it was stated:

> "...continued restrictions on access to Scarborough Reef; pressure on the long-standing Philippine presence at the Second Thomas Shoal; putting hydrocarbon blocks up for bid in an area close to another country's mainland and far away even from the islands that China is claiming; announcing administrative and even military districts in contested areas in the South China Sea; an unprecedented spike in risky activity by China's maritime agencies near the Senkaku Islands; the sudden, uncoordinated and unilateral imposition of regulations over contested airspace in the case of the East China Sea Air Defense Identification Zone; and the recent updating of fishing regulations covering disputed areas in the South China Sea."[6]

In 2014, the US Department of Defense (DOD) made a reference to the 1972 Convention on Preventing Collisions at Sea (COLREGs) to which both China and the US are members. The COLREGS which is binding in nature seek to regulate the prevention of collision of military vessels, paramilitary and law enforcement (i.e., coast guard) vessels, maritime militia vessels, and fishing boats, among other vessels at sea and applies "to all vessels upon the high seas and in all waters connected therewith navigable by seagoing vessels."[7] In the 2014 annual report the DOD stated that in December 2013, vessels of the Chinese navy and the US navy came into close proximity in the South China Sea. During the incident, the US naval vessel—the USS COWPENS (CG 63) was positioned lawfully around 32 nautical miles from the southeast of the Hainan Island and thus it was beyond the territorial sea of any nation. When it was approached by two Chinese naval vessels and one of them positioned itself directly in front of USS COWPENS forcing the latter to stop to prevent a collision; such conduct of the Chinese vessel was inconsistent with the norms and rules of maritime conduct as laid down in the COLREGS.[8]

Close on the heels of the incident involving the USS COWPENS, China, the US and 21 others agreed on a non-binding agreement called Code for Unplanned Encounters at Sea (CUES) on 22 April 2014 which provided a protocol of safety procedures, basic instructions for communications and manoeuvring for naval ships and aircraft in the event of encounters at sea which were unplanned with a goal to reduce the possibility of incidents due to such encounters.[9] In addition, in November 2014 the US-China MOU on Air and Maritime Encounters was signed by the US DOD and China's Ministry of National Defense which set rules of conduct for maritime and air safety in case of encounters.[10]

During a Testimony of Daniel Russell, Assistant Secretary of State, US Department, on 13 May 2015 it was pointed out that the US and China had attempted to cooperate to manage differences and that the US was welcoming of the peaceful rise of China and had been keen to ensure that China took greater lead in tackling global and regional challenges but also mentioned that the US could not ignore attempts by China's muscular policies towards the South China Sea aimed at dominating other countries and mentioned that the US consistently raised, "Concerns directly with China's leadership and urge China to manage and resolve differences with its neighbors peacefully and in accordance with international law. We also underscore that the United States will not hesitate to defend our national security interests and to honor our commitments to allies and partners in the Asia-Pacific."[11]

During the Obama period, China reiterated its understanding of freedom of navigation. China had consistently maintained that it supported freedom of navigation that was based on the freedom of navigation of commercial ships in international waters. On the other hand the US and the west defined freedom of navigation includes navigation freedom of military ships and aircrafts. When asked why China warned a US navy plane on 12 August 2015 which was operating near the Spratly Island in August 2015, Ambassador Zhao Jianhua said: "Freedom of navigation does not mean to allow other countries to intrude into the airspace or the sea which is sovereign. No country will allow that," He said. "We say freedom of navigation must be observed in accordance with international law. No freedom of navigation for warships and airplanes."[12] Similar arguments were forwarded by China during Trump's presidency.

In August 2015, the Asia-Pacific Maritime Security Strategy (MSS) was released which stated that for safeguarding the seas, preventing conflict and encouraging adherence to international law, the US would: strengthen its military capacity by "investing in new cutting-edge capabilities, deploying our finest maritime capabilities forward, and distributing these capabilities more widely across the region. The effort also involves enhancing our force posture and persistent presence in the region, to maintain a higher pace of training, transits, and operations". The MSS also stated that the US would also work with its allies and partners in the Indian Ocean and Northeast Asia to bolster their maritime capacities by "building greater interoperability, updating our combined exercises, developing more integrated operations, and cooperatively developing partner maritime domain awareness and maritime security capabilities, which will ensure a strong collective capacity to employ our maritime capabilities most effectively". It also mentioned that the US would pursue military diplomacy to ensure transparency, prevent miscalculation and promote maritime rules of conduct among the countries which would include "bilateral efforts with China as well as multilateral initiatives to develop stronger regional crisis management mechanisms" and "encourage countries to develop confidence-building measures with each other and to pursue diplomatic efforts to resolve disputed claims." Finally, the maritime strategy also sought to bolster security institutions of the regions and promote the creation of regional security architecture such as increasing the engagement of the US DOD in "ASEAN-based institutions such as the ASEAN Defense Ministers Meeting Plus (ADMM-Plus), ASEAN Regional Forum (ARF), and the Expanded ASEAN Maritime Forum (EAMF), as well as through wider forums like the Western Pacific Naval Symposium (WPNS) and Indian Ocean Naval Symposium (IONS)."[13] Regarding joint exercises with other countries in the region, it was stated in the MSS that US intends on "increasing the size, frequency, and sophistication of our regional exercise program, with a particular focus on developing new exercises with Southeast Asian partners and expanding our multilateral exercise program. We have also begun incorporating a maritime focus into many of these engagements in order to tailor our training to address regional partners' evolving requirements."[14]

US Defense Secretary Ashton Baldwin Carter had announced at the Shangri-La Dialogue on 30 May 2015, that the Southeast Asia Maritime Security Strategy of the US was an effort to cooperate with the US allies and partners to enable them to address changes in the maritime sphere.[15] In the MSS it was further elaborated that:

> "In particular, we are focused on several lines of effort: working with partners to expand regional maritime domain awareness capabilities, with an effort to work towards a regional common operating picture; providing the necessary infrastructure, logistics support, and operational procedures to enable more effective maritime response operations; further strengthening partner nation operational capabilities and resilience by deepening and expanding bilateral and regional maritime exercises and engagements;

> helping partners strengthen their maritime institutions, governance, and personnel training; and identifying modernisation or new system requirements for critical maritime security capabilities."[16]

With regard to the littoral countries in the SCS and Southeast Asia the MSS pointed out:

> "In the Philippines, the Department is providing coastal radar systems and assisting the Department of State with naval maintenance capacity building as well as providing interdiction vessels, naval fleet upgrades, communications equipment, and aircraft procurement. We are helping Vietnam bolster its maritime ISR and command and control within their maritime agencies, and we are working with Malaysia to build maritime law enforcement training capacity and interagency coordination to help improve their maritime domain awareness. The Department also is working with Indonesia to increase its patrol capacity, ISR integration, and maintenance capability. In 2015, we established new bilateral working groups with both Indonesia and Vietnam to help clarify their maritime defense requirements."[17]

The MSS also mentioned that the US was helping its allies generate institutional structure and procedures needed to manage maritime vessels including "unified maritime agencies, such as the Malaysian Maritime Enforcement Agency (MMEA)" and it stressed that "the Defense Threat Reduction Agency (DTRA) is helping to construct a Philippine National Coast Watch Center in Manila that will assist the Philippine Coast Guard (PCG) in assuming increased responsibility for enhancing information sharing and interagency coordination in maritime security operations."[18]

On 25 September 2015, Remarks by President Barack Obama and President Xi Jinping which were made during a Joint Press Conference were released. President Barack Obama's remarks, "reiterated the right of all countries to freedom of navigation and overflight and to unimpeded commerce... indicated that the United States will continue to sail, fly and operate anywhere that international law allows." President Barack Obama also mentioned the US's concerns over "land reclamation, construction and the militarisation of disputed areas" and "encouraged a resolution between claimants in these areas."[19] Xi, in his remarks, stated that China has, "the right to uphold our own territorial sovereignty and legitimate maritime rights and interests' and that China was "committed to respecting and upholding the freedom of navigation and overflight that countries enjoy according to international law."[20]

He also stated that, "Relevant construction activities that China are undertaking in the island of South—Nansha Islands do not target or impact any country, and China does not intend to pursue militarisation."[21] The declaration that China did not intend to militarise the South China Sea has however been considered as having been voided by China due to their recent activities in the SCS in the succeeding years.

Apart from such declarations, which reiterated US commitment towards its allies and freedom of navigation, the US, during President Barack Obama also undertook several Freedom of Navigation (FON) Operations in the SCS. The supporters of FON argue that such operations was consistent with the freedom of navigation which the US professed and it made it clear that the US did not accept China's sovereignty over the SCS. Four FONs were conducted under the Obama regime in the SCS.[22]

One of the most significant events during the Obama regime was the verdict of the tribunal in Hague on the South China Sea issue, which was delivered in July 2016. The tribunal found the construction of China's artificial islands, and its historical claims over the SCS as being without legal basis (Perlez 2016). In a Speech at the China-US Dialogue on South China Sea between Chinese and US Think Tanks on 5 July 2016, Dai Bingguo, who served as the State Councilor of the China, made China's disapproval of the ruling that Chinas historical rights claims in the SCS were without legal foundation, and that China's activities in the Exclusive Economic Zone (EEZ) of the Philippines which infringed the latters' sovereignty, by a tribunal at the Permanent Court of Arbitration (PCA) on the dispute brought by the Philippines against China clear by alluding to historic injustices and hegemonism of the West in this way:

> "The final award of the arbitration, which will come out in the next few days, amounts to nothing more than a piece of paper. China suffered enough from hegemonism, power politics and bullying by Western Powers since modern times. The Versailles peace conference at the end of World War I forced a sold-out of Shandong Province. The Lytton Commission, sent by the League of Nations when Japan invaded China's northeast provinces, only served to justify Japan's invasion. Even the US-led negotiations on San Francisco Peace Treaty excluded China. These episodes are still vivid in our memory. That is why China will grip its own future on issues of territorial sovereignty, and will never accept any solution imposed by a third party."[23]

He also made it clear that China did not intend to engage in 'strategic rivalry' and mentioned that China had "no ambition to rule Asia, still less the Earth.

Even in the context of the issue in question, we have never claimed we own the entire South China Sea. We only have one ambition, which is to manage our own affairs well and ensure a decent life and dignity for the nearly 1.4 billion Chinese people."[24] On 12 July 2016, in a Statement of the Ministry of Foreign Affairs of the People's Republic of China on the Award, it was asserted "China's territorial sovereignty and maritime rights and interests in the South China Sea shall under no circumstances be affected by those awards. China opposes and will never accept any claim or action based on those awards."[25]

The US endorsed the verdict in the Philippines versus China arbitration over the SCS. The US state department stated: "The decision today by the Tribunal in the Philippines-China arbitration is an important contribution to the shared goal of a peaceful resolution to disputes in the South China Sea."[26] The State Department reiterated its preference for adhering to the UNCLOS, which, as mentioned above, the US has not ratified but adheres to it as part of customary international law. It was also mentioned: "We encourage claimants to clarify their maritime claims in accordance with international law—as reflected in the Law of the Sea Convention—and to work together to manage and resolve their disputes. Such steps could provide the basis for further discussions aimed at narrowing the geographic scope of their maritime disputes, setting standards for behaviour in disputed areas, and ultimately resolving their underlying disputes free from coercion or the use or threat of force."[27]

US Approaches to the SCS: The Donald Trump Era

Donald Trump has followed much of Obama's policies in the SCS including FONOPS and maritime security cooperation with countries such as Vietnam and Indonesia. During the trump presidency, on 12 November 2017, the US and Vietnam signed a joint statement whereby they "underscored the strategic importance to the international community of free and open access to the South China Sea, the importance of unimpeded lawful commerce, the need to respect freedom of navigation and over-flight, and other lawful uses of the sea" and reiterated their stance on refraining "from escalatory actions, the militarisation of disputed features, and unlawful restrictions on freedom of the seas."[28] However, it has been pointed out that Vietnam apart from China has been militarising the SCS and the US "itself has increasingly raised tensions by militarising the region with its forward deployed troops, assets and patrols as part of the 'rebalance' of its defense forces" (Valencia: 2017).

In 2017, the US under Donald Trump released the National Security

Strategy (NSS) which alluded to China's position on the SCS and stated that China was one of the contenders for power. The NSS stated that: "A central continuity in history is the contest for power. The present time period is no different. Three main sets of challengers—the revisionist powers of China and Russia, the rogue states of Iran and North Korea, and transnational threat organisations, particularly jihadist terrorist groups—are actively competing against the United States and our allies and partners (National Security Strategy 2017: 46)." It further highlighted that, "Although differing in nature and magnitude, these rivals compete across political, economic, and military arenas, and use technology and information to accelerate these contests in order to shift regional balances of power in their favour. These are fundamentally political contests between those who favour repressive systems and those who favour free societies (National Security Strategy 2017: 46)." With regard to China the NSS mentioned that despite US overtures to cooperate with China, the latter was "using economic inducements and penalties, influence operations, and implied military threats to persuade other states to heed its political and security agenda. China's infrastructure investments and trade strategies reinforce its geopolitical aspirations" and stated that China's "efforts to build and militarise outposts in the South China Sea endanger the free flow of trade, threaten the sovereignty of other nations, and undermine regional stability. China has mounted a rapid military modernisation campaign designed to limit US access to the region and provide China a freer hand there (National Security Strategy 2017: 46)." It also ascertained that, "China presents its ambitions as mutually beneficial, but Chinese dominance risks diminishing the sovereignty of many states in the Indo-Pacific. States throughout the region are calling for sustained US leadership in a collective response that upholds a regional order respectful of sovereignty and independence" (National Security Strategy 2017: 46).

In September 2017, China's Four Sha Legal Claim, which critics have called lawfare or legal warfare, was unveiled by Ma Xinmin, deputy director general in the Foreign Ministry's department of treaty and law. According to this claim China, which had already claimed three of the island chains had also added a fourth zone known as the Pratas Islands situated near Hong Kong. China calls the island groups: *Dongsha, Xisha, Nansha*, and *Zhongsha*. Ma declared that China was legally claiming and thereby asserting sovereignty over the Four Sha. These claims were based on China's historical rights over these waters and as they fell inside China's EEZ. He stated the area falls under China's historical territorial waters and is also part of China's 200-mile EEZ.

In response to the new claims, the US State Department spokesman Justin Higgins said the US did not adopt any stand on competing claims on the SCS and reiterated US recognition of the pursuance of the UNCLOS (Gertz, 2017).

The National Defense Strategy (NDS) (2018:1) of the US released in 2018 notes:

> "China is a strategic competitor using predatory economics to intimidate its neighbors while militarising features in the South China Sea." The NDS (2018:2) mentioned the revisionism of China in the following way: "China is leveraging military modernisation, influence operations, and predatory economics to coerce neighboring countries to reorder the Indo-Pacific region to their advantage. As China continues its economic and military ascendance, asserting power through an all-of-nation long-term strategy, it will continue to pursue a military modernisation program that seeks Indo-Pacific regional hegemony in the near-term and displacement of the United States to achieve global preeminence in the future."

The overall aim of the NDS (2018:2) was stated as "set the military relationship between our two countries on a path of transparency and non-aggression." The NDS also articulated the China along with Russia was attempting to weaken the international order that was in place after the Second World War which was constructed by the US and its allies in the shape of an open order which sought to promote liberty and prevent coercion. It also stated that the main priorities for the US was, "Long-term strategic competitions with China and Russia" due to the threats they pose to ensure "common domains remain open and free (National Defense Strategy 2018:1)."

In February 2018, the Philippines President Rodrigo Duterte addressed the militarisation efforts of China in the Spratly group in the SCS in a manner inimical to the stands of the US as he asserted that China's militarisation efforts were not directed at states such as The Philippines but towards the US. Duterte had been attempting to bolster ties with China. Earlier, in October 2016 Rodrigo Duterte had announced his 'separation' from the US, and alignment with China and announced that China and his country had agreed to resolve the SCS issue though talks (Blancard, 2016). A presidential spokesperson of the Philippine's noted after a FONOP during the Trump administration that freedom of navigation was 'America's problem'. He also noted that: "We have reached a point where we have independent foreign relations, and a problem of America is no longer a problem of the Philippines" (Panda, 2018). President Duterte has also not taken steps to implement the 2016 decision on the SCS awarded by the tribunal of The Hague.

In May 2018, in response to continued militarisation of the SCS, the US disinvited China to the RIMPAC (Rim of the Pacific) exercises that China had participated in 2014 and 2016. The US DOD released a statement with regard to the withdrawal of the invitation sent to China to participate in the RIMPAC of 2018 that states:

> "The United States is committed to a free and open Indo-Pacific. China's continued militarisation of disputed features in the South China Sea only serve to raise tensions and destabilise the region. As an initial response to China's continued militarisation of the South China Sea we have disinvited the PLA Navy from the 2018 Rim of the Pacific (RIMPAC) Exercise. China's behaviour is inconsistent with the principles and purposes of the RIMPAC exercise."[29]

Addressing the disinvite to China over concerns of the US, due to deployment of anti-ship missiles, surface-to-air missiles, electronic jammers in the artificial features constructed by China and the landing of bomber aircraft in the Woody Island, James Mattison during the Shangrila dialogue of 2018 mentioned:

> "Despite China's claims to the contrary, the placement of these weapons systems is tied directly to military use for the purposes of intimidation and coercion. China's militarisation of the Spratlys is also in direct contradiction to President Xi's 2015 public assurances in the White House Rose Garden that they would not do this.... For these reasons, and as initial response to China's continued militarisation of the South China Sea, last week we disinvited the People's Liberation Army Navy from the 2018 Rim of the Pacific Exercise, as China's behaviour is inconsistent with the principals and the purposes of the RIMPAC exercise, the world's largest Naval exercise, and exercise in which transparency and cooperation are hallmarks."[30]

Supporters of the US decision to disinvite China from the RIMPAC outlined that not disinviting China would amount to rewarding China for militarising the SCS. They also underscored that the information, which China would obtain from the exercise about US forces, would be much more than the information that the US would gain about China's forces. Detractors of the move to rescind China's invitation, however, pointed out that China's participation helps in maintaining positive ties with China and would be of benefit in case of any incidents involving the two forces in the SCS.

Until April 2017 the US under President Donald Trump had not conducted any FON and there were reports that the DOD had turned down the Navy's proposals for an FON. However, since then the US has conducted multiple FONs which were met with warnings from Chinese warships. The FONs under the Trump administration included one on 25 May 2017 which involved US navy destroyer D*ewey which sailed* within six nautical miles of Mischief Reef, of the Spratly Islands; another on 2 July 2017, when the destroyer *Stethem* (DDG-63) sailed within 12 nautical miles of Triton Island in the Paracels; another on 10 August 2017, which involved *John S. McCain* (DDG-56) which was sent within 12 nautical miles of Mischief Reef; yet another on 10 October 2017, when destroyer *Chafee* (DDG-90) was sent near but not within 12 nautical miles of the Paracels; another FON was conducted on 17 January 2018 when the destroyer *Hopper* (DDG-70) sailed within 12 nautical miles of Scarborough Shoal; and on 23 March 2018 when the destroyer *Mustin* (DDG-89) sailed within 12 nautical miles of Mischief Reef. However, it has been commented by Bonnie Glaser, a senior adviser for Asia at the Center for Strategic and International Studies in Washington "FONOPs are not a full strategy" and "It was not enough in the Obama era and it's not enough under Trump," Glaser said.[31]

Conclusion

The US policy with regard to the disputes in the SCS has been fairly consistent. It has continued to emphasise on the peaceful resolution of disputes and management of competing claims. The US is against the use of threats, intimidation, coercion in matters related to the SCS and support stands which are consistent with international law and which support to the freedom of the seas principles including freedom of manoeuvre and navigation. The US asserts that claims on territorial waters and EEZ should be derived from land features and believes that land reclamation and militarisation of these features will upset peace. The US position also subscribes to the view that coastal states can regulate economic but not military activities of other states in their EEZ. The US beliefs that its military movements in the EEZs of other nations is lawful under international law.

China has been the only country which has been singled out by the US as it has formidable capabilities in terms of maritime prowess, and claims all the land features in the SCS and has not clarified the meaning of the nine dashed line. The US is also keen not to let the SCS issue dominate overall US-China ties and thereby maintains a neutral stance on sovereignty claims. US's overall stance and approach are based on maintaining the international order and principles, which it had created after the Second World War. Thereby the US intends to prevent China from creating a new order based on the latter's rules and principles which differ from that of the US as it evident from the difference in the manner in which both nations interpret the principle of freedom of navigation. It is unlikely that the competing claims over sovereignty will be resolved soon. The uncertainty brought in due to President Duterte's recent statements and overtures towards reappraising ties with China have added an element of uncertainty in the calculations of the US in matters related to the SCS. A final settlement seems to be beyond the foreseeable horizon and thus the SCS will continue to be a dominant feature in regional stability and security related matters. A code of conduct, which is binding, if achieved, would likely bring stability and security in the region. Continued assertiveness of China in the SCS region would continue to increase US declarations on China's actions as well as heighten US involvement with the militaries and navies of the other littorals, along with increased FONOPs and possible diplomatic sanctions but it is unlikely that it will segue into economic sanctions and much less into an all out war between the two nations given the deep economic ties between them, the cascading impact of a military response, and the gargantuan costs associated with the launch of a full scale military option not only for those directly involved but the region and beyond as well.

NOTES

1 U.S. Department of State 95/05/10 Daily Press Briefing Office of the Spokesman, available at http://dosfan.lib.uic.edu/ERC/briefing/daily_briefings/1995/9505/950510db.html.

2 Ibid.

3 Declaration On The Conduct Of Parties In The South China Sea, available at http://asean.org/?static_post=declaration-on-the-conduct-of-parties-in-the-south-china-sea.

4 Remarks at Press Availability by Hillary Clinton, US Secretary of State, in Vietnam, 23 July 2010, US Department of State, available at https://2009-2017.state.gov/secretary/20092013clinton/rm/2010/07/145095.htm.

5 Mentioned in T. Inoguchi and G. Ikenberry, (2013), eds. *The Troubled Triangle: Economic and Security Conerns for the United Sttaes, Japan and China*, Palgrave Macmillan: USA.

6 Testimony of Daniel Russel, Assistant Secretary of State Bureau of East Asian and Pacific Affairs U.S. Department of State Before the House Committee on Foreign Affairs Subcommittee on Asia and the Pacific Wednesday, February 5, 2014 Maritime Disputes in East Asia, available at https://docs.house.gov/meetings/FA/FA05/20140205/101715/HHRG-113-FA05-Wstate-RusselD-20140205.pdf.

7 Rule 1(a) of the convention.

8 Department of Defense, *Annual Report to Congress [on] Military and Security Developments Involving the People's Republic of China 2014*, p. 4.

9 "Navy Leaders Agree to CUES at 14th WPNS," *Navy News Services*, April 23, 2014.

10 Memorandum of Understanding Between The Department of Defense of the United States of America and the Ministry of National Defense of the People's Republic of

China Regarding the Rules of Behavior for Safety of Air and Maritime Encounters, November 12, 2014.

11 Testimony of Daniel RusselAssistant Secretary of State Bureau of East Asian and Pacific Affairs U.S. Department of State Before the Senate Foreign Relations Committee Wednesday, May 13, 2015 Maritime Issues in East Asia, p. 6.

12 Jim Gomez, "Chinese Diplomat Outlines Limits to Freedom of Navigation," *Military Times*, August 12, 2015.

13 Department of Defense, *Asia-Pacific Maritime Security Strategy*, undated but released August 2015, pp. 19-20.

14 Ibid., p. 24.

15 The White House, Office of the Press Secretary, Nov 17, 2015, available at https://obamawhitehouse.archives.gov/the-press-office/2015/11/17/fact-sheet-us-building-maritime-capacity-southeast-asia.

16 Department of Defense, *Asia-Pacific Maritime Security Strategy*, undated but released August 2015, p. 26.

17 Ibid.

18 Ibid., p. 27.

19 Remarks by President Obama and President Xi of the People's Republic of China in Joint Press Conference, available at https://obamawhitehouse.archives.gov/the-press-office/2015/09/25/remarks-president-obama-and-president-xi-peoples-republic-china-joint.

20 Ibid.

21 Ibid.

22 See CRS report for more information on FON

23 Speech by Dai Bingguo at China-US Dialogue on South China Sea Between Chinese and US Think Tanks, Ministry of Foreign Affiars of the people's republic of China, available at http://www.fmprc.gov.cn/mfa_eng/zxxx_662805/t1377747.shtml

24 Speech by Dai Bingguo at China-US Dialogue on South China Sea Between Chinese and US Think Tanks, Ministry of Foreign Affiars of the people's republic of China, http://www.fmprc.gov.cn/mfa_eng/zxxx_662805/t1377747.shtml.

25 Full text of statement of China's Foreign Ministry on award of South China Sea arbitration initiated by Philippines, 12.7.2016, available at http://www.xinhuanet.com/english/2016-07/12/c_135507744.htm.

26 Decision in the Philippines-China Arbitration, Press Statementby John Kirby, Assistant Secretary and Department Spokesperson, Bureau of Public Affairs Washington, DC, July 12, 2016, available at https://20092017.state.gov/r/pa/prs/ps/2016/07/259587.htm.

27 Ibid.

28 Joint Statement between the United States of America and the Socialist Republic of Vietna, Issued on: November 12, 2017

29 DOD statement as reprinted in Megan Eckstein, "China Disinvited from Participating in 2018 RIMPAC Exercise," *USNI News*, May 23, 2018.

30 Remarks by Secretary Mattis at Plenary Session of the 2018 Shangri-La Dialogue Press Operations, Secretary of Defense James N. Mattis; John Chipman, Director-General and Chief Executive, IISS, June 2, 2018,available at https://www.defense.gov/News/Transcripts/Transcript-View/Article/1538599/remarks-by-secretary-mattis-at-plenary-session-of-the-2018-shangri-la-dialogue/

31 Mentioned in Emily Rauhala, "The South China Sea fell off Trump's radar last year. He may have to pay attention in 2018", The Washington Post, available at https://www.washingtonpost.com/world/asia_pacific/the-south-china-sea-fell-off-trumps-radar-this-year-he-may-have-to-pay-attention-in-2018/2018/01/01/b7c9a27a-eb1e-11e7-956e-baea358f9725_story.html?utm_term=.ab12881bbeb2.

REFERENCES

Blancard, Ben, "Duterte aligns Philippines with China, says U.S. has lost", *Reuters*, 20 October 2016, available at https://www.reuters.com/article/us-china-philippines-idUSKCN12K0AS?.

Fravel, Taylor (2016), *U.S. Policy Towards the Disputes in the South China Sea Since 1995*, 389-402, in Enrico Fels and Truong-Minh Vu, (eds.), Power Politics in Asia's Contested Waters: Territorial Disputes in the South China Sea, Switzerland: Springer.

Gertz, B. "Beijing Adopts New Tactic for S. China Sea Claims," *Washington Free Beacon*, September 21, 2017, available at http://freebeacon.com/national-security/beijing-adopts-new-tactic-s-china-sea-claims/.

Jane Perlez, Tribunal Rejects Beijing's Claims in South China Sea, *The New York Times*, 12. July 2016, available at https://www.nytimes.com/2016/07/13/world/asia/south-china-sea-hague-ruling-philippines.html

National Security Strategy, 2017, USA, available at https://www.whitehouse.gov/wp-content/uploads/2017/12/NSS-Final-12-18-2017-0905.pdf.

National Defense Strategy, 2018, available at https://www.defense.gov/Portals/1/Documents/pubs/2018-National-Defense-Strategy-Summary.pdf.

Panda, Ankit, 2018, Duterte: China's South China Sea Installations Aimed at the United States, Not the Philippines, The Diplomat, available at https://thediplomat.com/2018/02/duterte-chinas-south-china-sea-installations-aimed-at-the-united-states-not-the-philippines/.

Storey, Ian 2017, Assessing the ASEAN-China Framework for the Code of Conduct for the South China Sea, *Yusof Ishak Institute, ISEAS*, 62, available at https://www.iseas.edu.sg/images/pdf/ISEAS_Perspective_2017_62.pdf.

Tiezzi, S. 2016, Official: China Will Start Civilian Flights to South China Sea in 2016, *The Diplomat*, available at https://thediplomat.com/2016/01/official-china-will-start-civilian-flights-to-south-china-sea-in-2016/.

Valencia, J. Mark, 2017, Parsing Trump's Recent Policy Statements on the South China Sea, *The Diplomat*, available at https://thediplomat.com/2017/11/parsing-trumps-recent-policy-statements-on-the-south-china-sea/

Wright, Thomas, 2012, Outlaw of the Sea: The US republicans UNCLOS Blunder, Brookings, available at https://www.brookings.edu/articles/outlaw-of-the-sea-the-senate-republicans-unclos-blunder/.

5

China's Role in Promoting Maritime Stability in the Indo-Pacific

Huo Wenle

ABSTRACT

In recent years, especially after US President Donald Trump's first visit to Asia in November 2017, the emerging geopolitical framework of Indo-Pacific has increasingly attracted scholars' attention and discussion in China. Given the leading role played by the US in the framework of Indo-Pacific, most Chinese materials related to this topic focus on American Indo-Pacific Strategy, and then Indian perspectives on Indo-Pacific. In general, most Chinese scholars hold negative attitude toward the concept of Indo-Pacific, which is viewed by them as a tool to contain China's rise in this region and beyond. Therefore, the Indo-Pacific strategy will pose huge potential threats to China's peripheral security in the regions of the South China Sea, the East China Sea and the Taiwan Strait, and also complicate Chinese relations with India, the ASEAN states, the US and others. Many Chinese scholars, however, argue that the concept of Indo-Pacific has not yet formed a complete strategic system, and it is less likely for the Quad to achieve the goal of containing China's rise through the so called Indo-Pacific strategy. Although Chinese government holds a cautious and skeptical attitude to the Indo-Pacific, many Chinese experts argue that China is a quintessential Indo-Pacific state and a part of the Indo-Pacific region. China has the capability and willingness to promote the stability in the Indo-Pacific region. However, China's capability and ambition will be restricted by maritime and territorial disputes and major power competition in the Indo-Pacific region.

Introduction

In recent years, the reemergence of the Indo-Pacific as a geostrategic term has led to increased attention and caused extensive discussions regarding this concept. Generally speaking, the term refers to a region spanning the Indian and Pacific oceans. The terminology of Indo-Pacific is hardly new, because it has a long-standing acceptance as a distinct biogeographic region or has been used in ethnography since the 1850s. In the early and mid-20th century, the Indo-Pacific as a geopolitical term was occasionally used but soon was neglected for decades. In recent years, the term Indo-Pacific has reemerged as scholars, commentators and officials frequently mention it.

The focus on Indo-Pacific studies among Chinese began in 2013. In that year, Chinese scholars, researchers and experts for the first time published journal articles on the Indo-Pacific. Since the American President Trump's visit to Asia and the holding of Quad meeting between the US, India, Japan and Australia in November 2017, the concept of Indo-Pacific has aroused widespread attention and discussion in the Chinese academic community. For example, between 2013 and 2017, an average of 7 Chinese journal articles focused on the Indo-Pacific have been published each year. However, this number surged to 24 in the first half of 2018.[1] This paper will firstly elaborate Chinese perspective on the Indo-Pacific, and then examine China's role in promoting maritime stability in the Indo-Pacific.

Chinese Perspective on the Indo-Pacific

From the Chinese perspective, the Indo-Pacific has four layers of meaning, namely, Indo Pacific as a concept, region, strategy, and epoch. Most Chinese research materials on this issue focus on the definition of the Indo-Pacific concept, elaboration of major powers' Indo-Pacific strategy and their strategic dynamics in the Indo-Pacific region, and prospective of the coming Indo-Pacific epoch.

Regarding the Indo-Pacific as a concept, many Chinese scholars believe that it has evolved from a geographical terminology to a geostrategic one, and that the Indo-Pacific reflects the geoeconomic and geopolitical developments in this region.[2] Firstly, the global geostrategic and geoeconomic centre of gravity is shifting to the Indo-Pacific region. Secondly, the significance of the Indian Ocean is increasing. Thirdly, the simultaneous rise of India and China and their cooperation and competition have connected the Indian Ocean and Pacific Ocean as a unified framework. Lastly, foreign policies of different states in this region also promote the emergence of the Indo-Pacific. Some scholars, however, argue that the term Indo-Pacific is artificially constructed. The Indo-Pacific is a concept of completely artificial construction for strategic and security purposes. It does not have a solid realistic basis of political geography and lacks both internal cohesion and social and cultural identity.[3]

Regarding the Indo-Pacific as a region, there is no consensus in the Chinese academic circle about its geographical range. Roughly speaking, there are four different geographical scopes about the Indo-Pacific region: Western Pacific Ocean plus Eastern Indian Ocean; Western Pacific Ocean plus the whole Indian Ocean; the whole Pacific Ocean plus the Eastern Indian Ocean; and the whole Pacific Ocean and Indian Ocean. The ambiguity in the definition of the Indo-Pacific provides 'space for power game'[4] in concept construction. This will also allow as many countries as possible to participate in the discussion and construction of the Indo-Pacific framework.

Regarding the Indo-Pacific as a strategy, most Chinese scholars believe complete Indo-Pacific strategy system has not been formed yet. However, in the Chinese Indo-Pacific studies, scholars, researchers and experts often use 'Indo-Pacific Strategy' to refer to different powers' Indo-Pacific polices. Generally speaking, Chinese scholars pay more attention to major powers' Indo-Pacific strategy including the US, India, Japan and Australia.

Most of the Chinese scholars realise the dual purpose of Trump's Indo-Pacific strategy. On one hand, the Indo-Pacific strategy is designed to maintain, secure, and consolidate the dominant role of the US in the Indo-Pacific region through comprehensive approaches including politics, diplomacy and military. On the other hand, the Indo-Pacific strategy is certainly directed at China and aimed at containing or balancing China's rise through both geoeconomics and geopolitics. Professor Liang Fang of National Defense University, argues that the intentions of the Indo-Pacific strategy proposed by the US are to prevent the extension of Chinese Belt and Road Initiative through the Indian Ocean; nudge India to increase containment of China's sea lines of communication (SLoCs) in the Indian Ocean; and avoid direct confrontation with China.[5] In addition, some Chinese scholars note that the Indo-Pacific strategy is not only against China, but also against India's rise. Wei Hongxia, Research Fellow at Chinese Academy of Social Sciences, contends that the strategic design of US Indo-Pacific strategy is aimed at preventing Sino-Indian strategic cooperation, and regulating the rise of China and India in the geopolitical structure dominated by the United States.[6]

From the Chinese perspective, the Indo-Pacific strategy will pose potential challenges to China in both geopolitical and geoeconomic aspects. The Indo-Pacific strategy is regarded as the "most serious external challenge to China since 1949".[7] Firstly, the Indo-Pacific strategy will not only complicate the situation in the South China Sea (SCS), East China Sea and Taiwan Strait, but also increases the security risks for China's SLOCs in this region as 90 percent of Chinese foreign trade is conducted by sea, and 75 percent of imported oil flows into the South China Sea from the Indian Ocean through the Malacca Strait.[8] Secondly, the Indo-Pacific strategy may deteriorate China's relations with neighbouring countries such as India, Japan and ASEAN states. The Indo-Pacific strategy proposed by the Trump administration will expose Sino-Indian relations to greater uncertainty and intensify competition between China and Japan in Africa and other regions.[9] Thirdly, the Indo-Pacific Strategy compete with China's Belt and Road Initiative (BRI), exposing the latter to uncertainties. Ye Hailin, Director of Center for South Asian Studies at the Chinese Academy of Social Sciences, examines the possibility and potential risks of China's two-line restraint from the Indo-Pacific strategy. He argues that the Indo-Pacific strategy will complicate the "relevant elements of China's major power diplomacy and neighboring diplomacy" and increase China's difficulty to "maintain strategic coordination between major strategic directions and minor strategic directions".[10]

Most Chinese scholars hold a negative or pessimistic attitude towards the implementation of Indo-Pacific strategy, and believe that containment of China in the Indo-Pacific region through the Quadrilateral understanding among the US, India, Japan and Australia (also referred to as the Quad) is bound to fail as a 'utopia' or 'bubble'. Firstly, the Indo-Pacific region is too broad to be a coherent strategic region, and it is extremely difficult for the Quad to take joint measures and even build powerful alliance to balance or contain China. From the Chinese points of view, the Western Pacific Ocean and the Indian Ocean Region (IOR) are very different in nature. The Western Pacific Ocean is characterised by traditional security issues such as maritime and territorial disputes in the SCS and East China Sea, Taiwan Strait crisis, North Korean nuclear crisis, while non-traditional security issues are more prominent in the IOR. Secondly, the Quad mechanism is still facing some uncertainties. The Quad lacks a strong economic structure like the Trans-Pacific Partnership (TPP) and ignores other middle powers' role in this region. The continuity of Quad security mechanism is also questioned. Thirdly, inside the Quad, the United States, India, Japan and Australia have differences and contradictions about the Indo-Pacific framework. The Trump administration has not reached a balance between the 'America First' and global governance imperatives, nor has a clear ranking of the three US global strategic priorities.[11] The Indo-

Pacific strategy is just a tool for Trump to appease the "demands of domestic strategic circles and public opinion circles", and "its allies and strategic partners", and "raise the domestic downturn public approval ratings". India has long pursued non-alignment policy and independent diplomatic strategy; and hence will not support an Indo-Pacific security architecture designed by other powers. Otherwise people will "fundamentally misread the political projects" of India.[12] Indian refusal of Australian request to join the Malabar naval exercise, American suggestion to increase troops to Afghanistan, sending ships to the SCS for joint patrol with the US are clear examples. Fourthly, the growing inter-dependence among countries in a globalised and economically interdependent world has made it difficult for any country or group to isolate or contain China. Many other countries in the Indo-Pacific region are reluctant to get involved in the power struggle between China and the US at the cost of economic benefits. All four countries of the Quad grouping: the US, Japan, Australia and India are close trading partners with China, and China is the largest trading partner of each of them. For example, China has been Australia's largest trading partner since 2010. In 2016, Sino-Australian trade volume reached 107.8 billion US dollars and Australia's trade surplus exceeded 33.5 billion US dollars. In 2016, Chinese tourists spent as much as 46 billion RMB in Australia.[13] Lastly, with the development of China's comprehensive national power in every aspect, many regional and global issues cannot be resolved without China's participation. The US and the international community need to cooperate with China on common significant security issues, such as climate change, counter-proliferation and counterterrorism.

Thus, Chinese scholars mainly study the Indo-Pacific issues from the perspective of other powers' Indo-Pacific strategy, especially the US, India, Japan and Australia. Chinese scholars should think about Indo-Pacific issue from the point of China's national condition and strategy. It gives rise to certain questions which are as follows: (1) What is Chinese government's stance on the Indo-Pacific? (2) What kind of role should China play in the Indo-Pacific region? (3) What China can benefit from the Indo-Pacific? (4) How should China design its own Indo-Pacific strategy?

China in the Indo-Pacific Region

The Chinese government has remained silent on the term Indo-Pacific for a long time, although it has been prevalent among the official circles of many other countries. It was not until November 2017 that it got an official response from the Chinese government. Even so, Chinese government shows a cautious and skeptical attitude toward Indo-Pacific. The traditional term Asia-Pacific seems more comfortable to Chinese officials, and the term Indo-Pacific has been rarely mentioned by them. Otherwise, it will give the public an impression of Chinese endorsement of Indo-Pacific.

Generally speaking, Chinese government supports any constructive strategy, and objects any geopolitical and geoeconomic arrangements designed to contain China. Since November 2017, Chinese Foreign Ministry spokespersons have responded several times regarding the Indo-Pacific issue. They stated that the Indo-Pacific strategy should conform to the trend of the times characterised by "peace, development and win-win cooperation" and help to "uphold and promote regional peace, stability and prosperity",[14] and "should be open and inclusive", and avoid being "politicized and exclusionary" and should not "target a third party".[15] In October 2017, the Chinese ambassador to America Cui Tiankai contended that "any attempt to form exclusive clubs in the region [Indo-Pacific] following a so-called zero-sum approach will help anybody", and no one could 'contain' China.[16] In March 2018, in response to opinions that 'Indo-Pacific strategy' is meant to contain China, the Chinese Foreign Minister Wang Yi expressed that the term Indo-Pacific strategy is "like the foam on the sea, and gets attention but will soon dissipate." "Nowadays stroking a new Cold War is out of sync with the times and inciting confrontation will find no market," he said.[17]

Chinese government may be reluctant to officially adopt the Indo-Pacific strategy in the near future. China's decision makers, however, have had one kind of Indo-Pacific vision for a long time. Geographically, China is not only a Western Pacific state, but also close to being an Indian Ocean state or Indian Ocean stakeholder. With the long-term rapid development, Chinese foreign trade and imported oil transportation is heavily relying on the SLoCs spanning from the Western Pacific to the Indian Ocean. China has core interests in the Indian Ocean Region through which 10,000 Chinese large merchant ships pass each year.[18] With continuous presence of Chinese People's Liberation Army (PLA) naval ships in the IOR and the establishment of first Chinese military base in Djibouti, there is a hot debate that PLA Navy should adopt a 'two-ocean' strategy, which largely overlaps with the Indo-Pacific region. Recently, Chinese economic initiative Maritime Silk Road in the 21st Century, which extends from China's coast to the SCS, and further to the IOR through Malacca Strait, has received great attention and success. All of these show that China should be and has been a major power in the Indo-Pacific region.

Although some Chinese experts have been concerned that the Indo-Pacific will introduce more powers to the Western Pacific impacting China's maritime and territorial disputes with its neighbors, the Indo-Pacific will also justify Chinese increasing maritime activity in the Indian Ocean and beyond. With China's rapid rise as a maritime or naval power in the last one or two decades, China's increasing maritime activities have been always exaggerated by some major powers in the Indo-Pacific region, especially in the Indian Ocean. The adoption of Indo-Pacific strategy can help China view the Pacific Ocean and Indian Ocean as a unified strategic framework. More importantly, the Indo-Pacific will provide China's rise as a maritime power in a bigger theatre in comparison with East Asia or Asia-Pacific. Just as Rory Medcalf says, as a 'quintessential Indo-Pacific power', although Chinese influence is 'more diluted' in the Indo-Pacific region than in an exclusively East Asia setting, the Indo-Pacific can also "be the wider regional context in which China is rising".[19]

China's Role in Promoting Maritime Stability in the Indo-Pacific

In the last 20 years, China's large-scale naval modernisation and increasingly frequent open sea activities have increased China's capability to contribute the stability in the Indo-Pacific region. The Chinese government constantly reiterates China's willing to actively participate in international maritime security dialogues and cooperation, and jointly deal with traditional and non-traditional maritime security threats.[20]

In the Western Pacific region, China is facing complicated and severe maritime and territorial disputes with some ASEAN states in the South China Sea, Japan in the East China Sea and South Korea in the Yellow Sea. For a long time, China has been committed to resolving disputes with its neighbors through dialogue and consultation. Recently, the situation in the South China Sea (SCS) has been improving steadily. China and ASEAN countries continue to comprehensively and effectively implement the Declaration on the Conduct of Parties in the South China Sea (DOC), actively promote the Code of Conduct (COC) consultations and jointly safeguard regional peace and stability. As of December 2017, China and Vietnam have conducted 23 joint patrols in the common fishing zone of Beibu Gulf in the SCS since 2006. On February 13, 2018, the second meeting of China-Philippines Bilateral Consultation Mechanism on the South China Sea (BCM) was held in Manila, the Philippines. In October 2017, China and ASEAN states held joint maritime search and rescue exercise in the South China Sea. It is reported that China and all the ASEAN states will hold ASEAN-China Maritime Exercise at the end of this year. In the East China Sea aspect, China and Japan have maintained dialogues on issues related to the East China Sea. As of April 2018, China and Japan have held 9 rounds of high-level consultations on maritime affairs since May 2012. In the Yellow Sea aspect, China and the South Korea have signed bilateral fishery agreement in 2000 and launched relevant negotiations on maritime demarcation in December 2015.

China's role in the Indian Ocean Region is increasing but still limited. There is no continuous PLA naval presence in the Indian Ocean region until December 2008. Since then, Chinese government has dispatched 29 naval task forces to conduct escort operations in the Gulf of Aden and waters off Somalia. Chinese maritime presence in the Northwestern Indian Ocean provides opportunity for the establishment of Chinese first overseas military base and network of replenishment sites, which will improve China's power projection capability to maintain the stability in the IOR. Chinese regular patrols of nuclear or conventional submarines also help PLA Navy to maintain strategic deterrence and contribute to the stability in the IOR. To a large extent, China's contributions to the stability in the Indian Ocean region is through the PLA Navy task forces. Firstly, they conduct anti-piracy operations and maintain the security of SLoCs. In the last 10 years, the PLA Navy task groups have escorted more than 6500 ships in the IOR. Chinese task groups also enhance exchanges and cooperation with naval task forces of other countries such as Russia, India, Japan and South Korea, and jointly secure international SLoCs. Secondly, they carry out naval diplomacy. Since 2008, Chinese task forces have visited 108 countries, of which more than half are Indo-Pacific states. During the ship visits, China also conducts bilateral or multilateral naval exercise or training with Indian Ocean states such as Pakistan, India, Sri Lanka, Bangladesh, South Africa and Tanzania. Lastly, they conduct Humanitarian Assistance and Disaster Relief (HADR) operations. For example, Chinese naval ships from the 7th, 17th, and 19th task forces participated in the Libya evacuation in 2011, search for Malaysian Airlines Flight MH370 in 2014, and Yemen evacuation in 2015. In addition to the PLA naval task forces, China also provides medical services to the states in the Indo-Pacific. Since 2010, Chinese naval hospital ship Ark Peace has carried out 7 Harmonious Missions and visited 37 countries and provided free medical services for more than 180000 people. 27 of these countries are from the Indo-Pacific region.

India is doing well in the Indian Ocean region in the last several decades.

China can learn how to design an Indo-Pacific strategy from India. Firstly, China should release its maritime security strategy, which can reassure or assuage its neighbours' fears about China's rising maritime or naval power. Secondly, China should initiate more constructive initiatives for the regional maritime security order in the Indo-Pacific region. Thirdly, China should establish regular institutional arrangements with major powers or middle powers in the Indo-Pacific region through bilateral or multilateral frameworks. Lastly, China should provide more public goods, especially for small and island states in the Indo-Pacific region.

In conclusion, Chinese scholars view the Indo-Pacific as a system including concept, region, strategy and epoch. Although the Indo-Pacific strategy will pose huge potential challenge to China, Chinese experts believe that the Indo-Pacific strategy which is aimed at containing or balancing China is bound to fail. Given the increasing national interests and maritime activities in the Pacific Ocean and Indian Ocean, China is a quintessential Indo-Pacific state. China has the capability and willingness to promote stability in the Indo-Pacific region. However, China's capability and ambition will be restricted by maritime and territorial disputes and major power competition in the Indo-Pacific region.

NOTES

1 The data was collected from the database of Chinese National Knowledge Infrastructure (CNKI).

2 Wu, Zhaoli (2014), "Indo-Pacific: Origins and Multinational Strategy Game" ["印太" 的缘起与多国战略博弈], *Pacific Journal [太平洋学报]*, 22 (1): 29-40.

3 Zhou, Fangyin and Wang, Wan (2018), "The Indo-Pacific Strategy from the Perspective of Australia and China's Response" [澳大利亚视角下的印太战略及中国的应对], *Contemporary International Relations [现代国际关系]*, (1): 29-36.

4 Lin, Minwang (2018), "The Construction of 'Indo-Pacific' and the Tension of Asian Geopolitics" ["印太" 的建构与亚洲地缘政治的张力], *Foreign Affairs Review [外交评论]*, (1): 16-35.

5 Liang, Fang (2017), "The United States Pushes the 'Indo-Pacific' concept, What does the US want to do?" [美国推 "印太" 构想，到底想干什么], *Huanqiu*, available at http://opinion.huanqiu.com/hqpl/2017-11/11405093.html.

6 Wei Hongxia (2017), "The Evolution of the Concept of 'Indo-Pacific'" ["印太"概念演变], *Xinhua Net*, available at http://www.xinhuanet.com/globe/2017-12/02/c_136788048.htm.

7 Ding, Dong (2018), "Trump's 'Indo-Pacific' Strategy Opens New Cold War Against China" [特朗普 "印太" 战略开启对华新型冷战], China in Perspective, available at http://www.chinainperspective.com/ArtShow.aspx?AID=189810.

8 Liang, Fang (2017), "The United States Pushes the 'Indo-Pacific' concept, What does

the US want to do?" [美国推 "印太" 构想，到底想干什么], *Huanqiu*, available at http://opinion.huanqiu.com/hqpl/2017-11/11405093.html.

9 Mei, Xiouting (2017), "'Indo-Pacific Strategy': The Essence of Shinzo Abe's New Diplomatic Strategy" ["印太战略"：安倍晋三新外交战略的实质], QS Theory, available at http://www.qstheory.cn/international/2017-02/20/c_1120496115.htm.

10 Ye, Hailin (2018), "The Sino-US Relations under the Concept of 'Indo-Pacific'" ["印太" 概念下的中美关系], *Haiwai Net*, available at http://opinion.haiwainet.cn/n/2018/0509/c353596-31312447.html.

11 Jin, Canrong (2017), "The Concept of 'Indo-Pacific' Is like a Bubble, and Is Gone under the Sunshine" ["印太" 概念像泡沫，太阳一晒就没了], *Huanqiu*, available at http://opinion.huanqiu.com/hqpl/2017-11/11391717.html.

12 Chacko, Priya (2016), "Three Countries, One Centre of Gravity", *The Hindu*, available https://www.thehindu.com/opinion/op-ed/three-countries-one-centre-of-gravity/article4188788.ece.

13 Wu, Minwen (2018), "'Indo-Pacific Strategy' Where to Go" ["印太战略" 将何去何从], *Xinhua Net*, available at http://www.xinhuanet.com/mil/2018-02/22/c_129814427.htm.

14 "Foreign Ministry Spokesperson Hua Chunying's Regular Press Conference on November 7, 2017", Ministry of Foreign Affairs of the People's Republic of China, 7 November 2017, available at http://www.fmprc.gov.cn/mfa_eng/xwfw_665399/s2510_665401/t1508304.shtml.

15 "Foreign Ministry Spokesperson Geng Shuang's Regular Press Conference on November 13, 2017", Ministry of Foreign Affairs of the People's Republic of China, 14 November 2017, available at http://www.fmprc.gov.cn/ce/cemd/eng/fyrth/t1510216.htm.

16 "No One Can Contain China: Beijing Envoy on US' Decision to Sell Weapons to India", *India Today*, 31 October 2017, available at https://www.indiatoday.in/india/story/no-one-can-contain-china-chinese-envoy-1078996-2017-10-31.

17 "'Quad' Move Will Dissipate Like Sea Foam: China", *Times of India*, 8 March 208, available at https://timesofindia.indiatimes.com/world/china/quad-move-will-dissipate-like-sea-foam-china/articleshow/63221055.cms.

18 "China also Belongs to South Asian State and Has Core Interests in the Indian Ocean Region" [中国也属南亚国家，印度洋存核心利益], *Takungpao*, 7 September, 2017, available at http://news.takungpao.com/society/topnews/2017-09/3491143.html.

19 Medcalf, Rory (2012), "A Term Whose Time Has Come: The Indo-Pacific", *The Diplomat*, available at https://thediplomat.com/2012/12/a-term-whose-time-has-come-the-indo-pacific/.

20 The State Council Information Office of the People's Republic of China (2015), *China's Military Strategy*, available at http://www.scio.gov.cn/zfbps/ndhf/2015/Document/1435159/1435159.htm.

REGIONAL SECURITY ISSUES

6

Unrelenting Challenge to Regional Stability: China's Push for Control over South China Sea

Dr. Netajee Abhinandan

ABSTRACT

The dispute over South China Sea best exemplifies the crisis in Asia. Among the maritime areas under contention, the South China Sea has emerged as the hotbed of severe political conflicts threatening the peace and stability of Asia. While China asserts its sovereignty over this entire area claiming it as part of its territory, the Association of Southeast Asian Nations (ASEAN) countries like Malaysia, the Philippines and Vietnam, along with Japan vehemently dispute the Chinese claims and seek equal rights to explore natural resources from it. The tensions arising out of these claims and counter claims in recent times have posed serious challenge to regional security raising grave concerns in the international community. The adamancy of China, the principal player in the region, coupled with its refusal to cede any space to its neighbors has precipitated the situation affecting the peace and stability not only of the maritime region but of entire Asia. In this context, India's role assumes crucial significance as it tries hard to leverage its strategic partnership with ASEAN to attain greater power for itself vis-à-vis China in South and South East Asian region. The paper would endeavour to analyze the dynamics of engagement between India and ASEAN on the one hand and India and China on the other in mitigating all the regional disputes and problems and also effecting greater Asian solidarity. It would look at India's role in shaping the regional strategic discourse that has been drifting towards uncertainty, mutual suspicion and deep distrust for each other and also increasing fight for control over natural resources.

Introduction

Economic diplomacy, of late, has emerged as the most important facet of international relations, guiding the foreign policy of a country and determining the nature of its engagement with the outside world. Foreign policy is no more determined by politico-ideological considerations, but is rather guided by economic imperatives. Asia's fast growing economies, despite having major political differences, have managed to foster closer economic interactions and commercial transactions, coordinating their policies and actions to carry forward the process of modernisation. However, the emergence of geopolitical conflicts; especially maritime disputes over seas, oceans and islands relations, has threatened to jeopardise the relations among countries across the south and southeast regions of Asia. Among the maritime areas under contention, the South China Sea has emerged as the hotbed of severe political conflicts threatening the peace and stability of Asia. While China asserts its sovereignty over this entire area claiming it as part of its territory, the ASEAN countries like Malaysia, the Philippines and Vietnam vehemently dispute the Chinese claims and seek equal rights to explore natural resources from it. The tensions arising out of these claims and counter claims in recent times have posed serious challenge to regional security raising grave concerns in the global community.

The dispute over South China Sea is reflective of the continuing politico-strategic tussle in Asia. On one side is China asserting its control and dominance, while on the other are India, Japan and other South East Asian countries trying their best to counter China. The crisis is not confined to Asia or Indo-Pacific only; it has acquired global dimensions with the US hardening its stand against Chinese moves and also the matter reaching International Court of Justice. China's continuing expansion in the disputed region creates grave concerns among the important stakeholders and has the potential to seriously affect peace and order. With the emergence of China as a regional hegemon asserting its dominance, South China Sea has become a flashpoint.

South China Sea: The Tussle for Power and Control

The South China Sea is the first leg of the long distance trans-Asian trade route leading from China to the Mediterranean. In *The Times Atlas and Encyclopedia of the Sea* it is identified as the largest sea in the world. It covers an area of 3.5 million square kilometers and has rich biodiversity and abundant natural resources. One hundred and twenty-five major rivers drain into the South China Sea and over 30 per cent of the world's coral reefs border it, especially around the archipelagos of Indonesia and the Philippines. The South China Sea could be considered as the focal point of Southeast Asia in terms of its location and geostrategic importance. It is semi-enclosed, with ninety percent of its circumference rimmed by land and surrounded by countries like the Philippines, Malaysia, Brunei, Indonesia, Singapore, and Thailand; countries in Indo-China such as Cambodia and Vietnam; and the People's Republic of China (PRC, or China) and Taiwan (the Republic of China). It is crisscrossed by major shipping routes and divides Southeast Asia into a maritime sphere (i.e. the Philippines, Indonesia, Brunei, Malaysia and Singapore) and a continental one (i.e. Thailand, Cambodia, Laos, Myanmar and Vietnam). The shipping routes through the South China Sea have great strategic and economic significance to major non-littoral countries, particularly Japan and the United States, as well as to the bordering countries themselves. According to UN, the international legal position of the South China Sea is the following:

> The South China Sea is classified as a semi-enclosed sea that comes within the regime for enclosed and semi-enclosed seas in Part IX of the 1982 UN Convention on the Law of the Sea (UNCLOS). UNCLOS Article 123 stipulates that states bordering an enclosed or semi-enclosed sea should cooperate with each other in the exercise of their rights and in the performance of their duties under this Convention. And they shall endeavour directly or through an appropriate regional organisation to achieve this goal. (UN, 2012)

There are seven countries bordering the South China Sea. Five of these, as well as Taiwan, lay claim to some or all of the offshore islands and reefs lying in midstream between the mainland of East Asia and the Indonesian and Philippine archipelagos. All these countries are parties to UNCLOS and thus have a clear obligation to cooperate with regard to the management of the South China Sea, including the maintenance of good order at sea. However, despite numerous efforts to do so, particularly in recent years, it has proven extremely difficult to establish effective management regimes for the sea. On the other hand, the conflicts have increased over jurisdiction and territorial control of this area (Rosenberg & Chung, 2008, p. 61).

The post-Cold War period witnessed the emergence of China as a major economic and military power making it the most dominant player in Asia. To achieve 'big power' status, it became more demanding and assertive in its relations with neighbours. It claimed large swathes of maritime space in the South China and East China Sea creating uneasiness among neighbouring countries like Japan, Vietnam, the Philippines, and Indonesia. China's assertions and territorial claims over South China Sea, and its rather aggressive push for control over the region made ASEAN adopt a 'Declaration on the South China Sea' in July 1992 that espoused for the peaceful resolution of "all sovereignty and jurisdictional issues pertaining to the South China Sea" (Joint Communique 25th ASEAN Ministerial Meeting Manila, Philippines, 21-22 July 1992, 2012). Although China agreed to adhere by the 'principles' of the Declaration, it refused to sign it despite tremendous pressure by the ASEAN countries to do so. The same year the Chinese legislature enacted a "Law on the Territorial Waters and their Contiguous Areas" which specifically authorised the use of force in defending and enforcing China's broad sweeping claim over all the island territories in the South China Sea, thereby undermining the role of the ASEAN in finding commonly acceptable and peaceful solutions (Law of the People's Republic of China on the Territorial Sea and the Contiguous Zone, 1992). Again in July 1996, the ASEAN foreign ministers, in a joint communiqué, "endorsed the idea of concluding a regional code of conduct in the South China Sea" as something that would "lay the foundation for long term stability in the area and foster understanding among claimant countries" (ASEAN, 1996). However, no such code of conduct could be agreed upon due to severe internal differences among the member countries and China continued to pursue independent activities in the disputed maritime area.

In 1999, the Spratly Islands dispute reemerged as a security flashpoint in the South China Sea. Conflict erupted between China and the Philippines over structures built on the aptly named Mischief Reef, a tiny land feature known locally as Panganiban and situated within the Philippines' 200-mile exclusive economic zone as defined by contemporary ocean law. Finally, in 1999, China agreed to discuss the South China Sea issue with ASEAN countries in a multilateral setting. These discussions led to the Declaration on the Conduct of Parties in the South China Sea (DoC) in 2002 (ASEAN, 2002). This Declaration was part of China's diplomatic strategy to assuage the regional fears and anxieties over its rising economic, military and political power.

In 2010, China intensified its claims over the South China Sea. During this period, Beijing's activities and official statements generated widespread concerns not only about the South China Sea, but about China's overall strategic direction. China made serious efforts to establish a maritime sphere of influence in the South China Sea. Towards this goal, it imposed a unilateral fishing ban in April 2010 that encroached upon Vietnam's territorial waters and announced plans to expand its fleet of ships for maritime law enforcement. There was also a spike in Chinese seizure, harassment, and detention of Vietnamese fishing boats. The 'Far Sea Defense' (*yuanyangfangyu*) doctrine has become an important element of China's foreign policy and it is meant to portray its power from its shores (Wong, 2010). Most significantly, as part of its broad strategic strategy, China declared almost the whole of South China Sea to be a 'core interest' (*hexinliyi*)—on par with Taiwan and Tibet—and an area over which it would exercise 'indisputable sovereignty'. These pronouncements repudiated the doctrine of the 2002 ASEAN-China Declaration on the Conduct of Parties in the South China Sea (Declaration on the Conduct of Parties in the South China Sea, 2012). China went to the extent of planting its flag on the South China Sea seabed, demonstrating the scope of its territorial ambitions. Reinforcing these claims, the PLA Navy conducted several concerning naval exercises focused on South China Sea war fighting scenarios. These include the *Jiaolong* amphibious assault exercise in November 2010, which showcased the PLA's growing ability to seize islands and project military power far beyond its shores. Beijing has let it be known that it would not tolerate another maritime power operating in the South China Sea. These projection of strength by China has been well documented by Collins (Collin, 2014) who says that the press in Japan indicated that the PLA had made outrageous plans whereby it plans to capture South China Sea islands using force. The year 2011 witnessed an increase in the clashes between China and other countries. A very pertinent example of Chinese high handedness is the harassment of oil exploration vessel of Philippines by the PLA patrol boats in Reed Bank. Philippine Air Force retaliated by launching OV-10 bomber and Islander aircraft and deployment of three coast guard ships. A diplomatic protest was also launched. A similar act of aggravation was performed with Vietnamese oil exploratory vessel when its cables were knowingly cut by China in the disputed area in May 2011. The escalation kept on happening and later Vietnam alleged that Chinese patrol boats fired on its fishing boats and that too in Vietnam's own territorial waters. These incidents made clear that China could go to any extent and even resort to military action to assert its claims over the disputed islands. This made the South East Asian having stakes in these islands beef up their sea defense capabilities.

Recently, China has significantly stepped up pressure to establish its control over the South China Sea notwithstanding the pressure to follow the path of negotiated settlement of all territorial and jurisdictional disputes. China employed its large and growing force of maritime and fishing security ships, targeted economic sanctions, and repeated diplomatic warnings to intimidate and coerce Philippine officials, security forces, and fishermen to respect China's claims to disputed Scarborough Shoal (Heydarian, 2018). It showed stronger resolve to exploit fishing resources in the South China Sea with the announced deployment of one of the world's largest (32,000 ton) fish processing ships to the area and the widely publicised dispatch of a fleet of 30 fishing boats supported by a supply ship to fish in disputed South China Sea areas. A new, multifaceted administrative structure was created backed by a new military garrison that covered wide swaths of disputed areas in the South China Sea.[1] The coverage was reported to be in line with China's broad historical claims depicted in Chinese maps with a nine-dashed line encompassing most of the South China Sea. The large claims laid out in Chinese maps also were seen by foreign experts to provide the justification for a state-controlled Chinese oil company to offer nine new blocks in the South China Sea for foreign oil companies development that were far from China but very close to Vietnam, with some of the areas already being developed by Vietnam. However, China put forward a very moderate exposition of its territorial claims as the Foreign Ministry spokesperson said on February 29, 2012 that China did not claim the 'entire South China Sea' but only its islands and adjacent waters (Foreign Ministry Spokesperson Hong Lei's Regular Press Conference on February 29, 2012). On the other hand, China advanced cooperative relations with the 2012 ASEAN chair, Cambodia, thereby ensuring that the South China Sea disputes did not receive prominent treatment in documents at the 2012 ASEAN Ministerial Meeting. A result was strong division within ASEAN on how to deal with China, as demonstrated in a remarkable display of ASEAN disunity—the first failure in the 45-year history of the annual ASEAN Ministerial Meeting to conclude with an agreed-upon communiqué.

On 12 July 2016, China's claimed 'historical rights' over the bulk of the South China Sea (SCS) was repudiated by an arbitral tribunal at the Permanent Court of Arbitration convened under Annex VII of the United Nations Convention of the Law of the Sea. The tribunal guaranteed the legal rights of smaller countries such as the Philippines and Vietnam to exploit the hydrocarbon and fish stocks located around their seaboards. The SCS was confirmed to be largely international waters-open to the right of the US Navy (and other actors) to carry out military patrols and surveillance flights. Despite the US warnings and negative judicial pronouncement, China has solidified its territorial claims in the region by establishing military installations on artificially constructed reefs that are large enough to harbor its entire navy. With installation of sophisticated weapon systems and advanced military facilities, China's control over the region is almost total and absolute.

America's Dilemma

Trump has adopted a tough stand on Chinese activities in South China Sea region as he views China as a 'strategic competitor', stated clearly in the 2018 National Defense Strategy (NDS), harping on aggressive strategy to contain its growing dominance (National Defense Strategy of USA, 2018). Significantly, the US National Security Strategy (NSS) released in December 2017 goes further and declares that China seeks to "challenge American power, influence, and interests, attempting to erode American security and prosperity" (National Security Strategy of the USA, 2017). Though Trump was rather evasive on the issue during his long Asia tour in November 2017making only a few obligatory and superfluous statements on the South China Sea, the joint statements issued during his visit to Vietnam and the Philippines reaffirmed "the importance of unimpeded lawful commerce and the need to respect freedom of navigation and over flight and other lawful uses of the sea "underscoring the strategic importance of free and open access to the South China Sea (Joint Statement, 2017). During this tour the American President clearly signaled his intent to work towards initiating a 'new security order' in Asia by strengthening Washington-Tokyo-New Delhi partnership as a counter to the developing Beijing-Pyongyang-Islamabad axis. It was significant that Trump decided to combine his visits to Japan, South Korea and Vietnam with three major regional summits—the Asia-Pacific Economic Cooperation (APEC) and the East Asia and ASEAN Summits-that involved all the major powers around the Indo-Pacific.

Donald Trump in his speech on November 10 at APEC Summit at Danang in Vietnam clearly spoke his larger vision for Asia when he floated the new territorial idea of 'Indo-Pacific' (Trump D., 2017). The idea, centered on the notion of a 'free and open Indo-Pacific', is considered as Trump's alternative to Obama's 'Pivot to Asia' strategy', at least in form, if not completely in substance. Appreciating India highly Trump presented the idea of "renewed partnership with America" in order to work together both in the region and also bilaterally so that the interests of Indo-Pacific can be realised (Trump D., 2017). For Donald Trump, the basis of this cooperation should be built on free and fair trading and commerce environment. What is important to note is that Trump's repeated referral to Indo-Pacific was not merely rhetorical in nature, but rather was part of a grand strategy to forge strategic coalition between the US, India, Japan and Australia that could counter growing power and influence of China in Asia. In this context, one of the most important strategic takeaways from Trump's trip was the revival of the Quadrilateral Dialogue comprising the four countries, which met at the level of senior officials on the sidelines of the ASEAN Summit in Manila almost after a decade. The United States, of late, has enhanced its military operations both in South China Sea and Korean peninsula emphasising freedom of navigations and resisting Chinese assertions. These issues were discussed throughout Trump's Asia trip and are likely to remain on top of his Asia agenda for some time. Still, doubt prevails over Trump's sincerity in pushing this strategy as the American President neither devised any concrete roadmap for its implementation nor suggested what exactly would be America's role in the proposed regional order. With Trump's focus on 'America first', the littoral countries like the Philippines and Vietnam do not feel assured of American support—military and financial—as they challenge Chinese claims. The South East Asian countries are concerned by the inability of the US to prevent China's rise and have begun to doubt the US security guarantee. Trump's rather passive and unenthusiastic stand was a major departure as all the previous Presidents had tried to push the US into the driver's seat as the guarantor of peace and stability in Asia. It might be construed as Trump's strategy to disengage America from different global crises-gradually withdrawing from conflict zones-and focus primarily upon augmenting its own national power and security.

Asia: The Conflict Zone

In recent times, the rapidly growing economic, political and military power of China has made many countries, including Japan, anxious, prompting them to invite other major external powers to engage in the region. Many believe that their political and strategic interests would be adversely affected with the rise of powerful China and its assertions over maritime resources in the region. These concerns have led to the promotion of the concepts of 'Asia-Pacific' and 'Indo-Pacific' as emphasised by President Trump during his Asian tour. The conflict among the major Asian powers has led to realignments of relations with each redefining its role and strategy to maximise interest and enhance power. The US wants to reposition itself as a dominant player in Asia Pacific region and thereby stem the rapid decline of its power and influence in the region—by building new partnerships and alliances with countries like India, Japan and Australia. The US wants to specifically push India towards playing a more vigorous role to ensure that the strategic balance in the Asia Pacific does not become Sino-centric and there is space and opportunity for other South East Asian countries for pursuing their economic goals.

Exploiting its dominant and hegemonic position in the region, China has initiated and is directing the course of disputes in South China Sea. Although, there are no overt wars among nations of South East Asia, there is no dearth of covert conflicts (skirmishes, proxy battles and secret operations) that is happening for the control over the abundant natural resources of this region. The adamancy of China, the principal player in the region, coupled with its refusal to cede any space to its neighbors has precipitated the situation affecting the peace and stability not only of the maritime region but of entire Asia. Until and unless rules, commonly acceptable to all the warring parties, are framed and implemented, the South China Sea would remain a perennial source of discord and conflicts. The lack of rules of engagement and confidence-building measures, unresolved disputes, competition for scarce resources, and status considerations and the jostling for greater power among the countries can lead towards an armed conflict. Since all maritime trading powers have a common interest in the freedom of navigation, there is an urgent need to frame the rules of engagement and naval confidence-building measures amongst regional navies to promote stability. South China Sea has become a potential minefield where one wrong move could lead to severe regional crisis and volatility. This is a very egregious situation and if not controlled can lead to results which are not at all beneficial for any of its claimants and stakeholders. Therefore, in order to obtain the larger goals of regional cooperation and security, it is pertinent that a legally binding COC is finalised between China and other ASEAN members. This would act as an assurance for the parties involved that no one would be bullied by the other and would ultimately result in enhanced cooperation in South China Sea.

With all the major powers including the US and South East Asian countries getting involved, South China Sea dispute has emerged as the most contentious issue affecting the power dynamics of Asia. On one side is China that claims sole control over the marine resources of South China Sea; on the other side are countries like Japan, Vietnam and the Philippines who challenge Chinese assertions and activities. Indo-Japanese maritime cooperation, in this context, becomes increasingly important. While India relies on continuous access to sea lines of communications (SLOCs) plying the Western Pacific waters for the commercial and trade transactions, Japan is dependent for its energy needs on the same access to SLOCs through the Indian Ocean region. SLOCs security therefore constitutes a key driver of this Indo-Japanese partnership in the maritime domain. China has sparred with Japan over the Senkaku Islands in the East China Sea, and India is concerned over Chinese moves to send submarines to Sri Lanka and build a port at Pakistan. Significantly, Indian Prime Minister Modi and his Japanese counterpart Shinzo Abe have called for a "peaceful, open, equitable, stable and rule-based order in the Indo-Pacific region and beyond" in their joint statement (MEA, Government of India, 2015). It specified regular participation of Japanese navy in the large-scale American-Indian naval military exercise MALABAR that has been annually conducted in Bay of Bengal (the Indian Ocean) since 2007. In addition, the document stated the mutual agreement on holding 'dialogues and joint events' in the tripartite format with the participation of the US.

As both India and China vie for marine and oil resources to augment their economic development, they are locked in a fierce, often vicious, competition for stakes in overseas oil/gas fields in Russia, Myanmar, Iran, Iraq, Sudan, Vietnam, and Libya. The competition between the two has also intensified in Central and Southeast Asia as both view these regions as vital sources of natural resources and markets for their goods. The predominance of the US and Indian navies along these sea-lanes of communication (SLOCs) is viewed as a major threat to Chinese security. Moreover, to safeguard its long-term economic security interests, China is actively preparing the ground for a naval presence along maritime chokepoints in the South China Sea, the Malacca Straits, the Indian Ocean, and the Strait of Hormuz in the Persian Gulf through acquisition of naval bases in Cambodia, Myanmar, Bangladesh, and Pakistan. To counter the Chinese efforts towards greater control over the region, India has been promoting defense cooperation with Iran, Oman, and Israel in the west while upgrading military ties with Myanmar, Singapore, the Maldives, Thailand, Vietnam, Taiwan, the Philippines, Australia, Japan, and the United States in the east (Malik, 2004). India is determined to challenge China's growing power, with the help of the US and other friendly Asian countries who are equally uncomfortable with China's rise, and develop a degree of regional dominance comparable with China.

Implications and Challenges for India

China's claims over South China Sea could not be isolated from its long standing territorial disputes with neighbors like Japan and India. Both Japan and India feel threatened by growing Chinese military assertions over international sea resources. While Japan looks towards the United States to take counter measures against China and help in maintaining stability in the region, India feels constrained to adopt a more proactive stand on such strategic conflicts. Though India is not a direct claimant to any territory in South China Sea, the sea routes have become very crucial for India's burgeoning trade links with South East Asian countries. Moreover, India also has stakes in the oil and gas exploration in the region and has been engaged in commercial energy transactions with countries like Vietnam since the late 1980s. Also, around 50 percent of Indian trade transits through the South China Sea with countries in the Asia Pacific region. With rapidly growing economic engagements and trade with ASEAN countries—which is expected to cross US$ 100 billion by 2015–16, India is keen to link the ocean spaces of the Indian Ocean and Pacific Ocean to maximise its geostrategic influence in the region. (Granados, 2017) India sees itself as an important stakeholder in the evolving security dynamics in South China Sea as any kind of conflict or instability in the region could seriously affect its trade and the economic transactions. Its economic development is dependent upon continuous supply of energy and secure trading routes in the region including the Straits of Malacca. Thus, it cannot afford to disengage itself from the ongoing conflicts and controversies related to South China Sea dispute.

India is worried that China, by controlling this Sea area, would gradually start asserting its claims over the disputed areas in its northern borders. On the other hand, as India, encouraged by the South-East Asian countries and Japan, moves forward to expand its presence in the geoeconomic and geopolitical space at the confluence of the two major oceans, China sees the move as a direct threat to its natural claims and sovereignty. China views India's growing bilateral relations with Vietnam, Indonesia and other Southeast Asian countries and growing strategic cooperation with Japan, with suspicion and as a strategic threat in its own backyard. India's strategic partnership with the US coupled with the US intentions to play a role in the region enhances this threat perception for China. India faces a real challenge—how to maintain its strategic leverage in the South China Sea region and growing relations with the South East Asian countries and at the same time not antagonize China or invite any major diplomatic row with it over the dispute.

The Future Scenario

The tussle over South China Sea is not merely a geopolitical struggle; it is a battle for supremacy, power and most importantly resources. It has the potential to radically alter the power-relations in Asia leading to a major military conflict. Trump administration's strong stand against Chinese assertions, India's growing engagement with ASEAN countries and evolving strategic partnership with Japan, mounting international pressure and adverse judicial verdict have made

China's position somewhat vulnerable in the region. However, it is difficult to believe that China could be anyway pushed to cede space or control in the region to any other player or claimant. The way China is expanding its power, influence and territory and has consolidated its control over South China Sea, it could soon upstage the US as the 'balancer of power' in global political system, triggering a new Cold War. This dispute is not an isolated case of China pushing hard to have its way, but rather part of an overall strategy to validate its growing power, capabilities and intent to protect its 'interests and sovereignty' at any cost. The dispute is also a litmus test for the US as it is presented with an opportunity to reestablish its preeminence vis-à-vis China, with friends and allies expecting it to play a more proactive role in the region to counter Chinese moves and protect their interests. The ASEAN countries, not capable of challenging China either militarily or financially, look towards the US to revitalise its engagement with the region and revive the security ties to put China at bay. Along with the US, India is also expected to play a major role in the region to counterbalance China's growing influence. The visit of all ten heads of state of ASEAN on the occasion of India's Republic Day signaled a new phase of partnership between India and ASEAN that may prove crucial for regional stability. In this scenario, until all the stakeholders come to the negotiating table to chart out a common code of conduct to regulate the activities around South China Sea region, peace would remain elusive.

NOTES

1 For some plausible interpretations of Chinese assertions, see Carlyle A. Thayer, "Recent Developments in the South China Sea: Grounds for Cautious Optimism?" RSIS Working Paper, no. 220 (December 14, 2010), pp. 2-6, http://www.rsis.edu.sg/publications/WorkingPapers/WP220.pdf; and Michael D. Swaine, "China's Assertive Behavior, Part One: On 'Core Interests'," China Leadership Monitor no. 34 (Fall 2010), pp. 8-11, http://carnegieendowment.org/files/Swaine_CLM_34_1114101.pdf.

REFERENCES

ASEAN (1992), available at https://asean.org/?static_post=joint-communique-25th-asean-ministerial-meeting-manila-philippines-21-22-july-1992. Retrieved August 12, 2018, from https://asean.org: https://asean.org

Collin, K.S. (2014, October 17), available at https://thediplomat.com/2014/10/southeast-asias-emerging-amphibious-forces/. Retrieved August 14, 2018, from https://thediplomat.com: https://thediplomat.com/2014/10/southeast-asias-emerging-amphibious-forces/

Trump (2017, November 10), available at https://www.hindustantimes.com/world-news/trump-praises-pm-modi-for-india-s-astounding-growth-at-apec-summit-in-vietnam/story-jf5EJlsfXVsntKOyEH2pJI.html. Retrieved September 15, 2018, from www.hindustantimes.com: https://www.hindustantimes.com/world-news/trump-praises-pm-modi-for-india-s-astounding-growth-at-apec-summit-in-vietnam/story-jf5EJlsfXVsntKOyEH2pJI.html

ASEAN (2002), *Declaration on Code of Conduct of Parties.*

MEA, Government of India. (2015). *Joint Statement on India and Japan Vision 2025.*

Joint Communique 25th ASEAN Ministerial Meeting Manila, Philippines, 21-22 July 1992. (2012, July 5). Retrieved March 30, 2018, available at https://asean.org/?static_post=joint-communique-25th-asean-ministerial-meeting-manila-philippines-21-22-july-1992

Declaration on the Conduct of Parties in the South China Sea. (2012, October 7). Retrieved April 26, 2018, available at https://asean.org/?static_post=declaration-on-the-conduct-of-parties-in-the-south-china-sea-2

Heydarian, R. (2018, June 23). How the Scarborough Shoal came back to haunt China-Philippines relations. *South China Morning Post.*

Granados, U. (2017), India's Approaches to the South China Sea: Priorities and Balances. *Asia and the Pacific Policy Studies, 5* (1), 122-137.

UN. (2012). *Part IX: Enclosed or Semi-enclosed Seas.* Retrieved July 21, 2018, available at www.un.org: http://www.un.org/Depts/los/convention_agreements/texts/unclos/part9.htm

Rosenberg, D., & Chung, C. (2008, February 11), Maritime Security in the South China Sea: Coordinating Coastal and User State Priorities. *Ocean Development and International Law, 39* (1), pp. 51-68.

(1992), *Law of the People's Republic of China on the Territorial Sea and the Contiguous Zone.* Government of PRC.

ASEAN. (1996). *Joint Communique of The 29th ASEAN Ministerial Meeting (AMM) Jakarta, 20-21 July 1996.* ASEAN.

Wong, E. (2010, April 23), Chinese Military Seeks to Extend its Naval Power. *The New York Times.*

(2012), *Foreign Ministry Spokesperson Hong Lei's Regular Press Conference on February 29, 2012.* Ministry of Foreign Affairs of the People's Republic of China.

Summary of the 2018 National Defense Strategy of The United States of America (2018). Retrieved September 15, 2018, available at https://dod.defense.gov/Portals/1/Documents/pubs/2018-National-Defense-Strategy-Summary.pdf

(2017), *National Security Strategy of the United States of America.* The White House.

Vietnam-US Joint Statement (2017, November 12). Retrieved September 15, 2018, available at http://en.nhandan.org.vn/politics/external-relations/item/5638502-vietnam-us-joint-statement.html

Trump, P. (2017, November 10), *Remarks by President Trump at APEC CEO Summit.* Retrieved September 15, 2018, available at https://www.whitehouse.gov/briefings-statements/remarks-president-trump-apec-ceo-summit-da-nang-vietnam/

Malik, M. (2004, October). India-China Relations: Giants Stir, Cooperate and Compete, *Asia-Pacific Centre for Security Studies.*

7

Rise of QUAD: Perspectives from Member Countries

Monish Tourangbam

ABSTRACT

The Quadrilateral understanding among India, the US, Japan and Australia is perhaps one of the most significant multilateral pronouncements in recent times, reaffirming the geopolitical relevance of the Indo-Pacific region. Officials from the four countries met for the second time, in Singapore in June this year, after the last meeting in Manila late last year. All these democratic countries have shown policy priorities to combine capabilities and intent in the Indo-Pacific region. America's embrace of the Indo-Pacific as a geopolitical theatre of priority have clearly given more heft to emerging convergence among these countries and the recent renaming of the US Pacific Command as the Indo-Pacific Command is a firm strategic signalling in this regard. In a symbolic message of strategic intent and purpose, the Naval Chiefs from all the Quad countries early this year, shared the same dais at the Raisina Dialogue in New Delhi. The Indo-Pacific partnership unfolding through the Quadrilateral grouping reflects the geopolitical imperatives of a rising China making its presence felt across the continental and maritime realms through its ambitious Belt and Road Initiative (BRI). In fact, many have called the Maritime Silk Road (MSR) of the BRI as the Indo-Pacific with Chinese characteristics.

Managing the rise of China in the Indo-Pacific and creating deterrence for its aggressive activities, is definitely a geopolitical determinant for the Quadrilateral understanding. However, a more overt call for countering China's rise might not be in the offing, given the complex interdependent relations that all four Quad members share with China. Quadrilateral grouping is being seen as a diplomatic manoeuvring to establish stability in the Indo-Pacific. Although all the four countries share the notion of a "free, open, prosperous and inclusive"

Indo-Pacific, they have been issuing different statements during their meetings. In this context, the paper will attempt to assess the finer nuances of what it means to have an Indo-Pacific strategy in a multipolar order, from the perspectives of all the four-member countries.

Further, it will understand the rationale behind the quadrilateral understanding and assess the debates revolving around its relevance to strategic calculations of the member countries. The paper will also make an attempt to analyse the feasible trajectory of the Quad and its limitations in view of the geopolitical and geoeconomic drivers in the Indo-Pacific region.

Geopolitics of the Indo-Pacific: Perspectives from Quad Countries

Ten years after Quadrilateral grouping was first mooted in 2007 and also died a very quick and premature death, the same four democratic countries came together in Manila in 2017 to revive the Quad. As in 2007, it is no rocket science to discern that the challenge of managing China's rise remains the focal point of this grouping. The Quadrilateral understanding among these countries is clearly in commensurate with the significance that the emerging geopolitical construct of the Indo-Pacific has been acquiring in the strategic calculations of these countries. Their convergence over the salience of the Indo-Pacific has been instrumental in the political leaderships in these countries coming together to revive the Quad again. Aligning interests among these countries and the managing of threats emerging as a consequence of China's rise remain important determinants of the Quadrilateral understanding in the Indo-Pacific region. China is rising and making its presence felt across the continental and maritime realms through its ambitious Belt and Road Initiative (BRI), that crisscrosses continental Eurasia and maritime Indo-Pacific. While the threat of a rising China showing aggressive intent brings some kind of a strategic unison among these countries, all the Quad members have their own interdependent ties with China which is too vital to be jeopardised to hyperbolic rhetoric and threatening actions. Indo-Pacific has quickly acquired the status of being perhaps the most prominent geopolitical construct of the 21st century because of the growing interconnectivity over trade and commerce, energy security and security concerns among countries in the Western Pacific and the Indian Ocean region. How to manage China's rise without escalating tensions with China remains an overriding concern for all these countries? Though the term Indo-Pacific has been doing the rounds of strategic circles in countries like India, Japan and Australia, the repeated references to Indo-Pacific from President Donald Trump and his administration officials have given a much-required strategic heft to the emerging convergences in the region. Earlier,

Washington showed some hesitations in officially embracing the term 'Indo-Pacific' often referring to it as the Indo-Asia-Pacific. However, the recent renaming of the US Pacific Command as the Indo-Pacific Command, if not immediately in operational terms, but in terms of optics, has left no one in doubt that Washington is completely invested in the idea and the implementation as far as peace and stability in the Indo-Pacific is concerned.

Geopolitical regions are constructed and reconstructed reflecting the fortunes of great powers in the international system, and the shifting balance of power games. The Indo-Pacific, in that sense, reflects a certain strategic purpose of all the Quad countries, with a single overriding determinant being the rise of China in this mega region and beyond. India, the United States, Japan and Australia aims to combine intent and capabilities that they can deploy across the region as some sort of a deterrence against China's unilateral activities in the region. However, the opportunities that emerge in the region also define the foreign policy priorities of these countries. If the region is theatre of an emerging balance of power, it also includes critical sea lanes through which most of international trade and commerce traverses and hence has to be kept open and transparent. India's Prime Minister Narendra Modi made a nuanced presentation of the complex notion of threats and opportunities inherent in the region, during his keynote speech at the Shangri La Dialogue in Singapore in June 2018. He said:

> "The Indo-Pacific is...home to a vast array of global opportunities and challenges. India does not see the Indo-Pacific Region as a strategy or as a club of limited members. Nor as a grouping that seeks to dominate. And by no means do we consider it as directed against any country. A geographical definition, as such, cannot be. India's vision for the Indo-Pacific Region is, therefore, a positive one."[1]

The US National Defense Strategy (NDS) 2018 has clearly emphasised the centrality of the Indo-Pacific region in the promotion of America's national interest. The 21st century geopolitics is seen as playing out in the Indo-Pacific theatre and America's resources and partnerships is seen as directed to this region in the times to come. According to the Defense Strategy, "a free and open Indo-Pacific region provides prosperity and security for all. We will strengthen our alliances and partnerships in the Indo-Pacific to a networked security architecture capable of deterring aggression, maintaining stability, and ensuring free access to common domains. With key countries in the region, we will bring together bilateral and multilateral security relationships to preserve the free and open international system."[2] The US National Security Strategy (NSS) 2017 also clearly stated that the United States welcomes "India's emergence as a leading global power and stronger strategic and defense partner. We will seek to increase quadrilateral cooperation with Japan, Australia, and India."[3] India's Ministry of External Affairs in its response, said,

> "We appreciate the strategic importance given to India-US relationship in the new National Security Strategy released by the US. As two responsible democracies, India and the US share common objectives, including combating terrorism and promoting peace and security throughout the world. A close partnership between India and the US contributes to peace, stability and prosperity in the Indo-Pacific region as well as to the economic progress of the two countries."[4]

Reflecting Australia's newly recalibrated role as an Indo-Pacific player, both the official circles as well the strategic cum academic community have embraced the Indo-Pacific in concept and practice. Australia, by dint of its geography, is seen as a quintessential Indo-Pacific player and having an Indo-Pacific strategy is natural to the country. Such a policy is seen an independent Australian foreign policy orientation that is neither predicated entirely on targeting China, nor on being fundamentally pro-American. It has been essentially seen as a whole of government approach to have an Indo-Pacific strategy all geared towards enabling Australia to maximise its interests in a multipolar world order.[5] The Australian Defence White Paper 2016, places Australia's third Strategic Defence Interests "in a stable Indo-Pacific region and rules-based global order which supports Australia's interests." "A stable rules-based regional order is critical to ensuring Australia's access to an open, free and secure trading system and minimising the risk of coercion and instability that would directly affect Australia's interests," the White Paper stated.[6]

Japanese Prime Minister Shinzo Abe, one of the original proponents of the Quadrilateral Understanding and one of the fiercest supporters of the Indo-Pacific relevance has been on the forefront of convergence among these four maritime democracies. Writing a very influential commentary in 2012 titled 'Asia's Democratic Security Diamond,' Abe argued that, "peace, stability, and freedom of navigation in the Pacific Ocean are inseparable from peace, stability, and freedom of navigation in the Indian Ocean. Japan, as one of the oldest sea-faring democracies in Asia, should play a greater role—alongside Australia, India, and the US—in preserving the common good in both regions."[7]

This was some sort of a follow-up to his more influential speech at the Indian Parliament in 2007 *Confluence of the Two Seas*, in which he argued that, "the Pacific and the Indian Oceans are now bringing about a dynamic coupling as seas of freedom and of prosperity. A 'broader Asia' that broke away geographical boundaries is now beginning to take on a distinct form. Our two countries have the ability—and the responsibility—to ensure that it broadens yet further and to nurture and enrich these seas to become seas of clearest transparence."[8] Japan's 'Free and Open Indo-Pacific Strategy' also aims to enhance development cooperation in the region, which it intends to implement through the much-debated Asia-Africa Growth Corridor (AAGC). This connectivity project spanning across Asia and Africa is a priority area of cooperation between India and Japan. This project essentially aims to broaden the horizons of Japan's foreign policy by combining two continents—Asia and Africa, and two oceans—the Indian and the Pacific oceans. The AAGC, took birth in a joint declaration issued by Prime Minister Narendra Modi and Prime Minister Shinzo Abe in November 2016. As opposed to China's BRI which is often accused of being unilateral in nature and having strategic intent, the AAGC is being envisioned as people centric, the specifics of which, will be developed through a number of consultations across Asia and Africa, aligned with the developmental priorities of different countries and sub-regions in Africa. The AAGC goals will be in commensurate with the commitments of the Sustainable Development Goals (SDGs), and raised on the four principle pillars of Development and Cooperation Projects, Quality Infrastructure and Institutional Connectivity, Enhancing Capacities and Skills and People-to-People partnership.[9] The Priority Policy for Development Cooperation Financial Year 2017 of the International Cooperation Bureau, Ministry of Foreign Affairs, Japan thus contends that, "to make the 'Free and Open Indo-Pacific Strategy' into shape, Japan will strengthen strategic collaboration with India, which has a historical relationship with East Africa, as well as the US and Australia."[10]

Strategic Rationale of the Quad

Since the last time in 2007, when the Quad was first initiated, and which was soon followed by the global financial crisis denting much of the economic power parameter of the United States, China's clout by dint of its economic growth and increasing military prowess has grown. China's growing military power has led to increasing aggression in the Indo-Pacific region, most particularly in the South and East China Seas, dealing a blow to the notion and practice of the freedom of navigation in the high seas. More overt intentions on China's part to become a global power has raised concerns regarding China's willingness to socialise itself into the global rules of road and norms, more particularly, when it comes to management of global commons. Its anti-access/area denial strategies in the East China Sea as seen in the imposition of the Air Defence Identification Zone (ADIZ) and its aggressive activities in the South China Sea have increased threat perceptions. Unlike Prime Minister Modi who was more nuanced and subtler in his references for the need for a free Indo-Pacific, US Secretary of Defense James Mattis speaking during the plenary session at the Shangri La Dialgoue was more direct in saying that "China's policy in the South China Sea stands in stark contrast to the openness of our strategy." "China's militarisation of artificial features in the South China Sea includes the deployment of anti-ship missiles, surface-to-air missiles, electronic jammers, and more recently, the landing of bomber aircraft at Woody Island. Despite China's claims to the contrary, the placement of these weapons systems is tied directly to military use for the purposes of intimidation and coercion," Mattis stated.[11] The US NSS was quite categorical in saying that, "China has mounted a rapid military modernisation campaign designed to limit US access to the region and provide China a freer hand there. China presents its ambitions as mutually beneficial, but Chinese dominance risks diminishing the sovereignty of many states in the Indo-Pacific. States throughout the region are calling for sustained US leadership in a collective response that upholds a regional order respectful of sovereignty and independence."[12] The US NDS considers "long-term strategic competitions with China and Russia are the principal priorities for the Department." "As China continues its economic and military ascendance, asserting power through an all-of-nation long-term strategy, it will continue to pursue a military modernisation program that seeks Indo-Pacific regional hegemony in the near-term and displacement of the United States to achieve global preeminence in the future," the NDS said.[13] Though the Indian Prime Minister was more nuanced and subtle in pointing out strategic challenges and did not resort to name calling, it was quite apparently clear that he was referring to China in many cases. "We should all have equal access as a right under international law to the use of common spaces on sea and in the air that would require freedom of navigation, unimpeded commerce and peaceful settlement of disputes in accordance with international law," Prime Minister Modi said.[14] Talking about connectivity in the Indo-Pacific region, he said,

> "There are many connectivity initiatives in the region. If these have to succeed, we must not only build infrastructure, we must also build bridges of trust. And for that, these initiatives must be based on respect for sovereignty and territorial integrity, consultation, good governance, transparency, viability and sustainability. They must empower nations, not place them under impossible debt burden. They must promote trade, not strategic competition."[15]

It is not very hard to discern that this was an indirect reference to China's BRI. A major project of the BRI is the China-Pakistan Economic Corridor (CPEC), which passes through disputed territory. India, even among the Quad countries, is perhaps the only one that has openly criticised the BRI and refused to endorse even during the Shanghai Cooperation Organisation (SCO) Summit in 2018 in Qingdao, China.[16] The Indian Ocean which forms a significant theatre of the Indo-Pacific security architecture, is not only an important international trade route, but is also fast becoming a region of interstate strategic contest. The regular entry of Chinese nuclear and conventional submarines in the Indian Ocean, the Sino-Pakistan nexus and also China's port investments in India's neighbourhood is becoming a concern for India. India's stated vision of mission-based deployment and the quest for an outcome oriented naval force by and large reflects its intention to develop capabilities to deter China's increasing presence in the Indian Ocean Region (IOR).[17] Developments in India's Maritime Domain Awareness (MDA) requires internal balancing, as well as external balancing with countries like the United States, Japan and now with Australia as well. Increasing interoperability among forces and cooperation towards growing intelligence, surveillance and reconnaissance (ISR) capabilities are seen as critical in this regard. While the Quad is clearly at an exploratory stage and developments have been largely diplomatic and cautious in nature not to antagonise China beyond a point, the signals have been clear that these band of democracies do not want to let China run unchecked in the Indo-Pacific region. While efforts have been pushed ahead to bring more understanding between India and China through initiatives like the Wuhan summit between Prime Minister Narendra Modi and President Xi Jinping, there is no denying that there remains a long shadow of mistrust between the two countries. Often, China has been seen to use the pretext of anti-piracy, counterterrorism and humanitarian disaster relief to justify its foray into the Indian Ocean waters.[18] The flagship Malabar exercises between India, the US and Japan or the signing of the India-US Logistics Exchange Memorandum of Agreement (LEMOA) are seen as major initiatives to increase cooperation between like-minded countries in the Indo-Pacific and the Quad is clearly an augmented step in that direction.[19] As the entry of Chinese submarines into the IOR is a major concern, India's maritime cooperation with the US and Japan is geared towards increasing its anti-submarine warfare capabilities.

India's Maritime Security Strategy 2015 in defining India's maritime interests covers a wide geographical area indicating the relevance of the Indo-Pacific region and "underscores the central importance of adequate power projection in and from the seas, and for sea control capability in 'blue waters', to safeguard interests and counter threats before they can bear upon India."[20] It is worth noting that *China's Military Strategy 2015* aims to abandon China's "traditional mentality that land outweighs sea" and attached importance "to managing the seas and oceans and protecting maritime rights and interests."[21] The PLA Navy has been aiming to spread influence not only in its near seas but also in the far seas. The establishment of the Gwadar Port in Pakistan, and the first Chinese overseas military base in Djibouti has been a matter of concern as far as Chinese presence in the IOR is concerned.[22]

Reports say that Australia will invest around US$5.2 billion to develop and buy high tech US drones to carry out joint military operations and to monitors vital waters including the South China Sea. The new acquisition is seen as important for enhancing Australia's anti-submarine warfare, maritime strike capability, and search and rescue capability. Australia's Minister of Defence Industry Christopher Pyne was quoted as saying, "Australia insists on its rights to be able to travel through the South China Sea, in international waters as we have always done, whether it is with surface ships or aircraft."[23] The Australian Defence White Paper 2016 while recognising the importance of its economic ties with China, also emphasises the threat perceived from China's military modernisation and its ambiguous intentions. It says, "as a major power, it will be important for regional stability that China provides reassurance to its neighbours by being more transparent about its defence policies." The Australian government seeks "to deepen and broaden" its "important defence relationship with China while recognising that" their "strategic interests may differ in relation to some regional and global security issues."[24] The following argument in the Defence White Paper could be easily aimed at China, although the country has not been named as such:

> "...newly powerful countries want greater influence and to challenge some of the rules in the global architecture established some 70 years ago. While

> it is natural for newly powerful countries to seek greater influence, they also have a responsibility to act in a way that constructively contributes to global stability, security and prosperity. The Government is committed to working with the United States and like-minded partners to maintain the rules-based order by making practical and meaningful military contributions where it is in our interest to do so."[25]

The Defence White Paper 2017 of the Japanese Government was also quite categorical in terms of pointing out Chinese activities "in sea areas and in airspace, including the East and South China Seas" that raise security concerns in the Indo-Pacific region and the international community. Japan, particularly under the leadership of Prime Minister Shinzo Abe, has been found to be more outspoken about China's unilateral activities and more supportive of the democratic countries coming together to counteract China's rise and spread of influence. Japan-China differences in the East China Sea, and China's announcement of an ADIZ there in 2013 infringing freedom of overflight, have fuelled tensions between the two countries. The Defence White paper emphasised,

> "China, particularly over maritime issues where its interests conflict with others', continues to act in an assertive manner, such as attempts at changing the status quo by coercion. China also remains poised to fulfil its unilateral demands without compromise, which has included making steady efforts to turn these coercive changes to the status quo into a fait accompli. Japan has great concerns over such Chinese military activities, etc., together with the lack of transparency in its military affairs and security issues, and needs to keep utmost attention to them."[26]

The Quad Redux: Taking Nascent Steps

Undoubtedly, more than anything, the emerging geopolitics of the Indo-Pacific is responsible for bringing the Quad back to life. The strategic community in India views the Indo-Pacific as a natural extension of India's foreign policy approach to South-east Asia under the Act East Policy. India's former Foreign Secretary Shyam Saran writing on the relevance of the region to India's interest maximisation commented that it "represents the inclusion of the Western Pacific within the range of India's security interests, thus stretching beyond the traditional focus on the Indian Ocean theatre." "In another sense, it is also a reflection of the concept of the Asia-Pacific, which hitherto excluded India, expanding westwards to encompass the subcontinent as its integral part. As India's regional and global profile increases, it will inevitably gravitate towards the centre of this expanded geopolitical and geoeconomic space. The concept of an Indo-Pacific theatre fits in neatly with this evolving trend," he wrote.[27] The increasing ambitions of the Chinese military and their capability enhancement have brought sharper focus to the new realignments in strategic vision and practice among other major powers in the Indo-Pacific. The Quadrilateral Understanding is a clear reflection which at present is in an exploratory stage, and much of what the Quad countries do currently shows cautious steps that do not want to overplay the China factor in the new initiative.

The focus on the Indo-Pacific is something that has often been a matter of concern to Beijing. An editorial in the *Global Times* argued, "The idea of 'Indo-Pacific' is a fresh one, but if reviewed carefully, it appears as another empty slogan. What is most important is that China is the biggest trade partner of all four countries.... The US and Japan have little leverage to play geopolitical games in the region, and few countries are willing to fall into the orbit of Washington and Tokyo." "India has its own trick to play. In the past, the mainstream media in India was obsessed with competing with China on GDP growth and international status. Now they are keen to compare their country to Australia or Japan to see which can curry more favour from the US. After the US began using the term 'Indo-Pacific', some Indian media outlets were ecstatic that their country had become an important pillar of this new US strategy," the editorial said.[28]

The four Quadrilateral countries India, the United States, Japan and Australia aim to combine capabilities and intent for a "free, open, prosperous and inclusive," Indo-Pacific; an effort also seen by and large, as a deterrent to China's rise in the region.[29] Many have criticised India's decision to block Australia's participation at the recently held India-US-Japan Malabar exercises off the coast of Guam, as a fatal blow to the Quad.[30] However, the Malabar exercises is not the Quad, and vice-versa and at a time, when the Quad is at an exploratory stage, it is wise not to confuse it with a military exercise, which has sustained for 22 years between India and the US, with and without Japan. Moreover, all the four countries which make up the Quad, in their separate official statements, have called their Manila and Singapore meetings as consultations among the four countries, and not Quad meetings.[31] So, it is too early and unwise to allege India alone, for going soft on China and harming the Quad.

Southeast Asia assumes a pivotal geographical area in the Indo-Pacific region and has played an important role in terms of how the Quad countries have defined their Indo-Pacific strategies. All the four countries have recognised and "reaffirmed their strong support for ASEAN centrality and the ASEAN-led regional architecture."[32] There may be differences in operationalising their respective Indo-Pacific strategies as can be seen in the four different statements issued in both the Quad consultation meetings held till now.[33] Hence, the finer nuances of the geopolitical game unfolding in the region have to be understood to assess the varying dimensions of each country's Indo-Pacific strategies. For instance, the maritime aspect of China's BRI, in practice, covers what is called the Indo-Pacific, leading many to call it the Indo-Pacific with Chinese characteristics.[34] Each country's approaches to China's ambitious BRI might bring out some differences among the countries, and hence the Quad countries in the near future, could make this an important agenda item in their discussions while discussing the potential of connectivity projects led by Quad countries.[35] Developing habits of cooperation among the Quad countries on non-military matters like Humanitarian Assistance and Disaster Relief (HADR) activities is a good way to take the initiative towards maturity. It is worthwhile remembering that the genesis of the Quad is often traced to HADR activities during the devastating Indian Ocean tsunami of 2004, involving these countries as the Tsunami Core Group.[36] Moreover, India, the US, Japan and Australia can further develop coordination and cooperation towards common maritime security challenges like piracy and maritime terrorism. On the road ahead, the Quad countries have to find ways to deal with China, with which all the four countries have intertwined economic ties, without accommodating China's hegemonic tendencies in the Indo-Pacific region.[37]

Conclusion

The emerging global geopolitics reflects the disruptions primarily brought about by China's rising power and intentions to shape global order, and the uncertain trajectory of US power parameters. The world is certainly no longer unipolar and, in many aspects, is entering an increasingly multipolar world order. In the strategic flux that the global order is going through, a number of bilateral, trilateral and multilateral relations are going through significant changes and the Quad has re-entered the lexicon of geopolitics and international relations. In many ways, perceptions are in a dynamic stage. Perceptions and misperceptions at this stage, by and large, reflect the views relating to the Indo-Pacific region. The Quad is certainly at a nascent stage and countries driving the initiative should be nimble footed in terms of adjusting their approaches according to shifting geopolitical circumstances to prevent another premature death of the group, like the one that happened the first time it was mooted in 2007. More explorations have to be done, in order to realign interests and manage threats in the Indo-Pacific region through this initiative. How to further develop consensus not only among the Quad countries, but also with ASEAN countries, in the face of China's increasing influence in the region remains a task cut out for the group. The Quad is about China, but it is also not only about China and how these complex dimensions drive cooperative behaviour among the four countries remains to be seen. As with many other multilateral initiatives, the debates around expansion of Quad membership in some sort of a Quad plus might feature in future consultations and this should clearly reflect what an expanded membership entails, and what it intends to achieve. The Indo-Pacific is also a confluence of strategic and economic factors, something clearly reflected in the varying positions towards China's BRI. How the Quad countries develop their own connectivity strategies and to what extent, they will converge or diverge with China's vision will put the Quad band on a test of fire. The Quad is just one of the many components of the emerging security architecture of the Indo-Pacific and how it fares in the complex permutations and combinations of strategic competition-cooperation in the region remains to be seen. In the end, the idea and practice of the Quad and what it envisions for the Indo-Pacific should outlive the current leaderships in these countries, and strive ahead through more institutionalised linkages, that are not at the mercy of leadership changes and domestic political dynamics.

NOTES

1 Ministry of External Affairs, "Prime Minister's Keynote Address at Shangri La Dialogue," June 1, 2018, http://www.mea.gov.in/Speeches-Statements.htm?dtl/29943/Prime+Ministers+Keynote+Address+at+Shangri+La+Dialogue+June+01+2018, accessed on June 20, 2018.

2 The Department of Defense, "Summary of the 2018 National Defense Strategy of the United States of America: Sharpening the American Military's Competitive Edge," https://www.defense.gov/Portals/1/Documents/pubs/2018-National-Defense-Strategy-Summary.pdf, 9, accessed on June 15, 2018.

3 The White House, "National Security Strategy of the United States of America," December 2017, https://www.whitehouse.gov/wp-content/uploads/2017/12/NSS-Final-12-18-2017-0905.pdf, 46, accessed on June 15, 2018.

4 Ministry of External Affairs, "Official Spokesperson's Response to Media Queries on Indo-US Relationship," December 19, 2017, http://www.mea.gov.in/media-

briefings.htm?dtl/29184/Official_Spokespersons_response_to_media_queries_on_IndoUS_ relationship, accessed on June 16, 2018.

5 Rory Medcalf, "Mapping our Indo-Pacific future: Rory Medcalf's Speech," Full text of the landmark Policy Forum and National Security College talk, Policy Forum, *Asia & the Pacific Policy Society,* June 5, 2018, https://www.policyforum.net/mapping-our-indo-pacific-future-rory-medcalfs-speech/, accessed on June 10, 2018.

6 Department of Defence, "The Defence White Paper," Australian Government, 2016, http://www.defence.gov.au/WhitePaper/Docs/2016-Defence-White-Paper.pdf, accessed on June 17, 2018.

7 Shinzo Abe, "Asia's Democratic Security Diamond," *Project Syndicate*, December 27, 2012, https://www.project-syndicate.org/commentary/a-strategic-alliance-for-japan-and-india-by-shinzo-abe?barrier=accesspaylog, accessed on June 14, 2018.

8 Ministry of the Foreign Affairs of Japan, "Confluence of the Two Seas: Speech by H.E. Mr. Shinzo Abe, Prime Minister of Japan at the Parliament of the Republic of India," August 22, 2007, https://www.mofa.go.jp/region/asia-paci/pmv0708/speech-2.html, accessed on June 12, 2018.

9 "Asia-Africa Economic Growth Corridor: Partnership for Sustainable and Innovative Development," A Vision Document, African Development Bank Meeting, May 22-26, 2017, http://www.eria.org/Asia-Africa-Growth-Corridor-Document.pdf, accessed on June 20, 2018.

10 International Cooperation Bureau, "Priority Policy for Development Cooperation, FY 2017," Ministry of Foreign Affairs of Japan, https://www.mofa.go.jp/files/000259285.pdf, accessed on June 18, 2018.

11 U.S. Department of Defense, Remarks by Secretary Mattis at Plenary Session of the 2018 Shangri-La Dialogue, June 2, 2018, https://www.defense.gov/News/Transcripts/Transcript-View/Article/1538599/remarks-by-secretary-mattis-at-plenary-session-of-the-2018-shangri-la-dialogue/, accessed on June 12, 2018.

12 The White House, "National Security Strategy of the United States of America," 46.

13 The Department of Defense, "Summary of the 2018 National Defense Strategy of the United States of America: Sharpening the American Military's Competitive Edge," 2-4.

14 Ministry of External Affairs, "Prime Minister's Keynote Address at Shangri La Dialogue."

15 Ibid.

16 Sutirtho Patranobis, "India refuses to endorse China's Belt and Road Initiative in SCO Summit Statement," *Hindustan Times*, June 10, 2018, https://www.hindustantimes.com/india-news/india-refuses-to-endorse-china-s-belt-and-road-initiative-in-sco-summit-statement/story-sk9cC8d1zD3Zwje6Rnh0uI.html, accessed on June 22, 2018.

17 Ministry of Defence, 'New Mission-Based Deployment Concept to Result in Greater Presence and Visibility in IOR—Admiral Sunil Lanba, CNS,' *Press Information Bureau*, Ministry of Defence, Government of India, October 27, 2017, http://pib.nic.in/newsite/PrintRelease.aspx?relid=171983, accessed on December 1, 2017.

18 Jabin Jacob, 'Does China Have a Maritime Strategy?,' *Center for Security Studies*, ETHZurich, November 13, 2017, http://www.css.ethz.ch/en/services/digital-library/articles/article.html/e6468897-903a-4cb5-a28c-e4a911fa7d2e/pdf, accessed on November 27, 2017.

19 Rajeswari Pillai Rajagopalan, 'Logistics Agreement with US: Why Signing LEMOA is

Significant for India,' *Hindustan Times*, August 31, 2016, http://www.hindustantimes.com/analysis/logistics-agreement-with-us-why-signing-lemoa-is-significant-for-india/story-btGO0oM2jVfxRZt6xkxHgJ.html, accessed on June 20, 2018.

20 Ministry of Defence, 'Ensuring Secure Seas: India's Maritime Security Strategy,' Integrated Headquarters, Ministry of Defence (Navy), October 2015, https://www.indiannavy.nic.in/sites/default/files/Indian_Maritime_Security_Strategy_Document_25Jan16.pdf, accessed on June 18, 2018.

21 Ministry of National Defense, 'China's Military Strategy,' Ministry of National Defense, The People's Republic of China, May 2015, http://eng.mod.gov.cn/Press/2015-05/26/content_4586805_6.htm, accessed on June 18, 2018.

22 Rajat Pandit, 'Eye on China: India Steps Up Naval Deployments, Kicks Off Nuclear Submarine Project.' *The Times of India*, Dec 2, 2017, https://timesofindia.indiatimes.com/india/eye-on-china-india-steps-up-naval-deployments-kicks-off-nuclear-submarines-project/articleshow/61882815.cms, accessed on June 21, 2018.

23 "Australia Buys High-Tech Drones To Monitor South China Sea, Pacific," *NDTV*, June 26, 2018, https://www.ndtv.com/world-news/australia-buys-high-tech-drones-to-monitor-south-china-sea-pacific-1873187, accessed on June 20, 2018.

24 Department of Defence, "The Defence White Paper," Australian Government, 2016, 43-44.

25 Ibid, 45-46.

26 Ministry of Defense, "Defense of Japan 2017", http://www.mod.go.jp/e/publ/w_paper/2017.html, 87.

27 Shyam Saran, "Mapping the Indo-Pacific," *The Indian Express*, October 29, 2011, https://indianexpress.com/article/opinion/columns/mapping-the-indopacific/

28 "'Indo-Pacific' a New Term for Old Anxieties," *Global Times*, November 14, 2017, http://www.globaltimes.cn/content/1075216.shtml, accessed on June 15, 2018.

29 "India, US, Japan and Australia Hold Talks on Key Issues in Indo-Pacific Region," *The Times of India*, June 7, 2018, https://timesofindia.indiatimes.com/india/india-us-japan-and-australia-hold-talks-on-key-issues-in-indo-pacific-region/articleshow/64497832.cms, accessed on June 18, 2018.

30 Emanuele Scimia, "Malabar 2018: India deals a blow to Australia and 'the Quad'," *Asia Times*, May 1, 2018, www.atimes.com/malabar-2018-india-deals-a-blow-to-australia-and-the-quad, accessed on June 21, 2018.

31 "Australia-India-Japan-U.S. Consultations on the Indo-Pacific," Department of State (U.S.A.) November 12, 2017, https://www.state.gov/r/pa/prs/ps/2017/11/275464.htm, accessed on June 22, 2018; "India-Australia-Japan-U.S. Consultations on Indo-Pacific," Ministry of External Affairs (India), November 12, 2017, http://mea.gov.in/press-releases.htm?dtl/29110/IndiaAustraliaJapanUS_Consultations_on_IndoPacific_November _12_2017, accessed on June 22, 2018; "Australia-India-Japan-United States consultations on the Indo-Pacific," Department of Foreign Affairs and Trade (Australia), November 12, 2017, http://dfat.gov.au/news/media/Pages/aus-india-japan-us-consultations-on-the-indo-pacific.aspx, accessed on June 22, 2018; "Australia-India-Japan-U.S. Consultations on the Indo-Pacific," Ministry of Foreign Affairs (Japan), November 12, 2017, https://www.mofa.go.jp/press/release/press4e_001789.html, accessed on June 22, 2018; "Australia-India-Japan-United States Consultations,"

Department of Foreign Affairs and Trade (Australia), June 7, 2018, http://dfat.gov.au/news/media/Pages/australia-india-japan-united-states-consultations.aspx, accessed on June 22, 2018; "U.S.-Australia-India-Japan Consultations," Department of State (U.S.A.), June 7, 2018, https://www.state.gov/r/pa/prs/ps/2018/06/283013.htm, accessed on June 22, 2018; "India-Australia-Japan-US Consultations, Ministry of External Affairs (India), June 7, 2018, https://www.mea.gov.in/press-releases.htm?dtl/29961/IndiaAustraliaJapan US+Consultations, accessed on June 22, 2018 and "Japan-Australia-India-U.S. Consultations," Ministry of Foreign Affairs (Japan), June 7, 2018, https://www.mofa.go.jp/press/release/press4e_002062.html, accessed on June 22, 2018.

32 Ibid.

33 Suhasini Haidar, "Quad Confusion," *The Hindu*, November 24, 2017, https://www.thehindu.com/opinion/op-ed/quad-confusion/article20723202.ece, accessed on June 24, 2018.

34 Rory Medcalf, "Mapping our Indo-Pacific future: Rory Medcalf's Speech."

35 Andrew Shearer, "Quad Redux: A New Agenda for Asia's Maritime Democracies," *The Interpreter*, Lowy Institute, https://www.lowyinstitute.org/the-interpreter/quad-redux-new-agenda-asia-maritime-democracies, accessed on June 26, 2018.

36 Marc Grossman, "The Tsunami Core Group: A Step toward a Transformed Diplomacy in Asia and Beyond," *Security Challenges* 1, no. 1 (2005): 11-14, https://www.regionalsecurity.org.au/Resources/Files/vol1no1Grossman.pdf, accessed on June 12, 2018.

37 Tanvi Madan, "The Rise, Fall and Rebirth of the 'Quad'," *War on the Rocks*, November 16, 2017, https://warontherocks.com/2017/11/rise-fall-rebirth-quad/, accessed on June 18, 2018; "Quad Meets Again, Discusses Rules-Based Order in 'Inclusive' Indo-Pacific," *The Wire*, June 8, 2018, https://thewire.in/diplomacy/quad-meets-again-discusses-rules-based-order-and-inclusive-indo-pacific, accessed on June 18, 2018 and Nayan Chanda, "Quad in Low Key: All Four Partners Hedge their Bets as they Look Over their Shoulders at China," *The Times of India*, November 18, 2017, https://blogs.timesofindia.indiatimes.com/toi-edit-page/quad-in-low-key-all-four-partners-hedge-their-bets-as-they-look-over-their-shoulders-at-china/, accessed on June 12, 2018.

8

Regional Responses to Quad

Urbi Das

ABSTRACT

International relations exemplify a complex game of changing equations, where nation-states are in a constant struggle to curve out their own area of influence. With the dawn of the 21st century, the world has witnessed the rising significance of the Asian nations such as India and China and the Indian Ocean region becoming the lifeline of global trade and commerce. While US influence in the Asia Pacific region is not new, what is interesting to note, is the expansion of the American zone of operation by coining the new terminology of Indo-Pacific. Indo-Pacific covers the continents of Asia, Africa and Australia and includes the Indian and the Pacific Ocean. The strategic and economic significance of the region, along with the presence of regional powers makes the region vulnerable to the changing dynamics of collaboration and conflict. As nation-states put forward their own vision for strategic and economic leverage, the Quadrilateral, better known as 'Quad' voices the common concerns of Japan, Australia, India and the United States in the Indo-Pacific region. Here, it should be noted that China is already playing an assertive role in the Indo-Pacific region. US-China competition is already evident and the ASEAN nations are also disunited in the game of alliances and counter-alliances. In light of the above, the paper seeks to analyse regional responses to the Quadrilateral cooperation in the Indo-Pacific. The paper while explaining the background behind the idea of the Quad, tries to investigate whether the Quad is sustainable in the long run given the diverse interest of the Quad members and their equations with other regional actors. The paper also endeavours to examine how the Southeast Asian nations and China will react to the actions of the Quad, and how will the other Quad members adjust themselves to the altering power equations, with China re-positioning itself and US trying to sustain its influence in the Indo-Pacific region.

Introduction

The term Indo-Pacific is a 21st century construct. Geographically, it is a huge area stretching from the tropical Indian Ocean, to the western and central Pacific Ocean, covering the equatorial seas of the Indonesian archipelago including the South China Sea. It is a super-region comprising sub-regional actors. If analyzed carefully, it is an arena there most of the intense competition since the major powers have their geopolitical interest in the geopolitical and economic security of the region. The United States has always had keen interest in the affairs of the region, beginning from its victory in the Spanish-American war of 1898 which established America as a Pacific power. Thereafter, America has always reiterated itself by economic and military means by establishing economic ties with some of the robust economies of the region such as Singapore, extending defence collaboration, for example with Japan and Australia and maintaining bases at crucial geostrategic locations in the region. In this sense, America's commitment to the region is nothing new. What is novel is the extension of the area of operation enunciated by the new terminology of Indo-Pacific that covers a huge geographical area and includes crucial geopolitical regions including some of the emerging powers and strategic sea-lanes which not long is essential for passage but also has vital energy reserves. Since, a lot of countries and their interests are attached to the vast stretch of Indo-Pacific, the region has become the hot-bed of competition, resulting in alliances and counter-alliances to gain more leverage and counter-balance the rise of competing powers.

Quad in the Indo-Pacific: The Background

Quadrilateral Framework or Quadrilateral Security Dialogue, often referred to as the Quad essentially suggests the convergence of the four important stakeholders of the Indo-Pacific region namely Japan, Australia, India and the United States of America on account of the geopolitical shift that ensued in the last decade. Its culmination is due to the growing concern of these four major powers owing to the rise of China and its unreliable intentions in the region. Against this backdrop, these four democracies have sought to be become one voice and unanimously counter the rise of any hegemonic forces in the region that sought to hamper their economic and strategic interests in the region.

The idea of the Quadrilateral Framework, however, is not new. The Quad grouping can be traced back to the Tsunami of 2004 that devastated the region and countries across the Indian Ocean. Often identified as one of the deadliest natural disasters in history, the tsunami brought devastation to 14 countries namely, Indonesia, Malaysia, Maldives, India, Myanmar, Thailand, Sri Lanka, Seychelles, Madagascar, Bangladesh, Somalia and South Africa, with Indonesia being the worst affected in terms of human and physical damage. According to Oxfam, the earthquake of 9.1 Richter Scale, with the epicentre being the western coast of the Indonesian province of Northern Sumatra, affected the lives of around 5 million people; of which more than 230,000 were killed and about 1.7 million became homeless (Oxfam 2014). It was during this period of crisis that countries joined their efforts to provide humanitarian assistance and disaster relief to the nations that were worst hit by the third largest earthquake in recorded history. The United States launched Operation Unified Assistance, playing a pivotal role along with the navies of Australia, Japan and India in providing some of the robust forces in the most devastating natural disaster of the present century. The four countries worked together somewhat like an ad-hoc group contributing over 40,000 military and humanitarian relief forces. It can be said that the effectiveness of the forces and the mutual coordination among the four countries paved the groundwork for furthering collaboration owing to the rising contingencies of the region (Chanlett-Avery 2018).

However, the formal proposal for the formation of a quadrilateral framework was expressed by Prime Minister Shinzo Abe, the then PM of Japan while addressing at the Parliament of India August 22, 2007. In his address titled 'Confluence of two Seas', PM Shinzo Abe enunciated the concept of 'broader Asia' that would include Japan, India along with Australia and the Unites States of America. He sought to build up 'an immense network spanning the entirety of the Pacific Ocean' that would be 'open and transparent' allowing 'people, goods, capital, and knowledge to flow freely'. In this regard, Prime Minister Abe wanted to build an 'Arc of Freedom and Prosperity' to secure the maritime interests and secure the sea lanes of communication of countries whose vital interests are linked to the Pacific and Indian Ocean, by calling for a joint effort and 'strategic global partnership' of like-minded democracies (Abe 2007). Along the same time, the United States too expressed the desire to establish a quadrilateral group in the Indo-Pacific. With similar designs in mind, the quad (consisting of an informal coalition of the democracies of the United States, Japan, India and Australia) met for the first time on the sidelines of the ASEAN Regional Forum meeting to set the tone for further cooperation in the diplomatic and maritime domain (Chanlett-Avery and Vaughn 2008). The Quad's heyday, however, remained limited to diplomatic discussions and few maritime exercises in the Bay of Bengal which included Singapore there making it 'Squad' and India executing its first trilateral naval exercises with the United States and Japan (Raja Mohan 2007). Thereafter the spirit of the Quad faded with the change in Australia's leadership and the end of the term of Prime Minister Shinzo Abe along with the change in US Presidency. The new Australian Prime Minister Kevin Rudd who wanted to avoid any bitterness in Australia's relationship with China, especially its economic ties, decided to withdraw participation from the quadrilateral arrangement (Chanlett-Avery 2018). It should be noted that China from the very beginning was sceptical of the idea of the Quad, and thought it to be an anti-China grouping. Both India and Australia did not want to upset China and the then Prime Minister of India Dr. Manmohan Singh stating the Quad actually 'never got going' (Madan 2017). Therefore the first initiative to establish a quadrilateral framework of like-minded and democracies died out without any substantial achievements.

Ten years later, the Quad revived themselves owing to the exigencies of the present environment. China has become more assertive, with its ramifications being felt in its mischief in the South China Sea, the proposal for the formation of One-Belt-One Road and the Maritime Silk Road, acting as a counter-hegemonic force and challenging America's force posture in the Indo-Pacific. All these led to the reviving of the Quad which till then had been in comma. In 2017, the Quad members revitalised their zeal to ensure 'free' and 'open' Indo-Pacific. While the meeting that was held a decade ago was termed as 'exploratory', this time, meeting on the sidelines of the East Asia Summit in Manila, the officials from India's Ministry of External Affairs (MEA), Australia's Department of Foreign Affairs, Japan's Ministry of Foreign Affairs and United State's Department of State affirmed 'cooperation based on their converging vision and values for promotion of peace, stability and prosperity in an increasingly inter-connected region that they share with each other and with other partner', and 'exchanged views on addressing common challenges of terrorism and proliferation linkages impacting the region as well as on enhancing connectivity' that would serve the long-term interest of the countries (MEA 2017). All the Quad countries expressed their common desires to maintain the respect for and uphold the international law, freedom of navigation and over flight, increasing connectivity, maintaining rule-based order, calling for peaceful resolution of disputes (Nauert 2017). They also expressed serious concerns against the rise of any aggressive powers that would hamper the interests of the countries whose stakes are vitally linked to the vast stretch of Indo-Pacific. They share the mutual distrust over China's aggressive policies in the South China Sea, where China has been engaged in reclaiming islands, issuing Air Defence Identification Zone and also refusing accept the international tribunal judgement.

The Quad and ASEAN: Figuring ASEAN's Response

While analyzing geopolitically, it can be said that Indo-Pacific is never complete without taking into consideration ASEAN member countries. ASEAN countries are the biggest bloc in the region and definitely one of the main stake-holders of the Indo-Pacific. Given their geographical location, their economic development and strategic goals are integrally linked to the vast stretches of the Indo-Pacific.

Founded in 1967, the Association of Southeast Asian Nations (ASEAN) is a regional grouping of ten members—Brunei, Cambodia, Indonesia, Laos, Malaysia, Myanmar, the Philippines, Singapore, Thailand, and Vietnam, that aims to promoting economic, political, and security cooperation. The ASEAN countries are positioned along the crucial geopolitical area covering the Indian Ocean, parts of the Pacific Ocean region and the South China Sea. Today, ASEAN is considered one of the most successful intergovernmental organisations in the developing world. Formed primarily by five countries, it has expanded to include other Southeast Asian states such as Brunei (1984), Vietnam (1995), Laos (1997), Myanmar (1997) and Cambodia (1999) (Khoman 1992). It is one of robust efforts towards regionalism in Southeast Asia.

The United States specifically had been instrumental, if not directly, in the formation of ASEAN. With the year 1967 marking a crucial period where the Cold War bipolar politics and the fear of spread of communism necessitated the American policy makers to push for a regional grouping that would follow the liberal order and also would contain China's influence in the soils of the Asia Pacific (Mahapatra 1990). Since then, US involvement in ASEAN has been increasing to encompass all dimensions of security arrangements—political, economic and military. Major US interests in Southeast Asia include maritime security, the promotion of democracy and human rights, the encouragement of liberal trade and investment regimes, counterterrorism, combating narcotics trafficking, and environmental preservation, among others.

ASEAN's economy is highly integrated with the United States. According to the reports by the Congressional Research Service (CRS), ASEAN's trade with the United States is dominated by electrical machinery and mechanical appliances. Some of the other top traded products are clothing, rubber and articles made of rubber aircraft, optical and scientific equipment and mineral fuels and oils. Collectively, ASEAN is one of the largest trading partners of United States', constituting about 5-6 per cent of total US trade. In 2008 trade flows between the United States and the ASEAN countries stood at $178 billion. Taken as a single trading unit, ASEAN ranks as the fourth largest US export market and the fifth largest source of US imports (CRS 2010). In 2009, the US under Obama Administration accessed to the Association of Southeast Asian Nations' (ASEAN) Treaty of Amity and Cooperation (TAC) through which Washington enhanced its economic relation with Southeast Asia by expanding the multilateral component of US policy in the region.

Therefore, it is quite clear that from the very beginning, USA has thoroughly maintained a firm standing in the affairs of Southeast Asia. The US statecraft was a judicious combination of hard and soft power characterised by diplomatic maneuvers, economic support and finally enhancing ties by attracting the ASEAN nations through its liberal economic model and market oriented policies.

India, although it did not have a coherent Southeast Asia Policy until 1991, did understand the significance of the Southeast Asian countries. The Look East Policy was enunciated by Prime Minister Narasimha Rao in lieu of the emerging economic and strategic significance of the Southeast Asian countries and the structural adjustment of the Indian economy which cleared the clouds of mistrust, giving way to increased economic integration and politico-security cooperation. With the Look East Policy gaining momentum, India's relations with Southeast Asia improved rapidly with India being made ASEAN's Sectoral Dialogue Partner in 1993 in three vital areas of trade, tourism and investment and then this was upgraded to Full Dialogue Partnership in 1995. India also participated in ASEAN's Post Ministerial Conference in July 1996 where the vision of mutual further cooperation in all fields such as science and technology, human resource development, infrastructure was envisaged. India was admitted to the ASEAN Regional Forum (ARF) in 1996 which enabled security cooperation between Indian and ASEAN, while signifying the recognition and acceptance of India's emerging power and its significant role in the Indo-Pacific. In the economic arena, India has signed Free Trade Agreement (FTA) with the 10 members of ASEAN. Further, the second phase of the Look East Policy has focused on widening the scope of integration with special emphasis on connectivity (Haokip 2011). With Prime Minister Modi coming into Office, the Look East Policy got rejuvenated under the name of Act East Policy. Noting the ever-expanding significance of ASEAN and addressing the opening ceremony of 15th ASEAN-India Summit at Manila, PM Modi restated that 'India's Act East Policy is shaped around the ASEAN, and its centrality in the regional security architecture of the Indo-Pacific region is evident'.[1] The Act East Policy focused on greater convergence of ideas, economics and enhancing connectivity and security including maritime security. With India inviting ASEAN to her Republic Day celebration and the ASEAN-India Commemorative Summit marking the 25th anniversary of the ASEAN-India dialogue partnership, India-ASEAN relationship is no doubt in its heyday.

Coming to Japan, the country that first articulated the idea of the Quadrilateral Framework, it can be said that Japan's partnership with ASEAN began in 1973 with the establishment of ASEAN-Japan Forum. Since then both of them have extended mutual cooperation to maintain peace, stability, bring about development and prosperity to Asia at large including East Asia and the Indo-Pacific. They have made business amounting to 248 billion US dollars in the year 2011 with the ASEAN countries being one of the favourite foreign direct investment destination for Japanese enterprises (Ministry of Foreign Affairs of Japan 2014). Japan and ASEAN share high level of integration in business and economic sector the ASEAN-Japan Centre playing a vital role in increase of exports, facilitating the low of investment and promoting tourism for the purpose of economic development between Japan and ASEAN Member States. They have collaboration in energy sector, at the socio-cultural level such as facilitating exchange student programs under the Japan East-Asia Network of Exchange for Students and Youths, the 'Kizuna' exchange programme among others. They have a highly integrated Information and Communication Technology which continues to grow; the establishment of Japan-ASEAN Integration Fund (JAIF) in 2006 that finances various projects in the areas of disaster management, counter terrorism, maritime cooperation, and economic integration, financing small and medium enterprises, facilitating people-to-people exchanges, training facilities among others (ASEAN 2017). Therefore, Japan and ASEAN can be said to enjoy a robust partnership that facilitates mutual development.

Australia on the other hand, became ASEAN's dialogue partner in 1974 and since then it has been a firm supporter of ASEAN's inclusive rule-based order while economically integrating the region. Like Japan, ASEAN has robust economic and strategic partnership in mutually gainful areas such as countering terrorism and the rise of extremism in the region, combating trafficking of all sorts and smuggling, and deepening regional integration through Free Trade

Agreements. ASEAN's economic significance lies in the fact that it is one of Australia's top three trading partners, accounting for around 15 per cent of Canberra's total trade, with ever-expanding areas of profitable trade and investment collaborations. Australia provides collaboration and exchange programs the in educational sector, which arguably is the cornerstone of strong bonding between Australia and ASEAN (Australian Government, Department of the Prime Minister and Cabinet 2018).

The Quad members have affirmed 'ASEAN's centrality' to a successful Indo-Pacific strategy and its indispensible role in the regional security. India has started intensifying their engagements with the ASEAN countries, especially with Indonesia, which is one of the largest countries in ASEAN, with both the countries pledging for 'free, open, transparent, rules-based, peaceful, prosperous and inclusive Indo-Pacific region' that would strengthen 'their maritime cooperation for promotion of peace, stability and bringing in robust economic growth and prosperity to the Indo-Pacific region', 'while reaffirming the importance of the ASEAN centrality and unity'.[2] Indonesia is quite enthusiastic regarding the idea of ASEAN Centrality floated by US counterpart. Indonesia is also working in close cooperation with Thailand to ensure a coordinate other members of ASEAN (Chongkittavorn 2018). It is definitely very important for the ASEAN countries to engage with the Quad members to enable proper enforcement in the areas of mutual concern, especially those issues such as combating terrorism and cyber security that cannot be dealt without joint action, and plan a broader strategy to maintaining statuesque in the regional security architecture with ASEAN at the core. This calls for partnering in maritime domain and combating the rise of unfriendly forces, dealing with the Korean nuclear crisis, intensifying economic ties, connectivity, inclusiveness and joint military exercises among others. Since, the very idea of Indo-Pacific is not complete without taking the ASEAN countries into confidence, it is very important for Quad to maintain and enhance their ties with the ten big shareholders of the region.

China's OBOR and the Quad: Is there a Flashpoint?

The interesting turn in the relationship among countries and the dilemma in establishing America favoured arrangements in the Indo-Pacific commences with the assertiveness and revisionist tendencies of the People's Republic of China (PRC) which has already emerged to challenge the orders at the sea and on land.

China's rise and mischievous activities in water and on soil is already making US blink. China's claims over the South China Sea have been a cause for anxiety US, Japan and Australia. Coupled with this, China has floated the plan of One-Belt-One-Road (OBOR), also known as the Belt and Road Initiative (BRI). Touted as the centerpiece to ensuring continuation of Chinese economic prosperity in the long run, OBOR is a grand plan that comprises 'Silk Road Economic Belt' (SREB) and the 21st century 'Maritime Silk Road' (MSR) that will link countries across Asia, Africa, Europe and South Pacific, and would entail massive investments in infrastructural projects, including financial integration, liberalisation of trade and investment, and enhanced connectivity among nations encompassing countries across continents including people-to-people connectivity (NDRC 2015). OBOR has made quite a tremor in international relations with some countries praising it because of its massive investment and connectivity blueprint while others are skeptical of their national interest being compromised. The United States Secretary of State Rex Tillerson has already tagged PRC's OBOR as 'predatory',[3] pointing specifically to Chinese economic statecraft warning smaller countries especially Latin American nations against the real Chinese ambitions.

The call for 'rules based order' and 'freedom of navigation' including the freedom of over flight as some of the primary goals of the Quad can be said to indirectly refer to China's aggressive actions in the South China Sea that is the nerve-centre of all transit routes. China has be engaged in reclaiming island across the South China Sea for causing bilateral disputes, for example, Japan and Philippines and causing turmoil in the region at large. While Chinese misadventures are already unraveling the existing statuesque, added to this was the OBOR grand plan, which took Quad leaders by surprise, if not pleasantly, and forced them to rethink their policies and equations in the Indo-Pacific region.

India is wary of China's OBOR project especially the proposed China-Pakistan Economic Corridor (CPEC) corridor that proposes to link Gwadar Port with Xinjiang, passing through the disputed territory of Gilgit-Baltistan region in the Pakistan Occupies Kashmir (POK) thereby compromising India's sovereignty. India is also worried about increased Chinese maritime power in the Indian Ocean. Even so, India does not want to annoy China directly. Chinese military strength and economic might is unmatched coupled with the sour historical experience of Chinese betrayal makes India unsure of Chinese designs in the region.

Historically, Sino-Japanese relationship has never been smooth sailing. In the 21st century, Chinese claims to the disputed island in the South China Sea and coupled with the Maritime Silk Road Initiative have brought renewed tensions in Tokyo as it compromises with Japan's energy security and therefore joins the call for a 'free and open Indo-Pacific'. Australia on the other hand, has been ambivalent, at least to some extent. Initially, Canberra's decision to participate in Asian Infrastructure Investment Bank (AIIB) and the sale of the Port of Darwin to a company linked to the One Belt, One Road strategy signalled its pro-China move. However, Australia has denied any formal links with China's One Belt One Road Initiative and is presently anxious about China's massive investment plans in the Pacific Islands (Gale and Shearer 2018).

America too does not want to go for any direct confrontation with China. US responses are limited to alliance and counter alliance formation in its efforts to control if not totally containing the rise of Chinese influence in the countries of the Indo-Pacific. The measure remain limited to fiery speech, redrawing of area of operation and is not seen to exceed beyond violating illegal steps untaken by Chinese counterpart such as the Air Defense Identification Zone (AIDZ) in the South China Sea. US measures serves two main purposes, one it avoids any direct confrontation with China, since China and the United States are intertwined when it comes to economics and secondly, it warns China against any aggressive steps in the Indo-Pacific.

China, too did not receive the idea of Quad in good taste. The use of the term 'Quadrilateral' has been unwelcoming to Chinese counterpart, as it signals the encircling and downplaying, if not containment of Chinese aspirations in the region. Reactions from the Chinese counterpart are not positive since China feels that the use of the very term Quad signals 'politicising and excluding'[4] other countries of the region. Though never accepted by Chinese officials, PRC is not in favour of any American alliance to lay down the rule of the game especially when it comes to Indo-Pacific region.

Conclusion

There is no doubt that the Quad was revived owing to China's assertive foreign policy measures in the Indo-Pacific and none of the Quad countries are in favour of a Chinese dominated Indo-Pacific order. Quad has already been labelled as playing the role of counter-balancing China's rise and an indirect measure to curtailing Beijing's game-plan. China's hegemonistic activities are soaring coupled with its charm offensive to win the support of the smaller states of the Indo-Pacific. China's also visions itself to be a 'Middle Kingdom' having historically backed authorisation to dominate the Southeast Asian countries and therefore has engaged itself to redraw the orders of the Indo-Pacific.

However, interestingly, none of the countries having geopolitical and strategic interest in the Indo-Pacific wants neither to anger China nor go for any direct or prolonged confrontation with China. China is a leading player in the region both economically and strategically. Each of the countries of the Indo-Pacific have intensive economic ties with China, which means that angering China will have wide-ranging ramifications for the economic and strategic balance of the region. The ASEAN countries are faced with a tough decision in the game of side-taking ASEAN members have historically seen the rule of the Big Brother in the Asia Pacific. However, with America's retreat from the Trans-Pacific Partnership (TPP) along with President Trump's 'America First' strategy, China found out a vacuum to engage with the ASEAN countries as evident with Philippines. However, it would be a mistake to say that America is no longer committed to the region. America's commitment has been revamped with increased area of operation under the banner of 'Indo-Pacific'.

It can be said that the Cold War politics has reappeared, with a new twist and added flavours. The political game of alliance and counter-alliances are still prevalent, and the two big powers of the Indo-Pacific namely, PRC and USA trying to woe more countries into their own zones of influence. The twist comes with the rise of regional powers such as India, Japan, Australia joining hands and each country adding its own flavour in the existing game of power-politics. Each of the Quad members wants to make sure that their own equations are not hampered and interests remain secured while engaging as a Quadrilateral Bloc. It's a careful gamble of side-taking that nations have to decide upon keeping their foreign policy imperatives and national interest ahead of all compulsions. It's definitely going to be a tight rope-walking as taming the Dragon is not possible. The question whether Quad can be a game changer in the Indo-Pacific will definitely depend on the judiciousness and diplomatic skills of the Quad members and how far they can act together in their endeavour to win maximum support and friends for their cause in the region while avoiding clashes and confrontation in the Indo-Pacific region.

NOTES

1 Prime Minister Narendra Modi's Opening Statement at 15th ASEAN-India Summit, Manila, 14 Nov, 2017, available at http://www.pmindia.gov.in/en/news_updates/pms-opening-statement-at-15th-asean-india-summit-manila/

2 Ministry of External Affairs: Government of India, "Shared Vision of India-Indonesia Maritime Cooperation in the Indo-Pacific", available at https://mea.gov.in/bilateral-documents.htm?dtl/29933/Shared_Vision_of_IndiaIndonesia_Maritime_Cooperation_in_the_IndoPacific

3 Remarks of Secretary of State Rex Tillerson on US Engagement in the Western Hemisphere made at the University of Texas at Austin, Austin, Texas, available at https://china.usembassy-china.org.cn/secretary-state-rex-tillerson-u-s-engagement-western-hemisphere/

4 Chinese Official remarks as reported in India Today, Dated November 13, 2017, available at https://www.indiatoday.in/world/story/asean-china-india-us-australia-japan-quad-meeting-indo-pacific-1085306-2017-11-13

REFERENCES

Ananth, Krishnan (2017), "China warns Quad meeting 'to avoid politicising or excluding parties'", available at https://www.indiatoday.in/world/story/asean-china-india-us-australia-japan-quad-meeting-indo-pacific-1085306-2017-11-13, accessed on 27 June 2018.

ASEAN (2017), "Overview of ASEAN-Japan Dialogue Relations", available at http://asean.org/storage/2012/05/Overview-ASEAN-Japan-Relations-As-of-8-March-2017.pdf, accessed on 26 June 2018.

Australian Government, Department of the Prime Minister and Cabinet (2018), "Australia-ASEAN Relations", available at https://aseanaustralia.pmc.gov.au/asean-australia/relations, accessed on June 27 2018.

Congressional Research Service (CRS) (2010), "United States Relations with the Association of Southeast Asian Nations (ASEAN)", *CRS Report for Congress,* R40933, available at https://www.everycrsreport.com/files/20100312_R40933_9057212b 408c4e 2531cc2423210da8c1ddb5611e.html, accessed on 27 June 2018.

Chanlett-Avery, Emma (2018), "Japan, the Indo-Pacific, and the "Quad", *The Chicago Council on Global Affairs,* available at https://www.thechicagocouncil.org/publication/japan-indo-pacific-and-quad, accessed on 25 June 2018.

Chanlett-Avery, Emma and Bruce Vaughn (2008), "Emerging Trend in the Security Architecture in Asia: Bilateral and Multilateral Ties among the United States, Japan, Australia, and India", *CRS Report,* available at https://www.everycrsreport.com/files/20080107_RL34312_18885b0a0ec70460f2f29d4c65f68b8a6c2c8a6e.pdf, accessed on 26 June 2018.

Chongkittavorn, Kavi (2018), "ASEAN's Role in the US Indo-Pacific Strategy", *Asia Pacific Bulletin, No. 425,* available at https://www.eastwestcenter.org/publications/aseans-role-in-the-us-indo-pacific-strategy, accessed on 27 June 2018.

Khoman, Thanet (2011), "Formation of ASEAN", *National Library Board, Singapore,* available at http://eresources.nlb.gov.sg/history/events/65bc5474-afba-4fcc-afc1-345457fa41a9, accessed on June 27, 2018.

Mahapatra, Chintamani (1990), *American Role in the Origin & Growth of ASEAN*, New Delhi: ABC Publication House

Ministry of External Affairs: Government of India (2018), "Shared Vision of India-Indonesia Maritime Cooperation in the Indo-Pacific", available at https://mea.gov.in/bilateral-documents.htm?dtl/29933/Shared_Vision_of_IndiaIndonesia_ Maritime_Cooperation_ in_the_IndoPacific, accessed on June 27 2018.

Ministry of Foreign Affairs of Japan (2007), "Confluence of the Two Seas", *Speech by H.E.Mr. Shinzo Abe, Prime Minister of Japan at the Parliament of the Republic of India*", available at https://www.mofa.go.jp/region/asia-paci/pmv0708/speech-2.html, accessed on 26 June 2018.

Ministry of Foreign Affairs of Japan, (2014) "40th Year of ASEAN-Japan Friendship and Cooperation", available at https://www.mofa.go.jp/region/asia-paci/asean/relation/ja40/index.html, accessed on 26 June 2018.

Madan, Tanvi (2017), "The Rise, Fall, and Rebirth of the 'Quad", *War on the Rocks*, available at https://warontherocks.com/2017/11/rise-fall-rebirth-quad/, accessed on 25 June 2018.

Ministry of External Affairs (MEA): Press Release, Government of India, "India-Australia-Japan-U.S. Consultations on Indo-Pacific (November 12, 2017)", available at http://mea.gov.in/press-releases.htm?dtl/29110/IndiaAustraliaJapanUS+Consultations+on+IndoPacific+November+12+2017, accessed on 26 June 2018

National Development and Reform Commission (NDRC), People's Republic of China (2015), "Vision and Actions on Jointly Building Silk Road Economic Belt and 21st-Century Maritime Silk Road", available at http://en.ndrc.gov.cn/newsrelease/201503/t20150330_669367.html, accessed on 27 June 2018.

National Informatics Centre (2017), "Prime Minister Narendra Modi's Opening Statement at 15th ASEAN-India Summit, Manila", available at http://www.pmindia.gov.in/en/news_updates/pms-opening-statement-at-15th-asean-india-summit-manila/, accessed on 27 June 2018.

Nauert, Heather (2017), "Australia-India-Japan-U.S. Consultations on the Indo-Pacific", US Department of States: Press Release, available at https://www.state.gov/r/pa/prs/ps/2017/11/275464.htm, accessed on 26 June 2018.

Oxfam (2014), "Ten years on: Boxing Day Tsunami response changed lives for good", available at https://www.oxfam.org.nz/blog/ten-years-boxing-day-tsunami-response-changed-lives-good, accessed on 25 June 2018.

Raja Mohan, C (2007), "East Asian Security: India's Rising Profile", S. Rajaratnam School of International Studies (RSIS), available at https://www.rsis.edu.sg/rsis-publication/rsis/964-east-asian-security-indias/, accessed on 26 June 2018.

Tsvetov, Anton (2017), "Will the Quad Mean the End of ASEAN Centrality?" *The Diplomat*, available at https://thediplomat.com/2017/11/will-the-quad-mean-the-end-of-asean-centrality/, accessed on 27 June 2018.

US Embassy and Consulates in China (2018), "Secretary of State Rex Tillerson On U.S. Engagement in the Western Hemisphere", available at https://china.usembassy-china.org.cn/secretary-state-rex-tillerson-u-s-engagement-western-hemisphere/, accessed on 27 June 2018.

9

Language as Soft Power in Indo-Pacific Area: Role of Technology in Promoting Chinese Language

Liu Jinxiu

ABSTRACT

Science and technology play a crucial role in the twenty-first century in varied scopes of our society, including the teaching and learning of a language, which has been the carrier of a culture and one of the embodiments of the soft power in a country. Introducing a language to other countries is to promote and proliferate that culture, ideology, and way of living behind that language. Examples can be seen in some languages: English, French, German, Japanese and Korean languages. The tremendous resonances afterward acquired and acknowledged more powerfully if accompanied by high technology, including hot and cold media likewise radio, movie, TV, and Internet. The debate on 'Two Cultures' by C.P. Snow and F.R. Leavis and their respective followers now is considered undoubtedly crucial in the modern world. The combination of the two cultures, i.e. 'science' and 'arts', at all levels of social life in China, including the academic level, has been significant in showcasing the Chinese language and has attracted foreign nationalities via mass media from the Indo-Pacific Area and other regions of the world. Mass media as the main representative of technology is utilised in language teaching and learning features through interactive, instant, and limitless information transitive analysis, hence, taken as an efficient means to demonstrate the soft power of China.

Introduction

Soft power, according to Joseph Nye in his book 'Bound to Lead' (1990), "Is the ability to attract and persuade without the need to resort to force or financial resources to get what you want", in other words, "when one country gets other countries to want what it wants—might be called co-optive or soft power in contrast with the hard or command power of ordering others to do what it wants" (Nye, 1990: 166). It takes non-coercive and persuasive means to influence other countries with its products, economic strength, diplomatic services, and cultural charm, in other words, to insert the influence through social and cultural ties. It's different from the hard power, which takes the means of forcing or giving money to influence the decision of other countries. Culture, political values, and foreign policies are its main angles. In the long term, culture becomes more and more important in the competition among countries. With the world more diversified, economies more globalised, and science and technology more advanced, the interexchange between cultures and economies, culture and politics are deeper than ever. The function of culture is more obvious, and it becomes a vital factor of a country's core competition strength.

Language as the carrier of a culture of one country can reveal the status and image of the country worldwide and as such language plays an important role in introducing the culture and improving the reputation of the host country. For example, promoting language is an efficient way to promote a country's socialist culture and to set the influence of that country in the world. Moreover, language as a special phenomenon has the function to express other aspects of culture. Not only language plays a radical role as a part of a culture and as the media of cultural transmission, but also as a means to integrate people of different cultures. The soft power represented by language and other factors interact with each other, these factors include GDP, without the development of language soft power cannot work at its best.

As the irreplaceable part of an overseas promotion, language is usually given the most importance, and major languages in the world have tried to enlarge their influence onto other countries. For instance, French, English, German, Korean, Japanese, just to name a few, have the experience of introducing themselves to the outside world. Francophone Alliance, started in Paris in 1883 when the imperial competition between France and Britain was still in its full swing, it was set up for the National Association to spread French language in Colonialised and Foreign Countries, directed by celebrities such as science fiction writer, Jules Verne, Ernest Renan, scientist Louis Pasteur and others in this 'National Association'. In Spain and Africa in the same year, the first office was established later and its scope of activities reached to Central and South America, Asia and the United States. The 'French Training Center' now has 1,072 centers in 130 countries that teach French. The British Culture and Education Association have set up 220 institutes, and the Goethe Institute has 149 offices for the promotion of English and German respectively. Both the institutes have long started operating specialised institutions that teach their own languages all over the world. The British Council estimates as follows:

> "English is spoken at a useful level by some 1.75 billion people worldwide that is one in every four people. By 2020, we forecast that two billion people will be using it—or learning to use it. It is the economically active, the thought leaders, the business decision-makers, the young, the movers and shakers present the future who are learning and speaking English. They are talking to each other more and more and English is the 'operating system' of that global conversation". (The English Effect: The Impact of English, What It's Worth to the UK and Why It Matters to World, British Council, 2).

The United Kingdom is considered to possess the 'greatest soft power' due to its diplomacy and cultural clout, which has led to the spreading of English language thus explaining the international acceptance of the British (and American) lifestyle.

In Asia, Japan decided to add 100 Japanese language learning centers for teaching and learning Japanese language. Korea also has Sejong Hakdang (Sejong Academy) set up by The Ministry of Culture and Tourism of Korean Government to teach Korean language overseas. With the heating up of the Korean Wave and the help of the worldwide network of Korean language, education experts who have participated in the operation of Sejong Hakdang, Korean language and culture have been introduced and spread in a rapid and wide scale. An example of the Korean Wave in Beijing shows that the Korean Cultural Center is crowded with Han people (the majority of Chinese people) who wants to learn the Korean language. The number of audience for lectures usually exceeds the accommodation capacity of the lecture venue and in places like Mongolia, the demand for the Korean language is even more. The advancement of South Korea's international status and the continuous expansion of the Korean Wave has made the Korean language highly popular around the world and is continually rising. The promotion of the language has made cultural impact and increased economic benefits and political influence of South Korea. According to the South China Morning Post in 2014, the K-pop boom led to the market ranking the 11th largest in the world with "creative content appealing global population" (Chow, 2014). The cultural contents exports change perceptions of Korean products, the dramas in particular create a lifestyle that is accessible by purchasing the products such as food, clothing and beauty item.

The main countries in the world are fastening their pace in promoting their languages. There are two reasons for this, one is an increase in the prosperity of a country by promoting language. Second, more and more countries and people are using languages that will contribute to the development in politics, economy, business, education, and technology. The world history is replete with examples in which the blooming of a language has concurred with the booming of its economy.

Chinese languages (Mandarin, Cantonese, with Tibetan and others) belong to the Sino-Tibetan language family; different from other families, likewise Indo-European (English, Russian, Hindi), Afro-Asiatic family (Arabic, Somali, Hebrew) and Malayo-Polynesian languages (Indonesia, Malay, Tagalog) and others. The Chinese language is the essence of the history of China's five thousand years; it has continuously evolved and improved with the evolution of Chinese society. Chinese Language as the mode of complex systems of communication among Chinese people, together with its functions in the development, acquisition and maintenance of these systems, it displays a certain culture behind it. It is also the representative of the overall image of China, likewise the whole nation working for the Chinese Dream in the current era and a way of China to influence the world.

The long history of China forms the strong base for the position of the cultural power. When the Chinese language is taught, the brilliant culture represented by Confucianism is also explained and implied. With multi-faceted ideas and values, the Chinese culture has built itself "in relationship of human and nature, of man and society", Chinese people emphasise the protection of nature, and consider that human has the same source and structure; and also emphasise the stability of society, collectivism and filial piety. Earlier Benevolence, justice, courtesy, wisdom, and faith was put with the greatest weight and in contemporary times socialist moral construction and in recent years Chinese Dream has caught the national attention.

The history of the transmission of Chinese language overseas started in ancient times. At that time and until the beginning of a modern era there were no technological means in learning Chinese, but many westerners themselves travelled to China for learning the language; this became the beginning of the western Sinology. With the improvement of the comprehensive national power, China started actively introducing and promoting Chinese language to the world in a peaceful tradition, unlike the countries in the east and west which tried to accomplish it through brutal wars (Huo Jiucang, 2003). The Silk Road is the wisdom of Chinese ancestors to attract the other part of the world with its brilliant ancient culture, which can be seen in records of Greek and Roman Empires and later in the writings of some Christian preachers or travellers who made great contribution to the mutual communication of the East and the West such as The Travels of Marco Polo, its four volumes talks about China's nature and costumes. From the 1540s to the 18th century we see that professional Chinese researchers to Western preachers, like Mendoza and Matteo Ricci, Voltaire to name a few, all have written works on China. In the nineteenth century, the Sinology was made as a subject in France, starting with the Chinese Lectures in some European universities by professors from the Institute of France. From then on the Sinology developed fast, before the WWII, there were a group of prestigious Sinologists, likewise Chavannes. In Britain, the development of Sinology is closely related to the Opium War, after which a certain amount of British academics and preachers entered China and did field work, collecting materials, many academic books appeared, such as Legge's Chinese Classics, at the same time, universities such as Oxford opened lectures on Chinese language and nurtured many sinologists such as Waley. In *History of Overseas Sinology* (2002), it states that after the latter half of the nineteenth century and the early twentieth century the Sinology in Britain entered a sustainable growth.

The several hundred years of overseas transmission of Chinese language underwent a process of change from outside towards inside in ancient times and in modern times from outside towards inside in contemporary times. China was isolated and was made China-centered by its rulers in ancient times, its culture was preserved from the outside world and was prevented from being exported to other places. But this changed soon when foreigners came as preachers, travelers, and scholars to China for business, study, introducing their religions or in search of hidden treasures. Thus gradually the Sinologist system was formed in a dynamic process of acknowledgment and understanding in some European countries: Great Britain, France, and Germany.

Different regions have their own specific communication in commerce and trade with China at different degrees, depending on the acceptance of

Chinese culture which is varied globally, therefore the promotion of Chinese language varies from region to region due to the gap in economic and social developments. Thus we need to take into consideration several factors like Chinese diaspora in the different regions of the world. In the Indo-Pacific area, there are countries as Afghanistan, Pakistan, China, Nepal, India, Myanmar, Thailand, Vietnam, Philippines, Malaysia, Indonesia, South Korea, Japan, Australia, and other countries. Among them, the Southeast Asian countries—Vietnam, Malaysia, Philippines, and Myanmar has the highest number of Chinese emigrants. After four waves of emigration in the past four centuries (Zhuang, 2008), the total number of Chinese emigrants are 33.48 million, which is 6 per cent of the total South Asian population, and 73.5 per cent of the whole 45.43 million Chinese emigrants (Zhuang, 2009). This area is the deepest, most durable area for the transmission of Chinese culture and Chinese language. The Chinese culture and language help them to maintain their own identity from which they belong to earlier. And Huntington once stated, language is the second factor to distinguish a group of people from other peoples after blood and before religion (Huntington, 1996:42).

The central Asia countries like Afghanistan and Pakistan have huge potentials in promoting the Chinese language. As these countries lie at a close proximity to the northwest part of China and since a long time there has been a positive and healthy relationship. Learners feel that English is comparatively an easier language to learn among language families making it the most widely spoken language internationally. Chinese language system is rich and often seen to be complicated in its usages even for the native speakers due to its large number of characters, and multiple meaning of a single character. One of the problems of these Central Asian countries is the lack of trained teachers and teaching methodology. Apart from these problems trade conflicts and competition coupled with regional instability are major challenges for the promotion of Chinese language promotion abroad.

Other countries of Indo-Pacific like Australia are comparatively better as the transmission of language took place due to the migration of Chinese population who went to study, work and/or settle down in Australia. Man as the carrier of language is the most significant factor in introducing and maintaining a language, the growing number of Chinese population in Australia led to Chinese Institutes/Departments in different areas, for instance, in Australian National University, Australian Capital Territory there are ANU China Institute, Australian Centre on China in the World, East Asian Studies,

School of Culture, History and Language; Chinese Studies Major and Chinese Language Major; in New South Wales, there are Chinese Studies in Macquarie University, University of New England, of New South Wales, of Newcastle, Sydney, Wollongong etc.

The Chinese language promotion is one of the national policy of China along with the communication and learning of daily life of Chinese people through Chinese teaching overseas. The countries covered by OBOR (One Belt One Road) has been given more weight in this regard. The OBOR initiative covers 65 countries, with which China's trade totalled to US$953.59 billion, 25.7 per cent of China's trade in global trade. ('One Belt, One Road' Trade Cooperation Big Data Report (2017)). The total number of Confucius Institutes and Confucius Classrooms totaled to 137 and 131 respectively by 2016, there were 2.32 million students in countries all over the world and about 12.72 million cultural events held globally. In the same year, there were 208,000 foreign students from OBOR countries, which is 46.92 per cent of the total number of international students coming to China. The ten countries with the largest number of students studying in China are South Korea, the United States, Thailand, Pakistan, India, Russia, Indonesia, Kazakhstan, Japan, and Vietnam. Among them, Pakistan, India, Indonesia, Japan, and Vietnam are Indo-Pacific countries. As one of the important country in the Indo-Pacific region, India is seen as a significant country China intends to include in its OBOR scheme. India has made progress in encouraging Chinese learning and/or China Studies in the past years, moreover, Chinese hi-tech electronic products like mobile phones have gained popularity in the Indian markets.

China and Chinese language should take the advantages of globalisation, industrialisation, and technologisation to reform the teaching materials, and create new means of Chinese transmission and revitalise it and enlarge the Chinese soft power. More importantly is to find a new way, instead of the old means of some western countries through colonisation to introduce Chinese culture and Chinese language to gain the trust and respect worldwide. The effects of the combination of administrative promotion with the natural transmission are highly fruitful like what the Tang Dynasty did, it introduced the Chinese language by attracting foreign people to its cultural values and charms and its liberal social environment. Now it's the post-industrial era with highly advanced technology. As the fourth factor, after human being, nature and society, technology is crucial in changing the world naturally and spiritually with its total interference. Technology most of the times function as the extension of the human body and it replaces certain parts of labours of a human. Technology nowadays performs like a new god as it can do almost anything. Nowadays there would be no more debates between the two camps of humanities and natural sciences, which can be traced back to the more obvious era of the enlightenment of the eighteenth century when Newton claimed that his achievement were made on the shoulder of his preceding giants, a kind of admission that those natural scientists were considered giants despite the elites in 20th century were still holding overconfidence of the orthodox of humanities and saw the uprising of natural sciences, alongside the technology, as a threat, though in ancient times inventions and applications of technology had already been recorded in varied disciplines. In twentieth and especially in the twenty-first century, science and technology play a vital role in the development of the economy, and progress of society and the forming of a new order whether it is social, political and even international. Language teaching and learning with technological means can be achieved with efficiency, high speed and lively interactions. These new means are hi-tech, printing media—papers, magazines, books and electronic media—radio, TV, movie and new media—web media, mobile text messages, and digital TV.

In the sense of language learning, "inevitably, (technologies in use) much has changed, especially with the introduction of multimedia, mobile technologies, and the advent of the Internet" (Levy, 2009:769). Currently, the online sources for Chinese learning include: 1. Comprehensive Resources, which update learning and exam information, latest news, materials of Chinese culture and tradition and else; websites likewise China Confucius Institute Headquarter, Chinese Education Foundation, Chinese Education Network, Chinese World, etc; 2. Teaching-Researching Networks: Overseas Chinese Teaching Interaction Network, Overseas Teaching and Exam Network; 3. There are colleges and organisations providing their own websites for teaching and learning Chinese; 4. Online Forum, blog, moments, status and microblog (Weibo), we can see Chinese International Forum, Chinese Teaching Community, Chinese World, Chinese Space Blog, etc.

Among them the online Chinese courses are more convenient to get access to and easy to use—online learning games, TV programmes and movies can greatly adjust the tedious learning process. One example here is during the Chinese Spring Festival, which is very important to most Chinese people, but often it is not represented in an accurate manner as there is very limited interaction and social gatherings between Chinese official representatives and

Chinese language learners. The very limited contents of their textbooks can hardly provide deep impression onto them. With the help of technology, they can easily watch the live programs by CCTV and get to know how the Chinese people celebrate the festival nowadays.

As web media is featured with interactive, speedy, vast coverage and is open to information transmission the singular and traditional ways of one-sided learning now turns to be two-sided communication between learning and teaching. The instantaneous response of words, sounds and images goes beyond the restrictions imposed by printing, thus learners can use information at anytime and anywhere provided by the internet. The traditional way of restriction of time and space becomes the large scope to global sharing of sources. The transmission of Chinese language with the help of technological means has been enlarged in received area and formed a super-big network.

Despite achievements made in recent years by improving and enlarging Chinese language learning scope, the disadvantages are still there. Firstly, the obstacles did not decrease and as compared to English language the Chinese language has less strength of science and technology and economy behind it. The Western languages have greater strength and influence when it comes to the development of science and technology than the Chinese language. English, French, German and other Western languages have always been stronger in scope globally. Second, the basic programming language of information technology is English; this situation hinders the proliferation of other languages, including Chinese. To solve these problems, more science and technology are to be applied to reduce the difficulties in learning Chinese, to improve the quality of Chinese media products. Chinese language embodies the national image of China and its cultural identity; its introduction and promotion motivate the understanding, economic and cultural exchange and cooperation between China and other countries. "The mass media of non-teaching content currently has a stronger communication effect, with the highest satisfaction with movies, music and animation."

As mentioned above, man is vital in introducing a language; hence, nowadays in the Universities of Beijing the around 300 language students are provided training for teaching Chinese language abroad and offer some MA degrees to students there. The first Confucius Institute was set up in Seoul Korea in 2004 and today there are more than 300 Confucius Institute and over 1000 Confucius classroom. Both Confucius Institute and Confucius Classrooms are foundations serve the demand for the study of Chinese language and to bridge China with the world by providing information and cultural exchange. They also reflect the significance of China's cultural communication strategy and the cultural soft power in the development of Chinese teaching in primary and middle school levels overseas.

The Chinese wave is now still in formation. To improve our soft power, the introduction of language is necessary. In recent years since 2001 both China and ASEAN countries claimed to form a free trade zone. Rapid achievements have been gained in several aspects: the economic and trade communication has increased, there is exchange of culture and arts among common people more frequently. The improvement of soft power at certain degrees impact economic power, in America and Japan the cultural products takes a big share of their GDP; through introduction of language it has increased the soft power of these countries and has made positive impacts. There are many aspects for improving the language transmission to the soft power: first, in the situation of globalisation, in the process of becoming an international superpower, the cultural soft power is vital for increasing China's influence and diversifying the cultural products. Second, the future development of China is close to the Asian-pacific zone and the area has many trade partners of China. With the improving soft power in this area China can tap more opportunities adding to its advantages. Last, the development of China is advantageous to the nearby area, the Asian-Pacific area is one of the most important areas: many of the trade partners and the culturally similar countries—Japan, Korea, Vietnam are located here.

Promoting Chinese language is also a good way to improve our soft power. It not only meets the requirements of the increasing demand of Chinese language learning, but also the need of China's own development. The promoting of the Chinese language, has to match the development and contribution China has made after its opening up to the world. The more connection with other countries, the more important role China can play in the global scene.

Conclusion

Soft power contains culture and other aspects; language as the embodiment of culture is vital for the improvement of the soft power of a country. Nowadays several countries are all trying to promote their own languages in order to increase the influence of their culture on other counties. Indo-Pacific area is strategically important to China's national policy as South East Asian countries have the most number of Chinese immigrants; Central Asia has a great potential for developing economic connection; in this post-industrial era technology is applied to improve the accessibility and better understanding in learning languages. The Chinese language should take the same step to help Chinese soft power in playing a bigger role in world affairs, though there are still advantages hindering the development of the transmission of the language.

REFERENCES

Chow, Vivienne (2014), Korean Cultural export success rooted in freedom and democracy, *South China Morning Post*, 9 December 2014, available at https://www.scmp.com/news/hong-kong/article/1658348/korean-cultural-export-success-rooted-freedom-and-democracy-industry

Huntington, S.P., The Clash of Civilizations and the Remarking of World Order, Simon & Schuster, NY, 1996.

Levy, Mike, "Technologies in use for Second Language Learning", *The Modern Language Journal*, Vol. 93, 2009, 769-782.

Nye, Joseph. Bound to Lead: The Changing Nature of American Power, New York: Basic Books, 1990.

"One Belt, One Road" Trade Cooperation Big Data Report (2017) available at https://www.scmp.com/news/hong-kong/article/1658348/korean-cultural-export-success-rooted-freedom-and-democracy-industry

The English Effect: The Impact of English, What It's Worth to the UK and Why It Matters to World, British Council.

Zhuang Guotu, "On The Four Waves of Chinese Emigrants to South-East Asia", *South Sea Studies*, 2008 (1).

Zhuang Guotu, "The New Estimation of the Number of Chinese Emigrants in South-East Asia", *Xiamen University Journal*, 2009 (3).

10

ASEAN Centrality in Promoting Harmony and Stability in the Indo-Pacific

Sachin Tiwari

ABSTRACT

ASEAN as a regional organization represents the collective interest of providing the platform for issue discussion and a form of an umbrella organization to forward peace, stability, and development for Southeast Asia and the broader region. In many ways, it provides a common identity to the disparate region with different historical experience, culture, and different forms of governance. Strategically, ASEAN states connect the Indian Ocean to the Pacific Ocean, and South Asia to East Asia, and the Pacific states. The position of it as 'middle region' leverages it, offering advantages and challenges at the same time. Reformulation of the strategy of the major powers as the US, Japan, India, and Australia focuses on the larger view of the region in the form of "Free and Open Indo-Pacific". The changing doctrine of major power elaborates on the broader strategic area encompassing the Pacific and the Indian Ocean. The idea is not being restricted to external power; rather large ASEAN states as Indonesia have pushed for their own vision of Indo-Pacific concept.

ASEAN as an originator of forums represents a large number of associations providing an extension for a meeting of the world power with developing states. The emergence of dynamic economy pushed the thrust of the organization becoming the driver for progress. However, the influence of the major power had a considerable effect since from its inception during the Cold War period. ASEAN remained a place for the major power contestation between great power, which now represents the US and China in the region. India's emergence as a leading power with a focus on the region in the form of Act East policy, Indo-Pacific policy are shaping the emerging order and India's greater share in the Indo-Pacific along with the established power. Efforts by the ASEAN along with ASEAN Regional Forum, East Asia Summit, and ASEAN Defense Minister Meeting are to drive more regional architecture where the area remains dynamic politically, economically and security wise. ASEAN role in shaping the Indo-Pacific have been driven from the internal cohesiveness and the external powers. The centrality can be seen from the perspective of the ASEAN remaining relevant providing extension of engagement through the multilateral framework of institutions and its position as the fulcrum of the region in the changing geopolitical landscape remaining relevant in the region. ASEAN leading role in the negotiation of free trade such as RCEP has pushed for the more economically driven region with the engagement of major economies. Yet, the reality of the China-led regionalism is pushing more China-centric order with financial institutions as Asian Infrastructure Investment Bank providing support to weakest ASEAN members with strategic interest. ASEAN consensus over the critical issues as the dispute over the South China Sea is divergent with individual members varying stand. The emerging maritime order of the Indo-Pacific region with militarization by major powers is creating a security dilemma, where the ability of ASEAN to remain neutral is being challenged and balancing between the US allies, partners, and China.

The chapter assesses the extent to which ASEAN provides peace and progress in the Indo-Pacific region. Examining the notion of ASEAN Centrality, the role of the important forums as ARF, East Asia Summit in dealing with important issues as economic cooperation, security architecture including terrorism, territorial issues will be analyzed. The emerging geopolitics of the Indo-Pacific region would be analyzed with ASEAN's own conception of it. It will also follow the relations of ASEAN with major powers such as the US, China, India, Australia and Japan in the emerging order.

Introduction

This chapter assesses the extent to which ASEAN provides peace and progress in the Indo-Pacific region. The first section, deals with the conceptual understanding, examining the notion of ASEAN Centrality including its emergence and understanding. The second section analyzes the emerging geopolitics of the Indo-Pacific that would be placed within the framework of different states including ASEAN own conception of it. The third section critically outlines the relations of ASEAN with major powers such as the US, China, India, Australia, and Japan within the context of ASEAN. The last section analyzes the role of the important forums like ARF, East Asia Summit in dealing with important issues, including economic cooperation, security architecture including terrorism, territorial issues.

ASEAN Centrality: Conceptual Framework

ASEAN was formed in 1967 as a regional organisation in the midst of the Cold War and the intensive fighting in the Indochina peninsula. The term Association of Southeast Asia Nations was coined by the American academic Russell H. Fifield with the emphasis on forming a loose coalition of non-communist states.[2] The association comprised of non-communist states which included Indonesia, Thailand, Philippines, Singapore, and Malaysia. ASEAN formed a zone of peace and stability in the region. The US position as the 'security guarantor' of the region led to the 'discreet guidance and support'[3] and provided a base for the regional institution's formation. During the period of Cold War, the US as the major security provided peace and stability to the region, where the economic development was pushed by major trade liberalisation efforts such as the Asia Pacific Economic Cooperation (APEC). Southeast Asia was the major center of the Cold war rivalry with intense fighting in the area. ASEAN has carved its own space and stability initiated in the Zone of Peace proposal in 1971,[4] though it had its limitation due to great power rivalry. ASEAN development was spurred by the emergence of the peaceful zone and promoting the development of institutions in the post-Cold War era.

The end of the Cold War was accompanied by a new set of challenges as the US relevance to the security of the region was being questioned. The formation of the ASEAN regional forum (ARF) forwarded the idea of an ASEAN plus structure in the regional security varied of the external control.[5] The composition of the member of ASEAN was representative of the states with varied visions, strategies playing their own role in carving out the regional order in the Asia Pacific. ASEAN led mechanisms provided a platform to discuss outstanding issues, which otherwise would not have been possible because of the strained relations between the states. ASEAN working principle described centrality had been reiterated by prominent leaders putting ASEAN at center.

Development of ASEAN Centrality

The establishment of ASEAN comprised of nations that were underdeveloped and weak financial conditions. The initial idea of the organisation was "not to burden itself with responsibilities forging the ideological, military and security problems of Southeast Asia" (Acharya, 2017). Lately, the organisation changed its structure with the inclusion of the communist and military-ruled states like Cambodia, Vietnam, Laos, and Myanmar, which stood in opposition to ASEAN during the Cold War period. By bringing all the Southeast Asian countries under a single roof, ASEAN became the collective representative organisation for the region. The integration also followed the formation of ASEAN-led institutions with security issues in form of ASEAN Regional forum in 1994 and economic expansion by formation of ASEAN PLUS Three (ASEAN+3) structures in 1997. ASEAN centrality has ensured that the member states remain in the 'driver's seat' for setting agenda.[6] East Asia Summit (EAS) was formed in 2005 with the agenda of 'leaders led forum' covering the strategic broad areas affecting the East Asia region. Initially, the topics covered for discussion were non-traditional security issues including energy and humanitarian crises. Officially the term ASEAN centrality is found in the 2007 ASEAN document describing it as the "primary driver for the wider region", encompassing the Asia Pacific regionalism. ASEAN Centrality can be related to similar concepts as the 'leader', 'architect', 'institutional hub', driving the institutional building process in the Asia-Pacific region.[7] Similarly, Herman Kraft in "Driving East Asian Regionalism: The reconstruction of ASEAN identity"[8] states that ASEAN accepted its centrality in engaging the major powers of the world which have a significant impact on the region. Similarly, Henrick Tsjeng of S. Rajaratnam School of International Studies argues that "ASEAN should engage with extra-regional players while upholding its interest and never allow the external player to push their agenda."[9] With the inclusion of the United States and Russia in 2011, the discussion agenda broadened with the US bringing the traditional security issues like territorial disputes including the South China Sea, Disarmament and Nonproliferation issues for agenda discussion. Hillary Clinton described it in terms of strategic significance "as the fulcrum for the emerging regional architecture".[10] For ASEAN, the centrality remains in the maintenance of its status as a dynamic region, with economic, politics activities deriving from it represented in form of multilateral engagement. All the major powers including the US, Australia, India, and Japan have reiterated the ASEAN as central to the maintenance of peace and prosperity in the region.

ASEAN Defense Minister Plus (ADMM) was convened in 2010 with the inclusion of the major powers including the United States and Russia. Largely, ADMM Plus represents the evolving structure of ASEAN with the changing dynamics of the region and challenges. ADMM Plus 2010 calls for consultation between the defense ministers on security issues and cooperation in form of the joint military exercise to build capacity and capability.[11] The members represent a balance of power including the United States, Russia, and China along with middle powers including India, Australia, South Korea, EU, and New Zealand in the grouping. The composition of the members represented discussion on varied issues due to the geopolitics tension intensified in wake of the Sino-American rivalry. On the role of ASEAN, Patrick Cronin of the Asia-Pacific security programme contends that the "role of ASEAN is to moderate the issues rather than being the object of growing great power competition".[12] Australia elevated its partnership with special ASEAN-Australia summit in 2018 and reaffirming the central role of ASEAN in the evolving regional architecture for maintaining peace and stability through the ASEAN-led mechanisms (Sydney Declaration, 2018).[13]

ASEAN in the Indo-Pacific

'Asia-Pacific' remained the terminology recognising the region since World War II. The envisioning of the region as Indo-Pacific defined the emerging realities of the 21st century and the shifts in the power structure with the emergence of China as a major power. Also, the emergence of the middle powers like India, Australia in the Indian Ocean is shaping the strategic order in the region. The conception was different from earlier narratives of development for a 'Pan Asian Identity' as conceived by Japan, India which was more based on moral integration rather than strategic outlook. The emergence of the Indo-Pacific strategy can be seen as the China balanced agenda and the validation of India's growing role.[14] Japan Prime Minister Shinzo Abe conceived the idea of Indo-Pacific as the 'confluence of two seas' in 2007 recognising the expanding horizon of the strategic area encompassing India and connecting to Africa. US 'Pivot to Asia' in 2009 aimed for the deeper engagement in the Asia Pacific region with 'ASEAN as the fulcrum' for its policies. *Australia Defense White Paper* 2013 recognises the importance of rising China, economic development of East Asia and the emergence of India as 'global power', as key factors shaping the Indo-Pacific.[15] The National Security Strategy (NSS) of the US published in December 2017 defined the Indo-Pacific region as, "the region which stretches from the West coast of India to the Western shores of the United States".[16] Australia Minister for Foreign Affairs Julie Bishop, defined the Indo-Pacific as "a term that reflects the strategic and economic reality that the most important part of the world embraced by Indian and the Pacific Ocean".[17] The earlier narrative of Asia-Pacific was not able to reflect the changes with India's emergence reflecting the shift in the geopolitics.

ASEAN forms the middle region encompassing a large region ranging from Myanmar connected to South Asia to Indonesia stretches from the Indian Ocean to the Pacific Ocean, thus forming a core strategic area in an evolving landscape. The ASEAN vision of the Indo-Pacific is emerging with Indonesia laying vision in the form of the maritime power and the promotion of the institutional based order with the network of alliances and forums. India has also laid its open and free Indo-Pacific policy recognising the importance of the Indian Ocean, The emergence of the groupings parallel to ASEAN undermines the role of it in moderating the issues. Quad compromising of the US, Australia, Japan, and India represents a zone of 'shared values' driven by the emerging geopolitics. China has strong reservations against any groupings serving against its interest and termed Indo-Pacific idea as a 'destitute' that 'will fade like foam'. Quad as a Quadrilateral Security Initiative (QSI) revived in 2017 at the backdrop of East Asia summit but the grouping saw no common joint statement by the member countries.

ASEAN Centrality and External Power Relations

ASEAN role as the originator of forums ensures the participation of member's states along with major powers. ASEAN soft balancing strategy, i.e. the process of engagement through the interconnected institutions has ensured ASEAN engaging members both internally and externally impacted by the great power rivalry in the region. The political engagement of ASEAN with the US, Australia, Japan, and India is shaping the geopolitics of Indo-Pacific which is discussed in context with ASEAN below.

East Asia was largely an American creation because it was the stability created by the US presence that was the foundation of the growth in what is otherwise a very "diverse region".[18] The US policy of 'Pivot' later renamed as 'Rebalance' in 2010 renewed the US focus in Asia-Pacific region with Southeast Asia at its core of security and economic policies. Establishing permanent secretariat in Jakarta in 2010, the US joined the East Asia Summit (EAS) considered a premier regional forum for security issues representing 27 members. Its inclusion saw the balance dynamics with the inclusion of the critical traditional security issues. US elevated its partnership with ASEAN in 2015 to 'strategic partnership' with increasing military forces with 60 per cent naval assets by 2020 in the Asia-Pacific region. The action of US under 'Asia-Pivot' strategy pushed for an assertive Chinese stand with the takeover of the South China Sea. The action was parallel to Obama's Rebalance Strategy in

Asia. Beijing views Indo-Pacific strategy as efforts by the US and its allies to encircle it, leading to an assertive behaviour and more escalation with the rise of the Quad states deploying the policy to encircle China.

Under Trump administration, the US has seen an increased defense budget and assured commitment for continued attention to the Indo-Pacific region. At the 5th ASEAN-US Summit in November 2017, former President Barack Obama stated that, "The United States remains committed to ASEAN's central role as a regional forum for total cooperation...advancing security and prosperity for the US and all the Indo-Pacific Nations".[19] The US engagement in changing regional security architecture is reflected by the Indo-Pacific strategy formally released by President Donald Trump at the ASEAN-US summit in Vietnam in 2017. The heavy lifting by the major powers as the US, Japan, Australia, and India has for ASEAN members to define the strategy and be able to prowess power. Indonesia has proclaimed itself to be the maritime power with the upgrade of the ports and closer defense association with Australia. The US uncertain behaviour under the Trump administration has been driven by the inclusion of India as a major partner for the US policy in the region. General Jim Mattis at the Shangri La Dialog 2018 reaffirmed the US commitment, "America is in the Indo-Pacific to stay".[20]

Australia became the first dialog partner in 1974 to ASEAN and has continuous engagement with the regional organisation. ASEAN is closely associated with Australia providing engagement to East Asia and ensuring economic engagement, people-people ties. The middle power as Australia has actively expanded its presence in the Indo-Pacific of which ASEAN remains an important partner. For it, the ASEAN centrality represents the main anchor for its 'big-tent diplomacy' with the organisation offering access to the initiatives as the ASEAN Defense minister, East Asia Summit.[21] China economic integration in the region through the efforts as the OBOR (One Belt One Road) extends through the ASEAN states. The position of Australia is the strategy to avoid any closed groupings where the choice has to be made between the US and China. Australia wielding influence through the extra-regional offering as Quad has signaled greater role of Australia in the Indo-Pacific region but with cautious steps to maintain relations with China which are linked with interdependent trade ties.

Japan's special adviser to Prime Minister Shinzo Abe, Kentaro Sonoura, outlined Japan's foreign on Free and Open Indo-Pacific (FOIP) "How can we realise this strategy [connecting Mekong nations to broader Indo-Pacific] without the cooperation of ASEAN that connect the Indian and Pacific Oceans?"[22] (Robinson, 2018) Efforts by Japan are pushing for greater infrastructure projects, free trade connecting Asia to Africa with ASEAN as the fulcrum. The intensification of the efforts by the external powers in the region has pushed for the expanded role of ASEAN from a regional organisation to the forum for agenda setting and discussion on key issues. Japan has invested in the Mekong region which represents the least developed states of Cambodia, Myanmar, Laos, and Vietnam (CLMV) in ASEAN. The region has seen huge investment in the form of Lancang-Mekong cooperation with China investing in 130 developmental projects.[23] Japan's international Cooperation agency has funded infrastructure projects including "major port projects including Mozambique (Nacala), Oman (Duqm), India (Mumbai) and Myanmar (Yangon)" increasing Japan's expanse amidst China OBOR plan.[24]

The role India had envisaged in the Indo-Pacific development remains among the most important. It was in Indian Parliament in 2007 that Japanese PM Shinzo Abe outlined the vision for Indo-Pacific[25] as 'Confluence of the Two Seas', placing the prominence of India in the growth of the region. India's' view of the region has expanded with the inclusion of the Indo-Pacific in the wider ambit of its policies. Its policies and practices in the past decade hold East Asia vital to its foreign policy. Look East Policy (LEP) over time has become embedded in India's foreign policy, and subsequent government pursuing to achieve it. In this series, 'Look East' policy founded more focused approach under the 'Act East' policy in 2014. The economic partnership has enlarged to the political and security alliance. It prioritized a bigger role for India as an emerging 'Middle' power. During PM Narendra Modi's visit to Indonesia, the vision for the maritime order was pushed with strengthening security architecture in Indo-Pacific through the ASEAN-led mechanism.[26] India 'strategic partnership' with ASEAN is pushed through the 30 dialogue mechanism and seven ministerial forums providing the greater connection.[27] India's foreign policy regards ASEAN centrality through its institution, especially East Asia summit and Regional Comprehensive Economic Partnership (RCEP) for the Indo-Pacific.

ASEAN Institutions and Economic Development in the Indo-Pacific

ASEAN represents a dynamic economy with the trade reached $2.2 Trillion with 6.9 per cent of the world share[28] and estimated to be the fourth largest economy by 2050. Consideration of the notion of the centrality also arises from the development of ASEAN as a major economic destination attracting the partners. 'Economics is security' has driven the ASEAN efforts for the regional integration and expansion in the form of the Free Trade Area. Major economies as the US, China, Japan, Australia, and India are integrated with the regional economies. Inter-ASEAN Trade forms 76.9 per cent as compared to the 23.1 per cent of Intra-ASEAN trade in 2016 showing the close association economy of ASEAN states with major powers.[29] ASEAN led process by setting principles and call for more extensive economic interaction with 'FTA Partner' including China, South Korea, Japan, and India. The economic liberalisation and the expansion of the economy were forwarded with several initiatives such as East Asia Economic Caucus (EAEC) in 1991 initiated by Malaysian Prime Minister Mahathir Mohamad.[30] The economic engagement was propagated by the Asian financial crisis in 1997 which "paved the way for ASEAN+3 initiative forming the way for a functional platform for East Asia Cooperation".[31] Several studies groups were initiated for the growth of the economy such as East Asia Vision Group (EAVS) in 2001 that laid the integration of Southeast Asia into a single integrated market. The vision expanded into the free trade agreement of ASEAN with China in 2004, India in 2010, South Korea in 2007, and Japan in 2008, and with the US through US-ASEAN connect to network and US-ASEAN Trade and Investment Framework (TIFA).

Emphasis on the economic dynamism of the region has progressed despite the difference among the members. The economic integration efforts as the TPP (Trans-Pacific Regional Partnership), China's OBOR has emerged as a major challenge to the ASEAN efforts. ASEAN economic efforts forwarded with the Regional Comprehensive Economic Partnership (RCEP) was endorsed by ASEAN leaders in 2011 at the 19th ASEAN summit. In perspective, RCEP constituted by ASEAN states, China and India represent the major economies forming an integrated economic zone. In the economic sphere, the groupings present collective will of the member's states for economic development in the Indo-Pacific region. ASEAN has developed efforts at maintaining its centrality with the parallel connecting model of economic policies. ASEAN Economic Community (AEC) Blueprint 2025 aims for "reinforcing ASEAN Centrality in the emerging regional economic architecture by maintaining ASEAN's role as the center and facilitator of economic integration in the East Asian region."[32] Maintenance of the economic dynamism is the model for the emerging Indo-Pacific region where the ASEAN lies at the center of the economic activities.

The ASEAN Free Trade Area paved the way for the liberalisation of the economies and the development of trade with the external partners.

China's economic model is not only the prevailing economic plan, rather other external players have approached for the economic development of the region with interest for integrated market access. The ASEAN Master Plan for Connectivity (AMPC) connectivity to integrate Southeast Asia requires financial support beyond its capacity. China has provided major financial investment through OBOR in the infrastructure projects which is much required for the Southeast Asia region. However, China connectivity model is not the role model for the region; rather Japan's 'Quality Infrastructure investment' has offered connectivity with the Mekong region. The plan included the investment of $110 Billion in aid[33] for the quality infrastructure and development of the local jobs with the expertise of Japan's high-end technology. The plan was unveiled in 2015 with the China investing through the Asian Infrastructure Investment bank (AIIB) which has been dubbed as 'twin sister of OBOR'. Similarly, India's Act East policy and Blue Economy has initiated projects for the development of connectivity.[34] Australia an important partner of ASEAN is also not behind the other players and has pushed for the investment in improving connecting in ASEAN states. ASEAN-Australia-New Zealand economic integration has been established broadened the ASEAN economic community for comprehensive regional integration. The ASEAN centrality is important in the context of centrality and managing the Thailand-Laos rail connectivity, China-Thailand, China-Singapore connectivity projects directly linking China to mainland Southeast Asia. Southeast Asian scholars have noted that the OBOR integration plan for connecting the ASEAN states on a bilateral basis to China, undermines the single integration, i.e. ASEAN to Chinese effort.

China led institutional order has gained in prominence with major initiatives like the One Belt One Road (OBOR) in 2013 connecting land and the maritime route across Asia, Africa, and Europe with over 60 countries joining the plan with funding of $124 Billion in investment to generate economic development with the building of the infrastructure project. Silk Road runs across from Xi'an in China to Europe forming a large integrated area, while the maritime route connects the countries via oceans connecting Southeast Asia, Africa and extending to Latin America. The bandwagoning of the important allies of US including the UK, Australia, New Zealand in AIIB led by China despite the wariness of the US, depicted the apprehension of allies towards US unilateral action of economic withdrawal notably Trans-

Pacific Partnership (TPP). Indonesia has welcomed to form part of the maritime Silk Road with the development of the ports. The push for the economic integration in form of the ASEAN Economic Community apart from the driving economic growth by easing trade barriers is that "without economic integration, the centrifugal forces generated by China's expansion will at least loosen and may well destroy the nascent development of a Southeast Asia identity".[35]

Limitation of Consensus

The failure of the 2012 ASEAN summit to release a Joint communiqué on the South China Sea reflected the limitation of the consensus, the bedrock of ASEAN decision making process. Cambodia was influenced by China for avoiding the stand on the code of conduct operations in the sea lanes. The influence of the external powers is a prominent factor in shaping the ASEAN states with smaller states of CMLV dependent on China for economic development. The institutional capacity to deal with the sensitive territorial claims is limited and reflects the divergences among the ASEAN members. Some Southeast Asia scholar authors as Amitav Acharya and Bilahari Kausikan[36] have dubbed ASEAN Centrality as a 'myth' dependent on the major powers. Rohingya refugee crisis in Myanmar has witnessed the large-scale human rights violation and migration flow due to prosecution in recent times has highlighted the limitation within ASEAN to act on a member state. Myanmar clearly had confronted any efforts by ASEAN to interference in its internal matter citing the principle of noninterference in the sovereignty of member states called 'ASEAN Way'.[37] Concerning the matters of security, ASEAN agenda is dependent on the chair selected.[38] Ability to form a decision on the important issues as ethnic violence has led to the undermining of the credibility of ASEAN as an organisation among the members and external member states.

Security Dynamics in the Indo-Pacific and the Context of ASEAN Centrality

Post-Cold War period constituted the rise of China and India pursuing the economic liberalisation programs. The emergence of the Indo-Pacific narrative is the outcome of the changing power structure with China rise as the revisionist power working towards alerting the US-based security order. The region of East Asia and Southeast Asia has been marked by hostilities with the issues of the Taiwan Strait, the Korean peninsula, South China Sea resulting in a direct confrontation between the US and China. Several security issues have continued the extension of the Cold War period and new issues have been added to it. In this emerging scenario, the policies of the states have been revised to accommodate the changes.

On the security front, external powers are having a deeper engagement in the Southeast Asia region. The result is that the external issues affect more ASEAN states than internal. The composition of the ASEAN led initiatives is indicative of these changes as the EAS and ADMM Plus for discussion of the regional security issues. ASEAN has remained wary of discussing the topics concerning sovereignty, territorial position due to the limited capacity to resolve the issues. This is evidenced in the case of the South China Sea (SCS) where ASEAN states are claimants to the territory in SCS with China's aggressive stand on the territorial waters claiming a major portion of the sea.

South China Sea Issue and ASEAN Centrality

South China Sea (SCS) has become a flashpoint for the contestation between ASEAN states followed by the US allies and partners for the freedom of navigation. SCS lies at the strategic position enabling its position as a major international waterway with the passing of the important sea lane of commerce and holds a 'strategic position' connecting the Pacific Ocean and the Indian Ocean.[39]

ASEAN has often been referred to a consensus on the matter concerning South China where the China economic and security leverage have overshadowed their claims. One of the key ebb points was the 2012 ASEAN summit chaired by Cambodia, where the parties failed to reach a consensus and no summit declaration due to China's aggressive. The primary reason for the ASEAN position was the principle of 'consensus', 'sovereignty' where each party holds an equal position in the decision-making process. The argument of the ASEAN as a limited organisation limits the working of how the organisation was formed and its function. The role of the ASEAN as a multilateral regional forum expands beyond the claims of its limitation as a 'talkshop'. China-ASEAN CUES ('Code for Unplanned Encounters at Sea') is a major principle on the South China Sea; the agreement is non-binding with flexibility in the implementation. US and China agreed to the CUES in 2014 under the Western Naval Pacific Symposium held at Qingdao in China. On the basis of the earlier CUES agreement, ASEAN and China reached an understanding in 2016 at Singapore Summit on the issue of conflict in South

China agreed "to use the safety and communication procedures for the safety of all our naval ships and naval aircraft when they encounter each other in the South China Sea" (ASEAN Secretariat, 2016). The Annunciation of the CUES is not only pushed by ASEAN but also due to China's international position and its effect on the ASEAN as asserted by Chinese foreign minister Wang Yi, "China wants a framework for COC by 2017."[40] ADMM Plus represented by the defense ministers of the ASEAN states, regional and extra-regional powers as a multilateral forum for resolving disputes and forwarded the CUES agenda at the Singapore security summit.

India's rise as the major economy with large security apparatus in the Indian Ocean has carved its direct role in the affairs of the region. India has embarked on a closer engagement with ASEAN actively engaging itself through the various forums. It opened the door for the logistic support on the strategic Changi Naval Base in Singapore through which trade passes to East Asia. With Vietnam, it provided a defense line of Credit, apart from the cooperation with ASEAN in the non-traditional security issues as Cybersecurity, Counterterrorism. The 2018 visit of Indian Prime Minister Narendra Modi placed strategic weight on the maritime cooperation with the agreement of the Sabang port in Indonesia as the defense base.[41] The maritime strategy of encircling China is to counter the 'string of pearls' strategy which involves the heavy Chinese presence in the Indian Ocean with strategic seaport being constructed in various nations inclusive of Sri Lanka, Pakistan, and East Africa. The actions have drawn criticism from China which could ignite 'military race' and "it might wrongfully entrap into a strategic competition with China and burn its own fingers."[42] The concern arises from the fact that sea lanes of communication pass through the Strait of Malacca and India's presence have raised China's anxiety.

Convergence on Countering Terrorism has emerged with the rise of global terrorism. 2017 ASEAN "Comprehensive Plan of Action on Counter Terrorism" places the emphasis on a joint effort to address the spread of Terrorism and violent extremism.[43] The cooperation has strengthened with developing capabilities of ASEAN states of coordination, reconnaissance undertaking major operations. Major Powers including US, Australia, and China supported the Philippines during the ISIS attack on Marawi city. ASEAN Multilateral Naval exercise was conducted in November 2017. These exercises demonstrate changing agenda for the grouping where the economic program remains a key concern. It included the ASEAN states with the agenda of readiness, capacity building, and interoperability amidst the rising threat of terrorism in Southeast Asia. ASEAN is more integrated with the external issues, where the coordination with the external members helps in resolving the transnational security issues as Drug Trafficking, Piracy, and the Environmental change is vital to the Indo-Pacific region.

The convergence of the major power is also driven by the factor of maintenance of stability in the Southeast region with the convergence of the external powers as India, Australia, US, and Japan. Joint exercises forming of the Indonesia designation of itself as the 'global maritime power' reflects the shift amidst the uncertainty and the proactive role which Indonesia wants to play in Indo-Pacific. The proposal has been passed to other ASEAN states for consideration for the Indo-Pacific. However, the distinct reality of the Chinese presence in the region depicts the challenge of balancing the ASEAN position on security issues.

Conclusion

The role of ASEAN has changed dramatically from its original inception of maintaining intra-affairs to a global approach. As a regional organisation, ASEAN has successfully continued for over 50 years maintaining a zone of peace stability and conditions for development supported by external powers. The security guarantee ensured by the US in the region led to the thriving economy with the phrasing of 'Asian Tigers'. Rapid economic development along with the neutral status of ASEAN states provided a condition for the major powers to converge in ASEAN-led institutions. ARF inception for regional security provided an expansion to ASEAN activities and transformed it into a multilateral forum with the inclusion of major powers in it. ASEAN has pushed for the Free Trade Area with major powers resulting in a reduction of trade barriers and easing of policies for economic expansion. The conception of the ASEAN centrality drives from the ability of the ASEAN as an organisation to drive the regional activities and influence the global affairs. External powers have influenced ASEAN especially the Sino-US rivalry which is shaping the Indo-Pacific region with emerging powers like India, Australia, and Japan. China led institutional order in form of economic; security development is limiting the thrust of the ASEAN led institutions. Selective picking of ASEAN states has resulted in form limited consensus on the issue especially concerning sovereignty where the states are depended on China for economic assistance. Ability to exert influence with the strategic interest of securing lines of communication for the economy, security establishment in the Indo-Pacific with assertive actions is driving the security anxiety. US military buildup also poses a security threat to the ASEAN region affecting economic development due to the environment of uncertainty. The case represents the mismatch of the reality and the expectations, where the power of great powers is reality and the ASEAN prominent role in resolving those issues is seen as an expectation. Indo-Pacific region conception of a wide region encompasses beyond the ASEAN which lies at its center. ASEAN continues to provide the platform for discussion of security and economic issues, with the external players driving the strategic policy through the ASEAN-led institutions using its centrality.

NOTES

1 Kuo, M.A. (2018), The Origin of Indo-Pacific as Geo-Political Construct, The Diplomat, January 25 2018, available at https://thediplomat.com/2018/01/the-origin-of-indo-pacific-as-geopolitical-construct/

2 Kausikan, Bilhari (2016), "Dealing with an Ambiguous World Lecture III: ASEAN & US-China Competition in Southeast Asia", IPS Nathan Lecture Series, 30 March 2016, available at https://lkyspp.nus.edu.sg/docs/default-source/ips/mr-bilahari-kausikan-s-speech7d7b0a7b46bc6210a3aaff0100138661.pdf?sfvrsn=cec7680a_0

3 Mahapatra, C. (1990), *American Role in the Origin & Growth of ASEAN*, ABC Publication: New Delhi.

4 Zone of Peace, Freedom and Neutrality declaration on 27th November 1971.

5 Final declaration on application of the Code for Unplanned Encounters at Sea in the South China Sea, Published on 7 September, 2016, available at http://www.fmprc.gov.cn/nanhai/eng/zcfg_1/P020170413336454220678.pdf.

6 Anthony, MC. (2014), "Understanding ASEAN's Centrality: Bases and Prospects in an evolving regional architecture", *The Pacific Review*, Vol. 27(4): 563-584.

7 Acharya, A. (2017), "The Myth of ASEAN Centrality, Project Muse, Contemporary Southeast Asia: A Journal of International and Strategic Affairs", Vol. 39 (2), available at https://muse.jhu.edu/article/667776/pdf.

8 Kraft, H.J. (2011) eds., Driving East Asia Regionalism: the reconstruction of ASEAN'S Identity, in ASEAN and Institualization of East Asia, Chapter 4, Routledge Press.

9 Tzeing, H. (2016), "ASEAN Centrality: Alive and Kicking", RSIS Commentary Vol. 48, 29 February 2016.

10 Department of State (2010), America's engagement in the Asia-Pacific by Former Secretary of State Hillary Clinton, US Department of State Archives (2009-2017).

11 ADMM PLUS Declaration (2010), Hai Noi, 12th October 2010, ASEAN Secretariat Publication, available at https://admm.asean.org/dmdocuments/JointDeclaration-ADMM-Plus-101012.pdf.

12 Cronin, P. (2016), Power and order in the South China Sea, Center for New American Security, November 10, 2016.

13 Joint Statement of the ASEAN-Australia Special Summit: The Sydney Declaration, March 2018, available at http://asean.org/joint-statement-of-the-asean-australia-special-summit-the-sydney-declaration/

14 Two versions have emerged for shift in terminology; one is reflecting India's growing role and second is strategy to balance China. Lloyd Adducul, "The Indo-Pacific Construct in Australia's White Papers: Reflections for ASEAN-Australia Future Strategic Partnership", CRISS Paper March 2018.

15 Australia Ministry of Defense (2013), Defense White Paper 2013, Commonwealth of Australia.

16 The White House (2017), National Security Strategy of the United States of America, Published on December 2017.

17 Julie Bishop, Minister of Foreign Affairs Australia, ASEAN: The nexus of the Indo-Pacific, New York: 8 March 2018.

18 Kausikan, Bilahari (2016), *Dealing with an Ambiguous World*, World, Scientific Publications: Singapore.

19 White House (2017), President Donald Trump Remarks at 5th ASEAN-US Summit, Danang, Vietnam, available at https://www.whitehouse.gov/briefings-statements/remarks-president-trump-5th-u-s-asean-summit/

20 U.S. Department of Defense (2018), Secretary of Defense General Jim Mattis remarks at the Shangri-La Dialog, 2 June 2018.

21 Graham, E. (2017), "IS ASEAN Central to Australia?", *The Interpreter*, 20 August 2018, available at https://www.lowyinstitute.org/the-interpreter/asean-still-central-australia

22 Nikkei Asian Review, "Japan's Indo-Pacific push galvanizes Mekong region", March 29, 2018.

23 Kuock, L. (2018), Negotiating the Indo-Pacific Security Landscape: What the Shangri-La Dialog Tells Us, Brookings Publication, 8 June 2018.

24 Brewster, D. (201), "A Free and Open Indo-Pacific" and what it means for Australia, The Interpreter.

25 Speech was delivered at Indian Parliament in 2007, See Confluence of Two Seas, August 22 2007, available at https://www.mofa.go.jp/region/asia-paci/pmv0708/speech-2.html

26 PM Narendra Modi visit to Indonesia, 30 May 2018. Ministry of External Affairs Publication: New Delhi.

27 Hartig, K. (2018), "Japan-US-Australia Relations in the Emerging Indo-Pacific Regional System", Perth US Asia Center, 20 March, 2018.

28 ASEAN ranks fourth in trade after China, US, Germany. Trade Statistics 2016, ASEAN Secretariat Publication.

29 ASEAN Economic Community Chart book 2017, The ASEAN Secretariat Publication, Jakarta.

30 The idea was strongly objected by the U.S. for any East Asia integration plan being the important trading partner. However, the idea was formed in ASEAN+3 economic grouping. (Siu Gua, 2011, East Asia Regionalism: The Review of Original Idea of ASEAN+3 Concepts, Journal of International Development and Corporation).

31 Hong, Z. (2016), How ASEAN's vision can jive with China's belt and road initiative, *Strait Times*, March 30 2017 Singapore.

32 ASEAN Economic Community Blueprint 2025, The ASEAN Secretariat Publication,

November 2015, available at http://www.asean.org/storage/images/2015/November/aec-page/AEC-Blueprint-2025-FINAL.pdf.

33 Keihara, L and L. Sieg, Japan unveils $110 Billion plan to fund Asia infrastructure, eye on AIIB, *Reuters,* March 15 2015.

34 Jetin, B. (2017), "One-Belt One-Road Initiative "and ASEAN Connectivity: Synergy Issues and Potentialities, Institute of Asian Studies, Brunei Darussalam.

35 Ibid, n. 18.

36 Acharya, A. (2017), "The Myth of ASEAN Centrality?" *Contemporary Southeast Asia: A Journal of International and Strategic Affairs,* Vol. 39 (2): 273-279.

37 Tobing, D.H. (2018), "The Limits and Possibilities of the ASEAN Way: The Case of Rohingya as Humanitarian Issue in Southeast Asia", available at DOI: 10.18502/kss.v3i5.2331

38 Santikajaya, A. (2013), Challenges to ASEAN as an Indo-Pacific connector, East Asia Forum, available at http://www.eastasiaforum.org/2013/06/29/challenges-to-asean-as-an-indo-pacific-security-connector/

39 The Strait Times (2016), Remarks by Ambassador Bilahari Kausikan on 'Consensus, centrality and relevance: ASEAN and the South China Sea', 6 August 2016, available at https://www.straitstimes.com/opinion/consensus-centrality-and-relevance-asean-and-the-south-china-sea

40 Tan, S. (2017), Can the ADMM-Plus do CUES in the South China Sea?, Center for Strategic and International Studies(CSIS), Pacnet #78 Paper.

41 India has strategic port at Duqm Oman, Chabahar port Iran, Assumption Island Seychelles extending its position from East Africa to Indonesia.

42 Weijia, Hu (2018), Investment in Indonesia's Sabang Port will be test of India's diplomatic wisdom, Global Times, Beijing.

43 Joint declaration on Terrorism, EAS leaders' statement on countering ideological challenges of terrorism and terrorist narratives and propaganda, available at http://asean.org/storage/2012/05/3.-FINAL_EAS-Leaders-Statement-on-CT-14-Nov-2017.pdf/

11

Regionalism and Evolving Coalition Building in Indo-Pacific Region

Prerna Chahar

ABSTRACT

In the changing geostrategic reality, the 'Indo-Pacific' region have become a significant theatre of Great Power rivalry. Amid these change as the region has come to acquire a central role, it demands that the existing regional mechanisms are-evaluated, emerging traditional and non-traditional threats be recognised and the contemporary strategic demands be realised. Given the geostrategic and geoeconomic significance of the region along with growing traditional and non-traditional security threats have compelled states to rethink their national strategies, to build a more secure, and rule-based order in 'Indo-Pacific'. The nature of such threats having regional and global implications has resulted into the convergence of member states for mutual cooperation and collaborations on common issues at different bilateral, trilateral and, multilateral level. Recently, the revival of the Quadrilateral Security Dialogue is a significant initiative to address the emerging challenges of maritime security, connectivity, terrorism, piracy, etc.

This chapter aims to address four key areas to assess emerging challenges and opportunities of cooperation among different regional and sub-regional powers in the 'Indo-Pacific'. First section overviews the historic power shift, fast changing balance of power and convergence of regional and sub-regional powers in the Indo-Pacific. Secondly, it outlines the significance of term 'regionalism' as a concept and the resultant strategic architecture shaped by the emerging challenges and threats in the region. Thirdly, it analyses the recent revival of Quadrilateral arrangement and the future challenges and opportunities for the member countries. Lastly, amid the changing regional security arrangements in the region it examines the geostrategic imperative for country like India that is regarded as a 'linchpin' in the security architecture of the Indo-Pacific.

Introduction

With the onset of the 21st century and changing geostrategic landscape, the world is abuzz with the talk of 'Indo-Pacific'. Today, the focus has shifted from the 'Pacific-Atlantic' to 'Pacific-Indian' Ocean with the region acquiring notable significance as one of the most important geostrategic theatres of global politics. It is not an exclusive definite geographic region but rather characterised as a 'super-region' in which the sub-regions equally matter. The region has emerged in a new way to look at maritime Asia with geographical extension extending from East coast of Africa, across Indian Ocean to the Western and Central Pacific Ocean with its geostrategic and geoeconomic significance gaining fast momentum. The increasing importance is evident by the different geostrategic equations of major players in the region, like China's ambitious 'Maritime Silk Road', Japan's poetic expression of 'Confluence of the Two Seas' or *futatsu no umi no majiwari*,[1] India's shift from 'Look-East' to 'Act-East Policy' and United States 'Rebalance/Pivot to Asia' strategy. Australia's policy establishment is one step further to name the region 'Indo-Pacific' to suit its two ocean geography. Though the strategic and diplomatic equations may vary, yet small regional and sub-regional players is exploring and espousing for common 'Indo-Pacific' ideas.

The ideas and primacy of the region is driven by the huge energy demands, countries economic interest, respect for international law, lawful commerce and freedom of navigation. In past few decades as the regional trade has surged and commerce has multiplied manifolds, the 'Indo-Pacific' has come to be characterised as constituting one of the busiest and insecure sea lanes in the world. According to Pradeep Kaushiva and Abhijit Singh, regions vast natural resources, energy and international trade render the stability of the region critical as "the looming threat of maritime crime and environmental crises in the region make it an area of vital concern for maritime forces".[2] Thus, they argue that though the roots of new 'Indo-Pacific' might be economical, but the consequences are deeply complex and strategic.

The regional security environment has become much more complicated due to the assertive rise of China, increasing number of dissension over maritime boundary and territorial waters, coupled with emerging non-military threats like terrorism, piracy, climate change, drug trafficking, etc. Robert O'Neill, a special US warfare operator defines these non-military or non-traditional threats as "the problems of unintended chaos that are not the direct result of conscious policies by national government"[3] but that do have the potential to damage the domestic peace and economies. Hence, the current conundrum being played out amidst the newly emerging security threats and the immediate prospect of instability have compelled states to rethink their national strategies to build a more secure and rule-based order in Indo-Pacific. It presents valuable opportunity of cooperation and new discourse of convergence at different strategic levels and recognition of the benefits of peaceful cooperation at regional and sub-regional level. The strategic concerns have prompted the emergence of new partnership at bilateral, trilateral, quadrilateral and multilateral level. But the effective solutions as argued by many lies in flexible coalition of few.

One key factor that have acted as a key driving force behind the convergence and cooperation among regional and extra-regional countries is quintessentially the 'rise of China'. China's assertive military policies and steady expansion of footprints in the region have raised serious security concerns for the major regional actors in the region. It acts as both the influencer as well as the architect. China's growing clout in Indo-Pacific is likely to persist given it's over ambitious and belligerent outlook and therefore prompts new security partnership, mutual cooperation and collaborations among regional and external-regional powers for long-term security of the region.

Regional Perspective: Old Dilemmas and New Challenges

The Asia-Pacific region is fraught with animosities and historical rivalries since the time of imperialist period. Unfortunately, the animosities did not end with the Cold War and regional players continue to exhibit major differences and contradictions impacting the regional security as a whole. The change in strategic culture and geopolitical discourse from 'Asia-Pacific' to 'Indo-Pacific' further broadened the scope of 'regional security' in the region.

The emergence of 'Indo-Pacific' region as a strategic landscape can be best understood as a structural concept where regional security has been the main concern of nation states. The debate over broadening of the 'regional security' studies emerged post-Cold War, when the geostrategic environment changed and military confrontation between US and Russia seemed less prominent. Since the end of the Cold War period, the tempo of regionalism increased, and the region saw the emergence of new arrangements and strengthening of existing institutions shaping the new security order. The changed security order came to be characterised by increasing stress from the rise of China and its growing economic, military, and maritime power. Moreover, during the same time new kind of threats and risks started emerging which caught the attention of people around the world. Threats like terrorism, domestic violence, crime, environmental contamination, etc., became a major cause of concern for ensuring peace and stability within states. As states acknowledge that these threats are no more a national issue that can be dealt by state actors alone rather they are transnational in nature which requires collective response by countries in a more coordinated and concerted manner. It raised the need for a reordering of the regional security architecture and a growing contestation for the space for rule setting, creation of norms and cooperation among nation states. Hence, collective and cooperative bilateral, trilateral, multilateral and recently Quadrilateral framework emerged to maintain balanced regional security order in the region.

The Indo-Pacific region has become a new geostrategic theatre for Asia where the idea of 'new security order' has come to be defined in differently by different countries. According to President Trump, new security order signals strengthening 'Washington-Tokyo-New Delhi' partnership as a counter to the 'Beijing-Pyongyang-Islamabad' axis. For China it is more about establishing "illiberal hegemonic regional order at the expense of the liberal rules-based order"[4] by opening overseas military bases and ports and building its ambitious connectivity Belt and Road infrastructure. Australia and Japan tend to cooperate through involving in military exercises, interoperability, logistics and intelligence. And for India as an emerging swing power it is primarily interested in geoeconomics engagement of countries to sustain its economic growth, free movement of people, goods and services. But common to all countries concern is the rise of assertive China and its increasing security, economic and military threat in the 'Indo-Pacific' region.

China's demographic, economic and increasing defense expenditure with its 1.3 billion population, the status of the second largest economy in the world and the world's biggest exporter makes its rise unique in history. However, its ambitions as a rising state coupled with historical territorial grievances, land and maritime claims affecting other neighbors in the region are enough reasons why other countries need to be wary of its rise. Though the rise of China has benefited many regional countries economically, its increasing power projection in the region through bourgeoning military expenditure and modernisation have increased concerns among countries particularly for India, Japan, US, and small island nations. According to Saroj Bishoy, China follows the "periphery strategy that aims at developing good relationship with its East, South and Western neighbors".[5] Today, it's the largest trading and investment partner of all the regional economies. It is refocusing on its periphery through its 'One Belt, One Road' idea. Chinese scholars have argued that China is a major factor for ensuring peace, development, stability in the region and will not compromise with its territorial sovereignty at any cost.

The analysts from US, Japan, Australia, etc., are wary of it and disapprove of China's nationalist rhetoric and assertive foreign policy. The Chinese administration belligerent foreign policy approach can be observed through arbitrarily drawing of the nine-dash line in the South China Sea, forcibly occupying the Scarborough Shoal, raising tensions over the Senkaku in the East China Sea with Japan, stoking them further by declaring an Air Defence Identification Zone (ADIZ) and artificially building islands claiming it as a historical right. It has clearly altered the geoeconomic and geostrategic landscape of the region and rightly being characterised as a major 'destabilising 'factor in the region.

In the backdrop of the United States 'Rebalancing' strategy in the region, Chinese policy has become much more 'self-assertive'. It perceives the growing engagements of the United States with its regional partners as an attempt to contain China. Though America's presence is equally crucial in dealing with the emerging threats, many regional partners including Japan, Thailand, Philippines, Australia are suspicious of any positive support from the US considering its relative decline vis-à-vis China. Bishoyi (2016) notes that though "most of the US regional allies and partners welcome the US presence in the region in balancing China's growing economic and military assertions but at the same time they also constructively engage with China".[6] It is clear that despite the US still being the most powerful country, China has managed to carve out strategic space for itself by growing its military power and economic influence. Apart from the China factor, the region is beset with challenging non-traditional threats like piracy, terrorism, human trafficking, illicit arms, and drug trade, etc. These non-traditional security challenges have significant transnational implications that make regional and sub-regional cooperative response necessary. It is imperative that countries see regional and extra-regional cooperation as a solution to fix this regional flux.

The balance of power in the region is fast changing. The United States has been a security provider in the Indo-Pacific region nearly for three decades but its power is relatively declining vis-à-vis China. Chinese focus on increasing development and economic cooperation through Asian Infrastructure Investment Bank (AIIB), Chiang Mai Initiative, New Development Bank

(BRICS), regional countries do realise that apart from economic development issues, peace and stability of the region is in the larger interest of the nation. Most of the nation states have woken up to an emerging reality that China's 'peaceful rise' is no longer peaceful. China has begun to throw its weight about the South China Sea, South Asia, the East China Sea, and the Indian Ocean, and thus, not-so-quietly, new power configurations are emerging.

The changing balance of power in the Indo-Pacific is reflected in dynamic interactions among major players of the region like India, US, Japan, South Korea, Australia, New Zealand and the ASEAN. During the Cold War times, the region witnessed only a few bilateral security arrangements and the traditional multilateral security arrangements of cooperative and collective security nature could not find roots. The cooperation in the 'Asia-Pacific' came mainly from sub-regional groupings like ASEAN, SAARC, Economic Cooperation Organisation (ECO), and the Pacific Islands Forum. It was only in the 1990s that the regional security landscape initially being dominated by bilateral alliances came to work along with other multilateral institution and states realised that the region is made for 'multipolarity' or 'ad-hoc multilateralism', as it is too vast for hegemony to be sustained or successful.[7]

Hence, new equations and deeper regional and extra-regional convergence is visible among the countries in the Indo-Pacific. In this regard, the revival of Quad along with existing regional and extra-regional organisations like the ASEAN Defence Ministers Meeting Plus (ADMM Plus), the East Asia Summit (EAS), ASEAN Regional Forum (ARF) are some regional mechanisms that continue to shape the strategic landscape of the Indo-Pacific. Apart from these arrangements the region consists of number of sub-regional groupings like the Asia Pacific Economic Cooperation (APEC), the Bay of Bengal Initiative for Multi-Sectoral Technical and Economic Cooperation (BIMSTEC), the Mekong-Ganga Cooperation, the Indian Ocean Rim Association (IORA), the Shanghai Cooperation Organisation (SCO), and the Australia, New Zealand, United States Security Treaty (ANZUS). The rapid economic growth in the region too resulted in the emergence of a bilateral economic partnership between Australia-New Zealand, the US-Japan, the Japan-India, the Japan-Singapore, and Singapore-New Zealand. The region views them as potential platforms for dialogue towards ensuring stability in the region. Moreover, for ensuring deeper maritime security countries cooperate through joint military exercise (RIMPAC, MALABAR) and biennial meetings (Indian Ocean Naval Symposium) that have recently received growing attention amidst the rise of belligerent China and are perceived as catalysts of 'change' and 'stability' in the Indo-Pacific. Thus, the regional architecture today is shaped by the interweaving of multiple dyads, triads, quad, and multilateral regional & sub-regional arrangements to ensure that security and peace of the Indo-Pacific continue to prevail amid the newly emerging challenges and threats.

The Emerging Security Architecture: Avoiding Strategic Hubris

Due to the changing geoeconomic and geostrategic discourse of the region, the idea of 'regionalism' and 'regional security arrangement' has emerged as a dominant feature. With the end of the Cold War, the bipolar world also came to an end and the concept of 'regionalism' acquired prominence among the strategic thinkers, business people, academic literature and policy-makers. In the Asia-Pacific region, in particular, emerged contesting perspectives on what defines 'regional goals, regional interests, and regional membership'. The idea of 'regionalism' remained highly contested and week concept as there existed some sub-regional groupings, but no region-wide grouping with uncontested goals. Today, we witness no definite 'regional security' arrangement but what exists is multiple regional arrangements at different scales shaping the regional strategic architecture of the region.

Regionalism can be conceptualised as formal or informal, multidimensional (strategic, political, economic) that "reflect and shape the strategies of governments, business corporations, non-governmental organisations, private sectors in three or more contiguous countries for mutual gains" (Alagappa, 1994; Katzenstein, 2000).[8] According to Dennis Rumley (2005), regionalism functions as, "An appropriate organising unit for international cooperation at a scale between unworkable global schemes and unsatisfactory national approaches…it can be seen as possessing an intermediary role between narrowly-defined nationalism and overly-broad globalism".[9] Furthermore, he argues that in the 21st Century, the challenges concerning human survival, economic and national development do require states and other stakeholders to cooperate and converge at the regional level. The cooperation in the region is also visible due to the availability of the rich regional resources and the intent to exploit these resources to meet member nation energy demands.

Rodrigo Tavares argues that regional organisations offer a real comparative advantage.[10] The benefits of regional connections and cooperation lead to 'greater understanding of the challenges' and result in 'fruitful dialogue' among the leaders because it is based on mutual trust and respect. It not only benefits in security terms by offering a timely response to overcome vital challenges and preserving regional stability it also benefits participating countries economically to expand their existing industries and domestic markets.[11] Hence, scholars call for regional and sub-regional countries to democratise security and establish their brand of 'new-new regionalism'[12] that can act as a vehicle for long-term regional security, stability and identity in Indo-Pacific.

Given the vastness of the region with different competitive and convergent interests, cooperation between central countries in form of new groupings and alliances is nothing but natural. US National Security Strategy report (2017) notes "the Association of Southeast Asian Nations (ASEAN) and Asia-Pacific Economic Cooperation (APEC) remain centerpieces of the Indo-Pacific's regional architecture and platforms for promoting an order based on freedom".[13] But the region which is the most turbulent regions of the world have had a limited history of security cooperation in the past. Today, the major geostrategic shifts in the region call for the emergence of strategic architecture in the region that is not constrained or shaped by any one country.

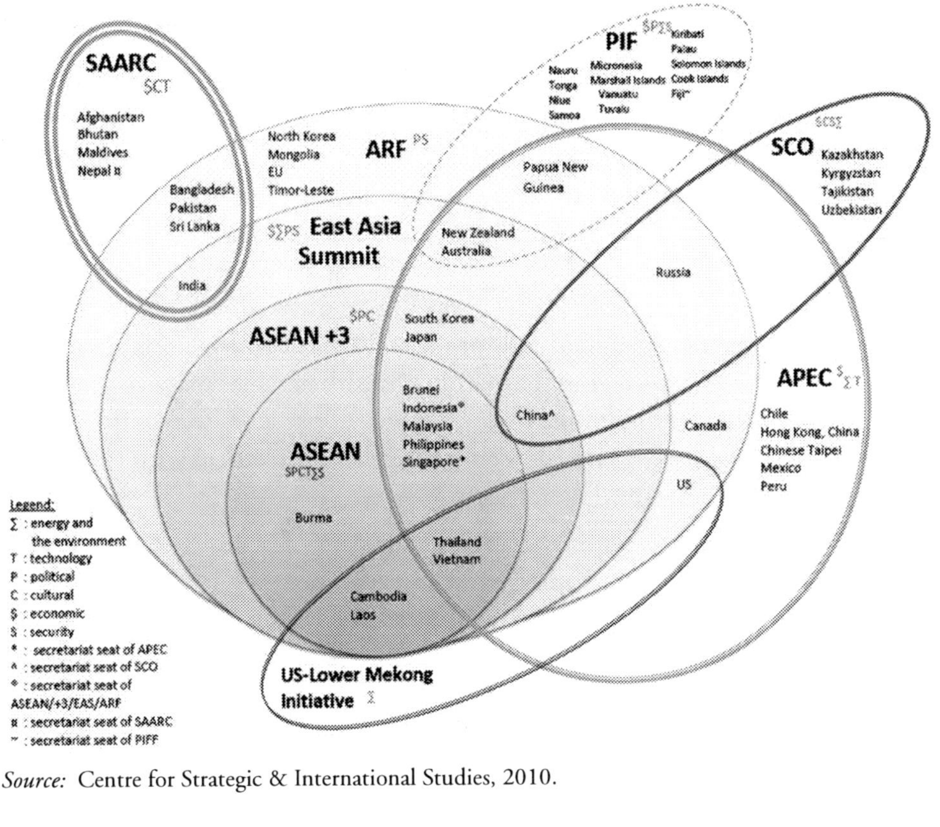

Source: Centre for Strategic & International Studies, 2010.

This raises some important questions as to what the future security architecture of the region should be? How do the various approaches to regional order relate to each other? Are they inherently competitive, or mutually exclusive, as many scholars would claim? For example, a debate in international relations theory and practice persists as to whether the interest in multilateralism could lead to the eventual supplanting of bilateral arrangements. Although some scholars have pointed to fundamental tensions between bilateral security alliances and multilateral institutions, others find them complementary. For long, bilateral alliances between the US and regional states dominated the security architecture but today there exists multiple layers of comprehensive and cooperative security approaches entwined with one another.

In the contemporary scenario, no single regional arrangement can be said to have the best hint of success. Apart from building an effective multilateral security cooperation framework (as it is always difficult to bring parties on building any immediate consensus), bilateral relations have once again gained prominence. William T. Tow argue for long time bilateral alliances have been successful in the region and will continue to remain the relevant and viable option of building cooperation in the region. According to him, the advantage bilateral alliance have is that they are already well established in the region and compared to multilateral security framework faceless contradictions. Apart from bilateral dialogues combinations of arrangement can help in building a new strategic arrangement to maintain stability and balance. This includes the formation of a trilateral dialogue between defense officials from the Australia, Japan, and the US, the newly emerging 'Paris-Delhi-Canberra' axis, re-emergence of Quad, military exercises among different member states, etc. The countries should partner with other regional or sub-regional parties on the issue by issue basis to build an ad-hoc multilateral security cooperation. According to Ron Huisken, the major regional approaches to security present today can best be summarised as "self-help, bilateral alliances with the United States, and a dash of multilateralism".[14]

William T. Tow argues the region consists of a "loose and complex patchwork of bilateral and multilateral arrangements that reflect primarily realist approaches to regional security supplemented by liberal and constructivist features".[15] According to him, the region is witnessing a "judicious mix of realist and liberal strategies," i.e. combining bilateral alliances and multilateral institutions, which he refer as 'convergent security' architecture.[16] The convergent security concept accepts the realist principle of the centrality of state interests but also promotes the liberal principle of co-operation. The concept connotes that any regional mechanism should focus on meeting aims rather than countering any specific threats. In this respect, he argues that alliances should go beyond mere deterrence of threats to the broader concern of establishing and maintaining a new regional order by including all the key players in the region especially China. To note United States historian Walter Russell Mead's preferred prescription, "while there can be no containment of China, there can be no hegemonic domination of Asia by China either".[17] Scholars like Hemant Krishan Singh and Sanjay Pulipaka (2013) argues that China's interest lies in realising "the inevitability of Asian multi-polarity and in joining hands with the US, India, Japan and ASEAN to reinvigorate efforts to advance a rule-based and balanced multilateral security architecture through the East Asia Summit (EAS) process".[18]

The emergence of Quad and its future success too should be seen in the light of this concept, where containing China should be regarded only as a 'crucial' factor but not a 'central' one. The emergence of the Quad as a dominant block is viewed as new power equilibrium in Asia that can change the contours of existing power relations. Many analysts, however, are critical of Quad's future course as no country in the region will be willing to be caught in a crossfire between the member countries on the one hand and China on the other. If the rebirth of Quad is seen to contain assertive China, then just being in its nascent stage it is bound to face challenges in the future.

The Quad Redux: Future Challenges and Opportunities

In the last decade, major geostrategic shifts resulted in the establishment of Quadrilateral Security Dialogue between mid-level foreign ministry officials of Australia, India, Japan and United State on sidelines of the ASEAN Regional Forum (ARF) in 2007. However, amid misgivings from the partner nation's foreign policy establishments, especially the reluctance from Canberra, changes in political circumstances, and most importantly protests from China, the initiative soon withered.

The revival of Quadrilateral Security Initiative (QSI) in Manila on the margins of ASEAN's East Asia Summit (EAS) 2017 got a new lease of life. Its member countries including Australia, India, Japan, and the USA committed to "free, open, prosperous, inclusive and rule-based order" in the Indo-Pacific region. The Quad countries sharing democratic values are more importantly driven by the common security concerns like the desire for maintaining freedom of navigation, enhancing connectivity, strategic balance, maritime security, respect for the international law but most importantly China's assertive maritime strategy. Its increasing aggression in the region offered unique concerns to Quad countries. Jesse Barker Gale (2018) points out some of the common concerns among member countries that led to the revitalisation of Quad initiative. He states,

> "Australia is concerned about Chinese interference in domestic politics and higher education…India fears encroachment on its zone of strategic interest as well as encirclement from Chinese projects in Pakistan…Japan is wary of China's ability to influence the energy supply chains on which East Asia depends…and the United States is seeking a way to counteract Chinese influence, particularly in the vacuum left by U.S. withdrawal from the TPP".[19]

The Quadrilateral arrangement among the member countries sharing common interests, values challenges and concerns is perceived as timely and necessary. It is regarded as a stabilising factor by deterring the use of force by any powerful country in order to ensure regional stability and balance in the region. According to Shyam Saran, Quadrilateral arrangement can be "the anchor for the Indo-Pacific with ASEAN centrality playing an indispensable role in regional security and making easier for ASEAN countries to accept the Indo-Pacific construct".[20] Moreover, the US President Donald Trump to calls for 'new security order' by strengthening 'Washington-Tokyo-New Delhi' partnership as a counter to the 'Beijing-Pyongyang-Islamabad' axis in the region. Hence, Quad is viewed as a dominant block and as a new power equilibrium that can change the contours of existing power relations in the Indo-Pacific region. Critics argue that the revival of Quadrilateral Security Initiative (Quad) is nothing but merely another extension of great-power rivalries occurring at the expense of the interests of ASEAN.[21] Looking ahead, the road for Quadrilateral dialogue is not devoid of challenges given the deep divisions and interest the countries has vis-à-vis China. Firstly, there has been no consensus or any joint statement with respect to the future vision of Quad. Analysts have argued that the rise of assertive China and its impact on Asian security was the driving reason for proposing the Quad arrangement. However, according to analysts China is not an important driver for the Quadrilateral initiative and arguably should not be, but it has definitely been a 'crucial' one. While China's concerns are central to the Quad members, it need not project the Quad as an anti-China group. If Quad is equated with China, there will be no purpose solved, and there are many chances of China being much more assertive in its foreign policy as happened in the past concerning US 'Asia-Pivot' policy.

Secondly, Quad as a strategic arrangement can still be successful but as an economic arrangement it cannot give the extensive economic trade ties the countries share with China. While security wise the countries have often perceived China as a challenge, economically it has often been seen as an opportunity. The countries might have differences and disputes with Beijing on economic issues, but each has also benefited from China's growth, albeit to different degrees. Tai Wei Lim argues, "when it comes to China and the Quad, the ASEAN and other regional countries are caught in the middle of this great power tug-of-war...Malaysia, Vietnam, Laos, and Cambodia are drawing closer to China economically, and the Philippines replaced the pro-Western Aquino administration with that of the Beijing-friendly strongman Rodrigo Duterte".[22] Therefore, he suggests that the Quad countries should aim at a policy of 'engaging' rather than 'containing' China.

Third, when it comes to fruition, analysts compare the Quadrilateral arrangement with NATO, which managed to keep "Russia out, the United States in and Germany down". If Quad have to be effective, rather then keeping its sole purpose to contain China, it should simultaneously focus on three other requirements, keep "China out, United States in and Japan down", which is currently not possible given the Great-Power rivalry game being played out in the region.[23]

Fourth, Quad countries cannot take United States action for granted given the unpredictable and uncertain nature of the administration under the Trump Presidency. The United States, the most powerful among all the countries of the Quadrilateral arrangement will have to ensure that it maintains its forward presence in the region through effective regional engagement and playing a key role in any regional strategy. If not, then other countries like India, Australia, Japan, and Indonesia should come together and convert this uncertainty as an opportunity to reshape the regional order.

Lastly, in the broader region as part of regional groupings, the Quad member countries are not part of any similar groupings. For example, in terms of the developing regional trade architecture, India is not a member of Asia-Pacific Economic Cooperation (APEC) while the US is not a member of the Regional Comprehensive Economic Partnership (RCEP). In terms of financing initiatives, Japan and the US are not members of the Asian Infrastructure Investment Bank (AIIB), while only India is a member of the New

Development Bank (NDB). In terms of regional connectivity side, India is highly skeptical of China's 'One Belt One Road' (OBOR).[24]

History has shown us time and again, the rise or dominance of any single power is always accompanied by the convergence of other powers in the region. Quad is one such convergence of power which can be regarded as a geopolitical move mainly to contain China's increasing prominence and bourgeoning military expenditure in the region. But the Quad is just a baby-step to counter any Chinese actions. According to Chinese Foreign Minister, Wang Yi "it as an attention-grabbing idea that would dissipate like the ocean foam". The idea of dissipating "like the ocean foam" or it has the potential of becoming a "powerful wave of resistance"[25] will finally depend on Quad countries and the path China chooses to traverse. Quad itself may not deliver the desired results and might lead to more assertive behaviour of China, but it is unquestionably an indication that countries are willing to be part of the common forum to maintain peace and maritime security in the region. Quad though regarded as baby-step can be a game changer. Its revival is a positive signal that shows countries willingness to work in a coordinated and cooperative manner.

However, amid the uncertainty of American policies and Chinese aggression, the Quadrilateral arrangement cannot be the only mechanism for ensuring regional security and balance. There is adequate room to strengthen the existing institution as well as for the other crucial pillars of 'multi-track' regional and extra-regional arrangements to work in symphony in order to establish long-term 'regional trust, norms and rule-based order' in the region. The major players in the region should perceive these threats alike and be akin to resolving the emerging challenges as they best know the local conditions, cultural values and conflict situations in the region than outsiders.

Geostrategic Imperatives for India

India's strategic location with a vast coastline, islands, bases, deployments, and economic development place India at the center of the 'Indo-Pacific' construct. According to the United States, India is a 'linchpin' to the regional security. Without India's 'economic growth' and 'expanded influence in the region this construct cannot be realised'.[26]

As an emerging 'swing power',[27] India is primarily interested in geoeconomics engagement with countries to sustain its "growth and development" in the region. It pursues a strategic partnership with the US, and despite having a long border dispute with China, have participated in

Chinese-led initiatives like the Shanghai Cooperation Organisation (SCO) and the Asia Infrastructure Investment Bank (AIIB). Its relation with countries of the region is also not new. India's traditional relationship continues since the early 1990s through 'Look East Policy', and recently the relationship revived under the Modi government through 'Act East Policy'. The Indian government has not officially enunciated any formal doctrine but the desire and actions have mostly been in the direction of free movement of investments, people, goods and services in the region. It has economic, defense, politico-diplomatic and strategic partnership with a number of countries at different levels. It has a bilateral relationship of 'strategic partnerships' level with countries like Australia, China, Indonesia, Japan, South Korea, and Vietnam. India also has security cooperation with countries like Indonesia, Japan, Sri Lanka, Vietnam, Philippines, Malaysia, etc. It maintains its multilateral circles of engagement through ASEAN, BRICS, and the Bay of Bengal Initiative for Multi-Sectoral Technical and Economic Cooperation (BIMSTEC), Indian Ocean Rim Association (IORA) and recently through revived Quadrilateral arrangement and gaining membership in SCO (Shanghai Cooperation Organisation). It gives India a platform with a high degree of flexibility, strategic autonomy and leverage vis-à-vis major powers in the region.

India's further successful integration would require reform in many of its trade and investment policy; renewed foreign policy and diplomatic strategy, and commitment to its maritime interests and global multilateralism. Nitin Pai, notes "to safeguard its interests, New Delhi has moved from being a passive ringside observer of East Asian multilateralism in the 1990s to an active, if conservative, contributor the balance of power".[28] Currently, India is part of many regional and sub-regional groupings and engage in regular dialogues and processes. On a bilateral level, the India-US have convergence on many issues especially when it comes to containing China and countering nuclear and terrorist threat perception from Afghanistan and Pakistan. India is also overcoming its military isolation trends and engaging in trilateral defense exercises with Japan and US, RIMPAC, ADMM+8. It seems the East Asia Summit and the ADMM Plus fora as the principal high tables of Indo-Pacific diplomacy. India led Indo-Pacific order through Indian Ocean naval Symposium and IOR-ARC must extend beyond and include other maritime security partners like Japan, Indonesia, Philippines, and Malaysia to take full advantage of its geographical location and extend its influence. Quad, a collective security framework of democratic countries that includes India is an important opportunity for India to raise its stakes in the region that is long enjoyed by other countries. Hence, India is an indispensable country in the region that "will continue to demonstrate its credibility through joint military exercises, patrolling, port calls, anti-piracy missions and humanitarian missions. It remains to be seen if such measures will be perceived as credible enough by the countries of the region, especially in the backdrop of China's assertive rise"[29] (Pai, 2016).

India has a proactive role to play in the Indo-Pacific given its geostrategic location and ties with strategic partners in the region. But the main concern for India as a 'rising power' is China's growing clout &military influence in the region. China's surge in military expenditure and its rapidly developing economic relationship with key countries of the region regarded as the "string of pearls" strategy pose a serious threat to India. It has not only developed an assertive maritime strategy but it also aims to dominate the region by increasing its influence through funding infrastructure projects like building Gwadar and Hambantota port in Pakistan and Sri Lanka respectively. China argues that these projects will help in increasing connectivity and will be used for varied commercial purposes. However, strategists like Suresh Mehta argue, that apart from commercial purposes, these infrastructure projects "have considerable scope for military applications". Furthermore, he notes "China's ability to put India under strain in the Indian Ocean is a growing factor shaping the broader dynamic of Asian security."[30] Apart from China, India also faces challenges from the rising non-traditional security threats, Great Power competition, and maritime boundary claims. India is aware of the fact that any neglect on its front in the maritime domain can cost its political sovereignty and economic interests. Hence, in order to successfully handle the challenges, India aims "to encourage and participate in cooperative approach which would enable all countries in the region to counter traditional and non-traditional security challenges and ensure that the critical sea lanes are kept open, secure and free for navigation and trade".[31]

India is one of the key players that has created significant geostrategic space for itself and has developed its own comprehensive strategy to promote its foreign policy interest in the region. It has developed its own way of multidirectional engagement and cooperation with regional and sub-regional countries in the region to respond to the challenges and protect its interests. It should continue to play an important role in regional institutions and acts as a key player in the rule-making process, failing to which can affect its long-term strategic interests and give China more strategic and economic space in the region.

India needs to come up at the center stage and take up leadership role by moving one step further in building economic cooperation, people to people exchanges, increase connectivity and capacity building with North East, South East Asia, and East Asian countries. It should try to exhibit more maturity and flexibility given the safety, security and national interest of the country in the region. This will increase India's commitment to its 'Act East' slogan and further extend its outreach to ASEAN nations. Its emergence as a 'pan-Asian power', as evidenced by its willingness to be a 'net provider of security' in the region, will definitely have a significant influence on the evolving architecture of security co-operation in the region.[32] Given the complex nature and acute competitiveness in Indo-Pacific, India should follow the policy of inclusive co-existence and work closely with other powers like Japan, China, and Australia at bilateral level, participate in trilateral engagements and intensify trade relation through mini-lateral collaboration with small island nations and like-minded countries to diversify their trade and reduce dependence on China. India should be ready to walk the new talk. It should not yield to any specific countries demand rather should focus on the inclusive approach of developing its relations with multiple countries with the main focus on its neighborhood policy.

Conclusion

The 'Indo-Pacific' strategic landscape has unfolded as the new 'power-zone' of the geopolitical system. Though the region always had a limited history of security cooperation the current strategic scenario of the region is varied and complex. The changing strategic landscape call for regional security architecture that aims to address constructively the emerging challenges and threats in the region. Thus, it requires the creation of fora and institutions that help bridge differences and creates an architecture which promotes peace, stability, and economic prosperity. Today, the regional security architecture can be viewed as the interweaving of unilateral military policies, bilateral arrangements, trilateral maritime exercises, multilateral organisations, and recently the redux of the Quadrilateral alliance. The regional security architecture of the Indo-Pacific is not for the development of any one single mechanism but it aims to create an 'ad-hoc' multilateral security cooperation framework based on cooperation among regional states. That is apart from the multilateral framework, bilateral mechanisms between countries like India-China, India-US, US-Japan, Japan-South Korea, US-South Korea, and India-China be strengthened to cooperate on multiple levels on the issue by issue basis.

Major regional players should remember that the security challenges the region is facing are distinctive, therefore their solutions should be distinctive as well to address the unique regional issues. An effective regional strategic architecture will require local cooperation and constructive engagement from countries in the region and beyond the region. The development of security mechanisms must not obscure the need to assure that an overall balance of power remains. The revival of the Quadrilateral Security Dialogue (Quad) is a significant step to ensure a strategic balance in the region. However, the Quad initiative being in its nascent stage and given the uncertainties in the region its potential future cannot be predicted. It is more of a security-oriented alignment that raises questions as to what broader cooperation on different strategic and economic front is feasible given different priorities and stakes for the four countries. It is a timely and necessary arrangement, but there is a need for the other crucial pillars of regional stability to play a secure and balanced role in the Indo-Pacific. It is imperative that main actors and institutions like Australia, China, Japan, India, US, and ASEAN come together to define a common 'rule-based' order that is not dictated by any one player in the region. China is a profound player in the region and should understand that it cannot continue with its assertive foreign policy in the region. Rather, it should be playing a key role along with other regional countries in defining 'new security architecture' and 'rule-based' order in the region.

Concerning China there exists pessimism and containing China is a strategic rationale but it should not be pushed to such a corner that might result in severe strategic confrontation. Many countries do share close economic relations with China, instead of side-lining China consensus must be built and groupings must try to accommodate China. Apart from the China factor, the region beyond doubt will continue to face different non-traditional security challenges and threats. The commitment from major actors in the region should be greater readiness and cooperation in building consensus among rival states. Due to political tensions or mistrust among countries in the Indo-Pacific, finding a common path and reaching for consensus will be difficult. But the success of any regional architecture will require a stable grouping among the countries and institutions based on collaborative efforts, clear goals, common principles, and governing standards.

Lastly, for long-term stability and peace, following considerations should guide any future convergence among the countries in the region; First, 'developmental' aspect combined with a system of 'rules and mutual respect' should be the priority of any regional arrangement. Second, there is a need to 'strengthen' the existing institutions like ASEAN for better cooperation in the region by including countries like Japan and India in the forum. Third, the regional countries should look 'beyond sub-regions' i.e. the process of cooperation and integration should be 'outward-looking'. For example, the recently talked about 'Paris-Delhi-Canberra' axis by French President Macron to respond to challenges in the region is a welcome step. Countries in the region should now be accommodative with the fact that the regional affairs have undergone tremendous changes and the existing and emerging institutions have to embed these changes. The onus lies on the emerging economies in the region to shape multilateralism and its institutions with the aim of forging more concentrated and stable democratise security process that has the potential to facilitate long-term regional stability, promote security and enhance economic integration by overcoming any of the existing misconceptions.

NOTES

1 Medcalf, Rory (2013), "The Indo-Pacific: Whats in a Name", *Brookings,* 10 October, 2013.

2 Kaushiva, Pradeep and Abhijit Singh (eds.) (2014), *GeoPolitics of the Indo-Pacific,* New Delhi, Knowledge World.

3 Roy, Denny (1997), *The New Security Agenda in the Asia-Pacific Region,* UK, Macmillan Press.

4 Chellany, Brahma (2008), "A New Order for the Indo-Pacific", *Project Syndicate,* March 11, 2008.

5 Bishoyi, Saroj (2016), "Geostrategic Imperative of the Indo-Pacific Region", *Institute for Defence Studies and Analysis,* March 2016, pp. 89-102.

6 Ibid.

7 Mahapatra, Chintamani (2017), "India and Shifting Power Equations in the Indo-Pacific", *Indian Foreign Affairs Journal,* June 2017, 12(2), pp. 93-118.

8 Alagappa, M. (1994), "Regionalism and Conflict Management: A Framework for Analysis", *Review of International Studies,* 21, pp. 359-387; Katzenstein, P. J. (2000), "Regionalism and Asia", *New Political Economy,*5 (3), pp. 353-368.

9 Rumley, Dennis (2005), "The Geopolitics of Asia-Pacific Regionalism in the 21stCentury", *The Otemon Journal of Australian Studies,* 31, pp. 5-27.

10 Tavares, Rodrigo (2008), "Understanding Regional Peace and Security: A Framework of Analysis", *Contemporary Politics,* 14 (2), pp. 107–27.

11 Pitsuwan, Surin (2011), "ASEAN Taming the Cycle of Conflict and Misery", *The Jakarta Post,* May 3, 2011.

12 Rumley, Dennis (2005), "The Geopolitics of Asia-Pacific Regionalism in the 21st Century", *The Otemon Journal of Australian Studies,* 31, pp. 5-27,

13 United States National Security Strategy (2017), "The Strategy in Regional Context", *NSS,* pp. 46.

14 Ron Huisken, "Accelerating the Evolutionary Process of Security Cooperation in the Asia-Pacific: An Australian Perspective," in See Seng Tan, Amitav Acharya, "*Asia-Pacific Security Cooperation: National Interests and Regional Order*", 2004.

15 William T. Tow, "Convergent Security Revisited: Reconciling Bilateral and Multilateral Security Approaches," in See Seng Tan, Amitav Acharya, "*Asia-Pacific Security Cooperation: National Interests and Regional Order*", 2004.

16 Ibid.

17 Subramanian, Nirupama and Arvind Sivaramakrishnan and Raghuvir Srinivasan Interview Walter Russell Mead, "Nobody shares Pakistan's vision for Afghanistan," *The Hindu,* 24 August 2012.

18 Singh, Hemant Krishan and Sanjay Pulipaka (eds) (2013), "Asia's Arc of Advantage: India, ASEAN and the US: Shaping Asian Architecture", New Delhi: ICRIER, August 2013.

19 Gale, Jesse Barker (2018), CSIS Brief, "The Quadrilateral Security Dialogue and the Maritime Silk Road Initiative" *Centre for Strategic & International Studies,* 2 April 2018.

20 Saran, Shyam (2018) "Quad can be the anchor for the Indo-Pacific region", *Hindustan Times,* 29 June 2108.

21 Saha, Premesha (2018), "The Quad in the Indo-Pacific: Why ASEAN remains cautious", *Observer Research Foundation,* 26 February 2018.

22 Lim,Tai Wei (2018), "China and the Quad: Challenges for Southeast Asia", *Asia Global Online,* 10 May 2018.

23 Sidhu, W.P.S. (2017), "The emerging Indo-Pacific architecture," *Livemint,* 20 November 2017.

24 Madan, Tanvi (2017) "Economic Cooperation among the Quad (Plus) Countries: Limits and Possibilities," *Quad Plus Dialogue, Brookings Institution,* 28 March, 2017.

25 Saran, Shyam (2018), "Quad can be the anchor for the Indo-Pacific region", *Hindustan Times,* June 29, 2108.

26 L. Gordon Flake et al. (2017), "Realising the Indo-Pacific: Tasks for India's Regional integration", Perth US Asia Centre at The University of Western Australia, June, 2017.

27 Henry Kissinger, *The White House Years,* Simon & Schuster, New York, 1979, p. 712.

28 Pai, Nitin (2017), "India and the Indo-Pacific Balance of Power", *Indian National Interest,* 1 August 2017.

29 Pai, Nitin (2016), "India and the Indo-Pacific Balance" in David Brewster (ed), "Indo-Pacific Maritime Security: Challenges and Cooperation", *Australia National Security,* July 2016, p. 86.

30 Mehta, Suresh (2014), 'The Indo-Pacific Imperative', in Pradeep Kaushiva and Abhijit Singh (eds), *Geopolitics of the Indo-Pacific,* New Delhi: KW Publishers Pvt. Ltd, p. 3.

31 Ministry of Defence, *Annual Report 2010–11,* p. 4, New Delhi: MoD.

32 PM's Speech at the Foundation Stone Laying Ceremony for the Indian National Defence University at Gurgaon," *Prime Minister's Office, Government of India,* 23 May 2013.

REFRENCES
(*indicates Primary Source)

Alagappa, M. (1994), "Regionalism and conflict management: a framework for analysis", *Review of International Studies,* Vol. 21, pp. 359-387.

Bishoyi, Saroj (2015), "Geostrategic Imperative of the Indo-Pacific Region", *Institute for Defence Studies and Analysis,* March 2016, pp. 89-102, available at https://idsa.in/system/files/jds/jds_10_1_2015_geostrategic-imperative-of-the-indo-pacific-region.pdf

Brewster, David (ed), "Indo-Pacific Maritime Security: Challenges and Cooperation", *Australian National Security,* July 2016, available at http://takshashila.org.in/wp-content/uploads/2016/08/Indo-Pacific-Maritime-Security-Challenges-Cooperation-final.pdf

Chellany, Brahma (2008), "A New Order for the Indo-Pacific", *Project Syndicate,* March 11, 2008, available at https://chellaney.net/2018/03/11/a-new-order-for-the-indo-pacific/

Dunne, T. and N. Wheeler (2004), "'We the People' contending discourse on security in human rights. theory and practise" *International Relations,* 18 (9), p. 11.

Gale, Jesse Barker (2018), CSIS Brief, "The Quadrilateral Security Dialogue and the Maritime Silk Road Initiative" *Centre for Strategic & International Studies,* April 2, 2018, available at https://www.csis.org/analysis/quadrilateral-security-dialogue-and-maritime-silk-road-initiative

Henry Kissinger, (1979), *The White House Years,* Simon & Schuster, New York, 1979, p. 712.

Katzenstein, P. J. (2000), 'Regionalism and Asia', *New Political Economy,* Vol. 5 (3), pp. 353-368.

Lim, Tai Wei (2018), "China and the Quad: Challenges for Southeast Asia", *Asia Global Online,* May 10, 2018, available at http://www.asiaglobalonline.hku.hk/china-quad-southeast-asia-asean/

Madan, Tanvi (2017), "Economic Cooperation among the Quad (Plus) Countries: Limits and Possibilities," *Quad Plus Dialogue, Brookings Institution,* 28 March, 2017.

Mahapatra, Chintamani (2017), "India and Shifting Power Equations in the Indo-Pacific", *Indian Foreign Affairs Journal,* Vol. 12, No. 2, April–June 2017, 93-118.

Medcalf, Rory (2013), "The Indo-Pacific: Whats in a Name", *Brookings,* 10 October, 2013, available at https://www.brookings.edu/articles/the-indo-pacific-whats-in-a-name/

Mehta, Suresh (2014), 'The Indo-Pacific Imperative', in Pradeep Kaushiva and Abhijit Singh (eds), *Geopolitics of the Indo-Pacific,* New Delhi: KW Publishers Pvt. Ltd., in association with National Maritime Foundation, 2014, p. 3.

*Ministry of Defence, *Annual Report 2010–11,* p. 4, New Delhi: MoD.

Mohan, C. Raja (2018), "New Indo-Pacific axis", Indian Express, 8 May 2018, available at https://indianexpress.com/article/opinion/columns/emmanuel-macron-india-france-relations-paris-delhi-canberra-axis-malcolm-turnbull-narendra-modi-5167221/

Mohan, C Raja, Rory Medcalf, Bruno Tertrais (2018), "New Indo-Pacific Axis" Carnegie India, 8 May 2018, available at https://carnegieindia.org/2018/05/08/new-indo-pacific-axis-pub-76279

Pai, Nitin (1991), "India and the Indo-Pacific Balance of Power", *Indian National Interest,* 1 August 2017, available at https://nationalinterest.in/india-and-the-indo-pacific-balance-of-power-1814c5a5f6a1

Palmer, N.D. (1991), *The New Regionalism in Asia and the Pacific,* Heath: Lexington.

Pitsuwan, Surin (2011), "ASEAN Taming the Cycle of Conflict and Misery", *The Jakarta Post,* 3 May 2011, available at http://www.thejakartapost.com/news/2011/05/03/asia-taming-cycle-conflict-and-misery.html

*PM's Speech at the Foundation Stone Laying Ceremony for the Indian National Defence University at Gurgaon," *Prime Minister's Office, Government of India,* 23 May 2013, available at http://pmindia.nic.in/ speech-details.php?nodeid=1316.

Roy, Denny (1997), *The New Security Agenda in the Asia-Pacific Region,* UK, Macmillan Press.

Rumley, Dennis (2005), "The Geopolitics of Asia-Pacific Regionalism in the 21st Century", *The Otemon Journal of Australian Studies,* Vol. 31, pp. 5-27, University of Western Australia, available at https://www.otemon.ac.jp/library/research/labo/cas/publication/pdf/31/2.pdf.

Saha, Premesha (2018), "The Quad in the Indo-Pacific: Why ASEAN remains cautious", Observer Research Foundation, 26 February 2018, available at https://www.orfonline.org/research/asean-quad/

Saran, Shyam, (2018), "Quad can be the anchor for the Indo-Pacific region", *Hindustan Times,* June 29, 2108, available at https://www.hindustantimes.com/analysis/quad-can-be-the-anchor-for-the-indo-pacific-region/story-IC5jc7fxAUdI3BtD5ULwXN.html

Sidhu, W.P.S. (2017), "The emerging Indo-Pacific architecture" *Livemint,* 20 November 2017, available at https://www.livemint.com/Opinion/moBrhtvotgcrUAyasMnscP/The-emerging-IndoPacific-architecture.html

Singh, Abhijit and Pradeep Kaushiva (eds), *Geopolitics of the Indo-Pacific,* 2014.

Singh, Hemant Krishan and Sanjay Pulipaka (eds), (2013), *Asia's Arc of Advantage: India, ASEAN and the US: Shaping Asian Architecture,* A Report of the ICRIER Wadhwani Chair in India–US Policy Studies, New Delhi: ICRIER, August 2013.

Sivaramakrishnan, Arvind, Nirupama Subramanian, and Raghuvir Srinivasan Interview Walter Russell Mead, (2012), "Nobody shares Pakistan's vision for Afghanistan," *The Hindu,* 24 August 2012, available at http://www. thehindu.com/opinion/interview/nobody-shares-pakistans-vision-for-afghanistan/article3813090.ece.

Tavares, Rodrigo (2008), 'Understanding regional peace and security: A Framework of analysis,' *Contemporary Politics,* 14 (2), 107–27.

Tuchman, M. (1989), 'Redefining security,' *Foreign Affairs,* 68 (2), 162–77; T. Sorensen (1990) 'Rethinking national security,' *Foreign Affairs,* 69 (3), 1–28.

*United States National Security Strategy (2017), "The Strategy in Regional Context" *NSS,* p. 46, available at https://www.whitehouse.gov/wp-content/uploads/2017/12/NSS-Final-12-18-2017-0905.pdf

NON-TRADITIONAL SECURITY THREATS

12

Complex Dynamics of Terrorism in the Indo-Pacific Region

Souravie Ghimiray

ABSTRACT

The threat from terrorism remains a complicated issue in the Indo-Pacific region. The problem of militancy and violence associated with several separatist and religious groups has existed since many years in the region. The countries in the region have witnessed amalgamation of various kinds of terrorism. Firstly, terrorism emanating from Islamic extremism remains a big threat; secondly support of terrorist groups by Pakistan is one major problem; thirdly, terrorism associated with ethno-nationalist and separatist movements is another problem; lastly, threat from transnational terrorism especially from ISIS in the present context remains the most alarming of all.

As a source of instability in the region the states of Indo-Pacific have relied on various policies ranging from security, socio-economic, ideological, law enforcement and educational policies. The approaches in countering terrorism by the states have varied in nature with some having a security approach while others favouring a comprehensive solution. Besides having differences and limitations in institutional capacities and understanding of terrorism by the countries of Indo-Pacific, these countries continue to develop policies and arrangements in the region to curb the threats emanating from terrorism through several efforts like policing, information sharing, regional cooperation, etc. Nevertheless the region continues facing threat from extremism and radicalisation. The aim of this paper will be to recognise the gaps that have made the region vulnerable to terrorist attacks. It will also seek to understand counterterrorism efforts led by the affected countries and how far has it been successful in addressing the problems rising from this issue.

Introduction

Prior to 9/11 countries in the Indo Pacific region experienced a significant threat from terrorism and after the attack there was an increase in the activities of terrorist groups. The networks of less dense organisations spread across the region. While the less dormant groups became active and new ones were born. The Bali bombings of October 2002 killed around 200 people, it was perpetrated by Jehmah Islamiya (JI) a jihadist organisation in Indonesia that had links with Al-Qaeda, this incident demonstrated the growing outreach and influence of Islamic extremism. One of the features of the terrorist groups in the region is its ability to have a transnational presence. Extremist groups like JI and Abu Sayyaf Group of Philippines which successfully spread across the national borders had an aim of establishing a pan-Islamic caliphate in South East Asia. What is unique about the regionalisation of extremist groups and in particular Jehmaah Islamiya is its connectivity with extremist groups those capable of posing serious threat to security of sates.

The region surrounding Afghanistan and Pakistan has remained one of the worst affected places by extremism. Pakistan has been described as the most dangerous place on earth due to the unending problem of terrorism. Before the infiltration of Al-Qaeda in Afghanistan and Pakistan the understanding of the region's problem for extremism was limited and this changed to a large extent after its arrival. Bangladesh too is currently facing an incremental growth of radicalisation. Home-grown extremist outfits have received support ideologically and strategically from the Islamic State of Iraq and Syria (ISIS) and Al-Qaeda in Indian Subcontinent (AQIS).

While in China the terrorism issue is intertwined with the ethno-separatist movement of the ethnic Uyghur Muslim in Xinjiang province. The Uyghur Muslims have not accepted the Chinese rule since decades now and is the result of various political, economic, and social grievances which has historical origins. This kind of separatist movement is common in Asia and in the case of Uyghur movement it got support by global jihadist movement under Al-Qaeda. In the early 1990s, Eastern Turkestan Islamic Movement (ETIM) was established with the aim of separating Xinjiang from. It was designated as a terrorist organisation in 2002 because of its connection with Al-Qaeda and since then the group has carried out attacks in China.

Another emerging threat comes from ISIS, in a report published by the UN Security council it maintained that the group loses in Iraq and Syria may shift the threat towards South East Asia. As such, group affiliated to ISIS has perpetrated terror attacks in the region and recently the attack in Marawi city of Philippines in May 2017 was inspired by the jihadist ideology of ISIS. The siege of the city by ISIS linked group resulted in the killing of around 1000 people that included civilians, government forces and the fighters. The number of foreign fighters joining ISIS was at large from the region itself, for example from Indonesia alone around 800 people including women and children travelled to Syria and Iraq to join ISIS. The formal branch of ISIS in Afghanistan and Pakistan, known as Islamic State's Khorasan Province, stayed active in 2016.[1]

Bangladesh has been experiencing a high level of transnational terrorist activity from both ISIS and al-Qaeda. The Muslim majority country is facing a growing threat from Islamist militant violence in the recent years. The targets of the extremist groups are mainly tourists, religious minorities and secular bloggers. In 2016, ISIS claimed responsibility for attacks in a restaurant in Dhaka which claimed the lives of 22 people. Australia has also faced homegrown jihadist threats notably after 2003 but due to its strong counterterrorism policies several terrorist attacks inspired by al-Qaeda were successfully aborted. Major threat came from individuals and small groups.

Causes of Terrorism in the Region

The direct threat in the Indo-Pacific stems from Islamic extremism. David C. Rapport[2] in his analysis of the four waves of terrorism asserts that Islam lies at the heart of the ongoing fourth wave which is postulated to last for at least four decades starting from the year 1979. While recognising the role of other religions contributing to violence in the world, he views that this wave's main driver will be Islam. This wave's timeline is to end by 2020 but so far there are no signs of the fourth wave coming to a rest. Moreover, with the coming of ISIS the religious wave has entered into a new phase and it seems to have an increasing role in the Indo-Pacific region. ISIS has affected the intensity of radicalisation in the region and has affected the vulnerable people with online propaganda to connect with the global cause of Islamic jihad. Especially in Kashmir the movement for freedom have recently been influenced by the radical ideology of ISIS which was evident in the upsurge of anti-India protests in Indian Kashmir and the raising[3] of ISIS flags.

Marginalisation and Discrimination

The reasons for support of terrorism in general tends to reveal the grievances arising out of socio-economic marginalisation as one of the major contributing factors. Dissatisfaction due to the failure of political methods in bringing about a change also acts as a driver in support of terrorism. Additionally the failure of State in fulfilling the issues of common nature may also lead to supporting terrorist groups who tend to provide an alternative method in fulfilling such needs. For example, according to a survey of 6000 respondents by Fair and Shapiro[4] urban Pakistanis support the militant organisation under two cases—one is the support of such groups in perpetrating violence for those issues thought to be of importance to them and two given the idea of their understanding of the political environment those respondents viewed violence was necessary to attain goals.

The failure of political leadership can also foment violent extremism, for instance in the Southern part of Malaysia the Malay Muslims have not been able to get their demands herd by the government which in turn has increased the danger of ethno-nationalist orientation to be supplanted by radical Islamism. Several studies[5] have shown that the discrimination of segment of the population by the government contributes in creating spaces for the affected ones to build grievances against the state. This leads the section of the affected population to use violence as a solution for discrimination and exclusion faced by the marginalised leading them to support terrorist groups. The presence of terrorist groups in Pakistan, Bangladesh and India reveal that marginalisation and discrimination has been one of the major reasons for their existence.

Insurgency and Terrorism

Most of the ethno-nationalist movements in the Indo-Pacific have been linked to jihadi terrorism. One such significant example is that of the ethnic Uyghur separatist movement under East Trukestan Islamic Movement[6] (ETIM) in the Xinjian province of China which has been allegedly linked to transnational jihadist organisation like Al-Qaeda especially after the 9/11 attacks. China has tried to portray[7] Uyghur separatism as 'terrorism' and 'extremism' since the mid-1990s. The events of 9/11 allowed China to approach this subject as an issue of global nature. The Uyghur separatist issue got a terrorist character once it got closely linked to the global 'war on terror', and the first official account[8] of Uyghur terrorism was published by the Chinese authorities in 2002. The ETIM is a umbrella organisation which has various groups operating in Central Asia and Pakistan and got listed as an 'international terrorist organisation' by the US State Department in 2002. The Turkestan Islamic Party (TIP) is one such prominent group formed by the members who escaped to Afghanistan and Pakistan in the 1990s. TIP has taken responsibility for various terror attacks inside China and has lately expanded its activities on the internet by putting up videos to join jihad by the Uyghurs in the Xinjiang region. China has linked ETIM to Al-Qaeda and Taliban and has been known to receive support from them through training and funding. In addition, China has continually feared concern from a radical Central Asian Islamic group called Hibz-ut-Tahrir al-Islami which calls for a formation of caliphate by uniting all the Muslims.

In southern Philippines the Moro Islamic Liberation Front (MILF) rebelled against the government demanding an autonomous region for decades. MILF has been involved with the government of Philippines for a peace deal which has been partially reached. Although MILF's main goal has been territorial and nationalistic rather than religious objectives but it got engaged with Al-Qaeda in the 1990s and received funding and training from it.[9] But after 2002 there was a change in MILF decisions, it cooperated with the Philippines government to end the problem of Abu Sayaaf Group (ASG) a violent jihadist group which broke up from MILF in 1991 that aims to establish a separate Islamic state. The positive attitude by MILF promoted the government to establish peace talks with MILF members. Despite the positive changes the groups renegade commanders have been known to give sanctuary to JI members. The presence of younger members in insurgent groups in the Philippines is of concern due to their leaning towards extremism. Hence, groups like MILF and MNLF, Abu Sayyaf and Rajah Sloaiman Movement will still have potential of being influenced by jihadist radicalisation leading to expansion of violence even if peace agreements have been reached.

The insurgency problem in Thailand's southern part has been going on for several decades and has shown no signs of abating. The conflict in Southern Thailand started in 1948 as an ethno-religious insurgency in the Malay Patani region. The annexation of the Patani Sultanate region by Bangkok has always been seen to be unjust by the people of that region. The forced annexation led to forced assimilation leaving the area disenfranchised. The heavy handed ruling of the government in the region in 2004 led to killing of Muslim youths, this incident has increased level of violence in Southern Thailand with rebels involving in bomb attacks over the years. The Thai government claimed the insurgents to have links with Al-Qaeda and there have been evidences of JI and Al-Qaeda operative to have found shelter in Southern Thailand among the religionist there but this claim has been disputed and the role of foreign militants have remained unclear. Failure of the political leadership in addressing the grievances of the Malay Muslims may transform the ethno-nationalistic outlook of the insurgency to be supplanted by the global jihadi orientations which can have even bigger repercussions in the region.

Women and Terrorism

More recently, the role of women in terrorist organisation has resurfaced mainly due to the sensationalisation of women as ISIS fighters in the media. The literature[10] that focuses on women in terrorist groups has shown that personal crisis is one of the main reasons leading them to be the path radicalisation. According to a finding[11] women migrant workers living in places like Singapore, Taiwan and Hong Kong experienced a 'cognitive opening' through personal crisis that increasingly made them rely on religion and they found a frame of resonance and community in ISIS. This finding is significant in revealing of a fact and contrary to the popular belief that women were coerced into joining the path of radicalisation. The motivations for women were mostly related to emotional or personal, unlike men who were driven by ideational factors. With the establishment of Islamic State women became increasingly important players in extremist ideology. Especially women from Indonesia became active participant in joining extremist groups like ISIS. Around 600 of them[12] travelled to Syria since the beginning of the conflict in 2012 to join ISIS. The women in the region have got radicalised and it is a growing concern for the countries in the Indo-Pacific. Initially it was perceived that the jihadist organisation like AQI were more conservative regarding the roles of women but lately ISIS position shifted[13] in allocating the roles of women by viewing that women were also obligated to fight in jihad.

Online Radicalisation Programmes

Internet is one of the main enablers for the spread of radicalisation in the region. One of the main reasons for the expansion of jihadist threat is due to the increase in the number of jihadist websites following the invasion of Iraq by the US. The global jihadist movement operated through internet and had a wide presence online but after the 9/11 incident it expanded even more rapidly. There was a rise in the number of jihadist websites and by late 2000s their presence in the social media increased.[14] The decentralisation of jihadist ideology is connected with the communication technologies which has empowered charismatic leaders to preach and has widened the scope for radicalisation process. Through the use of internet and social media enormous amount of content with sermons and lectures can be conveniently posted for the masses. Such content has motivated the drive for radicalisation and has facilitated 'self recruiting' to the adherents and individuals susceptible to fundamentalist ideologies.

The reliance in spreading jihadist ideology led to a decentralised strategy of promoting jihadism by the extremist groups. Strategists like Al Suri supported this idea even though it came at odds with Al-Qaeda's traditional centralised approach; nevertheless this approach became successful in spreading the broader movement and helped in mobilising the supporters from all around the globe. Australia has seen the lone wolf attack as the most common type of attack after 2000, the online spaces have provided platform for jihadi ideology to spread and have encouraged people to carry out attacks at individual will. In Australia after 2003 there were bigger incidents of terror plots that were influenced by the online propaganda of extremist groups. Even though there were no connections between the Pendennis plot and external jihadi group the plotter had extensively used internet materials to use in the attack. Its leader Abdul Nacer Benbrika had used the jihadi book *"The Guide to the Global Islamic Resistance"* to encourage and guide the operations.[15] Such self-starting plots in Australia became popular in incidents that led to terror attacks especially after 2003. There were about 21 people[16] involved in planning terror plots, apart from planning there were other individual who were involved in terrorist activities like fund-raising and distribution of instructional materials.

Countering Terrorism

Among most of the countries in the Indo-Pacific region Australia has developed a strong counter terror policy. Most of the terror attacks have been aborted successfully in Australia, operation Pendennis in 2005-06 was carried out to thwart a terror plot by jihadist group and in 2009 operation Neath avoided the local jihadist group from carrying out attacks. Globally Australia has been an active member in fighting war on terror, and has continually provided military support and humanitarian assistance to disrupt the efforts of foreign fighters. One area in which Australia has been successful in counterterror activities is by developing a leadership role to cut the financial support of jihadist groups. It is the member of Financial Task Action Task Force (FATA). Regionally Australia has given assistance to South East Asian countries through its financial intelligence unit by helping the regional countries to develop a financial profile of foreign fighters by detecting, preventing and deterring money laundering and financing activities of terrorist groups.

Australia has helped US in assisting in fight against Al-Qaeda due to which it has put itself in risk by becoming a target. Australia was increasingly targeted by jihadist groups other than Al-Qaeda post-9/11. Due to its support of US on war on terror it was perceived to be one of the western powers that had to be dismantled by extremist groups like LeT, ISIS, Al-Qaeda. Australia, since then, has focused mainly on jihadi terrorism and has built a comprehensive counterterrorism policy and has made legislative change that proscribes several terrorist offenses. There were many cases in which Australians have travelled to join ISIS in Syria and Iraq, through AUSTRAC i.e. their financial intelligence agency for anti-money laundering and counterterrorism financing, it identified persons linked to terrorist activities. Various government-led programmes have been in place to identify radicalised individuals at risk for who tailored services is provided to address the drivers of radicalisation.

Some countries have been successful in countering terrorism through preventive measures, for instance Malaysia and Singapore have prevented terror attacks by using forceful preventive measures by effectively making use of the existing preventive detention laws under their Internal Security Act. The governments of Indonesia, Philippines, Thailand have addressed terrorism in comprehensive manner through security, socio-economic and educational policies. In Malaysia the Southeast Asia Regional Centre for Counterterrorism was established. It provides research and training to officials against terrorist financing, and policing and also builds distributive policies of the developmental state to stop the spreading of religious extremism and terrorism. To stop the financing of terrorist groups Malaysian government has set up Financial Intelligence Unit which tracks suspicious transactions and is reported for further action.

The countries in Indo-Pacific have utilised affirmative action as a part of counterterrorism policy that acts in favour of underprivileged groups. Such interventionist policies have been formed as the cornerstone of the governments like Malaysia, Singapore, Philippines and Indonesia. It aims at improving the socio-economic conditions of the people in less developed regions. Apart from setting up security structures to curtail the terrorist cells various ideological, financial and educational responses has been introduced to stop violence from terrorism and is channelled[17] through the Muslim community. Following the Bali Bombings counterterrorism efforts in Indonesia has been revised. Indonesia has its elite special unit called Detachment 88 for carrying out counterterrorism efforts. It is a part of the law enforcement unit which detects, deter and prevents attacks from taking place. It has got support and training to build capacity for investigation and tactical skill form the US and Australia. This unit has been successful in greatly reducing the number of attacks especially by JI whose operational capabilities got a major blow in 2007. But apart from the special police forces Indonesia has introduced deradicalisation programmes which was initiated in 2007 and it aims at educating the population on extremism with the goal of stopping the radicalisation process. This programme goes beyond the traditional approach[18] of police surveillance and arrests of terror suspects in dealing with terrorism. This programme holistically approaches the issue of radicalisation and terrorism by actively involving Islamic teachers and scholars in conflict areas to stop radical ideologies from spreading further. Philippines has also used distributive policies in counterterrorism and has several developmental programs supported by countries like United States and Australia to address the larger socio-economic issues that has been the root cause of terrorism.

The Xinjiang Uighur Autonomous Region (XAUR) in China is under high surveillance and security systems. In the recent times the counterterrorism efforts have increased especially after the 9/11 incident. The intensified surveillance and security in the Xinjiang region has been viewed as China's heavy-handedness in dealing with the Uighur separatist movement. China has made amendments in its Criminal law and has deployed a wide definition of terrorism to curtail the activities of the Uyghurs. China also gave support to US on its 'war on terror' and since then it has used the Uyghur separatist movement to align with the discourse of Islamist inspired terrorism and has constantly tried to gain international support to suppress the insurgency. Moreover, the alleged links of ETIM and TIM to jihadist movement and their funding and training by Al-Qaeda have led China to crackdown on the Uyghurs which has been seen as violation of human rights[19] in the XAUR. The Chinese authorities to a great extent have got an opportunity to suppress not only the dissenting Uyghur but also Tibetans, Falun Gong members and protesting workers as terrorist. Shangai Cooperation Organisation (SCO) has cooperated with its member states for counterterror efforts at the regional level. The Regional Anti-terror Structure was established and has been effective in stopping terror attacks from taking place. SCO has adopted a convention on Countering Extremism to prevent the radicalisation of people in the region.

Through bilateral security arrangements with the countries of Central Asia like Kazakastan and Kyrgyzstan and through SCO a number of alleged Uyghur separatist have been extradited.

Bangladesh has relied on law enforcement agencies in countering the threat from Islamist terrorism. The efforts have mostly centred on policing and counterterror operations of suspects involved in jihadist networks. As Bangladesh is a member to the Asia-Pacific Group on money laundering, it has taken steps to curb the financing activities of terrorist groups through freezing accounts and further taking actions against criminal activities. Overall the counterterrorism efforts in Bangladesh remains limited due to a number of factors one being political rifts and dynamism that has encouraged the extremist groups to grow in strength. Another factor is the increasingly polarized political situation and politicisation of institutions that has allowed groups like ISIS and Al-Qaeda supported by home grown terrorist groups to thrive. In Pakistan the Counterterrorism Authority has banned several extremist groups as terrorist organisation. In Pakistan several areas were used as safe havens by terrorist groups and recently due to military operations in Khyber and North Waziristan, groups like Tahrik e-Taliban Pakistan (TTP) have been ousted and their hideouts destroyed. Pakistan counterterror policy is mainly relied on military option in eradicating the safe havens and it has been working on preventing financing of terrorism. LeT has been banned as a terrorist organisation but its wing called Jaamat ud Dawa continues to operate and has been involved in fund raising activities. Civilian deaths have been reduced in recent years compared to the number of deaths earlier. Most of the terrorist groups operate in Af-Pak border areas, the main concern is regarding the trafficking of WMD through its porous borders. With support from US Afghanistan has been working to counter the threat arising from nuclear terrorism through early detection and response to nuclear smuggling incidents.

India has faced greatest threat from the Pakistani based terrorist groups, with support from Pakistan's ISI these groups have been operating since decades in Kashmir to overthrow the Indian rule. India faces continuous threat from groups like Hibz ul-Mujahideen, Lashkar-e-Taiba, Jaish e-Mohammed. Islamist groups like LeT has combined jihad against India and West and is the most trusted allies of ISIS. It has multifaceted approach[20] for spreading extremism through educational and charitable activities. India established the National Investigation Agency (NIA) as the main counterterrorism institution which has been delegated with powers to investigate and arrest. Internationally India gave support to the US in its 'war on terror' and offered its airbases for carrying out operations in Afghanistan.[21] Counterterror cooperation between India and US has helped India to a great extent in developing its counterterrorism policies. Various bilateral agreements within two countries have helped India in developing its Intelligence agencies for terrorist screening that will provide the databases with names, date of birth, fingerprints of ever increasing number of terrorist suspects. United States in its 2010 Counterterrorism Cooperation Initiative (CCI) have promoted sharing of intelligence and supporting capacity building in the areas of transport security, terrorist financing, cybersecurity, and special units training.

Conclusion

The threat from jihadist extremism looms large in the Indo-Pacific region with the existing problems from sectarian violence and ethno-nationalism the countries in the region have to be alert about the growing trends of terrorism. Despite the efforts from every country that faces the danger from extremism the counterterror strategies needs to be developed effectively. Use of hard measures like raids, arrests and detentions may not effectively check on the rise of extremism. For instance in China the crackdown of Uyghur separatist in Xinjiang has led the militant to move in the areas of Pakistan where it can build links with jihadi organisations and have found safe haven in North Waziristan. In Bangladesh the failure of state to provide strong institutions have led the law enforcement agencies to use force as it lacks credible justice system and investigative capacity and corruption which has left no alternate option in dealing with the problem of extremism. Such a system has allowed hundreds of detained militant to escape punishment.

In cases where the government is involved in addressing the problem of terrorism through distributive policies like in Malaysia, Singapore, Thailand, Philippines the situation has seemed to improve to a certain degree. Moreover, the assistance from Western powers like US has helped these countries to understand the root causes of extremism. Various developmental programmes for socio-economic upliftment of the affected population has contributed in reducing the violence arising out of insurgencies and terrorism. In places like Indonesia the Salfi clerics are involved in Countering Violent Extremism programme, which can be effective in the long run with the clerics engaged in deradicalisation programmes and preventive campaigns. But this may also have its own drawback, Salafism might become a precursor to extremism in the future. In Philippines too despite the improved situation and agreement on a comprehensive peace deal with the MILF there are still number of radical groups in the Southern part that runs the risk for the continuation of violence. There are still some elements of extremist groups like Aby Sayaf Group that have got shelter in the areas ruled by extremist MNLF.

Terrorism emanating from Pakistan has the biggest potential for the escalation of terrorism in the region, without the Kashmir issue being resolved terror attacks from Pakistan will not cease against India. The rising extremism in the country with the spread of ISIS networking with the militant groups will increase terror related violence. Spread of terrorism with the presence of nuclear arms, the Pakistani establishment soft approach towards extremist groups has compounded the threat from terrorism further. India despite having a renewed counterterrorism policy and getting significant support from the US have produced few successes and has neither been able to contain Pakistani terrorists nor check homegrown terrorism. Hence, it needs to develop a resilient policy in the face of rising danger from transnational threats.

NOTES

1 Government of USA (2017), *Country Report on Terrorism: Middle East and North Africa.* U.S. Department of State, US.

2 Kaplan, J. (2016), "Waves of Political Terrorism", available at http://politics.oxfordre.com/view/10.1093/acrefore/9780190228637.001.0001/acrefore-9780190228637-e-24#acrefore-9780190228637-e-24-note-3, accessed on 12 July 2018.

3 DNA (2018), "Jammu and Kashmir: Terrorists Shoot Policeman Dead, ISIS Flags Raised in Srinagar", available at https://www.dnaindia.com/india/report-jammu-kashmir-terrorists-shoot-policeman-dead-isis-flags-raised-in-srinagar-2653145, accessed on 1 Sept. 2018.

4 Shapiro, J. and Fair C., (2010), "Understanding Support for Islamist Militancy in Pakistan," *International Security*, 34 (3): 83-118.

5 Hwang, J.C. (2018) "Pathways into Terrorism: Understanding Entry into and Support for Terrorism in Asia", *Terrorism and Political Violence,* In Press:1-7

6 Xu, B. (2014), "The East Turkestan Islamic Movement", available at https://www.cfr.org/backgrounder/east-turkestan-islamic-movement-etim, accessed on 6 July 2018.

7 Clarke, M. (2018), "China' Xinjiang and the Internationalization of the Uyghur Issue", *Global Change Peace and Security*, 22(2): 213-229.

8 Government of People Republic of China (2002), *East Turkistan Terrorist Forces Cannot Get Away with Impunity*, Information Ofce of the State Council of the PRC, PRC.

9 Abuza, Z. (2003), *Militant Islam in Southeast Asia: Crucible of Terror*, USA: Lynne Rienner Publishers.

10 Nuraniyah, N. (2018), "Not Just Brainwashed: Understanding the Radicalisation of

Indonesian Female Supporters of the Islamic State", *Terrorism and Political* Violence, 1-21. Scopus®, EBSCOhost, accessed on 8 August 2018.

11 Ibid 9.

12 Tempo.co (2017), "Immigration Helps Detecting 600 Indonesians Affiliated to ISIS,", 8 July available at https://en.tempo.co/read/news/2017/07/08/055889877/Immigration-Helps-Detecting-600-Indonesians-Affiliated-to-ISIS

13 Middle East Eye (2017), "Islamic States Call on Female Supporters to Take Part in Jihad", 6 October available at http://www.middleeasteye.net/news/islamic-state-called-female-supporters-take-part-jihad-934020595

14 Zelin, A. (2013), "The State of Global Jihad Online: A Qualitative, Quantitative and Cross Lingual Analysis", available at https://www.washington institute.org/uploads/Documents/opeds/Zelin20130201-NewAmericaFoundation.pdf, accessed on 2 July 2018.

15 Zammit, A. (2013), "Explaining a Turning Point in Australian Jihadism", *Studies in Conflict & Terrorism*, 36(9): 739-755.

16 Hogan, S.H. (2012), "Australian Neo-Jihadist Terrorism: Mapping the Network and Cell Analysis Using Wiretap Evidence," *Studies in Conict & Terrorism*, 35(4): 308–309.

17 Aldis, A. and Herd (eds) (2007), *Strategies for Counter-terrorism*, London: Routledge.

18 Emmers, R. (2009), "Comprehensive Security and Resilience in Southeast Asia: ASEAN's Approach to Terrorism", *The Pacific Review*, 22(2): 159-177.

19 Ibid., n. 6.

20 Tankel, S. (2011), Storming the World Stage: The story of Lashkar-e-Taiba, New York: Columbia University Press.

21 Pant, H.V. and Lidarev, I. (2018), "Indian Counterterrorism Policy and the Influence of the Global War on Terror", *India Review*, 17(2): 181-208.

13

Nuclear Proliferation in the Indo-Pacific: Role of the United States

Upma Kashyap

ABSTRACT

An intense geopolitical tussle among powers is underway in the Indo-Pacific region. The Indo-Pacific region comprises of area stretching from the western shore of North America to the west coast of India and has the highest population with booming economies. Today it is facing a wide array of security issues having the potential to impact region's political, economic and cultural traditions. An unprecedented mix of new security threats, like cybercrime, migration and drug trafficking, have affected the region along with other traditional security threats in the Korean peninsula, East and South China Sea and China's rise which has broader strategic implications—all have a bearing on the Indo-Pacific region. The region includes world's major nuclear-armed states. This article argues that the US nuclear deterrence as the only strategy to maintain peace and stability in the region cannot resolve the current regional situation. Hence, effectively maintaining the security of Indo-Pacific region has become a significant aspect in preserving peace and stability in the global context. The post-Cold War United States relations and bilateral alliances which had guaranteed deterrence and containment of the alliance partner is now evolving into a diverse set of alignments taking into consideration the changing nature of regional security issues. Until, now US nuclear deterrence in the Indo-Pacific had protected its allies from threats and had avoided the need to develop their nuclear capabilities. Of late, this situation has been contested due to the regional dominance of China and its military modernisation program that poses a major challenge to the interest of the US in Indo-Pacific. Recent international developments suggest that speculation on the success cannot be taken for granted. The advent of Trump administration has further created uncertainty all around and has made its allies, particularly Japan and South

Korea, anxious. Trump's pull out from the Iran Nuclear Deal and call for more security cost sharing has made them even more anxious. The recent Trump meeting with North Korean leadership and the joint statement affirming the denuclearisation of the North Korean peninsula is at best ' extremely premature'. The withdrawal of US from the 12 nations Trans-Pacific Partnership has already led the region into an uncharted territory. With this contextual backdrop, the aim of the paper is to analyse the US approach to nuclear non-proliferation in Indo-Pacific. The paper will attempt to assess the nonproliferation challenges faced by the Trump administration in the Indo-Pacific region. To look into various strategies tailored by the US to address the 21st century security threats in the Indo-Pacific. The paper would also consider the question whether the threat stemming from the North Korea's nuclear programme is over? The study in effect endeavours to examine how US will find the balance between its continued assurance of security to its allies through nuclear deterrence and its 'America First' policy. Also, how US plans to deal with China modernising its military and nuclear capability with the possible return of great power competition.

Introduction

Since relatively early in the nuclear age, preventing the acquisition of nuclear weapons by additional countries has been a major goal for the US in its national security and foreign policies. The main foundation for preventing the spread of nuclear weapons through international effort in the 1970 is Nuclear Non-Proliferation Treaty (NPT), which prevents the non-nuclear weapon states (NNWS) from acquiring nuclear weapons, and gives assurance for developing nuclear energy for peaceful use, it requires that its five nuclear weapon state (NWS) parties i.e. United States, United Kingdom, France, Russia and China continue efforts in good faith to achieve nuclear disarmament.[1] Whether the NPT has been a success or failure is a glass half-full, empty debate. Supporters argue that NPT has slowed the spread of nuclear weapons and should be further strengthened.[2] Today there are nine countries with nuclear weapons, the five NPT Nuclear Weapon States (NWS), Pakistan, India, North Korea and Israel, far fewer than United States leaders had feared. Not even one country has obtained nuclear weapons in the roughly twenty-five years since North Korea achieved its nuclear capability.[3] On the other side critics view NPT as failed in places like South Asia, Korean Peninsula and the Middle East. The reason for such a state is late in addressing the nonproliferation issues and using 'problem management' approach at a mature state instead of 'problem solving'. One of the problems is also the shifting standard often driven by political and domestic considerations, while in the past the only concern was 'no more nuclear weapon states and the nuclear ones should disarm'.[4] Thomas P. Cavanna questions how much does the United States care about nonproliferation? He does not agree with the scholarship analysis that the US grand strategy during the Cold War was driven by the fear of spread of nuclear weapons. He argues that geopolitics was important over nonproliferation policy that encouraged India and Pakistan to go nuclear, as often nonproliferation was relegated to the backburner whenever the strategic goals of the US came in conflict with it.[5] In my view the Nonproliferation Regime was stressed in the era of globalisation and faces various challenges today. Even though the recent international developments provide with an optimistic assessment but may be premature and that continued success cannot be overlooked.[6] The Nonproliferation policy seems to be in a flux and the game of the regime is changing. Increase in North Korea's nuclear missile programs has raised threats in the Indo-Pacific region and it is important to observe whether the US can influence Japan and South Korea in reconsidering their nuclear options.

The current uncertain security environment with very few countries challenging the international order; governments may not be keen on reevaluating their security choices. An intense geopolitical contest among the major powers is underway in the Indo-Pacific. The Indo-Pacific region is the most populated and has rising economies in the world. Today it is facing wide array of security threats. An unprecedented mix of threats, ranging from conventional, biological, chemical, cyber threats, space, nuclear and violent state actors. New security threats in the Korean peninsula, East and South China Sea and the broader strategic implications of China's rise all have a bearing on the Indo-Pacific region. One can say international relations are volatile. New developments have produced increased ambiguity and risk. China's military modernisation has led to increase in nuclear force, and is less transparent to its intentions. Russia and China are contesting international norms and order; US has build to assure security of its allies. For the first time in twenty-five years, the US is facing a return to great power competition. As Russia and China both have improved their military capabilities this evolving and uncertain international security environment has lead to shift in US security thinking. Keeping the current threat environment and uncertain future in mind US is emphasising on have effective and modern nuclear forces, along with the infrastructural support. US is aware that developments in new technologies have changed the nature of threats that are being faced today and the capabilities required to address them effectively.[7]

Today there is a potential for shifts in how other countries view America and its allies. The alignment among other states seems to be changing which can lead to relative power shifts in the international system. The Indo-Pacific includes most of the world's nuclear-armed states—the United States, China, Russia, India, Pakistan and North Korea. Gareth Evans explains that the major powers in the Indo-Pacific seeks to neutralise threat from each other. Non-nuclear allies like South Korea, Japan and Australia in the region seek to nuclear protection from various threats contingencies. Whereas vulnerable states Pakistan and North Korea are seeking to strategic equalizer.[8] Further, Michael Krepon argues that Asia's nuclear relationships can be understood two triangles—India-Pakistan-China triangle and US-Russia-China triangle. These nuclear weapons are connected with number of important non-nuclear weapons states. This adds further two triangles—US-China-Taiwan, US-China-Japan and one quadrilateral US-China-South Korea-North Korea quadrilateral to Asia's nuclear equation. US and China are central in all of these relationships. Both these major powers influence other states' nuclear deterrence choices and behaviour.

Shift in US Strategic Thinking

Nuclear weapons have served extremely important purpose for the past 70 years in America's National Security Strategy. Nuclear weapons are seen as the foundation of US strategy to maintain stability and peace by deterring any kind of aggression against America, its partners. Though nuclear deterrence strategies alone may not be able to prevent all conflicts, they have been significant in preventing nuclear attack, non-nuclear strategic attacks and large-scale conventional attacks. For the past several years US has been extending nuclear deterrence to more than 30 allies and partners that have helped them to assure their security and reduce their need to possess the or own nuclear capabilities. Until now US nuclear deterrence in the Indo-Pacific had helped assure allies security and avoided their need to own nuclear capabilities. US nuclear capabilities make necessary contributions to the deterrence of both nuclear and non-nuclear aggression. US allies have always placed enormous value on US extended nuclear deterrence for their own security. US nuclear deterrence also contributes to US nonproliferation goals. The US conventional approach to nonproliferation in the Indo-Pacific has been extended nuclear deterrence.[9] President Trump's foreign policy has raised questions about whether the United States will continue to play a pivotal role in the region. Despite US still being a major power its ability to influence appears to be diminishing.

Trump's call for strategic allies such as South Korea and Japan to share burden of supporting US troops in their countries has put geopolitics of the Indo-Pacific in flux.[10] In the year 2015 Defense Secretary James Mattis in testimony to the US Senate asked some important questions about the role of US nuclear weapons ? 'Do they serve solely to deter nuclear war'?[11]

The Nuclear Posture Review 2010, public report under the Obama's administration has viewed world to be a safer place without nuclear weapons and essential in maintaining the peace and stability in the world. The report maintains that reducing the number and role of nuclear weapons to be the objective of the US and use of nuclear weapons in extreme circumstances and avoid developing new nuclear warheads or capabilities. These objectives were clearly reflected in the Obama's speech in Prague in April 2009.[12] President Donald Trump has redefined US nuclear weapons policy. He calls to greatly expand and strengthen US nuclear capability in contrast with his predecessors.[13]

Today we are witnessing big policy changes under the Trump presidency. The decision to withdraw the US from the 12 nations Trans-Pacific Partnership has lead the region into the unchartered territory. The implications of the US pull out from the Iran Nuclear Deal is May 2018 on the future nonproliferation discourse is yet to be seen. There shift in the US policy in the Indo-Pacific and US nuclear policy has created uncertainty in the region. The recent Trump meeting with the North Korean leader Kim Jong-Un and the joint statement affirming the denuclearizing of the North Korean peninsula is at best 'extremely premature'.[14] Hence, Nonproliferation policy today faces new challenges such as the emergence of proliferating states, emergence of new technology and increasing threat from non-state actors. The section ahead analyzes the various challenges to US nonproliferation within Indo-Pacific.

Challenges to US Strategic Stability and Nonproliferation

(i) An Unstable International Environment

A geopolitical tussle between the old established world order and new emerging world order is taking place in the Indo-Pacific region. America's foreign policy started focusing in the Indo-Pacific in late 2011, when US President Obama announced a foreign policy 'pivot' to Asia. Though US emphasises the relevance of the region to a broader global politics in making, some analysts interpreted it as a policy to contain rising power of China. Using economic inducements, military threats to influence other states for its own political and military agendas, marks China assertion. China's heavy investment in infrastructure and trade strategies reflects its geopolitical aspirations. Japan and India are anxious about the geopolitical situation in the Indo-Pacific and are of the view that China must not be allowed to undermine the existing 'rule-based order'. North Korea is rapidly accelerating its nuclear and ballistic missiles programmes to acquire nuclear capability. US sees its pursuit of nuclear weapons as a global threat and call for an immediate global response. Japan, Australia, New Zealand, continue to reinforce security and economic arrangements that support US interests across the region. India has emerged as a stronger defense and strategic partner of America. Indo-Pacific security issues are still centered on US foreign policy. The bilateral security alliances with the US are seen as the basis of regional security and US presence is vital for Indo-Pacific security and stability. But President Trump's direction of foreign policy has raised doubts about the US commitment to the Indo-Pacific region.[15] Geopolitical uncertainty has arisen about the future security environment, which US will have to take into account. There is a fear of potential shift in how US allies and partners view US, leading to change in alignments among states and entire relative power shift in the international relations. The new technological developments have also led to change in the nature of threats. Such geopolitical and technological uncertainties has made the Indo-Pacific region security environment unstable. US certainly needs capabilities to address them effectively.[16]

(ii) North Korea's Nuclear Programme

North Korea first conducted its nuclear test on October 9, 2009, despite United States and international community efforts to contain North Korea's nuclear program for more than a decade. Security analysts speculated that North Korea might provoke other non-nuclear weapon states in Indo-Pacific to embark their own nuclear weapons. The so-called 'nuclear cascade' might begin with South Korea and Japan reconsidering its nuclear option.[17] In the year 2013 North Korea accelerated its pace of ballistic missile developments. In response United States approached South Korea for stationing Terminal High-Altitude Area Defense (THAAD) missile defense batteries and associated radar systems on their territory. After much debate, South Korea went ahead with THAAD deployment, but China levied informal economic penalties against South Korea in 2017 and warned against any future actions that threaten China's security. The opacity of North Korean programme further makes it policymakers difficult to analyze North Korea's intentions. North Korea's motivation behind its nuclear and ballistic missiles program, whether it is defensive or offensive is still subject of speculation.[18] Over the years North Korea has used its nuclear and missile capabilities as a leverage to improve diplomatic relations with the US and Japan.[19] The Obama administration strengthened US regional ballistic missile defenses and homeland defense by positioning key capabilities in Japan and South Korea and Ground Based Interceptors in the Western United States.[20]

North Korea's nuclear and the ballistic missile testing progressed faster than what was predicted by the foreign policy analysts. According to the July 2017, US Defense Intelligence Agency, North Korea has successfully conducted hydrogen bomb tests, and has produced a miniaturised nuclear warhead that can be installed onto its ballistic missiles. The Defense Intelligence Agency analysis further says that North Korea could be possessing around sixty nuclear weapons and could produce twelve more weapons annually. North Korea's ability to target South Korea, Japan and US military bases in East Asia, US facilities in Guam, eventually the US homeland with nuclear weapons raises security concerns for US in the Indo-Pacific.[21] In the Testimony by "Kelly E. Magsamen Senate Armed Services Committee, April 2017", titled "US Policy and Strategy in the Asia Pacific: Challenges and Opportunities" stated North Korea as a most urgent challenge. It says the most pressing challenge facing the United States is the Pyongyang's persistent ambition of its ballistic and nuclear missile programs. The challenge is that North Korea has proven to withstand international sanctions in the past especially two tough UN Security Council sanctions resolutions in the year 2016. The US acknowledges the fact that Korean leadership will not suddenly unilaterally arm.[22]

The North Korea challenge has become more difficult in recent years due to some factors as China's unwillingness to apply decisive pressure against the Kim Jong Un regime. North Korea has a greater ability to grapple with International pressures as its economy strengthened in recent years due to the relaxation of few government controls on private economic activity.[23] The Trump administration put North Korea issue in top priority of its foreign policy and perceives it as an urgent national security threat.[24] The United States wanted to give diplomacy a time. The denuclearisation of North Korea still remains a long-term goal of the US.

The recent Trump meeting with Pyongyang's leadership Kim Jong Un and the joint statement affirming the roll back of the North Korea nuclear programme is at best 'extremely premature'. In the recent June 12 Singapore summit on denuclearisation of North Korea only of its 13 action items relate explicitly to the North Korea's nuclear weapons and its wording is deliberately vague. Kim has agreed to freeze warhead testing, but after almost six tests it is questionable whether North Korea needs further testing. Experts on North Korea opine that the statement lacks the specifics on denuclearisation, lacks substance, the outcome of the summit was ambiguous and that the threat of North Korea hasn't gone away yet. Few analysts argue that the problem is not over yet; rather the threat has increased since the Singapore summit. In the following weeks since the summit North Korea has been upgrading missile and nuclear facilities, increasing fuel for nuclear weapons on unknown sites, building new long-range missiles and hiding all the activities from the US.[25]

The Trump administration's current North Korea policy is eroding international support, narrowing US options. North Korea seems to be taking advantage of the situation and playing a longer strategic game and is trying to build a bilateral relation with the US and keep the nuclear weapons as well. North Korea has embodied its nuclear armed status in its constitution, raised the role of its 'national nuclear force' in its self-defense and declared it has 'completed' the development of its ballistic missile and nuclear arsenal. Analysts are not supporting President Trump's confidence of end of the North Korean threat. US options to solve North Korea issue seem to be narrowing as one of its options, i.e. military action is now off the table, and the strategy of ' maximum pressure' is weakening due to lack of international support and decline of US international credibility and moral authority. The coming days will be a test of the nonproliferation policy and US policy to secure the denuclearisation of the North Korea.[26]

(iii) Anxious Allies Questioning US Security Assurances

US allies and security partners in the Indo-Pacific, mainly Japan and South Korea has depended significantly on US security assurances in the region and so far continue to forgo their own path of acquiring nuclear weapons.[27] Recent South Korean political discourse reflects the possibility of country going nuclear and prompt to advocate an independent nuclear weapons capability. The debate in South Korea about going nuclear started with its concern with the security threats emanating from nuclear programme in its neighborhood, China's expansionist behaviour and Japan's unclear security policy. President Obama assured the security of US and its allies, and stated to maintain a credible and strong strategic deterrence in Berlin in the year 2012. At present the credibility of US extended deterrence is under stress due to constant changing strategic landscape in Indo-Pacific. Rather America's nuclear umbrella has become questionable among its allies. US established the Extended Deterrence Dialogue (EDD) with Japan and Extended Deterrence Policy Committee (EDPC) with South Korea to address anxiety of the allies. The North Korea nuclear tests in 2013 created uneasiness in its neighborhoods and started a debate both in Japan and South Korea advocating that they should also go for nuclear weapons. However, a small section of people support the idea of possessing nuclear weapons. For example some members of the Saenuri Party took a hard approach on North Korea and called South Korea to be able to deal with the increasing threat from the North Korea by building its own nuclear deterrence capability. Some experts from South Korea questioned the credibility of America's extended deterrence in Indo-Pacific at the 28th Annual Conference of the Council on US-Korean Security Studies in July 2013.

According to a survey conducted by The Asian Institute for Policy Studies (AIPS) 2013, 67 per cent of the South Korean population agreed to reintroduce tactical nuclear weapons in their country. In reality reintroducing tactical nuclear weapons will be violating the Nuclear Non-Proliferation Treaty (NPT). Hence, according to Shin Chang-hoon, director of the Nuclear Policy and Technology Centre at AIPS, South Korea is not trying to break free or come out from the US 'nuclear umbrella'. The nuclear debate demonstrates a sense of insecurity among South Koreans. In order to deter threat stemming from its neighborhood, South Korea has developed homegrown cruise missiles, has unveiled ship-to-shore and submarine-to-ground cruise missiles, developed with South Korea's own technology.[28] The South Koreans are certainly skeptic about the US extended deterrence in the region and now share a close trade relation with China. Its economy hugely benefited from trading with China. This has put South Korea in a difficult position and also raises a question whether US allies are drifting to China in the Indo-Pacific region? China is however suspicious about the America's strategic intentions on the Korean peninsula. Many Chinese scholars opine that US goal is to just keep North Korea's nuclear problem under control and not resolve it. The North Korean problem serves US interest to maintain its military presence in the Indo-Pacific region and contain China.[29]

The proposal of establishing own nuclear deterrence in Japan is much more silent than in South Korea, because of the continuing vibration in the national political culture of Hiroshima and Nagasaki, but the voices to exist.[30] Japan hosts US military bases and has assigned a mission 'Japan's Self Defense

Forces' to support American forces during a Korean contingency. Japan has already spent about $18 billion on missile defense systems, which will protect both Japanese citizens and US military personnel bases in their country. Japan reinterpreted its constitution in the year 2014 which made Japan possible to exercise the right of collective defense. The new security legislation enacted in the year 2015 enables Japan to provide combat support to US forces, to further shoot down North Korean ballistic missiles targeted at Hawaii or Guam. In order to deter threat arising from North Korea, Japan deployed the land-based Patriot Advanced Capability Three (PAC-3) system and the sea-based Standard Missile Three (SM-3) Block IA Aegis system. Japan's security policy is the source of uncertainty for US, and how it will impact the US role as a security and alliance partner. Observers opine that Japan's potential capability to strike targets inside North Korea is to grow over time. Japan has been constantly worrying about the US disengagement from the Asian region and desires to enhance US-South Korea-Japan trilateral cooperation, whereas China sees such an engagement as a direct threat.[31] Japan supports The Nuclear Posture Review 2018, but to understand Japan's security policy at present is like to look into the hazy crystal ball. The Japan's unclear security policy can turn out to be a challenge for the US extended deterrence policy in near future.[32] Hence, US nuclear deterrence as the only strategy to maintain peace and stability in the region cannot resolve the current regional situation.

(iv) Downturn in US Relations with China and Russia

Another challenge to affecting US Nonproliferation approach in the Indo-Pacific region is the deteriorating US bilateral relations with China and Russia. Both China and Russia are important players to help sustain the nonproliferation regime.[33] Since 2010 analysts have observed a kind of Great Power Competition, and both China and Russia challenging the existing post-Cold War international norms and behaviour.[34] China has been using economic inducements and penalties and influencing operations to head its political and security agenda in the Indo-Pacific. China's trade strategies and infrastructure investments reflect its geopolitical aspirations. China is often alleged to build and militarise outposts in the South China Sea jeopardising the free flow of trade and undermining the regional stability. Analysts argue that China can discipline North Korea through economic and trade policies and curb its nuclear programme. China's efforts in this direction so far have been only symbolic. US is worried about China continuous efforts to expand the number and capabilities and of its nuclear forces. The ambiguity of its scope and extent of nuclear modernisation raises further questions about its future intentions. According to Nuclear Posture Review 2018, China has developed a new road-mobile strategic intercontinental ballistic missile (ICBM); a ballistic missile submarine armed with new submarine-launched ballistic missiles (SLBM) and a new multi-warhead version of its DF-5 silo-based ICBM. China possesses theater-range ballistic missile capable of reaching the US region, forces, partners and military bases in the region.[35] Chinese thinking on war fighting rather than in favour of a minimal deterrence posture has continued to influence China's nuclear modernisation efforts.

Russia violated international commitments political and legal; that can impact the security of other states, including the Intermediate-Range Nuclear Forces (INF) 1987, the Presidential Nuclear Initiatives 1991, and the 2002 Open Skies Treaty. Russia violated 1994 Budapest Memorandum by occupying Crimea and supporting Russia-led forces in Eastern Ukraine. Thus, Russia has been following lopsided ways and means to counter US capabilities and increasing the potential of a military conflict with America, its partners and allies. Russia is also developing counter-space military capabilities to weaken the US capability to conduct space-based intelligence, surveillance and reconnaissance (ISR), nuclear command, control; and communications (NC3), and positioning, timing and navigation. Russia's strategic policies, capabilities and nuclear policy pose a challenge to the American nuclear capabilities that is needed to protect the US states, partners and allies.[36]

The US-Tailored Strategies to Deter Challenges

America has tailored different diplomatic, military and economic strategies to deter the new threats of the 21st century challenging the US nonproliferation policy. The aim of United States is to maintain the deterrence capability to threaten all intolerable damages. According to Secretary of Defense James N. Mattis, "a safe, secure, and effective nuclear deterrent is there to ensure a war that can never be won, is never fought." US is prepared to respond precisely to China's both nuclear and non-nuclear aggressive ambition. US military exercises in the Indo-Pacific clearly demonstrate its preparedness to meet challenges or any kind of aggression in the region. US is looking forward for a meaningful dialogue with China on issues like countries nuclear policies, capabilities and doctrine in quest of a safe and peaceful security environment with an ambition to stable relations between both the states. It has responded to Russia's INF Treaty Violation by taking diplomatic, economic and military measures. It continues to seek a diplomatic resolution through INF's Special Verification Commission, the US also imposed sanctions on Russian companies involved in the making of Russia's prohibited cruise missile system. It is reviewing its military concepts, themes and options for conventional, ground-launched, intermediate-range missile systems.

US wants to give diplomacy a time to deal with the North Korea problem. US has made it clear that actions against the US or it allies will be unacceptable and will lead to end of that regime. It already has offensive and defensive capabilities to stop and defeat Pyongyang's missile programs. America will maintain its extended deterrence by working on common nuclear threats with the allies, holding joint military exercises and through meaningful consultative dialogues. President Obama followed a policy of 'strategic patience' to deal with the North Korea's nuclear programme. Despite several prior arms-control efforts followed by President Obama, the US recently launched an extensive modernisation program for its nuclear weapons, which involves nuclear warheads, support infrastructure and delivery systems. The new modernisation program aims to renew the entire nuclear triad i.e. new generations of bombers, intercontinental ballistic missiles, nuclear-armed cruise missiles and ballistic submarines. Trump administration has expressed an urgent need of modernisation US nuclear arsenal. According to the Trump administration by the year 2020 there will be a sharp increase in budgetary spending to modernise all three legs of the US Nuclear Triad. Such a spike in the defense budget will be seen after the mid 1980's during the peak of the Cold War under the President Reagan administration. The Trump administration made an overall 11 per cent increase for the National Nuclear Security Administration in the White House Office of Management and Budget.[37] According to critics focus of "modernisation of US nuclear weapons is a technological leap and increasing America" capacity to fight and win a nuclear war.

President Obama pursued a policy of 'strategic patience' toward North Korea in opposition to the North Korea's assiduous pursuit of its nuclear program. North Korea conducted a series of test of long-range ballistic missile in the beginning of 2009. In reaction to the tests, the UN Security Council collectively adopted Resolution 1874 to impose further economic sanctions on Pyongyang, authorising nuclear programme. In this backdrop Obama administration formulated the policy of 'strategic patience' based on key principle that the US would not engage in negotiations with Pyongyang until the latter shows the evidence of committing to denuclearisation. Analysts argue that Obama's policy failed in making North Korea move towards denuclearisation because of US miscalculations about the North Korea's circumstances and intentions. Also China remained reluctant to pressure North Korea to give up its nuclear program. Trump administration adopted a policy of 'strategic accountability' to tackle the North Korean crisis. The policy centered on' maximum pressure and engagement toward the denuclearisation of Kim Jong Un regime. Trump administration has tightened pressure on North Korea through tough unilateral and multilateral sanctions, by engaging China to exert pressure on Pyongyang to change its behaviour, strengthened its military preparedness and defense posture in cooperation with Japan and South Korea.[38]

Trump argues that China has a great economic power over North Korea. China has not been exerting maximum pressure on North Korea. He further adds that US still has tremendous power over China. Here he means the 'power of trade'. It appears to the analysts that Trump intends to use the 'trade policy' to pressurise China to persuade North Korea to stop its nuclear programme.[39]

Opportunities

What about the role of India and Pakistan in the region? I argue India is a mature nuclear power. India has performed better than other NPT member states in upholding the NPT norms despite being a non-member of the NPT. In an interesting article 'Geopolitics over Proliferation' by Thomas P. Cavanna the writer draws a theoretical debate to highlight the primacy of geopolitics over nonproliferation in South Asia at different technological, security and identity inter-connected levels. The writer argues that various geopolitical interests and engagements could not stop Pakistan and India from going nuclear. In a major policy change the July US-Joint Statement notably highlighted that India is a responsible country with advanced technology and must be given the same benefits as other states.[40]

The 48-nations Nuclear Suppliers Group (NSG) has been debating whether to include non-NPT countries like India and Pakistan. Since the year 2010, the US has supported India's membership in the four multilateral export control regimes, i.e. NSG, Australia Group, the missile technology control regime and Wassennar Arrangement. At present US is finding out ways to support India's membership bid to the NSG. US perceives India as a big opportunity in the Indo-Pacific region. India can become a reliable partner of the US in the region helping to strengthen the nonproliferation tool kit.[41]

Further experts opine India does not intend to engage with any nuclear arms race with Pakistan. Further, Pakistan cannot think of engaging in a nuclear arms race with India. Also it is unlikely that Japan will go nuclear.[42]

Conclusion

The Nonproliferation Policy seems to be in a flux and the game of the regime is changing. The recent international developments like the June 12 Singapore summit suggest an optimistic assessment may be premature and that continued success cannot be taken for granted. Solving the North Korea nuclear issue would be the real success for the Nonproliferation Regime. We see a major shift in the US Strategic Thinking today as critical questions about the role of US nuclear weapons in the US national security are being raised. President Trump has redefined US nuclear weapons policy by greatly calling to expand and strengthen US nuclear capability in contrast with his predecessors. US is aware that it faces new challenges like an unstable international environment, North Korea nuclear programme, and change in behaviour of its old trusted allies in the indo-pacific. The June 12 Singapore Summit can be considered unprecedented or historic as it marks a major shift in the US foreign policy approach. Though the North Korea threat has not entirely gone away yet. As we live in the age of uncertainty and fast changing world, US nuclear deterrence as the only strategy to maintain peace and stability in the region cannot solely resolve the current regional situation. Understanding the issues complexity, US has tailored various diplomatic, economic and military strategies to deter the new threats of the 21st century challenging US nonproliferation policy. US expresses a desire to maintain extended deterrence through military exercises to work with its allies to improve shared understanding of nuclear threats, aims to modernise its entire nuclear arsenal, and exert maximum pressure on North Korea to denuclearise its nuclear programme. President Trump is aware of the US economic power and intend to use the 'trade policy' to pressurise China to persuade North Korea to roll back its nuclear programme. India is seen as a big opportunity in US strategic calculations. India is capable of supporting US to maintain the credibility of nonproliferation policy in the Indo-Pacific region. The US today has less leverage than it once had to influence developments in the nonproliferation field. Nevertheless US leadership remains indispensable, especially pressurising North Korea to curb its nuclear programme.

NOTES

1 Brookings (2017), Non Proliferation Challenges Facing the Trump Administration 2017, Arms Control and Non-Proliferation Series, New York.
2 Kashyap, Upma (2016), *U.S.-Iran Nuclear Negotiations since 2009*, M.Phil. Dissertation, New Delhi: Jawaharlal Nehru University.
3 Brookings (2017), n. 1
4 Kashyap, Upma (2016), n. 2.
5 Cavanna, P. Thomas (2018), "Geopolitics over Proliferation: the origins of U.S. Grand Strategy and their implications for the spread of nuclear weapons in South Asia", *Journal of Strategic Studies*, 41(4): 576-603.
6 Brookings (2017), n. 1
7 Department of Defense (2018), Nuclear Posture Review, Department of Defense, Washington D.C.
8 Evans, Gareth (2013), "Nuclear Deterrence in Asia and the Pacific", *Asia and the Pacific Policy Studies,* 1(1): 91-111.
9 Department of Defense (2018), n. 7.
10 Seth, Ranjit (2018), "Asia Pacific Security in the Trump Era", available at http://cenjows.gov.in, accessed on 2 July 2018.
11 Glaser Alexander and Mian Zia (2017), "Japan and U.S. Nuclear Arms Control and Disarmament Policy under the Trump Administration; A Look into the Cloudy Crystal Ball", *The Asia Pacific Journal*, 15 (8).
12 Ibid.
13 The British American Security Information Council (BASIC) (2017), Changing Nuclear Weapons Policy in the Trump Era, The British American Security Information Council (BASIC), Westminster, London.
14 Seth, Ranjit (2018), n. 10.
15 Ibid.
16 Department of Defense (2018), n. 7.
17 Huges W., Christopher (2007), "North Korea's Nuclear Weapons: Implications for the Nuclear Ambitions of Japan, South Korea and Taiwan", *Asia Policy*, 3, 75-104.
18 Brookings (2017), n. 1.
19 Carnegie Endowment for International Peace (2018), Security Spillover: Regional Implications of Evolving Deterrence on the Korean Peninsula, Washington, DC.
20 Congressional Hearings, I (2017), U.S. 115th Congress, Session 1st Senate, Committee on Armed Services, Hearings, "U.S. Policy and Strategy in the Asia Pacific: Challenges and Opportunities", April 25, 2017, (U.S. Government Printing Office: Washington DC).
21 Carnegie Endowment for International Peace (2018), n. 19.
22 Congressional Hearings, I (2017), n. 20.
23 Brookings (2017), n. 1.
24 Hyun, Kim (2017), "Comparing North Korea Policies of the Obama and Trump Administrations", *Nanzan Review of American Studies*, vol 39: 45-69.
25 Hass, Rayan (2018), "Trump did not Solve the North Korea Problem in Singapore- in

fact, the threat has grown", available at www. Brookings.edu, accessed on 18 August 2018.

26 Revera, J.R. Evans (2018), "U.S. Policy and Pyongyang's Game Plan: Will we expect Nuclear Armed North Korea?", available at www.brookings.edu, accessed on August 2018.

27 Brookings (2017), n. 1.

28 Panda, Rajaram (2015), "Should South Korea go Nuclear?"*Asia-Pacific Review*, 22(1), 448-176.

29 Carnegie Endowment for International Peace (2018), n. 19.

30 Evans, Gareth (2013), n. 8.

31 Carnegie Endowment for International Peace (2018), n. 19.

32 Glaser Alexander and Mian Zia (2017), n. 11.

33 Brookings (2017), n. 1.

34 Department of Defense (2018), n. 7.

35 Ibid.

36 Ibid.

37 Glaser Alexander and Mian Zia (2017), n. 11.

38 Hyun, Kim (2017), n. 24.

39 Glaser Alexander and Mian Zia (2017), n. 11.

40 Cavanna, P. Thomas (2018), n. 5.

41 Brookings (2017), n. 1.

42 Balachandran, G. (2018), "Nuclear Arms Race in South Asia ?- An Analysis", *Strategic Analysis*, 42(3), 281-292.

REFERENCES

Brookings (2017), Non Proliferation Challenges Facing the Trump Administration 2017, Arms Control and Non-Proliferation Series, New York.

Balachandran, G. (2018), "Nuclear Arms Race in South Asia?: An Analysis", *Strategic Analysis*, 42(3), 281-292.

Carnegie Endowment for International Peace (2018), Security Spillover: Regional Implications of Evolving Deterrence on the Korean Peninsula, Washington, DC.

Cavanna, P. Thomas (2018), "Geopolitics over Proliferation:the origins of U.S. Grand Strategy and their implications for the spread of nuclear weapons in South Asia", *Journal of Strategic Studies*, 41(4): 576-603.

Congressional Hearings, I, (2017), U.S. 115th Congress, Session 1st Senate, Committee on Armed Services, Hearings, "U.S. Policy and Strategy in the Asia Pacific: Challenges and Opportunities", April 25, 2017 (U.S. Government Printing Office: Washington DC).

Department of Defense (2018), Nuclear Posture Review, Department of Defense, Washington D.C.

Evans, Gareth (2013), "Nuclear Deterrence in Asia and the Pacific", Asia and the *Pacific Policy Studies*, 1(1): 91-111.

Glaser Alexander and Mian Zia (2017), "Japan and U.S. Nuclear Arms Control and Disarmament Policy under the Trump Administration; A Look into the Cloudy Crystal Ball", *The Asia Pacific Journal*, 15 (8).

Hass, Rayan (2018), "Trump did not Solve the North Korea Problem in Singapore- in fact, the threat has grown", available at www. Brookings.edu, accessed on 18 August 2018.

Huges W., Christopher (2007), "North Korea's Nuclear Weapons: Implications for the Nuclear Ambitions of Japan, South Korea and Taiwan", *Asia Policy*, 3, 75-104.

Hyun, Kim (2017), "Comparing North Korea Policies of the Obama and Trump Administrations", *Nanzan Review of American Studies*, vol 39: 45-69.

Kashyap, Upma (2016), *U.S.-Iran Nuclear Negotiations since 2009*, M.Phil. Dissertation, New Delhi: Jawaharlal Nehru University.

McDonald, Matt (2017), "Critical Security in the Asia-Pacific: an Introduction", *Critical Studies on Security*, 5(3), 237-252.

Panda, Rajaram (2015), "Should South Korea go Nuclear?", *Asia-Pacific Review*, 22(1), 448-176.

Revera, J.R. Evans (2018), "U.S. Policy and Pyongyang's game plan: will we expect nuclear armed North Korea?" available at www.brookings.edu, accessed on August 2018.

Seth, Ranjit (2018), "Asia Pacific Security in the Trump Era", available at http://cenjows.gov.in, accessed on 2 July, 2018.

The British American Security Information Council (BASIC) (2017), Changing Nuclear Weapons Policy in the Trump Era, The British American Security Information Council (BASIC), Westminster, London.

14

Environmental Insecurity in the Indo-Pacific Region: Regional Cooperation and Challenges

Merieleen Engtipi

ABSTRACT

Stretching from the Pacific Basin, to the African coast of the Indian Ocean, the Indo-Pacific region represents a unique blend of abundant natural resources and extreme weather events. The region is known for its biodiversity, richness of species and marine ecosystem; it is home to numerous flora and fauna, mainly due to the presence of rainforest, wetlands and also desert vegetation. However, much of these resources are used for its economic development and most often leading to excessive stress to the environment and its resources. In the pursuit of economic development, the region was faced with a threat of overuse of its resources; and simultaneously, due to the rapid growth of industrialization, much of the industrial waste lacks proper disposal sites. These waste materials are disposed in open ground or in the sea leading to marine pollution and contamination of groundwater and also are a threat to already scarce water resources. Due to increasing population, deforestation is carried out for farming practices to feed the needs of the people and also urbanizing the rural spaces. With deforestation there is a growing concern about the endangered species losing their natural habitat, as the forest areas destroyed include mainly rainforests which have biologically diverse ecosystems. Simultaneously, deforestation also disrupts the natural harmony with growing carbon emissions in the air due to industrialization and less forest to reap the benefits.

The region had also suffered from extreme climatic events; it is prone to natural disasters as most countries sit in the Pacific ring of fire where 90 per cent seismic activity of the world originates. Marine pollution and Air pollution was also one of the major concerns facing the region; due to rapid industrialization and clearing up of lands, "slash-and-burn" for economic plantation, environmental hazards such as haze has become a problem not only to the individual states but to the neighbouring states as well. Dumping of radioactive and electronic waste, oil spill, and overfishing were the foremost reasons for the depletion of marine resources and the disruption and destruction of coral reefs. However, these environmental problems have become a part of greater security studies due to its conflicting nature over scarce resources, which directly affects the socio-economic livelihood of the people, and also the transboundary nature of environmental impact itself.

This chapter focuses on three aspects of environmental security that relates to marine pollution, air pollution and natural disasters. Firstly, it explores the concept of environmental security and its applicability in the region. Why is environmental security an important issue to deal with? This section analyses the human security perspectives and also national security concern of the individual states. Secondly, what are the growing environmental security concerns in the region? A descriptive analysis will be given on three aspects of environmental problems- marine pollution, mostly from the toxic chemical waste, oil spill and blast fishing; air pollution causing from "slash-and-burn" practises, deforestation, rapid growth of industries; and, environmental hazards caused by tsunami, earthquakes, typhoons, and also nuclear accidents. Lastly, it also analyses the regional framework for cooperation towards a more sustainable environment and developmental practises and its challenges.

Environmental Security as a Concept

The concept of environmental security has emerged in the 1980s, until then 'security studies' was focused on the security of the states from external threats. However, in the early 1960s, the concern for environment was prevalent in the works of some environmental thinkers such as Rachel Carson, Murray Bookchin, and Ralph Nader. Rachel Carson's Silent Spring has garnered much focus on the environmental issues bringing awareness on the environmental consequences based on our actions. The 1960s and 1970s saw the history of environmental awareness and also the environmental problem such as pollution of water, air, and soil, depletion of the ozone layer and enhanced greenhouse gases caused by human activity, and a realistic proposal to address the issue through sustainable development.[1] Simultaneously, the academic community mainly dealing with 'security studies' tried to broaden the concept of security. Barry Buzan et al. (1998), in "Security: A New Framework for Analysis," wrote about the widening and deepening of the security concept. Buzan et al., suggested five components of security that are military, economic, societal, political and environmental security.[2] Environmental Security is the protection of the human environment and their infrastructure against natural disasters. It includes the security of the natural resources in the form of depletion of freshwater resources and loss of fertile land by the soil erosion.[3] Environmental Security is also most often, defined as the protection of the people by the state, from the environmental threats and threats that have an environmental origin.[4]

In Hans Gunter Branch (2005), Security has been a critical concept in two competing schools: 1) from a Hobbesian perspective of war, military, strategic or security studies; and 2) from a Kantian or Grotian standpoint of peace and conflict research that has focused on conflict prevention. Since the 1990s, the distance between the two schools has been narrowed with "new approaches and inter-paradigm debates relevant to security have emerged between traditional approaches, critical security studies, and constructive approaches."[5] Alongside the scope of 'securitisation', the referent object has also been changed from 'national' to 'human-centric' security concept, and in the academic community, the concept of security is peace-focused.

Scholars have clubbed the environmental security issues on the human security agenda over the years. The United Nations have also incorporated the environmental dimension of human security. The UNDP's Human Development Report of 1994 consolidated the concept of Human Security in its agenda. Seven core areas fall under the purview of human security—food security, political security, economic security, health security, personal security, community security, and environmental security.[6] In the report of the Secretary General's high-level panel on Threats, Challenges, and Change on 2 December 2004, environmental degradation has sought to enhance the occurrence, and destructive potential of natural disaster, which have taken a toll on human lives and affected millions of people and the economic toll surpassed the previous four decades.[7]

Environmental security has the credibility to engage in an isolated approach of study because it is directly or indirectly related to the national security issue.[8] Brauch (2008) emphasises on the environment as a 'new threat to national security' and environment as a contributing factor to hazards, crises, migration and also in some cases leads to conflict. Brauch cited the works of Mathews (1989) and Myers (1989), following the end of the Cold War, debates on the issue of widening the concept of security concept in the US. In the works of Myers (1989), environmental factors such as ozone layer depletion, soil erosion, and climate change have a legitimate cause for international concern and may have repercussions for US security policy. He moreover pointed that environmental issue leading to a conflict are population growth, mass extinction of species, global warming and ozone layer depletion which have an indirect impact, and on the other hand, environmental refugees as a direct consequence. In the US, whether environmental security is a part of a broader national security strategy can be known from the National Security Strategy, published by the incumbent administration.[9]

Dokken (2001), in his study on environmental security issues, and the driving force to regional integration, noted that "it is issues of politico-military security that are likely to generate calls for closer international cooperation. Increasingly, problems of environmental security will do the same. Regional environmental problems may be considered concerning shared hazards and shared resources: both categories are now poised to acquire significant integrative potential."[10] According to him, this concept does not make a contradiction between the 'international environmental regimes and vital national interest,' but instead cooperation on environmental issues could sustain these natural resources for the next generation.

Environmental Problem is a Matter of 'Security' and not just an 'Issue'

The environmental issue is not a standalone problem; it is interconnected and tends to evolve into several issues concerning security. There are several reasons why it has been termed as a matter of security and just a problem. Environmental Security is essential for a state to protect its citizens caused by threats posed by the neighboring countries through their hazardous practices. The new challenges faced after the end of the Cold War such as environment meant, security of the individuals as a human being and not just as a citizen of a state.[11] Simultaneously, when states are forced to take extraordinary measures to remove the threats caused by the environmental problem, it becomes a security issue.[12]

In most scenarios, the region suffers from a transboundary or spillover effects of pollution. The countries of the region have their own standards of conducting their industrial practices. Some nations are strict in their industrial regulations, while others loosely follow any industrial regulations. In East Asia, due to the air pollution caused by the coal-fired plants and industrial activities of China, there seemed to be a tension between Japan, South Korea, and

China. Transboundary pollution can be measured as an external environmental threat and can be considered as a matter of security for the immediate neighbors that are victims of this transboundary pollution.

Scarcity of resources is also an essential environmental security concerns. There has been an increasing number of cross-boundary migration and refugee flows due to the shortage of resources like water, land, and wood for fuel caused by land degradation due to soil erosion, over cultivation and deforestation. Studies show that the primary drivers for cross-boundary migration from North Korea into China and South Korea are political subjugation and environmental disruption such as resource scarcity. Fishing in regional water is also an issue because states in the region share the exclusive economic zones concerning maritime boundary.[13]

Environmental Problems facing the Indo-Pacific Region

Despite the vastness, the region had shared both common and specific environmental issues pertaining to the region. This section focuses on the various environmental issues concerning the region due to alarming levels of pollution both on land and in water caused by the rapid growth of industrialisation and commercialisation. Under the broader umbrella of atmospheric and marine pollution, region-specific activities will be analyzed. Natural disasters have proven to be an essential component in the destruction and loss of lives, property, and also to the natural environment itself.

Due to the growth of the tourism industry, the region is much aware of the marine environment through which the coastal countries generate much of the revenue. Due to the vastness of the Oceans, it was assumed to be unpollutable despite the dumping of harmful elements in the ocean surface. However, in the recent past, a severe agenda of securing the marine environment and its resources have become an issue of grave concern. The region is known for its biodiversity, and there has been an increasing number of human activities in the flourishing and yet sensitive environment. However, there has been growing concern about the loss of biodiversity and also the also the depletion of coral reefs due to the various activities conducted by humans both on land and offshore. These activities have over the years taken a toll on the marine environment.

Overfishing and the Methods of Fishing: The fish stocks of the world are considered to be at risk due to excessive fishing, and also the methods carried in fishing. Illegal, Unreported and Unregulated (IUU) fishing are carried out as a large-scale profitable business in the region. Illegal fishing creates an order of fishing beyond nature's capacity to produce, therefore disrupting the natural order.[14] Several hotspots in the region that have a medium to high risk of facing severe threats of food security, since fish is consumed in large quantity by the people of the region.[15] However, the issue here relating to pollution is the methods used for fishing in the high seas. In the African coast of the Indian Ocean region, blast fishing is a common tactic used by the illegal fishers.[16] Blast fishing as a method of fishing was seen as a convenient method for the fisherman to secure their catches in huge numbers. However, it destroys the marine habitat, reducing the sustainability of the aquatic creatures and also reducing the possibility of future catches, which might affect the food security and the communities that depend on fishing as a livelihood. The fishing industry is regulated in the European countries; however, it is not the case in most developing countries which is mainly witnessed in the African coast of the Indian Ocean and the South-east Asian region.[17]

South-east Asia's marine ecosystem is diverse and attracts tourists from all over the world. However, this is threatened by over and destructive fishing which is carried out in no small number, and most often unregulated. Recent studies suggest that over 64 per cent of the resource base of the fisheries is calculated at a medium to high risk from overfishing. Cambodia and the Philippines are amongst the most to be profoundly affected. The methods of fishing here also include poison fishing, and this is because of the high demand for live fish. The poison fishing has become a commercial fishing method for live reef fish; sodium cyanide stuns the fish which makes them easier to catch.[18]

Oils spill in the High Seas: Oil pollution is also one of the major concerns, as the region hosts some of the busiest shipping lanes. The region has some of the major sea lanes in the world, the Indian Ocean through which major international trade is carried, out and also the Malacca Straits which is one of the busiest sea lanes in the world.[19] An oil spill has the most destructive effects on the marine environment. Most often oil tankers face the problem of leakage which creates a surface of greasy oil that puts a barrier to the marine ecosystem that has harmful effects on their health. It continues to increase due to the sheer scope of oil operation stems from an ever increasing demand for energy. The level of oil pollution was seen worst in the Sea of Japan, and its level of pollution was most often 2.5 times the level than the unpolluted waters. Likewise, marine oil pollution had been tripled along the coast of South Korea, and apparently, the 'yellow sea' is termed as one of the 'dying seas' of the world.[20] One of the studies conducted by ITOPF shows that 50 per cent of the oil spill from the period 1970 to 2017 occurred when the vessels were underway in the open waters. Allisions, collisions, and grounding accounted for 59 per cent of the oil spilled. Simultaneously, this percentage goes even higher when the vessels were underway in inland or restricted waters.[21]

Radioactive and Industrial Waste: The Indo-Pacific region is one of the fastest growing economies of the world with industrial and economic development ranging from developmental stage to the highest stages of technological progress. History suggests that much of the advancements are seen usually in the region that has accessibility to cheap means of transportation such as sea lanes. Some of the highly industrialised countries are Japan, Singapore, China, South Korea, and Taiwan. Simultaneously, the region is home to the world's nuclear power countries such as China, India, Japan, South Korea, and Pakistan. In recent years, dumping of the radioactive and industrial waste in the Oceans has put severe concern in the environmental agenda of the region. Energy consumption has increased over the years due to economic development, which resulted in an increasing demand for energy, and nuclear power was developed to fill the need.[22] With the increasing number of nuclear power plants in operation, the problem of radioactive waste accumulation has become more serious, and so the case for nuclear waste management. The problem arising from the nuclear management and disposal has been due to the shortage of storage space for radioactive waste and also the inability to find a suitable place to build storage facilities for some countries.[23]

Radioactive waste that contains radioactive nuclear substance is generated from industries like mining, scientific research, medicine, defense, a nuclear power generator that produce by-products that include radioactive waste. These radioactive wastes are classified into—high level, low level, and intermediate level. Today, 90 per cent of the radioactive waste is low-level waste from the nuclear reactors, hospitals, etc. Industrial waste such as plastics, chemicals, and toxic pollutant have in addition contributed the largest to marine pollution and concurrently caused harmful effects to the marine environment due to the lack of proper waste management system. A US-based non-profit environmental organisation observed that five countries contribute to 60 per cent of all plastics that enter the world's ocean—China, Indonesia, the Philippines, Thailand, and Vietnam.[24]

Parallel to the industrial growth, the region has been facing serious health issues relating to air pollution caused by a number of factors in relation to the industrial activities, coupled with deforestation and the slash-and-burn tactics used for clearing the lands.

Industrial Activities: The industrial and manufacturing activities carried out in the region emit high levels of smoke and sulphur dioxide in the air. The industrial plants, power plants, and factories release organic compound, carbon monoxide, chemicals into the air. Oil refineries, cement factories, steel and aluminum plants, chemical factories, and producers of plastics are amongst the industries that release most harmful materials into the air. In addition to this, burning of woods, charcoal, and fuel produced from crop waste is also a contributor especially taken up for household activity such as cooking and heating.[25] Mining has also contributed to the overall atmospheric pollution; it had caused severe environmental damage leading to contamination of water, and eventually killing or poisoning fish, as well as damaging crops on the land. The sulphur dioxide emitted in the air from coal-burning factories, and power plants emanate dangers of acid rain, to which the East Asian nations are vulnerable.[26] Simultaneously, carbon dioxide released from the coal-fired plants caused the greenhouse effect—global warming, a rise in the sea level and climate change. The consumption and production of some of the hazardous industrial products are some of the reasons for the emission of chlorofluorocarbons (CFCs) that depletes the ozone layer.[27]

Deforestation and Desertification: Despite the presence of enormous rainforest, vast desert vegetation, and tropical climate, the concern is, however, the fast pace by which deforestation is carried out. Most of the forest cover has been clear either for making space for human habitat or for farming purposes. The efforts for forestation by the government have proven little to improve the situation. Deforestation is an alarming concern not only for the loss of biodiversity but it is an existential crisis for already endangered species which may occur at a fast pace due to loss of natural habitat.[28] In places where deforestation is acute, natural hazards such as landslides is a common phenomenon, it causes the soil to lose it firmness, and correspondingly degrading the quality of the land.

Deforestation also leads to degradation of natural forest and desertification; it is a problem due to overcutting beyond the levels of sustainability. All these are perceived to be environmental consequences due to failures in preserving the natural forest environment. Illegal logging carried out in most countries of the region is one of the reasons behind deforestation. The efforts for reforestation are also affected due to frequent logging. The increase in deforestation has been linked to the increasing demands for forest timbers and substantial timber industries. Deforestation in the region was at its peak in the 1990s, however, in the 2000s there has been some decline in logging, with an annual average of 5.9 million acres in the 1990s to 1.73 million acres in the 2000s.[29] However, it stills continue to threaten some biodiversity hotspots in the region, and also the endangered species.

Transboundary Haze Pollution: Haze pollution is prevalent in the countries of the region that subscribe to the method of clearing uplands such as 'slash-and-burn.' It affects human health and shows symptoms in the forms of sore throats, itchy eyes and blocked noses. Slash-and-burn is used by farmers to clear up patches of land for plantation. It is a method where the farmers cut down vegetation from a piece of land, and the rest of the residues are set on fire. The biomass produce after cutting the vegetation degrade faster when set on fire. In the short run, it is cost-effective and also helpful in getting rid of any diseases that might have affected the previous vegetation. However, it is due to the uncontrollable nature of fire during the dry seasons, which leads to forest fires and creates haze. These fires produce thick smog which releases a significant volume of greenhouse gases. Countries like Indonesia and Malaysia face the severe issue of haze due to the slash-and-burn method used by the farmers. Due to the transboundary nature of haze pollution, it has become a problem to the neighboring countries like Singapore and the Southern part of Thailand.[30]

However, other than the ignorant farmers, there are also illegal activities carried out by the palm oil companies. The concern has been that the palm oil companies have been using the slash-and-burn tactics to clear up more lands for the palm oil plantation. Palm oil has been in high demand, and also there has been a growing need for more plantation space. Therefore, it has been hard to decipher who is behind the slash-and-burn, the ignorant farmers or the greedy palm oil companies. There were deliberate attempts to burn the rainforest so that the companies could get their hands on the abundant lands for the palm oil plantation.[31] Indonesia is one of the largest producers of palm oil and the demand for palm oil has been increasing due to its utilities in various products from shampoos, to cosmetics, and biscuits to biofuels, etc.

Natural Disasters and their Effects on the Socio-Economic and Natural Environment

Natural disasters are a challenge the region in tackling with, and mostly due to its frequent occurrences. Extreme weather events had previously caused loss of lives, damages to property and severe strains to socio-economic development, which comes to a standstill. The other problem that can be seen is the varying degree by which a country could respond and also reduce the risk of these natural disasters. Typhoons and Cyclones have become part of some countries climatic conditions such as the Philippines. Frequent occurrences create an economy that sought for reconstruction and redevelopment after every natural hazard than actually moving ahead with developing its economy. The Pacific islands nation is primarily vulnerable to environmental hazards such as tropical cyclones, typhoons, and floods, and would be highly exposed to sea level rises resulting from global warming.[32] Extreme weather conditions also jeopardise gains in access to water and sanitation. Drought reduces drinking water availability, and floods and storms caused damages to basic water infrastructure and spread disease.

Earthquakes of low intensity are also common phenomenon in the region, however, when occurred on higher scale they disrupt the community and its infrastructure coupled with the loss of lives. These create serious damages to the basic infrastructure as most concrete structures are not equipped to deal with a high intensity earthquake, and are likely to be damaged. The process of clearing the debris, rebuilding communities and its infrastructures is also a costly affair.[33]

Natural disasters such as the tsunamis are also not alien to the region. One of the most massive tsunamis that had affected more than two countries of the region is the Indian Ocean Tsunami which occurred in the year 2006. Simultaneously, the tsunami that took place in Japan in 2011 was noted as the costliest disaster regarding the infrastructural damage it causes and also the process of clearing the debris.[34] Japan is familiar with earthquakes, and most buildings are constructed to withstand the shock of an earthquake. Before 2011, Japan faced instances of Tsunami. However, the nature and scale of the 2011 tsunami was nothing sort of an ordinary. The tsunami created serious damage to the nuclear reactor cooling facilities leading to series of meltdown.[35] The 2006 tsunami, on the other hand, affected several countries with loss of lives and a state of chaos. The international community had to lend their support for the damages caused by the hazards of this scale.

Floods are also frequent in the region due to lowlands and untamed waterways. Monsoons are also one of the reasons for the floods to occur. These floods have a serious effect on communities residing beside the river and even low lying plains. India, Bangladesh, and China suffered more frequently from flooding, leading to several deaths and affecting millions, and also contributing to substantial economic losses.[36] The Ganges, Brahmaputra, and Yangtze are the three Himalayan Rivers that contributes to the flooding in these three countries. As major cities are built alongside the rivers for availing the ports and alongside massive losses occur in the cities when increased flooding takes place beyond their resilience capacity.[37]

Regional Cooperation and Challenges on Environmental Issues

The industrial and economic growth of the region is juxtaposed with the rising concern for the health of the earth's atmosphere. The region has several mechanisms through which the cooperation on environmental issues is carried. Regional cooperation on environmental problems has been crucial in highlighting the issues based on transboundary pollution, sharing information based on lessons learned and collectively adopting measures to effectively tackle disasters with proper management.

Indian Ocean Region

The Indian Ocean region is uniquely diverse in size, culture and language, and economic strength. It is vital to maintain the security of the Indian Ocean for the socio-economic development and also to reap its uninterrupted benefits. For the sustainable growth and development of the countries in the region, the Indian Ocean Rim Association (IORA) was established in March 1997. In 2011, the IORA made Maritime Safety and Security (MSS) as the chief area of focus.[38] The Indian Ocean derives its importance from being a transit to trade vessels and where international trade is carried out. Therefore, it required specific attention for the safety of the region and for international peace and security. The security dimension of MSS focus on the security from crime at seas; security of natural resources and environmental security falls within the purview. The MSS focuses on the issue of IUU fishing, natural disasters, oil spills and effects on climate change.

IORA's counterpart the Indian Ocean Commission is an intergovernmental organisation uniting the five island countries of Comoros, Madagascar, Mauritius, Reunion/France, and Seychelles. The IOC acknowledges the dependence on the marine resources which also plays a considerable role in poverty reduction and improving the living condition of the society. Sustainability and management of the marine resources have been the core focus since two key economic generators such as fisheries and tourism depend on the very resources.[39] The IOC emphasises monitoring and management of the fisheries, its biodiversity and also its natural resources. Simultaneously, the IOC seeks to enhance the awareness of the policymakers, NGOs, and the civil society on the issue of coastal zone management. In order to tackle marine pollution, the IOC engages itself with various multilateral bodies for the primary purpose of "capacity building for prevention of coastal and marine contamination" and "building capacity for regional oil and chemical spill response."[40] For the marine ecosystem to flourish there is a delicate balance between the land and the seas. The activities on land can hamper the resources on seas; this is where waste management comes to play an important role. Since the region is not industrialised, less concern has been shown for proper waste management which leads to the accumulation of polluting material. The toxic waste is mostly for the consumption of imported goods such as batteries etc. However, a majority of its waste are mainly organic waste; therefore, converting the organic waste into bio-fertiliser is their first strategy, followed by reuse and recycle and also promotes ecotourism.[41]

The Indian Ocean Commission (IOC) in collaboration with *Stop Illegal Fishing* has been working to stop IUU fishing. IUU fishing is a concern not only for the marine ecosystems. However, it has been a shield to various illegal activities carried out from human trafficking to money laundering.[42] The Indian Ocean Commission along with Stop Illegal Fishing looked into the matter to best sustain the fishing activities without carrying any harmful methods. They also encourage sea farming because there is a risk of more demand and less supply due to activities carried out by humans. Blast fishing is prohibited by the governments of six nations in the Indian Ocean Commission.[43] Tanzania carries out the highest number of IUU fishing through blast fishing. The Indian Ocean-Pacific Rim countries also sees IUU fishing and its methods as a security concern. Relating to natural hazards, the IORA is seeking to provide a better Humanitarian Assistance, and Disaster Relief (HADR) to the victims through bilateral or multilateral exercises of HADR carried out in the Indian Ocean region.

East-Asian Region

Japan, South and North Korea, Mongolia, China, Taiwan categorically fall in the East-Asia region. The region is industrially developed and also highly prone to extreme climatic events. The primary concerns of the region are the marine pollution caused by radioactive waste and industrial waste dumping, oil spills, and agricultural chemicals in the Yellow and South China Sea, Sea of Japan, and the East China Sea. Since the time the East Asian states became a nuclear power, issues had been raised on the proper storage for the radioactive waste. In recent history, debates rose on the dumping of radioactive materials by Russia and Taiwan in the seas of the region close to Japan.[44] Simultaneously, Japan after the failure of the nuclear reactor had a problem with leakage and also sought to dump its radioactive material in the Ocean. However, there has been lots of opposition from the fishermen due to fear of contamination from the fish. Though several tests were conducted to prove there it has no harmful effects on the fish, however, the concern shown by the fishermen is that it would not play well with the psychology of the consumers.

Due to transboundary pollution, these countries suffer from the negative effects of industrial activities, and harmful effect on the environment. The region cooperates through the Northeast Asia Subregional Programme for Environmental Cooperation (NEASPEC); it is an intergovernmental effort to address issues and challenges in the North-east. NEASPEC organises conferences and also high-level visits of foreign dignitaries to discuss relevant environmental issues and seek regional cooperation for information sharing, conducting research and training, and monitoring conditions such as marine pollution, acid rain, biodiversity, etc.[45] NEASPEC has worked in the areas of nature conservation, transboundary air pollution, desertification, and land degradation, and managing the marine protected areas. The effort has also been made on adopting and advancing low carbon cities in the sub-region.

There has been no intergovernmental mechanism to tackle the challenges posed by disasters that have occurred in the region prior to 2008. Japan, China, and South Korea have made a trilateral engagement on disaster management to conduct research, share information on projects, and initiatives based on lessons learned. Development framework for comprehensive disaster management, adopting measures and systems for reducing and minimising damages from disasters, and strengthening the disaster management at the national, local, and community level are the three core areas the trilateral engagement sought to enhance cooperation.[46]

South-East Asian Region

The Association for South-East Asian Nation (ASEAN) is regional intergovernmental cooperation which deals with numerous issues relating to the region. The ASEAN also focuses on the environmental issue relating to the region. Since 1977, ASEAN has cooperated closely with its member states on promoting environmental cooperation among its member states. ASEAN's institutional framework on the cooperation on environment consists of ASEAN Ministerial Meeting on Environment (AMME) and ASEAN Senior Officials on Environment (ASOEN). Under ASOEN, there are seven subsidiaries/ working groups—ASEAN working group on Climate Change, on Chemicals and Waste, Coastal and Marine Environment, Environmental Education, on Environmentally Sustainable Cities, Nature Conservation, and Biodiversity, and on Water Recourses Management.[47]

The ASEAN Agreement on Transboundary Haze Pollution (AATHP) was signed on 10 June 2002 in Kuala Lumpur, following severe land and forest fires in 1997-98. In the 12th meeting of the Conference of the Parties (COP-12) to the ASEAN Agreement on Transboundary Haze Pollution (AATHP) held in 2016 in Kuala Lumpur, which adopted the roadmap on ASEAN cooperation towards transboundary haze pollution control with means of implementation.[48] The roadmap provided strategic, action-oriented, a time-bound framework with a vision to achieve Transboundary Haze free ASEAN by 2020.

Prone to disasters, ASEAN countries consider disaster management and humanitarian assistance as one of their top priorities. On 7 December 2004, ASEAN Ministerial Meeting on Disaster Management (AMMDM) met for the first time in Phnom Penh, Cambodia, in which they agreed upon on negotiating the ASEAN Agreement on Disaster Management and Emergency Response (AADMER). The ASEAN Agreement on Disaster Management and Emergency Response were signed by the foreign ministers of ASEAN in Vientiane, Lao PDR in July 2005.[49] ASEAN has also made efforts to work together in cohesion within and outside the region such as India and the UN.

Pacific Island Countries

Pacific Island countries are prone to natural hazards and shared environmental problems such as cyclones, tropical storms, flood, sea level fluctuation, land degradation, and the shortage of natural resources. The Island countries do not contribute to the air or marine pollution in comparison to its counterpart in the region. They are small island countries and least industrially development with the modest economy. Regional Organisations were formed as a mechanism to coordinate common environmental problems faced by the region. The

Council for Regional Organisations of the Pacific (CROP) is a formal mechanism to ensure synergies of goals and initiatives taken by the region.[50] The member organisations are: South Pacific Regional Environment Programme (SPREP); Forum Secretariat; Forum Fisheries Agency; South Pacific Applied Geoscience Commission; Secretariat of the Pacific Community; Tourism Council of the South Pacific; University of South Pacific; and Pacific Island Development Programme.

SPREP has helped to develop the island countries in capacity building and improving environmental management strategies. It has focused on issues relating to waste management, climate change, and impact assessment. Forum Fisheries Agency looks into the sustainability of fishery resources. Regional organisations such as Secretariat of the Regional Environmental Programme, based in Samoa have lately focused their attention on improving energy efficiency. Alongside the regional cooperation, various state and non-state entities outside the region also helped in building sustainability in the region. The United Nations with the support from Japan was implementing the coastal zone management programmes in Fiji, Marshall Islands, Tuvalu, and Samoa. Some of the national programmes conducted in Tonga, Vanuatu, and the Solomon Islands include promotion of eco-tourism activities and the establishment of species and habitat conservation areas.[51]

Challenges in Conducting the Environmental Cooperation Mechanisms

The uniqueness of the Indo-Pacific region lies in its diversity, diversity in race, culture, history, governmental policies, etc. However, this diverse environment has also played to its weaknesses and simultaneously it a challenge the region has to overcome to form a multilateral cooperation on issues such as the environment. In most governments, the barriers to including environmental security in its policies are not economic, legal, or technological but it is, however, cultural.[52] Firstly, the differences in capabilities and capacity of the countries in the region to handle the environmental hazards of greater scale have put an uneven footing in overall effectiveness. The region is splendid with commitments made in the Vienna Convention, Montreal Protocol, UNFCCC, Kyoto Protocol and also various others chemical related conventions. However, despite the pledges, technical constraints are what the regions' member states have been facing. With commitments came many obligations which weigh heavily on the financial and human resources of member countries.

For the multilateral cooperation to succeed, the focus should be on the operability of the policies decided upon. Operability is a key to ensure proper management of resources, policies that do not disrupt proper functioning in times of calamity and cooperation in hazards. Secondly, like-mindedness of the leaders alike is a crucial ingredient in creating a successful multilateral cooperation on the environmental problems. Since the region has a unique blend of governance, the leaders' ability to cut across different ideologies will remove many hurdles in putting across ideas. Thirdly, transparency, in addition, is a critical element in building trust and engaging in building a common future. If a proper account of the countries activities in emanating pollution is put forward in faith, the cooperation on the environment can be enhanced with proper knowledge and management. Lastly, accountability is necessary for engaging in the multilateral platform for the overall success. Where transboundary pollution is unavoidable, accountability helps in ensuring the future course of actions.

NOTES

1 Environmental history timeline, available at http://environmentalhistory.org/20th-century/sixties-1960-1969/

2 Buzan, Barry, Ole Waever, and Jaap de Wilde (1998), "Security: A New Framework for Analysis." Published by: Lynne Rienner Publishers, London.

3 Akhram, Mehwish (2017), "How human security is Linked with environmental security," in Foreign Policy News, available at http://foreignpolicynews.org/2017/09/14/human-security-linked-environmental-security/

4 Bae, Young Ja (2005), "Environmental Security in East Asia: The case of Radioactive waste," in Asian Perspective, Vol. 29, No. 2, pp. 73-79. Published by Lynne Rienner Publishers, available at http:/www.jstor.org/stable/42704503

5 Brauch, Hans G. (2005), "Environment and human security: towards freedom from hazard impacts," in UN U-EHS InterSections, Vol. 2, Published by UNU-EHS: Bonn.

6 United Nations Development Programme—Human Development Report 1994, Published for United Nations Development Programme by Oxford University Press, available at http://hdr.undp.org/sites/default/files/reports/255/hdr_1994_en_complete_nostats.pdf

7 United Nations and the Rule of Law (2004), "The Secretary-General's High-Level Panel Report on Threats, Challenges, and Change, A more secure world: our shared responsibility." Source: wed, available at https://www.un.org/ruleoflaw/blog/document/the-secretary-generals-high-level-panel-report-on-threats-challenges-and-change-a-more-secure-world-our-shared-responsibility/

8 Levy, Marc A. (1995), "Is the Environment a National Security Issue?" in International Security, Vol. 20, No.2, pp. 35-62. Published by the MIT Press, available at http://www.jstor.org/stable/2539228

9 Brauch, Hans Gunter (2008), "Conceptualising the environmental dimension of human security in the UN," Vol. 5, No 1, pp. 19-48. Published by Wiley Online Library, available at https://onlinelibrary.wiley.com/doi/abs/10.1111/j.1468-2451.2008.00631.x

10 Dokken, Karin (2001), "Environment, Security, and regionalism in the Asia-Pacific: is environmental security a useful concept?", *The Pacific Review*, Vol. 14, No. 4, pp. 509-530.

11 Graeger, Nina (1996), "Environmental Security?", *Journal of Peace Research*, Vol. 33, No.1, pp.109-116. Published by Sage Publication, ltd. Stable available at https:/www.jstor.org/stable/425137

12 Bae, Young Ja (2005), "Environmental Security in East Asia: The case of Radioactive waste," *Asian Perspective*, Vol. 29, No. 2, pp. 73-79. Published by Lynne Rienner Publishers, available at http:/www.jstor.org/stable/42704503

13 Haque, M. Shamsul (2001), "Environmental Security in East Asia: A critical view," *The Journal of Strategic Studies*, Vol. 24, No. 4, pp. 203-234.

14 FAO Newsroom (2004), Overfishing on the increase in Asia-Pacific seas, available at http://www.fao.org/newsroom/en/news/2004/49367/index.html

15 DeRidder, Kim J. and Santi Nindang (2018), "Southeast Asia's Fisheries Near Collapse from Overfishing," *The Asia Foundation*, available at https://asiafoundation.org/2018/03/28/southeast-asias-fisheries-near-collapse-overfishing/

16 Stop illegal fishing, Blast Fishing, available at https://stopillegalfishing.com/issues/blast-fishing/

17 FAO, Selected issues facing fisheries and aquaculture in Asia and the Pacific, available at http://www.fao.org/docrep/009/ag110e/AG110E08.htm

18 DeRidder, Kim J. and Santi Nindang (2018), "Southeast Asia's Fisheries near Collapse from Overfishing," *The Asia Foundation*, available at https://asiafoundation.org/2018/03/28/southeast-asias-fisheries-near-collapse-overfishing/

19 Stewart, Paige (2018), "Major Shipping Routes for Global Trade," *ArcBest*, available at https://arcb.com/blog/major-shipping-routes-for-global-trade

20 Haque, M. Shamsul (2001), "Environmental Security in East Asia: A critical view," The Journal of Strategic Studies, Vol. 24, No. 4, pp. 203-234; Lee, Geun (2002), "Environmental Security in East Asia: The Regional Environmental Security Complex Approach," *Asian Perspective*, Vol. 26, No. 2, pp. 77-99. Published by Lynne Rienner Publishers. Stable available at https://www.jstor.org/stable/42704361

21 ITOPF, Oil Tanker Spill Statistics 2017, available at http://www.itopf.org/knowledge-resources/data-statistics/statistics/

22 Chen, Nai Y. (2001), "Energy in the 21st Century," *Chemical Innovation*, Vol. 31, No.1, Published by ACS Publications, available at http://pubs.acs.org/subscribe/archive/ci/31/i01/toc/toc_i01.html

23 Bae, Young Ja (2005), "Environmental Security in East Asia: The case of Radioactive waste," *Asian Perspective*, Vol. 29, No. 2, pp. 73-79. Published by Lynne Rienner Publishers, available at http:/www.jstor.org/stable/42704503

24 Winn, Patrick (2016), "5 Countries spew more plastics into the oceans than the rest of the world together," *Global Post*, available at https://www.pri.org/stories/2016-01-12/5-countries-spew-more-plastic-oceans-rest-world-together

25 World Health Organizations (2018), Household air pollution and health, available at http://www.who.int/news-room/fact-sheets/detail/household-air-pollution-and-health

26 Library Index, Acid Rain—A Global Problem, available at https://www.libraryindex.com/pages/1144/Acid-Rain-GLOBAL-PROBLEM.html

27 ACS Chemistry for Life, Chlorofluorocarbons and Ozone Depletion, available at https://www.acs.org/content/acs/en/education/whatischemistry/landmarks/cfcs-ozone.html

28 National Geographic, Climate 101: Deforestation, available at https://www.nationalgeographic.com/environment/global-warming/deforestation/

29 Brown, Vanda Felbab (2011), "Not as Easy as Falling off a log: The Illegal Logging Trade in the Asia-Pacific Region and Possible Mitigation Strategies," Foreign Policy at Brookings, Working Paper No. 5, available at https://www.brookings.edu/wp-content/uploads/2016/06/03_illegal_logging_felbabbrown.pdf

30 *BBC News* (2013), South East Asia Haze: What is slash-and-burn? Source: web, available at https://www.bbc.com/news/business-23026219

31 Ibid.

32 UNESCO Media Services (2012), Water Resources in the Asia-Pacific are increasingly threatened by pollution and vulnerable to natural disasters, available at http://www.unesco.org/new/en/media-services/single-view/news/water_resources_in_ the_asia_pacific_region_are_increasingly/

33 *BBC News* (2011), Japan says quake rebuilding to cost as much as 25tn yen, available at https://www.bbc.com/news/business-12828181

34 Ibid.

35 CNN (2011), three nuclear reactors melted down after the quake, Japan Confirms, available at http://edition.cnn.com/2011/WORLD/asiapcf/06/06/japan.nuclear.meltdown/index.html

36 Wescott, Ben and Steve George (2017), "Asia under water: How 137 million people's lives are being put at risk," *CNN News*, August 20, 2017, available at https://edition.cnn.com/2017/07/24/asia/climate-change-floods-asia/index.html

37 Asia Development Bank, Fighting Poverty in Asia and the Pacific. Source: Web, available at https://www.adb.org/green-cities/index.html

38 IORA, Marine Safety, and Security, available at http://www.iora.int/en/priorities-focus-areas/maritime-safety-and-security

39 Indian Ocean Commission, Archives, available at http://www.commissionoceanindien.org/archives/environment.ioconline.org/home.html

40 Ibid.

41 Ibid.

42 Stop Illegal Fishing, Issues, available at https://stopillegalfishing.com/all-issues/

43 Ibid.

44 Haque, M. Shamsul (2001), "Environmental Security in East Asia: A critical view," *The Journal of Strategic Studies*, Vol. 24, No. 4, pp. 203-234.

45 NEASPEC, about NEASPEC, available at http://neaspec.org/about-neaspec

46 UNISDR, China-Japan-Republic of Korea Trilateral Cooperation on Disaster Management, available at https://www.unescap.org/sites/default/files/S4-2_Kim.pdf

47 ASEAN Annual Report 2016, ASEAN Cooperation on Environment at a glance, available

at http://environment.asean.org/wp-content/uploads/2018/02/ASEAN-Cooperation-on-Environment-At-A-Glance-Dec-2017.pdf

48 ASEAN, Conference of the Parties to the ASEAN Agreement on Transboundary Haze, available at http://asean.org/asean-socio-cultural/cop-to-aathp-conference-of-the-parties-to-the-asean-agreement-on-transboundary-haze-pollution/

49 ASEAN, ASEAN Ministerial Meeting on Disaster Management, available at http://asean.org/asean-socio-cultural/asean-ministerial-meeting-on-disaster-management-ammdm/overview/

50 UNESCAP, Chapter 18, available at https://www.unescap.org/sites/default/files/CH18.pdf

51 Ibid.

52 Allenby, Braden R. (2001), "Environmental Security: Concept and Implementation," *International Political Science Review*, Vol. 21, No. 1, pp. 5-21. Published by Sage Publication, Ltd, available at http://www.jstor.org/1601426

15

Health in Foreign Policy: A Study of the Indo-Pacific Region

Shantesh K. Singh

ABSTRACT

In 1999 WHO Director-General, Gro Harlem Brundtland rightly stated that the world had changed and that furthering national interests in health requires international cooperation. Followed by another similar event in 2006 when the ministers of foreign affairs from France, Indonesia, Norway, Senegal, South Africa and Thailand announced to adopt the cooperative measures on health and foreign policy. The result of this meeting was 'Oslo Declaration', which stated that 'health is one of the most important foreign policy issue of our time. To link health and foreign policy, the UN General Assembly validated the Oslo Declaration at the multinational political level by adopting Resolution 64/108. Further the link between health and foreign policy was also affirmed by the US government.

Since 2011, the BRICS Health Ministers have held annual meetings to discuss their cooperation for health. Major countries from the Indo-pacific region, i. e. Japan, China and India have also considered health as a foreign policy priority in the tune of developed countries. The recent Japanese global health policy states that "contributing toward global health is an integral part of Japan's foreign policy strategy". Foreign policy makers of Japan have been agreed to set out the values and priorities for global health action and establish mechanisms for cooperation. Another rising super power of the region, China, has pushed health cooperation more broadly as part of its foreign policy outreach. Through its foreign policy, it is trying to maximise its national interest by engaging developing countries of Asia and Africa in heath discussions and related initiatives. Being a recent arena of diplomacy, Indian diplomats and foreign policy practitioners have started growing an understanding and developing

India's diplomatic initiatives in the health sector. With the dynamism brought into foreign policy decision making in India, health is turning into a major fulcrum which will be playing a major determinant in building relations between nations. Nations from the Indo-Pacific region have several national interest goals, i.e. humanitarian, security and economic, which they want to achieve by linking health and foreign policy. The paper will discuss the relationship between health and foreign policy and will make the case that health is an integral part of the foreign policy agenda in Indo-Pacific region.

Introduction

A country's foreign policy must necessarily have domestic implications, which play a critical role in its activities, particularly its democratic polity. With the rapid unification of regions, both domestic and international borders keep changing, while at other times, due to nationalistic compulsions, it becomes protectionist. Policy initiatives are increasingly being dictated by new non-traditional challenges that are fast gaining ground. In such circumstances, foreign policy has to address subjects that were not discussed or dealt with earlier. Decision makers are searching for avenues that have scope for empirical investigation in developing a political space for policymakers to enable them to make the right policy choices during periods of peace, transition as well as crisis. The discourse on democratic polity centres on strengthening structures that would be able to effectively respond to conditions that threaten the social, political and financial elements within states, locally as well as globally.

With the United States taking on the dominant role in world affairs after the conclusion of World War II, its foreign policy concerning global health developed rapidly. During, and immediately after the war, the United States Army and Navy were confronted with great challenges with regard to civilian health in the far-flung war-ravaged areas. In Europe, during the course of the war, epidemic typhus fever broke out in Naples in 1943.[1] Prompt and proper use of DDT and anti-typhus vaccine rapidly brought the epidemic under control, and a pandemic was averted. Later, when the campaign in North-Western Europe was being planned, the public health and preventive remedy personnel of Supreme Headquarters Allied Expeditionary Force anticipated an outbreak of typhus fever in German-occupied territory. Plans were immediately put in place to deal with this possibility. Epidemic typhus was rampant in the German concentration camps, and, as the Germans deserted the camps after their defeat, the prisoners still in camps, continued to spread the disease to surrounding areas. By administering the same vaccines that had worked so well in Naples, a possible epidemic was averted, saving tens of thousands of lives.[2] These events are mentioned here to assert that health issues that have the capacity of turning into a pandemic overlaps borders.

Today, health challenges are treated as a national security issue, and appear consistently on the agenda of meetings of leading economic powers; affecting the bilateral and regional political relationships between developed and developing countries, which gives an impetus to alter the strategies wherever required by international non-state actors like the United Nations.[3] This paper will determine that health is an important issue, which plays a key role in foreign policy thinking, both as a security concept as well as an essential element of diplomacy.

Health in Foreign Policy: A Conceptual Overview

Health was always a part of foreign policy, but due to inattention, it became more of a domestic policy measure across the world. With the rise in infectious diseases and the end of the Cold War, in the 1990s, health became an increasing concern of foreign policy. After that, an epistemological change was seen in both policy and academic circles. This highlights the fact that health is an essential element of development and security. In September 2006, the foreign ministers of seven countries launched the Foreign Policy and Global Health Initiative (FPGHI). The ministers emphasised the importance of global health security, describing health as a 'defining lens' which countries could use as important elements in foreign policy and development strategies. They declared that "health is one of the most important, yet still broadly neglected, long-term foreign policy issues of our time." The emerging economies in global health politics appear to have overcome the potential health challenges and the unsustainability of the existing health financing model. Their share of the global gross domestic product (GDP) rose from 17 per cent in the 1960s to nearly 40 per cent today.[4]

Hillary Clinton once stated that, "there are four ways in which foreign policy and health can interact. Foreign policy can endanger health when diplomacy breaks down or when trade considerations trump health; health can be used as an instrument of foreign policy to achieve other goals; health can be an integral part of foreign policy, and foreign policy can be used to promote health".[5]

Former UN Secretary-General Ban Ki-moon stated that the core function of 21st-century foreign policy is "achieving security, creating economic wealth, supporting development in low-income countries, and protecting human dignity".[6] Health is identified as a specific objective of foreign policy that is on a par with security or trade. The instruments developed over the past 160 years to control the spread of infectious diseases and narcotic drugs or to address occupational safety and health, testify to the historical importance of global health diplomacy in foreign policy.[7] These instruments were specifically designed to protect international commerce, promote political stability, and ensure economic security; at a time when health was not a distinct foreign policy objective. The health focus is not limited to the prevention and treatment of specific diseases; it involves a larger view of the social determinants of health as well as the economic, commercial, and security implications related to public health.[8] Infections such as pandemic influenza virus A, subtype H1N1, and severe acute respiratory syndrome (SARS) are considered as risks that could severely disrupt commerce and curtail the movement of peoples; besides the specific health consequences of these illnesses, especially for vulnerable persons.[9]

Health as an objective of foreign policy requires new perceptions of global solidarity to change or transform "the conditions in which people are born, grow, live, work, and age."[10] These are in turn "shaped by the distribution of money, power, and resources at global, national, and local levels," and they may radically transform the nature of foreign policy.[11]

Health Scenario of the Indo-Pacific Region: Foreign Policy Perspective

Two formerly separate areas of tropical waters of the Indian Ocean and the Pacific Ocean, have come together to form the Indo-Pacific region which links Asia through mutually beneficial interactions and interdependence. Since 2010, Australia, India, Japan and the US, four major powers in the region, formally adopted the term Indo-Pacific into their foreign policy and defence strategies.[12]

The Indo-Pacific combines the Indian Ocean Region (IOR) and the Western Pacific Region (WPR) into a single regional construct. There are specific geopolitical and geoeconomical differences between the IOR and the WPR, which also include the security environment. The WPR faces severe and persistent military threats, unlike the IOR. This is a result of the dominant military governments who have been in power in most of the countries in the region since the 20th century. For example, one witnessed heightened nationalism in Japan, and now it is the turn of China. These were and are attempts to redraw sovereign boundaries, including 'territorialisation' of the seas. The attempts at hegemonic domination grew due to their economic advancement. It began with Japan, which later influenced the other East Asian economies to grow through outsourcing of lower-end manufacturing industries —the so-called 'Flying Geese Paradigm'.

Japan had been openly propagating its regional strategy of an 'open and free Indo-Pacific', which was soon emulated by the Indian leadership when they agreed to interact with an 'Indo-Pacific strategy' in its 'Act East Policy'. In December 2017, the United States adopted a similar approach in its National Security Strategy. Australia had referred to the Indo-Pacific in it's 2013 and 2016 Defence White Papers and again cited it in its 2017 Foreign Policy White Paper. In January 2018, Indonesia, while outlining its foreign policy priorities, included the term Indo-Pacific. The above-mentioned points reinforce the growing geostrategic significance and acceptance of the Indo-Pacific concept.[13]

Albeit Indo does not refer to India, but the entire Indian Ocean; the term Indo-Pacific strengthens India's growing ambition for regional hegemony. While some feel that the dominant Asia-Pacific construct is not a true indicator of India's increasing role in the region, others connect the Indo-Pacific construct to a China-balancing agenda. But all said and done; the term can be read as a validation of India's regional hegemony, downplaying a Sino-centric regional order.[14]

Several health-related issues have emerged in the Indo-Pacific region which has resulted in deterioration in its health parameters despite the economic progress made by some of these countries. The high level of deaths due to diseases in the region are shocking. Though India is a rising power in the region, 1.2 million children died of preventable diseases in 2015, which is a staggeringly high number.

Often, healthcare facilities are unreliable and grossly inadequate in many developing or under-developed countries in the Asia-Pacific region. Access to basic health services for the very poor is still at a nascent stage; for the relatively well-off it is a matter of making health-related choices based on availability or access to resources and choosing between government or private facilities. Though it is essential for the government to provide free or affordable health services, the private sector has an equally important role to play in the health sector. There is a need for a coordinated understanding of the challenges faced by the nations and its people in the Indo-Pacific region. Systems such as the

Asia Pacific Strategy for Emerging Diseases under the World Health Organisation, try to connect the countries in the Indo-Pacific region, by strategising on a wider global health response.

The Indo-Pacific region is host to several of the world's fastest growing as well as four of 12 biggest economies—China, Japan, India and South Korea—both in terms of nominal GDP and GDP (PPP) criteria.[15] Growing integration with the global economy has meant the region is experienced rapid economic transformation, with domestic GDP growth rates for much of the region in the past decade being in the close to around 5 per cent per annum. The fact that most of the emerging Asian economies were relatively untouched by the global financial crisis of 2008 also spurred foreign investment and consequent growth.[16] The exceptional pace of growth assumes even greater significance when viewed in light of the fact that this region is home to 60 per cent of the global population (approx. 4.2 billion).[17]

Parameters and definitions of public health and the associated challenges constantly evolve. With the advent of the Industrial Revolution, Europe underwent tremendous growth, albeit accompanied by major social upheavals and rising inequalities. These inequalities, especially in the fast urbanising rural and semi-urban spaces, necessitated policies and strategies to deal with the growing problems in the public domain, such as education and health, the latter made urgent by frequent outbreak of diseases, like plague and cholera. One important response was the establishment of national health systems across European states in the period immediately after World War II. Policy makers understood that an adequate and responsive public health infrastructure was essential to attain sustainable economic development. Similar challenges and responses are being witnessed today in the Indo-Pacific region. These challenges are made more daunting by the widespread inequalities, especially rampant poverty, with 1.63 billion people of the region living below the poverty line, subsisting at US$ 2 or less per day.[18] Decision makers recognise that the pursuit of wealth must be balanced by building healthy societies.[19]

The present fiscal challenges that are being experienced by nations are because of the rise in health care costs due to population growth, demographic shifts and technological developments. Across population groups, changing patterns of health and disease, coupled with epidemiological changes in lifestyles, work patterns and dietary practices, are increasingly being seen. Given the diversity of health needs across the Indo-Pacific region, what measures must countries adapt for their health policies was the question agitating the minds of policy and decision makers. Particularly so, in an era of globalisation where many of the health determinants, risks and outcomes cannot be geographically confined since health policies have local, regional and even global implications.

Given the variations in the geographical composition of Indo-Pacific, and unavailability of standardised data, it is indeed a challenge to undertake a detailed and long-term assessment of the health needs of specific population groups in the region. Equally challenging is the question of how best to respond to the changing health needs, in the face of rapid epidemiological transition witnessed across the region.[20]

Growing economic development and rising living standards have led to a marked improvement in heath indicators across the region. In the period of 1970-2010, life expectancy in 22 Indo-Pacific countries, excluding the much more developed Japan, South Korea, Australia and New Zealand, recorded a remarkable growth of an average 15 years, the figure for 2010 standing at an average 72.2 years. Similarly, Infant Mortality Rates have declined at an average of 26 deaths per 1000 live births, during 1980-2010. Further, maternal mortality rates have been halved since the 1990s.[21]

The impressive improvements in the field of health indicators is dampened by the wide regional disparities across the region. Life expectancy at birth varies from over 80 years in Australia, Japan and Singapore to less than 65 years in Cambodia, India and Myanmar. Even countries with higher than regional average for national wealth, such as Malaysia and Brunei Darrussalam, record lower life expectancy than economically weaker countries like Vietnam, highlighting the fact that factors besides national GDP and wealth contribute to such health indicators. In general, health indicators are better in East Asian as compared to countries in South and South-East Asia. For example, in 2010, Infant Mortality rates in Japan and South Korea were less than 5 deaths per 1000 live births, whereas in countries like Cambodia, India, Myanmar and Pakistan, the rates were in excess of 40. As per WHO reports only 4 out of 43 countries in the region had reduced their Under 5 Mortality Rates (U5MRs) and IMRs to one-third of 1990 values by 2010, and 28 of them could not even meet the Millennium Development Goal target by 2015.[22]

Inter-regional comparisons also highlight the differences in terms of causes of death, a special focus here being on the deaths caused by communicable vis-à-vis non-communicable diseases. In 2010, the average mortality in 20 selected Asian countries, from all causes, was 90.2 per 1000 people, which was almost twice the rate for the developed OECD countries.[23] Within the Indo-Pacific region, high-income countries/territories such as Hong Kong, Singapore and South Korea have witnessed an epidemiological transition from communicable to non-communicable diseases as the more prevalent cause of death,[24] while in the low- and middle-income countries, such as China and India, communicable diseases remain a major cause along with the growing prevalence of non-communicable diseases. In lower-income countries of the Asia-pacific region, communicable diseases have an especially higher prevalence.[25] In 2009, Papua New Guinea had the highest prevalence of HIV among 15- to 49-year-olds (0.9 per cent), followed by Southeast Asian countries like Thailand (1.3 per cent), Myanmar (0.6 per cent), Cambodia (0.5 per cent) and Malaysia (0.5 per cent). Access to medication for HIV, primarily anti-retroviral drugs is also abysmal. Affected individuals in countries like Papua New Guinea and Thailand only had 50 per cent access to such life-saving medicines, and even this was the highest in the region. The Global Burden of Disease Study (1990–2010) affirms the link between economic and epidemiological trends in Indo-Pacific Region defined as South-East Asian Region, Eastern Mediterranean Region and Western Pacific Region (Figure 1).

Owing to the distinct rural environmental settings and socio-economic lifestyle, where human and animals—both wild and domesticated—are in close contact, the region is also susceptible to relatively unknown communicable diseases called Zoonoses—diseases that are transmitted from animals to humans.[27] Diseases in the broad category of Zoonoses are caused by more than 800 pathogens. In the recent decades, several new zoonotic pathogens have been identified including the avian-origin H5N1, severe acute respiratory syndrome (SARS) and Nipah viruses. The factors that have contributed to the spread of Zoonoses in the Indo-Pacific region: widespread poverty, accompanied by poor housing; close proximity of humans and animals; weak public health infrastructure; diversification in the farming sector including animal husbandry; destruction of natural animal habitats, etc. Rapid urbanisation and industrialisation and the resultant change in food habits and lifestyles also indirectly impact the spread of Zoonoses.

The Indo-Pacific region has produced a wide diversity of health needs across countries which need to be addressed. The 'double burden' of dealing with alarming increases in both communicable and non-communicable diseases put additional pressure on governments.[28] Countries will need to diversify their health policies to tackle the shifting burden of disease, and link them

Figure 1: 10 Causes of Deaths in Indo-Pacific Region (1990–2010)[26]

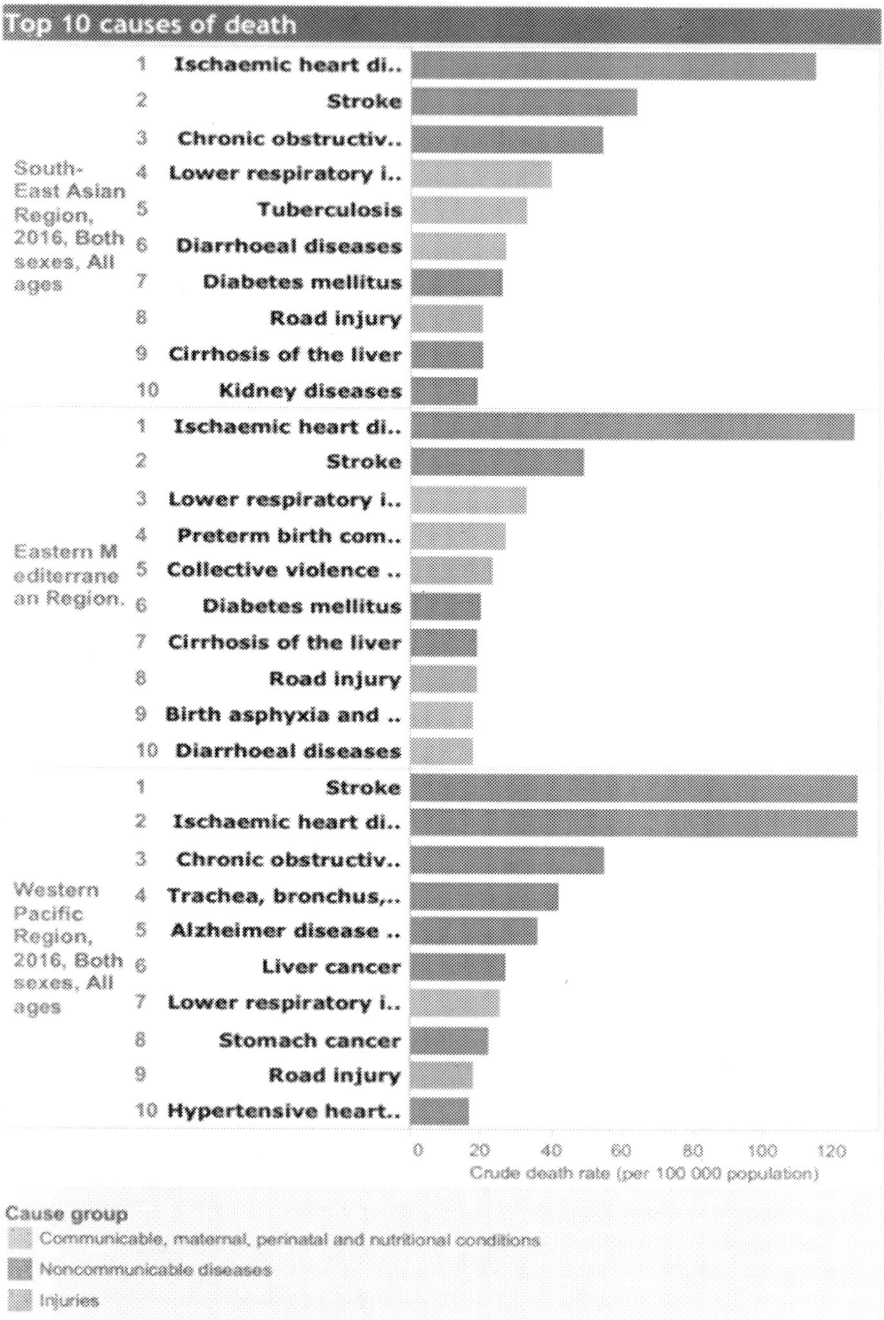

Source: http://www.who.int/gho/mortality_burden_disease/causes_death/top_10/en/

with economic policies to better understand the broader context of these epidemiological trends?

In this dynamic global environment, health policy has not been given sufficient attention. The negative effects of the major outbreak of diseases, like SARS and pandemic influenza, on the economy of affected countries, have attracted significant concern within the trading community, which has also be seen in recent past during the spread of diseases, such as H1N1, Ebola and Zika, etc.[29] There has been a lack of interest in understanding and examining the possible links between regional/global trade on the one hand and the rise in the spread of non-communicable diseases on the other. For example, the opening up of the market in this region to multinational tobacco companies has resulted in an increase in the spread of infections from tobacco-related diseases.[30]

While insufficient data on the issue makes it hard to draw definite conclusions on the links between changing dietary habits in the Indo-Pacific region and consequent health risks,[31] it is clear that the rapid rise in the incidents of non-communicable diseases has coincided with globalisation. Obesity and Diabetes, once considered disorders confined to the developed societies of the Western world, have become seen a rise in several low- and middle-income countries of this region.[32] Many factors, such as sedentary lifestyles and increased intake of food products with high dietary fat and high sugar content, have contributed to this trend. For example, the Pacific Island countries have among the world's highest rates of obesity (75%) and diabetes (47%). A marked shift from traditional high-protein diets to processed foods of low nutritional value.[33]

Health and Foreign Policy in the Indo-Pacific: As an Instrument to Advance National Interest

Development assistance, a vital component of foreign policy, serves the national interests and humanitarian needs of countries in the Indo-Pacific region. In this context, in the field of health policy and diplomacy, the role of Japan, China and India remain significant.

In Japan, a generation of people have grown up with a strong sense of pacifism that arose from firsthand experience of the devastation of World War II. The Japanese need to develop a new motivation to overcome their pacifism. Attempts to secure its position in an ever-changing world, Japan realised that human security offers a framework for future-oriented pragmatic pacifism in its politics. 'The evolution of the human security concept into a pillar of Japanese foreign policy thus reflects Japan's quest to solidify its position in the international community as a global civilian power'.[34]

Japan is particularly well-placed to play a leading role in promoting global health in the Indo-Pacific region since it has the longest life expectancy and the lowest infant mortality among the G8 nations. It was Japan that first put global health on the G8 agenda. At the 2000 Kyushu-Okinawa G8 Summit, Japan drew the world's attention to infectious diseases around the world.[35] The discussions led to the creation of the Global Fund to Fight AIDS, Tuberculosis and Malaria, which has contributed to saving 2.5 million lives until 2007. Since 2000, global health has had a continuous presence on the G8 agenda and resources deployed in the field globally have increased dramatically from $6 billion in 2000 to $14 billion in 2005.[36]

According to a Japanese estimate, 6 million people, or one person every 5 seconds, die of AIDs, tuberculosis and malaria around the world annually. Half a million mothers die during pregnancy and delivery, and 10 million children under 5 die each year. These preventable deaths are concentrated in poor regions of Sub-Sahara Africa where infant mortality is 50 times that of Japan, and maternal mortality more than 200 times.[37] Being a soft power, Japan firstly raised the issue of global health in the G8 and allocated a dedicated fund of $60 billion to fight against infectious diseases and strengthen health systems in Africa. It has also promised to provide 100 million insecticide-embedded bed nets by 2010 to fight against malaria to achieve the target of 2.3 health practitioners per 1,000 patients in Africa. Japan established a review mechanism to monitor and asses the past commitments, which are being implemented.[38]

According to James M Kondo[39] (2009), three things made Japan a public health leader in the Indo-Pacific region:[40]

1. *The Japanese political leaders stepped up and carried the G8 agenda forward:* Foreign Minister Masahiko Koumura, writing in the medical journal *The Lancet,* almost a year before the G8 summit, rallied the world to take immediate steps to address global health. In January 2008, Japanese Prime Minister Yasuo Fukuda announced global health as a G8 agenda in front of world leaders at Davos. Meanwhile, former Prime Minister Junichiro Koizumi created the Hideyo Noguchi Africa Prize to honour eminent global health researchers. Another former Prime Minister Yoshiro Mori chaired a discussion on health issues with

some African heads of state at the annual Tokyo International Conference on African Development.

2. *Other Japanese stakeholders also contributed:* For example, in business, Sumitomo Chemical, the producer of the innovative insecticide-embedded malaria bed nets central to the global fight against malaria, was one of the two companies named by Bill Gates as embodying 'creative capitalism' to address critical global issues. In the non-government organisation sector, more than 140 NGOs gathered to create the G8 Summit NGO Forum whose special task-force on global health organised events to galvanize the public, led advocacy, and built up a global coalition to demand G8 action.
3. *Multi-stakeholder platforms were created to connect government, business, NGOs, academia and the media:* One was the Global Health Summit co-organised by Health Policy Institute, Japan and the World Bank, six months before the G8 Summit, to build national momentum for the G8. Another was a cross-stakeholder working group organised by the Japan Centre for International Exchange that identified better coordination among various disease-specific initiatives, and a renewed focus on strengthening the overall health system (as opposed to building disjointed and suboptimal systems for each disease-specific initiative), as a key issue to be addressed at the island town of Toyako.

In the case of China, it is facing multiple challenges to its health care system on account of the changing demographics and politics of the country, the evolving dynamics of health care, and the emerging epidemiology of health as well as diseases. While China accounts for one-fifth of the world's population, its disease burden, measured in years of healthy life lost, is one-seventh in the world. Historically, China has been home to some of the world's major epidemics—the 1957 Asian flu, the 1968 Hong Kong flu, the 1977 Russian influenza, and the 2003 acute respiratory syndrome (SARS) epidemic.[41] Since 1949, the People's Republic of China has successfully used health as a tool to promote foreign relations. On April 6, 1963, Premier Zhou Enlai sent the country's very first medical team to Algeria.[42] Over the years it has continued to send medical teams to Africa and West Asia.[43] Such humanitarian efforts have helped generate favourable images of China globally; at the same time, helping it to improve its diplomatic relations. China is playing a vital role in ensuring global health security in the 21st century.

Its rise as a major economic power in the region, since the 1990s, generated strong interest in China to use foreign aid as a diplomatic tool to expand its influence in global health governance.[44] Since the 1990s, China has prioritised the economic side of foreign aid and encouraged the use of Development Assistance for Health (DAH) to secure its economic interests. One of the senior officials of the Ministry of Health rightly said that China's health assistance should "not only serve China's foreign policy but also act as a broker for economic development in China and recipient countries."[45] A major characteristic of China's new foreign policy, especially pertaining to health, centres on multilateral diplomacy with active international participation. With ongoing globalisation, inter-regional transmission of diseases has become a reality, requiring concerted remedial efforts at the global level.[46]

China understood the importance of ASEAN nations to its health security, and therefore, started paying special attention to the ASEAN nations. Putting public health on its priority list, China set up a Sino-ASEAN Foundation on Public Health Cooperation in April 2003, spending 10 million RMB (Malaysian Ringgit). In March 2008, information sharing among China and ASEAN countries became a reality when they put into operation information technology to enable prior notification of emerging infectious diseases. This made it possible to predict and respond to disease outbreaks well in advance.[47]

India, another important player in the Indo-Pacific region, also adopted a robust global health policy after Indian diplomats and foreign policy mandarins pushed for diplomatic initiatives in the health sector. The United Nations (UN) and the World Health Organisation (WHO) are the nerve centres for global health initiatives. Considering the importance of health in foreign policy dialogues, many countries have added permanent health attaché to their diplomatic staff, besides appointing diplomats to international health departments. Their brief is to take quick decisions and manoeuvre negotiations when faced with outbreaks of disease, security threats or other serious health-related issues that have global ramifications.[48]

Health is turning out to be a major determinant in relation-building between nations. With the infusion of new dynamism into foreign policy deliberations, India has started taking an interest in global health aid politics, making it an integral part of India's foreign assistance program and its impact has been growing exponentially over the years. Believing that the program will continue to expand in the coming years, Indian policymakers want to involve the country's private health sector players in health assistance initiatives.[49] Health assistance typically encompasses bilateral health support, health IT and Pharma etc., and involves infrastructure, human resources, education and capacity building. It is commendable that since 2009, India has committed at least US$100 million to several health programmes in the countries across South Asia, Southeast Asia and Africa. India, with its reputation as an IT expert hub, could help develop things like pan-Africa tele-medicine and tele-education networks, where hospitals and universities throughout Western Africa would be linked with counterparts in India to facilitate sharing of best medical practices.[50]

Policy makers in India are committed to strengthening cooperation and sharing of experiences in the public health sector. India uses foreign assistance as a diplomatic tool to further global trade and investment and offers a stable relationship with many emerging countries from Asia and Africa. India believes in the concept of south-south cooperation and is critical about the Western donor-aid model. Indian foreign aid includes technical assistance, grants and contributions to international organisations, soft loans, and Export-Import (EXIM) Bank credit with subsidized interest rates.[51] India's engagement with global health diplomacy is predominantly to increase its political presence internationally, though it has been formulated and implemented in a limited sense to also generate revenue.[52]

Rising Health Concerns and Indo-Pacific: Issues and Challenges

Another area of policy concern for all countries in the region, including Japan, China and India, is trade and investment in health-related goods and services. Health-related businesses such as pharmaceutical and biotechnology companies, health insurers, medical equipment manufacturers, and e-health providers would gain from a more prosperous Asia-Pacific. Four of the world's largest drug companies—Pfizer, Novartis, Sanofi and GlaxoSmithKline—earn a third of their revenue from outside their domestic markets. Established local pharmaceutical companies in Asia are competing with 'Big Pharma' companies to capture the region's markets by expanding their presence beyond their home bases. China, for example, is expected to overtake Japan to become the world's second-largest market for pharmaceutical products by the year 2016, with sales of around US$160 billion, while a relatively less-developed country like Indonesia promises to become the sixth largest pharmaceutical market.[53]

Since the 1990s, access to medicines in the Indo-Pacific region has been adversely impacted by trade liberalisation and become a subject of concern to NGOs such as Oxfam. Global trade dialogues and negotiations under the

World Trade Organisation have been continually interrupted. INGOs and human rights organisations argue that the new forms of intellectual property rights are being adopted under local (bilateral) and regional trade negotiations,[54] which, in turn, affects the access to medicines by the poor. As governments of the Indo-Pacific region have made integration with the world economy their priority, economic policy has taken precedence over health policy. Asserting that health policy is constrained by a lack of transparency, resources, technical expertise and regulatory frameworks, the public health community of the Indo-Pacific region has justified its non-participant in trade negotiations.

Despite, an alarming number of deaths from NCDs, the challenge for the region in the coming decades would be to see how best the region's growth can take a healthier course. More comprehensive data and analyses are needed to improve regulatory measures such as labelling, taxation and social marketing related to health. For instance, a report by the Asian Development Bank found that increasing tobacco pricing by 50 per cent through taxation in the five highest burdened countries from Asia would reduce the number of users by almost 70 million and tobacco-related casualties by 30 million.[55] Equally revealing was the fact that higher taxes would generate a tax revenue average of 0.30 per cent of GDP (US$24 billion per year), enough to cover the direct medical costs of treating tobacco-related illnesses.

Concluding Observations

The Indo-Pacific region is seen largely as a major source of global health 'threats' in the form of disease outbreaks, and unregulated use of tainted products such as illicit drugs, cigarettes or counterfeit medicines. The region has been categorised in relation to the concept of 'vulnerability', defined by Woodward as sensitivity to displacement (resistance) and adaptation (or resilience).[56] The two are closely linked. Similar to the upheavals of the Industrial Revolution, the large-scale de-territorialisation brought about by contemporary globalisation have made some human populations vulnerable to newer forms of diseases, both communicable and non-communicable.

New research needs to be conducted to ascertain the impact on human health resulting from the rapid transitions taking place. Governments must measure and monitor national well-being at the individual and population levels. The differing concepts of well-being have developed as a reaction to the limitations of economic indicators such as gross domestic products (GDP) as a measure of a society's achievements and progress.[57] Definitions of well-being are inspiring new approaches to defining and measuring economic and social goals, and how best to achieve them. The adaptation and implementation of such a way in the Indo-Pacific region are both timely and urgent.

NOTES

1 Conlon Joseph M. "The Historical Impact of Epidemic Typhus", p. 16. Available at http://www.montana.edu/historybug/documents/TYPHUS-Conlon.pdf.

2 Leonard A. Scheele, "Public Health and Foreign Policy", *The Annals of the American Academy of Political and Social Science*, Vol. 278, The Search for National Security (Nov., 1951), p. 64.

3 Fidler D.P. & Nick Drager (2006), "Health as Foreign Policy", *Bulletin of the World Health Organization*, September 2006, 84 (9), p. 687.

4 Yanzhong Huang, "Enter the Dragon and the Elephant China's and India's Participation in Global Health Governance," *Working Paper* (April 2013), p. 4.

5 Ilona Kickbusch, "How Foreign Policy Can Influence Health", *British Medical Journal* (BMJ), Vol. 342, No. 7811 (18 June 2011), p. 1345.

6 UN Secretary-General (2009). Note by the Secretary-General 64/365, "Global Health and Foreign Policy: Strategic Opportunities and Challenges". Available at www.who.int/trade/ foreign policy/en/.

7 Fidler D.P. (2001), "The Globalization of Public Health: The First 100 Years of International Health Diplomacy", *Bull World Health Organ*, 79(9): 842–849.

8 World Health Organization (2008), "Closing the Gap in a Generation: Health Equity Through Action on the Social Determinants of Health. Commission on Social Determinants of Health", *Final Report*, World Health Organization, Available at http://www.who.int/social_determinants/final_report.en.

9 Santiago Alcázar and Paulo Buss, "Health is an Integral Part of Foreign Policy", in Thomas E. Novotny et al. (eds.) (2013), *21st Century Global Health Diplomacy*, World Scientific Publishing Co., London, p. 150.

10 World Health Organization (2008), "Closing the Gap".

11 Ibid.

12 Michael Auslin (2010), Security in the Indo-Pacific Commons: Towards a Regional Strategy, Washington, D.C.: American Enterprise Institute.

13 Adducul Lloyd Alexander M., "The Indo-Pacific Construct in Australia's White Papers: Reflections for ASEAN-Australia Future Strategic Partnership", *Center for International Relations and Strategic Studies,* Vol. V, No. 6, March 2018, Available at http://www.fsi.gov.ph/the-indo-pacific-construct-in-australias-white-papers-reflections-for-asean-australia-future-strategic-partnership/

14 Ibid.

15 World Economic Forum (2018), "The World's Biggest Economies in 2018", 18 April 2018. Available at https://www.weforum.org/agenda/2018/04/the-worlds-biggest-economies-in-2018/. Also see, Prableen Bajpai (2018), "The World's Top 20 Economies", *Investopedia*, 16 August 2018, Available at https://www.investopedia.com/insights/worlds-top-economies/

16 Hale G, Kennedy A (2012), "Emerging Asia: Two Paths Through the Storm". *FRBSF Economic Letter*, 26 March.

17 Lee Kelly (2013). "Health Policy in Asia and the Pacific: Navigating Local Needs and Global Challenges", *Asia and the Pacific Policy Studies,* Vol. 1, No. 1, p. 45.

18 Asian Development Bank (2011), "Poverty in Asia and the Pacific: An Update", No. 267, *ADB Economics Working Paper Series,* Manila. Available at http://sites.asia society.org/asia21summit/wpcontent/uploads/2010/11/ADBPovertyinAsiaand thePacific 8.2011.pdf

19 Kelley "Health Policy in Asia", p. 46.

20 Ibid.

21 OECD/WHO (2012), "Health at a Glance: Asia/Pacific 2012", *OECD Publishing*, pp. 12-18, Available at http://dx.doi.org/10.1787/9789264183902 en.

22 WHO (2008), "Health in Asia and the Pacific, World Health Organization", *Regional Office for Southeast Asia,* New Delhi, Available at http://www.wpro.who.int/health_information_evidence/documents/Health_in_Asia_Pacific.pdf.

23 OECD/WHO (2012), "Health at a Glance: Asia/Pacific 2012", *OECD Publishing,* p. 18, Available at http://dx.doi.org/10.1787/9789264183902en.

24 Khoo S, Morris T (2012), "Physical Activity and Obesity Research in the AsiaPacific: A Review", *AsiaPacific Journal of Public Health* 24(3), pp. 435–449.

25 Bandara A (2005), "Emerging Health Issues in Asia and the Pacific: Implications for Public Health Policy", *AsiaPacific Development Journal* 12(2), pp. 33–58.

26 Lozano R, Naghavi M, Foreman K etal. (2012)' "Global and Regional Mortality from 235 Causes of Death for 20 Age Groups in 1990 and 2010: A Systematic Analysis for the Global Burden of Disease Study2010",. *Lance*t 380(9859), Figure 9.

27 Bhatia R, Narain JP (2010) "The Challenge of Emerging Zoonoses in Asia Pacific", *AsiaPacific Journal of Public Health* 22(4), pp. 388–394.

28 Lozano R, Naghavi M, Foreman K etal. (2012) "Global and Regional Mortality from 235 Causes of Death for 20 Age Groups in 1990 and 2010: A Systematic Analysis for the Global Burden of Disease Study 2010", *Lancet* 380(9859), pp. 2095–2128.

29 Brahmbhatt M, Dutta A (2008) "On SARS Type Economic Effects during Infectious Disease Outbreaks", *Policy Research Working Paper* 4466, World Bank, Washington DC.

30 Knight J, Chapman S (2004), "Asian Yuppies ... are Always Looking for Something New and Different: Creating a Tobacco Culture among Young Asians" *Tobacco Control* 13(Suppl 2), ii, pp. 22–29.

31 Ebrahim S, Pearce N, Smeeth L, Casas JP, Jaffar S, Piot P. (2013), "Tackling NonCommunicable Diseases in Low-and MiddleIncome Countries: Is the Evidence from HighIncome Countries All We Need?", *PLoS Medicine* 10(1), e1001377.

32 Asia Pacific Cohort Studies Collaboration (2007), "The Burden of Overweight and Obesity in the AsiaPacific Region", *Obesity Reviews* 8, pp. 191–196.

33 Parry J (2010), "Pacific Islanders Pay Heavy Price for Abandoning Traditional Diet", *Bulletin of the World Health Organization* 88(7), pp. 481–560.

34 Takemi, Keizo, et al., (2007), "Challenges in Global Health and Japan's Contribution", *Japan Centre for International Exchange,* Tokyo.

35 Ibid.

36 Kondo, M. James (2009), "Japan as the Catalyst for Improving Global Public Health", *The Japan Times*, 12 Feb. 2009.

37 Ibid.
38 Ibid.
39 Ibid.
40 Singh, Shantesh Kumar Singh (2014), *Emerging United States Policy of Global Public Health: A Study of US Approach Towards HIV/AIDS in India*, Manak Publications, New Delhi, 2014.
41 Huang, "Enter the Dragon", p. 86.
42 Chinese medical teams (Zhongguo Yuanwai Viliaodui). Available at http://news.xinhuanet.com/ziliao/2009-04/13/content_11178783.htm.
43 Xu Jing, Liu Peilong, and Guo Yan (2011), "Health Diplomacy in China", *Global Health Governance*, Volume 4, No. 2 (Spring), pp. 1-12
44 Huang, "Enter the Dragon", p. 6.
45 Ibid., p. 7.
46 Jing, Peilong, and Yan, "Health Diplomacy in China", pp. 1-12
47 Ibid.
48 Singh, Shantesh Kumar, "Global Health Diplomacy: A Strategic Opportunity to India", *India Foundation Journal*, Sep-Oct-2017. Available at https://www.indiafoundation.in/global-health-diplomacy-a-strategic-opportunity-for-india/.
49 Ibid.
50 Madhu Raghavendra and Reddy Srikanth, (2014), "An Opportune time for India to play the Global Health Diplomacy Card", *Global Policy*, September 22, Available at http://www.globalpolicyjournal.com/blog/22/09/2014/opportune-time-india-play-global-health-diplomacy-card.
51 Ibid.
52 Singh "Global Health Diplomacy".
53 LaSalle, Jones Lang (2011), "Global Life Sciences Cluster Report", Available at https://www.joneslanglasalle.com/ResearchLevel1/Global_Life%20Sciences%20 Cluster%20 Report_2011_gb.pdf.
54 Oxfam International/Health Action International (2009), "Trading away Access to Medicines: How the European Union's Trade Agenda has Taken a Wrong Turn", *Briefing Paper*, London, viewed 26 February 2013. Available at http://www.oxfam.org/sites/www.oxfam.org/files/bptradingawayaccesstomedicines.pdf.
55 Asian Development Bank (2012), "Tobacco Taxes: A WinWin Measure for Fiscal Space and Health", ADB, Manila.
56 Woodward A, Hales S, Weinstein P (1998), "Climate Change and Human Health in the Asia Pacific Region: Who Will be Most Vulnerable?", *Climate Research* 11, 31–38.
57 UK Parliamentary Office of Science and Technology (2012), "Measuring National Wellbeing", PostNote 421, Houses of Parliament, London.

16

Unorganising the 'Organised': Drug Trafficking in the Indo-Pacific Region as a Non-Traditional Security Threat

Sweta Kumari Thakur

ABSTRACT

From the 19th century's historic 'Opium Wars' in China to the ruthless 'War on Drugs' currently taking place in the Philippines, drug trafficking has always been a menace to the Indo-Pacific region. With a huge demand internationally, billions of dollars are extracted from this illicit business. A number of geo-political factors in the region favour drug trafficking that have led to its evolution as a transnational organized crime. Geographically, favourable climatic conditions in areas like the 'Golden Triangle' in the growing of illicit drugs, porous borders, and the availability of the Pacific Ocean, make this region suitable for the production and transportation of narcotics like heroin, opium, methamphetamines and cannabis. Chronic poverty, money laundering, corruption, firmly established racketeering with political backing, and existing rivalries among the countries in the region, further contribute to its unchecked growth. As a non-traditional security (NTS) threat, drug trafficking poses serious danger to the national security as well as human security in many countries within the region and beyond. Although, a number of legislations have been passed both at the domestic and the international level, substantive goals have not been achieved. Attempts made by the Western countries particularly, the United States and Australia, for instance, the 'supply control or source control', have not been successful. On the other hand, China's narcotics policy of coercive crackdown in its Yunnan region bordering Laos & Myanmar and developmental assistance to the 'Golden Triangle' has shown some positive results. The guidelines of the United Nations Convention Against Transnational Organized Crimes (UNCTOC) or the Palermo Convention (2000) could be promising as they seek to eliminate the differences in the legislations which deal with the tackling of drug trafficking offences among various countries and to facilitate exchange of the evidences against transnational racketeers. However, these guidelines stay in limbo because the small economies in the region are not competent enough to take punitive measures against this highly organized illicit business whose profit exceeds GDPs of many of them; and the capable ones are not willing to cooperate with their rivals. Thus, the region lacks a coherent anti-drug trafficking strategy that seeks regional and international cooperation.

Drug Trafficking Scenario in the Indo-Pacific

The trafficking of illicit drugs has always shown itself to be a huge impediment to the growth and development of the Indo-Pacific region. The region not only produces both natural and synthetic drugs but it also has a high consumption rate of the same. The natural drugs include mostly opium and cannabis. Opium is extracted from the latex of poppy and is mainly used in the manufacturing of heroin, one of the most popular drugs in the world. Among synthetic drugs, methamphetamines and its variants are very common and widely produced in the region. In order to understand the drug trafficking scenario, it is important to understand the region first. Although the Indo-Pacific has different definitions for different nations, it basically comprises most of the nations that border with either the Indian or the Pacific Ocean The countries in this region are very different from each other and sometimes are opposites in various aspects. For instance, in terms of geography and economy, Australia, China, and the United States can be considered as giants in comparison to countries like Laos, Philippines, and Myanmar. Not only this, but they also differ in the kinds of political establishments, law enforcement mechanisms, and border management practices. These factors determine the status of these countries as the manufacturers or the consumers or both with regards to the illicit drugs. India, which is situated in the close proximity of Afghanistan and Southeast faces the influx of drugs from both the sides. Myanmar is the largest producer of opium in the region, while China manufactures the largest amount of methamphetamines. According to the UNODC, currently, heroin and methamphetamines collectively contribute to approximately 40 billion dollars to the regional drug market.[1] This market is being controlled by well-organised transnational criminal groups. The drug syndicates transport illicit drugs across the borders within the region and also to different parts of the world. The Pacific Ocean facilitates the transportation of drugs and is often referred to as the 'transshipment point' for drug trafficking in the Indo-Pacific.[2] The region itself has a well-developed demand and supply mechanism for the drug trafficking market. First of all, the production of these drugs needs to be studied along with the factors behind them.

The Golden Triangle: Cultivation of Poppy and the Regional Determinants

Indo-Pacific region is the second largest producer of opium in the world after Afghanistan. Specifically, the region called the Golden Triangle, comprising the areas of Myanmar, Laos, and Thailand, is inflicted with the production and smuggling of opium. As the region is situated in the Greater Mekong Sub-region, it has a very suitable climatic condition for the cultivation of opium. While the cultivation takes place in the Shan province of Myanmar, the northern part of Laos and Thailand are mostly involved with the smuggling and distribution of opium within the region. For the last few decades, the demand for finer forms of opiates has increased in the range of the drug market. Heroin has become very popular in this regard. Its composition includes opium and other precursor chemicals. It is manufactured mostly in Myanmar and China. Myanmar producers the opium while other chemicals required for heroin are produced in China. The exchange of these two prerequisites take place across the border and thus, heroin is manufactured in large quantities. A number of regional factors which contribute towards the production of opium and opiates in this part of the Indo-Pacific also needs to be assessed. Some of them have been highlighted below.

Poverty and Isolation

There are a number of regional factors that contribute towards the cultivation of opium. Myanmar is one of the poorest countries in the region. And poverty is directly linked with the cultivation of opium poppy in Myanmar. It contributes both as the cause and consequence of the opium poppy cultivation which has led to the formation of a vicious cycle that does not allow the farmers to quit this activity. Chronic poverty threatens the survival and livelihood of people in Myanmar. The surveys have found out that most of the regions that cultivate opium are economically deprived. Along with this, they are situated in the remotest parts of the country which lack proper connectivity the markets and the mainland. Being an agrarian, society, livelihood depends on agriculture. Rice is mostly grown as the staple food in the region, but it has been found that the lack of connectivity to market deters farmers from continuing the cultivation of rice. On the other hand, the cultivation of poppy provides them buyers who are basically drug smugglers. It has been found that in this region 10 per cent of the households are directly involved with the cultivation of opium poppy.[3] Because these areas are isolated, the people are not able to avail basic facilities like education and health services from the government, which not only affects the farmers involved with cultivation but also determines the fate of the next generation who would get caught in this poverty and poppy cultivation trap.

Armed Rebellion

Myanmar for decades has been suffering from the ethnic armed rebellion that has inhibited its growth and development. It has been found that various regions in the country which cultivate poppy and extracts opium, like Shan state, are inflicted with armed rebellion. The trading of illegal drugs has become the major economic strength of various rebel and terrorist groups in Myanmar and other parts of Southeast Asia. These rebel groups control the local region and facilitate opium production so that they can easily acquire huge sums of money for the arms supplies and other needs. Often they perform the role of intermediaries in the drug trafficking market. They buy opium from the farmers at a very low cost and sell it to the drug syndicates at a handsome price, gaining millions of dollars. As a lot of money is gained very conveniently from this business, they promote the cultivation of poppy rather than illicit crops among farmers, either by luring them or sometimes forcing them. Their presence and dominance in these regions have also become the major hindrance between the ordinary people and government agencies. It has been observed that the income of the leaders of these rebellious ethnic groups and common soldiers have a huge economic gap. These warlords and their families enjoy a luxurious lifestyle because of the drug trafficking business and hence they keep the tensions alive so that they could gain maximum personal benefits from the cultivation of opium.[4] Thus, they avoid peace negotiations and keep creating the circumstances which leave no option for the farmers but to grow illicit crops.

Porous Borders and Mismanagement

The complex geography of the Golden Triangle further supports drug trafficking. The borders are porous and not properly managed. Because of this, the traffickers do not face much trouble in crossing the borders to buy opium and then take it back. They take the route from Lao PDR and Thailand to cross the borders of Myanmar. Similarly, the borders are not properly managed and many corrupt practices normally take place. The bribing of border security personnel and local authorities is also very common.

Fig. 1: Myanmar Heroin Flows in the Greater Mekong Sub-region

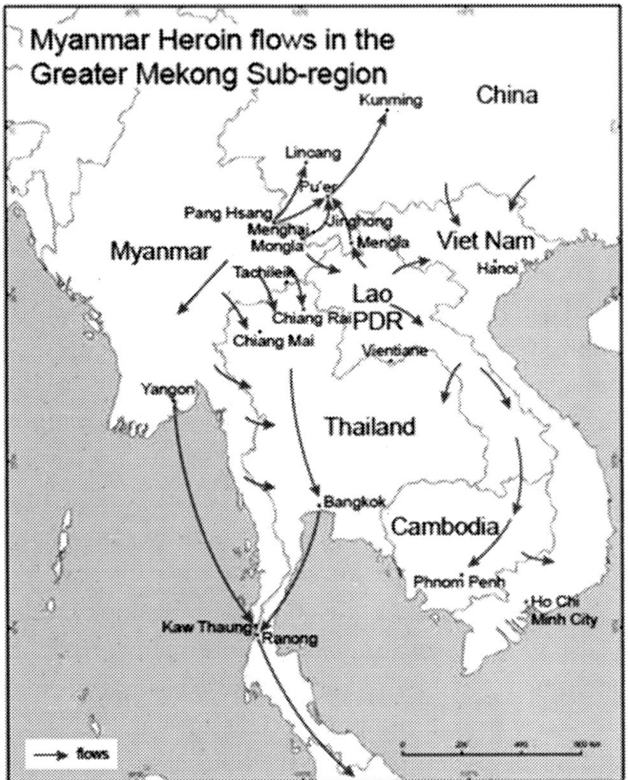

The boundaries and names shown and the designations used on this map do not imply official endorsement or acceptance by the United Nations.
Source: UNODC

Manufacturing of Synthetic Drugs and New Psychoactive Substances (UNDOC 2013 Report)

Synthetic drugs have mushroomed in the drug trafficking business in the past few decades. It poses a grave danger to human security in the region. Two of the prominent synthetic drugs in the region are Methamphetamines and Amphetamine-Type Stimulants (ATS). China is the largest manufacturer of methamphetamines in the region. Almost all the countries in the region are more or less associated with the production of methamphetamines in the region. The rapid expansion of synthetic drugs can be estimated by the figures provided by the UNODC 2013 report. According to this, the number of ATS labs which have been busted in the region increased from 83 in the year 2006 to more than 400 in the year 2013. The methamphetamines are being manufactured in both tablet (locally known as yaba tablets) and crystalline form. Another category of synthetic drugs which is emerging these days is known as the New Psychotropic Substances (NPS) which are under study in order to understand their harmful effect in the body. Even small amounts cause serious hallucinations.[5] This is the reason that they are very much in demand in the international drug market. Some of the NPS are Ecstasy, Flakka, and many others.

Fig. 2: Global Emergence of New Psychoactive Substances up to December 2017

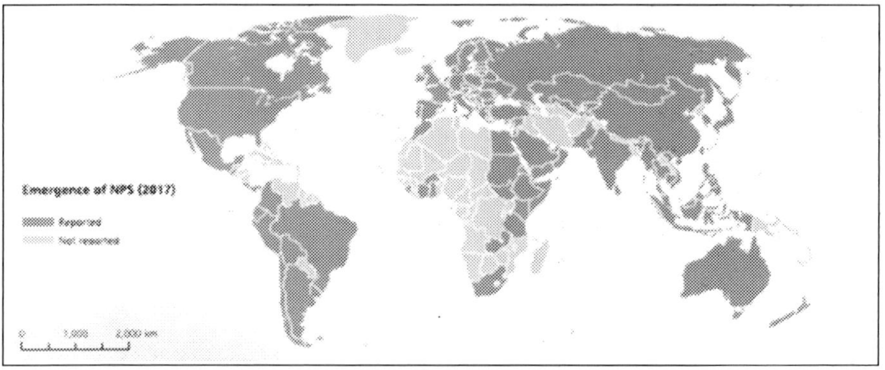

Source: United Nations Office on Drugs and Crime, Early Warning Advisory on NPS, 2017.

The production of synthetic drugs is much easier and flexible in comparison to updating and other natural drugs, as it does not require plant extract and the production is mobile. The most important elements required in the manufacturing of these drugs are the precursor chemicals. The problem which the authorities are confronting is how to detect these chemicals. The UNODC in the World Drug Report 2014 highlights some of the strategies that the operators of drug syndicates apply in the manufacturing of synthetic drugs and NPS. These are as follows:

- The use of more sophisticated ways to obtain precursor chemicals.
- The use of transit countries with weak control systems.
- The emergence of organised criminal groups specialised in the supply of precursor chemicals.
- The creation of front companies to conceal illegal imports.
- The domestic diversion and subsequent smuggling of precursor chemicals to final destinations in order to bypass the international control system.

- The use of the Internet.
- The misuse of pharmaceutical preparations (notably preparations containing ephedrine or pseudoephedrine).
- The emergence of non-scheduled precursor chemicals, including various pre-precursors that can be easily converted into the required precursors.[6]

The Nexus between Drug Trafficking and Other Transnational Organised Crimes

Drug trafficking is not the only organised crime taking place in the region. In fact, the money extracted from this business helps to conduct other transnational organised crimes. The United Nations office of drugs and crime (UNODC) has outlined four categories of transnational organised crimes rampant in this region including the drug trafficking. The other three are:

- Human trafficking and the smuggling of migrants.
- Resources (wildlife, wood products) and pollution crime (e-waste, ozone-depleting substances).
- Products (counterfeit goods, fraudulent medicines).[7]

All these criminal activities are controlled by the transnational racketeers and drugs syndicates that are extremely powerful in the region. The large amounts of money that are generated from these contribute to large-scale corruption and money laundering and hence ensures them to a large extent from the scrutiny of law enforcing bodies. There are various criminal organisations associated with these activities. Some of them belong to specific countries with the region while some of the networks extend beyond it. For instance, the regional criminal associations like the infamous *Triads* and *Yakuza* are active in China and Japan respectively. The Vietnamese organised criminal groups are active in most of the area of Southeast Asia. The international drug dealers like the Colombian drug cartels and Russian and Italian mafias have links in Australia and New Zealand. Similarly, the West African criminal groups have been engaged with trafficking in countries like Indonesia.[8] These racketeers play a very important role in the global distribution of illicit drugs and their precursor chemicals. For instance, flakka, a bath salt, commonly known as Zombie drug, is smuggled into the US from Mexico, but the key chemical components are manufactured in China and then transported to Mexico. There the final composition of the drug takes place and then it is exported across the borders of the United States by these drug syndicates.

Involvement of Technology in Illegal Drug Dealing

The dealing of illegal drugs on the Internet has become very popular. The virtual cyberspace also known as the 'darknet' is used for the buying and selling of the drugs. The drug syndicates are also transported drugs through "mail or express delivery, and pay via online trading platforms."[9] These save them from coming within the radar of the authorities and also increases the pace of trafficking. It has been found out that cryptocurrency like 'Bitcoin' is used for the payment of drugs orders.[10] Thus, the identities of both buyers and sellers remain hidden, which the conventional security measures cannot deal with and hence, need a technological upgrade.

Drug Consumption and an Assessment of the Drug Control Policies

The manner in which chronic poverty in the region contributes to the cultivation and manufacturing of both natural and synthetic drugs so does the rapid economic growth dictates the consumption of illegal drugs in the Indo-Pacific region. In the past few decades, many of the countries in the region have witnessed rapid economic growth. As seen in the above-mentioned map, almost all the countries in the Pacific region are deeply affected by illicit drugs. As per the statistics, there are more than 3 million heroin users and over 5 million methamphetamines users in the region. This region has the largest number of consumers and the demand for new psychotropic substances have skyrocketed in the regional market. If looked into the seizures, around 2.4 million pills of ecstasy were seized off the Myanmar coast in 2014.[11]

Fig. 3: ATS seizures reported in East and South-East Asia and Oceania, 2008-2013

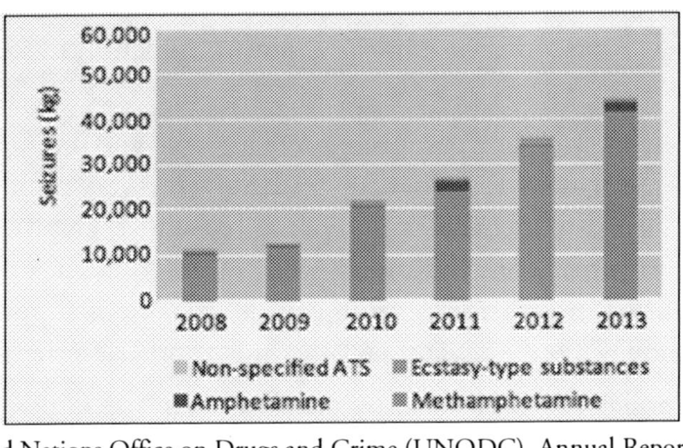

Source(s): United Nations Office on Drugs and Crime (UNODC), Annual Report Questionnaire 2008-2013.

The popularity of illegal drugs poses a direct threat to the human security of a country. In the United States, cocaine, heroin, methamphetamines, ecstasy, and other new psychotropic substances are commonly used drugs which threatens the well-being of common citizens. Apart from cocaine, most of the drugs are associated with the Indo-Pacific region. As per the American Society of Addiction Medicine (ASAM), in 2015, approximately 586,000 Americans were detected with a substance use disorder that included heroin consumption.[12] Similarly, in China, the reports tell that more than 2.5 million people are drug addicts and the growth rate for the same is about 1.9 per cent per year. The majority of the afflicted ones include the younger generation between the age group of 18 to 35 years.[13] The trend follows alike in other countries as well.

As a major non-traditional security threat, from time to time, a number of steps have been taken by various governments and the international organisations in the region. In the lieu of human security crisis created by drug consumption, countries like the United States and Australia have been actively involved in curbing the drug trafficking in the region. They have formulated several domestic legislation to curb drug addiction and its entry and distribution in their territories. In terms of foreign policy, they have focused on the supply reduction mostly through the tightening of Border Security but this has not proved as successful due to the ever-increasing demand for drugs among the population. Because of this huge demand, it has been practically impossible to stop the influx of illegal drugs within their territories. Attempts made by individual countries have shown some positive results. Myanmar in the last two years has witnessed a decline in the poppy cultivation. The present Myanmar government has been working in association with the UNODC. The total area under cultivation has reduced to a quarter from its 2015 estimate. Also, there has been a decrease in the opium production in 2017 by 14 per cent.[14]

Because of the lack of a comprehensive regional and an international law enforcement mechanism towards drug trafficking it is very difficult for a single country to curb this menace as is represented above graph. Transnational organised crime operations are intertwined with each other; one single crime cannot be curbed in isolation. Even if drug trafficking is suppressed to some extent, the money, weapons, and racketeering of other crimes revive it again.

China's policy towards the drug eradication in the Golden Triangle has been impressive. China National Narcotics Control Commission has followed

Fig. 4: Opium Production in Myanmar with the Decreasing Level of Production and Cultivation (1996-2017)

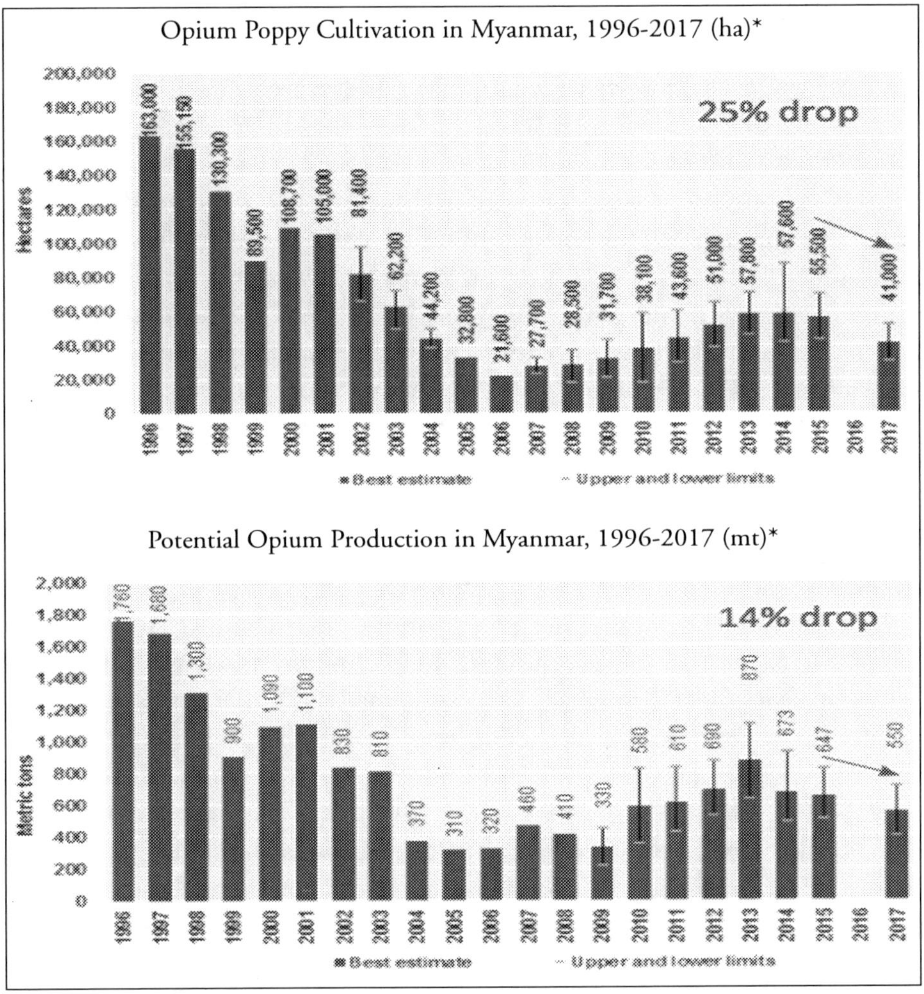

a two-way policy so that it can find a permanent solution to the drug entry problem in China through its Yunnan region. Firstly, the coercive crackdown of regional drug syndicates has been done by punishing the drug lords and traffickers. Secondly, with the support of Chinese agricultural enterprises, the government has taken initiative to provide developmental assistance to the farmers in the poppy cultivation area. Farmers can use these incentives in shifting towards the legitimate cash crops and hence help them in their social and economic development.[15] Individual efforts have been made by Vietnam, Laos, Cambodia, and Thailand which also grab the illegal drug market in their countries to some extent. But the 'War on Drugs' which is being carried in the Philippines is quite disturbing because of the violence inflicted on groups, individuals and also adversaries by the government forces.

The Organisational Efforts to Curb Illicit Drug Trafficking

The United Nations

The United Nations is deeply engaged in the region in order to eradicate drug trafficking through its United Nations office of drugs and crime. Its regional unit known as the regional office for South East Asia and Pacific works in collaboration with the governments in the region. The United Nations facilitated the Mekong Memorandum of Understanding (MoU) on Drug Control in 1997. It became a platform for six major countries in the region affected by drug trafficking to work in cooperation in tackling this issue. The six countries include Cambodia, China, Lao PDR, Myanmar, Thailand, and Vietnam. The UNODC is the non-signatory seventh partner which coordinates the task. Although this partnership has not been able to eradicate drug problem in the region, it has, to some extent been able to control it.[16]

The UNODC helps the government authorities to conduct various service in order to get evidence about the cultivation of poppy and manufacturing of synthetic drugs. And through these surveys, the UNODC has found out that good security conditions and a stable government play an important role in the reduction of poppy cultivation. A pilot project to conduct in the micro level detailed analysis in the Shan state of Myanmar discovered that a targeted situation analysis can provide effective solutions. It was found that government ban and the fear of eradication of poppy cultivation by the government has in some positive ways made many of the farmers in the region stop this cultivation. The UN guiding principles on alternative development recommends "target illicit cultivation [...], and address related factors, by alleviating poverty, by strengthening the rule of law and institutional frameworks, as appropriate, and by promoting sustainable development aimed at enhancing the welfare of the population" and to implement alternative development in concert with broader drug control policies, including demand reduction, law enforcement, illicit crop elimination and awarenessraising."[17] The UNODC Global Synthetics Monitoring: Analyses, Reporting, and Trends (SMART) program focuses on dealing with synthetic drugs and the new psychotropic substances.[18]

ASEAN

The ASEAN countries came up with an elaborate plan to eradicate the menace of drug trafficking in the region known as the ASEAN Work Plan on Combating Illicit Drug Production, Trafficking, and Use (2009-2015). The goal of this action plan was 'ASEAN Drug-Free 2015' through monitoring and evaluation mechanism.[19] Although this goal looks far from being realised. ASEAN is also engaged with UNODC in the various platform to work towards the tackling of transnational organised crimes through the strengthening of law enforcement mechanism.

Underlying Problems

In terms of policy formulation, a lot has experimented for decades at an individual regional and international level. Despite that, drug trafficking still exists as a thriving non-traditional security threats in Indo-Pacific policies life source control for a while being affected but because of the complex intertwining of poverty, transnational organised crime, corruption money laundering, and unregulated borders reignite this phenomenon again and again. At all three levels there exist some technical deficiencies that need to be addressed in order to get success over this draconian problem.

Firstly, at the individual level, no country in the region even with the stringent most anti-drug policy, has not been able to tackle either one or both the production and consumption of illicit drugs from there countries. Since very wealthy and powerful transnational drugs syndicates are involved in this business, they easily find one way or other to penetrate inside a territory and carry out the drug transaction process. Governments of smaller economies in the region would not be able to at the individual level because many of the racket involved have more income than their GDPs and because of that they are able to influence the government from inside through corruption and money laundering. In bigger economies, porous borders combined with mismanagement of borders and unlawful practices of security personnel leave a country vulnerable to these traffickers.

Secondly, the regional forums like the ASEAN have not been very successful in tackling production consumption and transportation of drugs in the region because of the incompatibility among the law enforcement mechanisms of various countries. Often they even contradict each other. At a very subtle level, some nations intentionally neglect the recommendations so that they can use it as a tool to hamper the economy and security of the regional Rivals.

These have been the reasons that even if these action plans seem highly ambitious on paper but they never get implemented in spirit.

Lastly, at the international level, the major challenge which the United Nations faces the scarcity of funds. Technology has become one of the most powerful weapons in the transnational organised crime. In order to be with that, a proper structural framework is required which needs a large amount of money. But most of the countries, even the advanced ones, like the US and China, are hesitant in providing sufficient assistance and focus inwardly towards their national drug policy.

Future Possibilities

With all the analysis and assessments, it has been found out that in order to disrupt the well-organised drug trafficking there is need of proper coordinated regional and international mechanisms. One thing that is evident is that the drug trafficking cannot be solved in isolation; other organised crimes will have to be with dealt simultaneously. The United Nations convention against transnational organised crime (UNCTOC), 2000, commonly known as the Palermo convention came out with some of the concrete solutions to tackle these crimes. It recommends the elimination of difference among these legal systems of various countries in the region and also standardises domestic laws that can deal with these crimes in an effective manner. Another major recommendation of this convention was to have a regional or international forum that could work towards the cross-border investigation of transnational organised crimes along with the exchange of evidences witnesses and the extradition of offenders.[20]

The drug situation is more alarming than ever. One, because it is severely affecting the human security within the Nations, especially with the upcoming of the fatal synthetic drugs and new psychotropic substances along with the increased rate of diseases like HIV. Another is the national security concern as there has been the rise of various non-state actors in the region, especially the terrorist groups, whose activities are fueled by the billions of dollars extracted from this business.

The countries in the Indo-Pacific region need to work with each other to eradicate the drug trafficking menace. The bigger economies like the US, China, Australia, New Zealand, and even India should invest money in training and capacity building of border security personnel of their own country as well as of the weaker countries and act as a helping partner in the peacebuilding mechanism of the countries affected with armed rebellion and work together in order to bring political stability. They need to act as the link between the programs of the United Nations and the smaller countries so that they can come up with the infrastructure like education awareness employment, rehabilitation mechanism, and other health services. Stringent actions should be taken against drug mafia and they should not be used as a tool to support other country security and economy. But in doing that human rights should not be violated as it is presently being done in the Philippines. This can never be an option in dealing with the illicit drug trade.

As suggested by UNODC, *emphasis* needs to be given on helping the farmers in the poppy cultivation region shift towards the cultivation of licit cash crops through the alternative development process. In terms of synthetic drugs and new psychotropic substances which are rather new, law enforcement legislation should be brought up in order to identify and destroy both the product and their laboratories. One of the major roles which these giant countries in the region can play is to develop the capabilities to detect and destroy the darknet kind of cyber crimes. All these options seem very ambitious, but they need to be implemented on an urgent basis so that within the right time frame, the 'organised' gets 'unorganised' and a major security threat can be averted.

NOTES

1 https://www.unodc.org/southeastasiaandpacific/en/myanmar/2018/05/mekong-region-drug-conference/story.html
2 "Situational Analysis of Illicit Drug Issues and Responses in Asia and the Pacific".
3 https://www.unodc.org/documents/southeastasiaandpacific//Publications/2017/2016_Myanmar_Shan_Opium_Poppy_web.pdf
4 https://thediplomat.com/2017/09/war-drugs-and-peace-afghanistan-and-myanmar/
5 https://www.unodc.org/LSS/Page/NPS
6 https://www.unodc.org/documents/wdr2014/World_Drug_Report_2014_web.pdf
7 Transnational Organized Crime in East Asia and the Pacific: A Threat Assessment.
8 Schloenhardt, Andreas. "Fighting Organized Crime in the Asia Pacific Region: New Weapons, Lost Wars," *Asian Journal of International Law*, Vol. 2, No. 1, 2012, pp. 137–167., doi:10.1017/S2044251311000075.
9 http://www.chinadaily.com.cn/a/201806/26/WS5b31e428a3103349141dee03_6.html
10 https://www.unodc.org/documents/wdr2014/World_Drug_Report_2014_web.pdf
11 https://www.unodc.org/documents/ungass2016/CND_Preparations/Brown_bag_lunch/Asia/2014.11.19_CND_preparation_for_UNGASS_2016_final.pdf
12 https://americanaddictioncenters.org/rehab-guide/addiction-statistics/
13 http://www.chinadaily.com.cn/a/201806/26/WS5b31e428a3103349141dee03_5.html

14 https://www.unodc.org/documents/southeastasiaandpacific/Publications/2017/Myanmar_OPS_2017_Fact_Sheet_web.pdf
15 https://www.unodc.org/southeastasiaandpacific/en/what-we-do/toc/mou.html
16 Ibid.
17 Op. cit., n. 3
18 https://www.unodc.org/southeastasiaandpacific/en/smart.htmln
19 http://asean.org/storage/2017/07/Doc-1-ASEAN-WP-on-Combating-Illicit-Drug-Production-2009-2015.pdf
20 Op. cit., n. 7.

Index